SMALL BUSINESSES

Philip Clarke

SMALL BUSINESSES

How they survive and succeed

DAVID & CHARLES
NEWTON ABBOT

0 7153 5603 8

Set in Plantin
and printed in Great Britain
by Latimer Trend & Co Ltd, Plymouth
for David & Charles (Publishers) Limited
South Devon House Newton Abbot Devon

To my wife Enid

who contributed so much
and gave up such a lot

Contents

Author's notes

1 Like most books this one has a beginning and an ending. The first five chapters consist for the most part of general material, as do the last two chapters, while chapters 6 to 15 inclusive are in the main devoted to profiles of small firms. But there is no reason why readers should not dip into the stories of individual small businesses before tackling the introductory chapters. In any case many of the people and firms covered in detail in the profiles make brief appearances, illustrating specific points and experiences, in the earlier chapters.

2 While this book was being written there were many changes and developments in the world of small business. By the time it is published there will have been more, and in a number of places I have no doubt that events will have overtaken my text. That apart, however, I must take the blame for any omissions, inaccuracies or imperfections. Obviously every care has been taken to minimise this risk but I feel it is important to warn readers that on financial, taxation and legal matters, which are very much subject to change, no guarantees can be given. It is essential that readers should consult their own professional advisers before embarking on any course of action in which these subjects are of moment.

Introduction

The public image of the small firm. Past disinterest and neglect. The new climate of interest. The Bolton Committee. The threat to small business and discrimination against it. Change and its effect on old attitudes and traditional markets. New opportunities for new-style entrepreneurs. The lack of research on small business. The arbitrariness of definitions of size. The common denominator: the owner-manager. Independence and quality of life.

THERE are several reasons for writing a book about small businesses. The first is that there are so many of them, and they go largely unremarked or unnoticed because unlike big business, about which there are many books, they seldom do anything notable or remarkable enough to attract national attention. When they do it tends to be in the nature of a single, ritualised performance like hearing the first cuckoo. The cuckoo call may come in the shape of something like the Queen's Award to Industry, or the British National Export Council's Award for small manufacturers. Then the newspapers are full of stories about small firms and their splendid export records. Everyone applauds their enterprise, their contribution to the national good and then closes their newspapers and promptly forgets about them—until next year. The other occasions on which small firms attract the public eye is when their enterprise has gone sadly wrong. When the Department of Trade and Industry publishes its annual report on bankruptcy there follows a spate of depressing headlines which identify the woes of characteristic areas of small business. Headlines like 'SHARP RISE IN BANKRUPTCIES—BUILDERS HEAD THE LIST' or 'MORE BANKRUPTCY FAILURES AMONG GROCERS' are typical.

The second reason for writing this book is entangled with the first, because the subject has long been one of grey disinterest. Government concern about small businesses, which flickered into life in the later years of Mr Wilson's administration and which was one of the main planks of Mr Heath's electoral platform, came none too soon. Since then small business has had some powerful spotlights focused upon it, and these have illuminated some dark corners and revealed the special problems and difficulties of the small firm. It has been shown that such firms are important to have around for the sake of the economy as a whole, and it is now accepted that since there are trials and tribulations which they find especially upsetting and destructive, something should be done to help them meet these. The plea of the small firm never has been that it should receive preferential treatment, only that it should not be discriminated against because of its size.

In July 1969 the government set up the Bolton Committee which, to give it its full and official title, was the Government Committee of Inquiry on Small Firms. Its common usage name came from its chairman, John Bolton, a former chairman of the British Institute of Management. He first made his name—and his money—from Solartron, the electronics company which he helped build up from a small fifteen-man concern in 1951, to a medium-sized international firm by the time it was eventually taken over by a big conglomerate company with interests in electronics. Just prior to the publication of his committee's report in November 1971 Bolton was appointed chairman of the Small Business Capital Fund, a company backed by the Co-operative Insurance Society to finance promising small businesses.

The Bolton Committee was charged with the task of considering the role of small firms in the national economy, the facilities available to them and the problems confronting them—and to make recommendations. Its job was also to examine the profitability of small firms, the availability of finance for them and the function of small firms as innovators and specialist suppliers. The committee patiently took evidence from every Tom, Dick and Harry on the small business scene; so much evidence that its report long overran the original publication date. Exhaustive and revealing though it was, there is, however, little doubt that it will remain unread by hordes of small businessmen largely because they are so busy running their own companies that they do not have time to read reports—even if they are the heroes of the piece.

For precisely the same reason many small businessmen to whom I sent a questionnaire while gathering material for this book were either unable to respond or did so too late. One of the very real and singular problems of the man running a small firm is that he is snowed under with an unwanted plenitude of forms and returns, emanating from everyone from the taxman to government departments, requiring statistical information. On top of this there is the required reading of his business, with which he can never keep abreast. His position is quite unlike the executive in an oil company, or a large electronics concern, who has a commercial intelligence department, a staff of librarians or a personal assistant to read for him, mark the relevant passages and draw them to his attention. The man running his own show has to read and mark himself—if and when he can spare the time.

It is this man who has felt increasingly in recent years that his livelihood and way of life is being threatened, that he is unwanted and unloved, that he is being assailed on all sides and conveniently used as an Aunt Sally by government and big business alike. If he has one single, raw spot, it is the conviction that as a breed he is being unfairly discriminated against. To him the arch villains in the economic thicket are the stupidities of the tax system and big firms who, slow in settling their bills, display in his eyes a callous disregard for his difficulties. To precisely what extent these factors, aggravated by successive credit squeezes, have been responsible for the high levels of failures in business in recent years it is impossible to say. But the fact is that in 1970 bankruptcies totalled 4,656, the highest figure for ten years. On the other hand it has to be recognised that a clumsy tax system and apparently callous trading associates can make very convenient scapegoats for sheer management ineptitude and inertia. Even if the financial pressures which weigh so heavily on some small businesses were totally relaxed, it is still doubtful whether their owners would see an end to their misgivings and difficulties.

This is because small businessmen are confused and uneasy by what is happening to their traditional markets in this fast-moving commercial world. The retailer, for instance, must wonder on occasions what has hit him. The fierce assault of supermarkets, discount trading, franchising and the mounting popularity of home-selling activities by housewives for firms like Avon cosmetics, the abolition of resale price maintenance—all of these have combined to make the traditional small retailer feel all the more that the ground is being cut from beneath his feet. For every one small business which has not gone bust there must be heaven knows how many more who are attempting to weather their difficulties by stringently cutting back and squeezing costs where they are almost impossible to be squeezed, by making personal sacrifices, by not taking salaries out of the business when things are bad, or by hanging on to what little profitability they do enjoy by sacrificing some of their sovereignty and independence and bringing in outside shareholders and money.

Yet in any accounting of the status of small business the writing is not all in balance-sheet red. It may seem something of a paradox but at a time when giant corporations are part of the accepted order and when there are fewer and fewer companies each becoming larger and larger in industries like brewing, shipbuilding, hotels and catering, aircraft manufacture and textiles, opportunities for small firms abound. An editorial entitled 'The New Entrepreneur' in the January 1970 issue of *Management Today* states the position thus: 'The giants must concentrate their scarce entrepreneurial talents and their abundant cash flow on the areas of maximum commitment. Their corporate climate, with ongoing activities of enormous scale demanding intensive day to day management, does not encourage entrepreneurship in the classic sense of one bright man exploiting one new idea.' In other words the small business is still the last stronghold of the man with the gut feeling which demands that he should strike out on his own and back his hunch with everything he has. Yet in recent years the tax climate and the government's industrial policies have placed serious restraints on such men and the opportunities available to them. Whether more sympathetic policies would have seen more new businesses initiated, and arrested the long-term decline which has occurred in the small business population, is open to debate.

Even if a lot of people for whom the Bolton Committee's report would make salutary reading do not get around to inwardly digesting it, it is clearly better to have such a document than none at all, so that some sort of balanced and accurate picture of small business is available. Prior to the appointment of the committee there had never been a comprehensive study, official or otherwise, of the small-firm sector in the United Kingdom. The bulk of this book, for example, was written before the publication of the Bolton Report, and my own spade-work soon revealed that it was an area which had been little researched and poorly documented. The report itself, in its opening paragraphs, made the point that inevitably this meant the formulation of industrial policy had proceeded without adequate knowledge of the functions performed by small firms, of their efficiency and of the likely effects upon them of the actions of government.

I quickly discovered that even a simple matter of the numbers employed in the country by small businesses was a subject which was full of pitfalls and required a lot of digging in a variety of sources, since it was not gathered together in a concise and single form. In their book, *The Private Company Today*, A. J. Merrett and M. E. Lehr make the point that information on employment accounted for by small firms is misleading because in the first place the definition of small is a purely arbitrary one, and secondly, the coverage of statistics is limited. The authors single out the Confederation of British Industry's pamphlet, *Britain's Small Firms—Their Vital Role in the Economy*, as an example. 'The information relates only to individuals employed in the so-called census industries, which account for little more than half the total employment in the United Kingdom. They [the statistics] wholly exclude those employed in agriculture, transportation, wholesaling, insurance, banking, finance, catering and hotels,' say Merrett and Lehr. 'Moreover, some 1·6 million people, 8 per cent of the labour force in the private sectors, are self-employed and less than half of these are in the census of production and distribution figures. Official figures do not attempt to allocate employment between the unquoted and quoted sectors, and attention thus tends to be directed towards the sector for which detailed figures of profits, assets etc are available —namely quoted public industrial companies.'

The first point they raise, the arbitrariness of the definition of a small firm, is a quagmire for the unwary. Trying to define what is a small firm with precision and exactitude is a fruitless task. You could go on producing a torrent of words on the subject and succeed only in driving your readers into the ground with boredom. This can be avoided by disposing now of this awkward problem so that it does not tug at our sleeves on every other page hereafter.

This book is concerned primarily with the spirit and character of small business rather than with inflexible definitions of its size. Whatever yardstick of size you employ—turnover, profits, assets, numbers employed—it is not very realistic or convincing standing on its own. In any case people have their own ideas as to what 'small' means. The charter of the Confederation of British Industry defines a small firm as one with less than 200 employees. The Rural Industries Bureau sees it as one with less than twenty skilled employees. When the 1967 Companies Act was under discussion in the House of Commons, the CBI suggested an annual turnover of up to £1 million might be taken as a criterion. In the event the government finally adopted a figure of £50,000. Taken in isolation all these measures are equally arbitrary. The Board of Trade's terms of reference for the Bolton Committee defined a small firm as one with not more than 200 employees but made the point that this should not be regarded as a rigid definition. It was not, and the committee modified it to suit the various industrial groups it studied. All the units of measurement mentioned are useful markers to have at the back of your mind when discussing small businesses, but there is no virtue in leaning on them too heavily.

There are certainly companies in this book with more than 200 employees on their payrolls and more than £50,000 of annual sales going through their books. Furthermore, there are enormous differences as to what people understand by 'small' between industry and industry. Clearly it means something different in retailing, when you are talking about a small corner shop, from what it does in the petro-chemical industry when you are talking about a small refinery. Again a highly automated chemical plant with on-the-ground assets worth millions of pounds might employ fewer personnel than a small firm in a highly labour intensive business like the rag trade. A small business can be one man with a market stall, or it can be a company on the verge of going public.

Perhaps the best indicator of all to what is meant by 'small' in this context comes from examining the nature and the character of a firm. There is one characteristic which, in contrast to public companies, small firms do seem to have in common. This is that major policy decisions are taken by one or two people who usually own, manage and risk their own money in the business. As it stands it is still not an exact definition of what constitutes a small firm, but used in concert with the yardsticks previously mentioned it does go a long way to help towards an understanding of the kind of animal it is we are studying.

I cannot claim that this modest work is as comprehensive as the Bolton Committee's report—with all the resources which were open to it. In any case Bolton's expenditure, including the printing and publishing of the report, was nearly £150,000. I can promise you I have not spent quite so much on my inquiries. None the less both our publications are in some measure part of the reaction against the cult of size and the merger mania with which both government and large lumps of industry were obsessed in the 1960s. For my part I have tried to extend the conventional discussions about small business beyond the usual terms of pressures, problems and panaceas. I have attempted to show that above all else small business is very much a matter of people and not cogs in a machine, that it is so often intertwined with family life, bound up with personal goals and ambitions, all of which are highly relevant themes in the story, yet which you will scarcely find taken into account in a business-school case study. It may be a hard point for some people to grasp, but after listening on the one hand to the arguments about small firms being more efficient than large ones and winning a higher return on their capital than public companies, it has to be accepted that running a small business is often less a matter of maximising returns on capital employed, and much more a question of individuals profiting from intangibles such as independence, creative satisfaction and a particular style and quality of life which can never be quantified in a profit and loss account.

The life of a small businessman is compounded both of anxiety and triumph, despair and euphoria, but for the great majority of them it is a consciously chosen, deliberate and meaningful existence which they would not change for the world.

My qualifications for writing this book are neither a doctorate on the subject, nor membership of the Bolton Committee. Nor am I a small businessman, though my father was. All that I can offer is the fact that for a number of years now, in my job writing a regular column called 'Prufrock' in the *Sunday Times Business News*, I have talked with, commiserated with, argued with, fallen out with, eaten with, travelled with, stayed with, become friends with and written about more small businessmen and their businesses than I care to count. Which brings me to the last selfish reason for this book. It is that I find small businessmen, with all their considerable virtues and all their considerable failings, a fascinating breed.

Chapter 1

A view of small business

The story of Caterpillar Products, the archetypal small firm. The small business population. The strengths of small firms —adaptability, flexibility, serving specialist markets and large firms, the development of new ideas. Personal motivations and personal involvement. The weaknesses of small firms—lack of money, unskilled and overburdened management—their special problems and vulnerability. The adverse effect of government policies.

CATERPILLAR Products is a small business. Very small. It has a workforce of three people. To be absolutely accurate it has a workforce of one, because the other two own and manage the firm. In the 1963 Census of Production, in the section which breaks down manufacturing establishments according to the number of employees they have, Caterpillar Products comes into the 1–5 category. It is hidden there, a single establishment along with 17,718 other firms like it. Between them they give employment to 62,000 people out of the United Kingdom's total working population of over 22 million. If there were a smaller category, say 0–1, then Caterpillar Products would go into it. But there isn't. So lacking a pigeon hole for the firm's single employee you might as well ignore the impersonality of government statistics and give her name instead. She is Heather Brownsell, and she has been with Caterpillar for over five years, cycling through the Hertfordshire country lanes to work each day, from the village of Chipperfield where she lives, to the village of Flaunden where Caterpillar Products lives. The rest of the combined workforce, managers and proprietors are Tony and Eve Nyboer.

Tony's father was Dutch and Tony started life as a musician, playing the violin in the old silent cinemas when he was fourteen. Eve's father was an electrical engineer, and, although she has had no formal training in engineering, quite a lot of engineering knowledge rubbed off on her as a result of life with dad. In addition, as Tony says, she is very good at organising. They first met during the war when Tony, unable to serve in the Forces because of his medical grading, was working as a fitter at Handley-Page, the aircraft firm. In 1942 he and Eve were married and, of all improbable beginnings to setting up home, they bought a pantechnicon for £10 and lived in it. Their business career together started when they decided to do some sparetime work for the war effort, making components for Eve's father's firm. To do so they set up a workshop in an old chicken shed.

Of the two Tony is the optimist. If he has a business philosophy it approximates to 'everything-will-turn-out-for-the-best-in-the-end.' Both of them have had a happy business life, despite a never-ending procession of ups and downs, shortages of money and excruciating labour troubles which were neither of their own nor their employees' making. They still thoroughly enjoy doing what they are doing, and if they were ever to change Caterpillar Products into a private limited company, instead of working as individual owners trading on their own account, an appropriate alternative name for it might be Resilience Ltd.

At the present time the firm's product is artificial paper flowers; rather unusual ones, different from others you see on the market in that they are specially stiffened, don't become bedraggled and sad-looking with wear, can be rinsed free of dust and dirt and are perfumed. But the firm hasn't always made paper flowers. What it has made at different times of its history couldn't be more varied. Once it was undercarriages for Oxford Airspeed training aircraft, for example. For like scores of other firms throughout the country Caterpillar Products was spawned out of the war effort in the 1940s, when small engineering shops and factories were set up in towns and villages, in barns, garden sheds, lock-up garages and church halls, all part of the enormous drive to supply the nuts and bolts of the war machine. It was the few bits and pieces made in the chicken shed which started Caterpillar Products off. The few started to mount into many, which necessitated some help, and it was then that the Nyboers realised that in their part of the country pockets of untapped labour, especially women, existed in the surrounding villages like Bovingdon, Belsize, Chipperfield and Sarratt, all more or less within bicycling distance of Flaunden. The Ministry of Aircraft Production was sufficiently impressed by the Nyboers' argument about the availability of labour to build them a small factory, the same old army-style hut, suffering a little from the depredations of time and weather, which they still occupy.

It shows how long memories take to fade because letters still occasionally arrive there with the official wartime sounding address on the envelope. It wasn't of course known as Caterpillar Products in those days. This was a post-war refinement. In the 1940s it sported not so much a name but more a designation: Ministry of Aircraft Production, Flaunden Unit.

Some of these old wartime businesses ultimately grew large, waxed and flourished, and today still trade but in conditions and surroundings unrecognisable from their hurried and humble beginnings. Others faded away when people wanted their lock-up garages and church halls back again. Yet others, like Caterpillar Products, no longer able to depend on producing components for the engines of war, turned to anything they could to bring in some money to keep the business going and preserve their owner's independence.

So between the undercarriages and the artificial flowers is the story of a small business, not always so small as it is now, which preserves much of the quintessential flavour and style of hordes of other small businesses everywhere. In many ways Caterpillar Products is the raw material for a cheerful, human, scenario of all the classic strengths and all the disturbing weaknesses of the small firm. It is one of those bouncy little concerns which are always coming back for more, which show formidable powers of survival and which stay very much in the small business league, committed to it by the nature of its product and the desires or the abilities of its owners. In all honesty it is not a firm throbbing with some outstanding inner dynamic. Nor is it particularly distinguishable from cohorts of other small concerns. Nor is it of any great moment in the weight of its contribution to the gross national product, the balance of payments or to the wellbeing of the populace at large. It may not account for much in the broad sweep of British manufacturing industry, but in Flaunden it does—and has. At times it has been the largest single employer of labour in the village, providing the only bit of industry that Flaunden—a handful of houses, a shop, a pub and some farms—has ever had. At those various times it has represented a tiny fragmented offshoot of a fairly wide range of industrial effort and it has tried its hand at pretty nearly everything.

When the war was over and there were more undercarriages than anyone could possibly need, the Nyboers sat down and said to themselves, 'Now what shall we make?' In 1945 Eve persuaded the Ministry of Aircraft Production to let her take over the building and she reached an oral agreement with an old lady who lived in the village on whose land the factory had been built to let her rent it. This agreement still stands.

At the time there was a lot of poaching going on in the district and the Nyboers got the idea of making bird brooches using genuine feathers. As soon as it was known that they were setting up a pheasant poaching by-product business, both feathers and poachers started to arrive at the door. But in the end they had to get their feather supplies on a proper footing, from a fly-fishing firm, rather than relying on the haphazard results of a night's raiding.

It was at about this time that Tony invented the caterpillar-tracked sandal made of wooden slats with rubber buffers between which provided the firm with its name. 'Wearing them was like walking on a cushion,' says Eve, who strode off to Leicester to see about getting someone to make the uppers. But there wasn't much interest. People had gone off wooden footwear because of wooden-soled shoes in wartime Britain. So the caterpillar-tracked sandal came to naught. But some good came from it because the chap in Leicester saw the bird brooch Eve was wearing and said he would buy them in pairs for shoe trimmings. So in no time at all the Nyboers were employing twenty women making miniature wild ducks in left-wing and right-wing pairs for shoes.

It was a business which depended on fashion, and as everyone knows, fashions change. By the early 1950s the big new thing on the scene was television and the market for sets was starting to take off. So Caterpillar Products shifted from feathers to making one of the mysterious bits of a TV set, a thing called an ion trap. This was contract work and it gradually took them into other areas of the electronics industry, first making transformer windings and after that switches and control units for lifts.

From all this it is plain that the last thing of which you could accuse Caterpillar Products is lack of versatility. It is one of those firms which, when you are running through textbook lists of the advantages and disadvantages of being small, keep insistently popping up in your mind's eye. The thing about Caterpillar Products is that it has demonstrated an ability to endure and to soldier on fuelled by a mixture of optimism, innovation and adaptability. It is just one of a legion of small businesses which are neither abject failures, nor runaway successes. It is the archetypal persistent firm, and there are many others like it, without which the fabric of Britain's industrial life would be a great deal less colourful than it is.

If numbers alone are anything to go by small firms dominate the industrial scene. John Bolton has said[1] there are 1·25 million of them in the country with 6 million employees and 20 per cent of the gross national product. The Census of Production for 1963 shows that of a total of 84,000 manufacturing establishments in the United Kingdom over 76,000 of them employ less than 200 workers. These firms account for a total net output of £2,869 million, out of a total of £10,708 million and they provide employment for nearly 2·4 million out of the manufacturing working population of nearly 7·75 million. These figures are for manufacturing alone and take no account of the enormous span of activity from retailing and transportation to the service industries and professional practices.

The Confederation of British Industry, which has 5,000 individual firms employing less than 200 workers as direct members, has calculated that 97 per cent of all United Kingdom manufacturing establishments have less than 500 workers, that these small firms provide work for 50 per cent of the total manufacturing labour force and that they account for 45 per cent of industrial sales in terms of value.[2] A sample of 300 small firms aided and studied by the Industrial and Commercial Finance Corporation showed an average increase in profits of 38 per cent compared with the average increase in profits of all UK companies of about 21 per cent.[3] This was for the period between 1960–61 and 1963–4. A later and similar survey, the Small Firm Survey 1970 by ICFC, showed that as between 1964–5 and 1967–8 the overall increase in UK company profits was 1·7 per cent as compared with 21·8 per cent for 304 ICFC firms. Another way of looking at the small business population is to remember there are over 50,000 small factories and workshops with up to twenty-four employees where the boss probably knows all his workers on first-name terms. This is one of the matey characteristics of small businesses.

What these small companies do has absolutely no relevance to the economies of scale which characterise large concerns. The nature of their service and product is such that there are not any economies of scale to enjoy. What they tend to do is to fulfil functions that large firms cannot or do not wish to fulfil. In the case of Caterpillar Products you are involved in a craft with a heavy dependence on hand labour. Compared with a motor-car factory it is pure cottage industry, doing a different job from a large concern, in a different way and in a manner which would neither pay the corporation nor be possible for it. It can serve its own special market—the buyers of the paper flowers at Harrods, John Lewis and other large department stores—very well indeed, but in the end it is the size of the market which must limit the size of Caterpillar Products. Depending on the state of this market the firm swells and grows when there's a flush of orders, contracts and takes on a thinner aspect when business goes slack.

Thus, when out of the blue Cadbury's telephoned to say they had heard about the flowers and they were making inquiries about a special order for a promotion for Roses chocolates—they wanted 20,000 paper roses a week during the campaign—the

Nyboers jumped about a bit, worried whether they could handle the order, bought a petal-cutting machine for £850 and got eighty outworkers in the surrounding villages working for them in their own homes. The order provided six months' work and was worth about £12,000. As an illustration of why small firms manage to exist beside and service much larger neighbours it could hardly be better.

Another reason for peaceful co-existence is that even when competing, small firms usually only take a minute portion of a large company's market, so even if there were a giant artificial flower-making plant the impact on its sales from the activities of a smaller concern would be marginal. This kind of situation, where small firms exist side by side with large ones, is typical of industries like engineering. Think of the dozens of small metal-cutting shops in the Midlands turning out one or two components for the car factories. Thus while a small firm stays small, sticks to its last, and performs a useful function for large-scale industry, it will be tolerated. But if it is ambitious and rapidly en route to becoming big then the story is likely to be a different one, especially if its product or service threatens the business of the larger concerns. Then big brother will start to cock a wary eye in the small man's direction. Ultimately he might remove the threat by mopping it up, though there are certain pressures against excessive tactics of this sort. Big companies are often sensitive about their image, and do not like to get a name for buying up anyone who gets in their way.

Besides, there is always the Monopolies Commission huffing and puffing over the skyline.

One of the specific characteristics of small firms which give them a market advantage over large ones is flexibility. When market conditions demand a change in design of product, or indeed a change of product itself, the large plant is often handicapped by highly planned and expensive production lines, whereas the small firm with a smaller commitment to fixed equipment can switch more easily from making one product to another. And, as in the case of Caterpillar Products, it often switches with endearing insouciance from making control gear for lifts to artificial paper flowers. This happened at a time when the lift industry took a hammering after a government clampdown on office development in city centres. It was a harsh experience for the Nyboers, an experience which made them determined to slough off their dependence as contract workers on others and take up something which they could both produce and sell for themselves. Increasingly over the years they had come to realise that working under contract for other people, making bits and pieces to specification, placed them in an acutely vulnerable position.

At the first sign of business slackening the firms supplying work tend to cut back. As small concerns themselves, they are exercising this special small business attribute of flexibility. But their small contract workers, like Caterpillar Products, are the first to suffer. This was a constant source of worry to the Nyboers and eventually put them off assembling for others.

The lift crisis was the final straw. 'We had to lay off thirty girls and we found this very distressing and upsetting because we knew them all by their christian names, and used to meet them and their husbands and have a drink in the village pub with them on a Saturday night,' says Eve. 'When you all live in the same village it makes it very difficult, although they were all very nice about it, and felt as sorry for us as we did for them.'

Personal motivation, personal service, personal identity are common threads which run through almost all small businesses and there is little doubt that these induce a degree of loyalty where the word means something deeper and different from what it does in a giant corporation. When you talk to the owners of small firms it is noticeable how the majority of them attach considerable importance to the loyalty shown by employees. Often this is rooted in the past with the long-serving faithful employee who is still faithful but frankly a passenger being carried by others in the firm, a fact which owners are well aware of but content to leave like that.

The point about loyalty, comforting and reassuring though it is, goes deeper than mere benevolence and pleasant human relationships. It is a valuable lubricant to efficiency and is clearly an important factor in employees giving of their best. A survey of its members conducted by the Smaller Businesses Association showed that small firms suffered less than average from absenteeism and trade disputes. The survey also claimed that the work done over a year by an employee in a small firm was greater than that done by an employee in a large one, because from the employee's point of view satisfaction was more readily obtained by working for a small concern. In such a climate work was not considered solely as a means to obtaining a pay packet.

The co-operative spirit which exists in many small firms not only makes employees realise that their absence or slackness will increase the work of their colleagues, but it will bring forth extra effort and endeavour in crunch situations. People working in the factory often know customers by name. The word goes round that Mr So-and-So needs this order urgently in two days. Everyone buckles to because they know him and there is a sense of personal involvement with his predicament.

Nor is a small firm only able to get the best from its manpower. It frequently operates with economy and thrift in the use of machines and equipment, though taken too far this can be a double-edged weapon, especially if the machines start falling to bits or endangering workpeople. But the fact is that small firms are often very good at improvising. Tony Nyboer made a machine to wind paper on to the stems of the paper flowers instead of doing it more slowly by hand. He did this out of nothing more than a few bits of metal and wire and the motor from an old Singer sewing machine.

But as well as the virtues and strengths of the small firm there are a whole lot of weaknesses on the other side of the scale. Lack of money and difficulty in raising it is one of the overriding problems. It is a problem which always seems to be hanging round the necks of small businessmen. It springs precisely from having a limited base which makes it difficult to raise funds. It is also a problem of timing, of getting the right sort of money, at the right terms, in the right amounts, at the various important stages of its development.

It is not merely the machinery of the money market, which so many small businessmen tend to feel is designed for the exclusive benefit and use of large firms, which is cast in a villainous role, but so are the larger firms themselves. A small firm is always vulnerable because of a lack of ready cash and this can be the result in some measure of the actions of larger firms, customers of the smaller concern, which are slow payers. It produces an awkward sort of vulnerability because here the small firm's valued and important customers are using it as an unofficial banker and are trying to live off its trade credit for as long as they can. Because it is small, diffident and worried about losing business, it is reluctant about banging on doors and demanding its money. The small firms also believe that they are vulnerable because of the actions of bankers who in times of credit squeezes and directives from the Bank of England to reduce the level of overdrafts are more likely to put pressure on the small man whose overdraft may be counted in a few hundreds or a couple of thousand pounds than a giant corporation whose account is in the millions. Money to keep going and money to expand is invariably a major bugbear.

Management is a further weakness. By its nature a small firm is more often than not driven by one man, responsible for everything from policy decisions to details about his product or service. In the early days of developing his firm he is alone, bears the brunt on his own shoulders, sometimes under the sort of physical and mental pressure for sustained periods which can make home life and marriage creak, produce ulcers or even more deadly stress diseases. By the time the firm does grow, can afford some sort of management assistance, this kind of highly individualistic and energetic owner may find it extremely hard to delegate, impossible to keep his fingers off management functions which were once his province and which he cannot really credit anyone else could discharge as well as he. Another consideration which is overlooked or underestimated is the sheer loneliness of the man running a one-man-band firm, because no matter how hard-working and loyal his staff, there comes a point where they cannot help, where in a difficult, confused, or dangerous business situation the decision must be his and his alone.

So often it is the relentless pressure of day-to-day affairs which is responsible for the owner of a firm not seeing the wood for the trees. The sheer burden of getting out orders may preclude an investigation to see whether they are being executed profitably. Working incredibly long hours is no substitute for an efficient cost control system. There are many perfectly sensible, intelligent people who cheerfully admit there is a trace of this in their business, and they really ought to do something about it, but do not. You could argue that they like things the way they are.

They are not particularly anxious to recruit someone, to bring in an outsider to help put the problem right. In their hearts they are afraid the change may take from them something which is personally theirs. Possibly they feel the change may subtract from them some of the satisfactions of being their own boss, which is something above all else they like being.

In many small concerns these trials and tribulations are inherent in running a business and are those which most businessmen expect to have to take into account. A completely different bunch of problems are caused by events over which the businessmen have little or no control, by the course of international events or by government policy or particular economic doctrines.

In Britain there has probably been more opprobrium heaped on the heads of those who determine fiscal policy by small businessmen than by any other section of the community. The main complaints have been levelled at the effect of estate duty on small businesses—often causing them to go into liquidation in order that the duty be paid—and the provisions which require that certain categories of small business must distribute their profits. The effect of this has been, according to those who suffer from it, to make it well-nigh impossible for companies to plough back money into the business in order to finance expansion and future developments which, in turn, has meant that they have had to seek outside finance often at rates which they can't really afford.

The problems produced for small business by government fiscal and monetary policies have been summed up by one writer thus: 'Apart from the notorious close company provisions, the change to investment grants has worked to the disadvantage of small companies. The continuous and usually intensifying credit squeezes characteristic of Labour's term of office had much more serious effects on small companies than upon their larger brethren.'

'Confiscatory measures such as the special charge on investment income imposed in the 1968 Budget and the forced loans required under SET and the Imports Deposit Scheme also had disproportionately large effects on the small firm.'[4]

Another writer, this time in one of the classic areas of small business, the restaurant trade, outlined his disenchantment with fiscal policy even more tellingly. Towards the end of 1968, diners at the Genevieve, a French restaurant in London's Thayer Street, found that before their eyes had even alighted on the pâté de canard à l'ail, the menu was addressing them thus:

'Congratulations, you are supporting the following good causes:
Company Tax, Corporation Tax, Customs and Excise Tax, Income Tax/PAYE, Graduated Pension Contribution, Licence Duty, Import Duty, National Health Contribution.

'You are also contributing towards: Purchase Tax, Profits Tax, Rates, Reduction in Investment Allowance, Selective Employment Tax, Surtax, Surcharge, Water Rates, Wine and Spirits Tax, National Training Board Levy.

'Did we mention: Shortfall Tax, Distribution Tax (Schedule F), Short Terms Gains Tax, Capital Tax, Betterment Levy, Redundancy Fund Contribution, Special Charge (Schedule D), Increase in SET?

'And us.'

There is little doubt that in recent years a special feature of the small business scene in the United Kingdom has been the way in which the threat of estate duty has produced a business landscape dotted with examples of men who have built up a successful business from nothing and then sold out to a larger company, often staying on to run it with a fat service contract in their inside pocket. In situations where the business is heavy in assets the threat has been all the greater. This has been particularly true of family firms with large numbers of family shareholders.

In these conditions it only needs two or three deaths of substantial shareholders to occur close to each other and the burden of death duties immediately hazards the continuing existence of the firm. This is why in the brewery industry which is heavy in assets, where breweries are up to their ears in pubs, the examples of small breweries selling out to larger ones are legion. Transport and haulage is another field in which this trend is discernible, and there is at least one publicly quoted company, the Transport Development Group, which has sustained a steady annual growth rate, keeping its shareholders happy, by following a policy of acquisition, buying good, well-run transport concerns which come on to the market.

It would be reckless to claim that the sole reason for these sellouts was the prospect of estate duty looming up, but certainly the tax structure today has put a premium on this kind of sale. While the 1971 budget went some way to making small businessmen feel that at last the government was for them rather than against them, the relaxations and changes which were made by no means went as far as many people running small businesses had hoped. The peculiarities of the tax system and the problems produced by it for small companies will be examined in more detail in Chapter 16.

NOTES

1 Page 23. 'Men and Matters', *Financial Times* (17 September 1971).
2 Page 24. Confederation of British Industry. *Britain's Small Firms: Their Vital Role in the Economy* (November 1970).
3 Page 24. J. S. Boswell. *Small Firm Survey*. Industrial and Commercial Finance Corporation (November 1967).
4 Page 30. Frank Broadway. *State Intervention in British Industry, 1964–1968*. Kaye Ward (1969).

Chapter 2

The persistence of small business

The enduring nature of small business. Its position in the United Kingdom and other countries. Its sensitivity to change—how it adjusts, adapts and exploits. How its common problems and common attributes transcend frontiers and oceans. The UK economic background. Interventionist policies. Mr Heath's disengagement. Big business versus little business. Economic circumstances favouring small firms. The European economic climate. The long-term decline of small business. Small business failures.

SMALL businessmen have been around ever since bartering began, accommodating themselves to the circumstances and opportunities of their times, carrying over the broad thread of their business affairs from century to century, the craftsman and the pedlar giving pedigree to today's manufacturer and shopkeeper, and there is no reason to suppose they will not be with us for a long time to come.

In the future the function they perform and the areas in which they perform it may well be different from those to which we are accustomed now. Technological change will see to this, the way it has in the past. When the discovery of electricity was applied for the benefit of mankind, there was inevitably a fall-off in the number of small businesses concerned with the esoteric mysteries of lamp and wickmaking, with supplying paraffin oil, with making candles for everyday use.

But equally there grew up a whole spread of new small industries serving the needs and application of electricity—electrical retailers and television repairers, lampshade manufacturers, producers of fuse wire. The motor car brought an end to the dependence of cities like London on horse-drawn transport. The ramifications of this for small business, the changing nature of a whole important sector of it, was enormous. Fodder merchants, carriage repairers and horse dealers gave way to garages and motor mechanics. The Norfolk reed industry declined, along with the horse population of the cities, because the reed was no longer required for stable litter.

Small business has demonstrated an unquestionable historic persistence. It has also suffered a fair bit of persistent historic questioning too. As long ago as the tenth century in Constantinople, for instance, if you were in a small way of business it did not pay to be growth minded. The authorities held the view that businesses should be regulated and kept small, and they fostered the notion that competition was rather beyond the pale and dangerous. It certainly was.

If you happened to put someone out of business you were likely to lose your hands and ears. In more recent times the trend towards concentration, the preoccupation of both governments and economic planners with the restructuring of industry into units of greater size and therefore (so the argument goes) efficiency has made many small businessmen feel that their presence and value was being sharply questioned. But at least as a small man if you got caught up in the backwash from one of the Industrial Reorganisation Corporation's cataclystic merger operations all you might lose was your livelihood, not your ears.

As a matter of balance it has to be said that while fundamental changes—industrial or social—may kill off one set of opportunities for small business, the change itself deposits new ones in its wake. The establishment of new industries, for example, is a powerful stimulus for the establishment of new sorts of small businesses to serve them. The coming of the computer has produced a flush of small companies to serve its special needs, ranging from air-conditioning engineers who specialise in seeing computers get the clean, dust-free air they need to firms like Computer Field Maintenance which has a flying squad of seventy engineers ready to attend any computer which feels one degree under.

In the last century the revolution in public health, improved sanitation and piped water supplies, brought forth a small army of new businesses dedicated to plumbing in U-bends and seeing to it that Twyfords wc basins flushed the way they were intended to. Today the tremendous increase in housebuilding and the increasing number of older properties being renovated and refurbished has created a demand for a drain-cleaning operation which could not be met by conventional plumbing services. So a system of drain clearing called Dyno-Rod, with a nationwide coverage, is franchised to owner-managers, and has provided a new specialist area of small business which has all the benefits of public identification on a national scale. There is more about this in Chapter 9.

Everywhere in the industrial societies of the western world small businesses have demonstrated their propensity for hitching themselves to the bandwagon of change. It would be wrong, however, to fall into the trap of imagining that the special characteristics and problems of small business were somehow a peculiarly British phenomenon.

In May 1971 the Organisation for Economic Co-operation and Development in Paris published a report on the basis of evidence submitted by sixteen countries—Austria, Belgium, Canada, Denmark, Finland, France, Germany, Ireland, Italy, Japan, Norway, Portugal, Sweden, Switzerland, United Kingdom and the United States—on small and medium-sized businesses which is the nearest thing we have to a world picture of the small business population and what is happening to it.

Small and medium-sized businesses predominate in all the countries concerned and in Austria, Belgium, Denmark, Japan, Norway, Sweden and Switzerland firms with less than 50 employees account for over 90 per cent of the total. In Canada, Germany and the United States such firms represent between 74 and 80 per cent of the total. In Finland industrial enterprises having a maximum of 100 employees counted for 97 per cent of the total in 1967. In Ireland 60 per cent of firms employ less than 20 people, and in Portugal 85 per cent of firms employ between 3 and 20 people. In the United Kingdom 97 per cent of manufacturing enterprises employ less than 500 people. Within the distribution trade sector in the United Kingdom nearly two thirds of total retail sales are accounted for by establishments employing 10 or fewer people.

Definitions as to what constitutes a small business vary in the different countries, but the figures do assist in giving a general view, even if it is not a strictly comparable one. In a number of European countries (Austria, Belgium, France, Sweden, Switzerland) small and medium-sized businesses are generally understood to be those with less than 50 employees; in Denmark and Norway less than 20; and in Germany and Italy generally up to 100 employees. In Japan the Fundamental Law of Medium and Small Enterprises gives a definition which covers either having capital not exceeding 70 million yen or having not more than 300 employees in manufacturing industry, and either having capital not exceeding 10 million yen or having not more than 50 employees in the commerce and services sector. Using these national yardsticks it is interesting to see that despite all you hear about giant trading companies in Japan like Mitsubishi, some 99·5 per cent of total establishments in the economy as a whole in 1966 were accounted for by small and medium-sized businesses which employed 25 million people or 80 per cent of the non-agricultural working population, and contributed 40 per cent of Japan's exports in value.

The contribution made to the economy, the share of small businesses in production and employment, varies considerably between countries, which reflects differences in industrial structure. Firms with less than 50 employees account for large proportions of employment in manufacturing in Japan (43 per cent), Norway and Portugal (36 per cent), Austria (29 per cent). On the other hand firms with less than 50 employees account for only 12 per cent of industrial employment in Germany and they contribute only about 10 per cent of the total industrial turnover. In the USA firms with less than 50 employees account for 16 per cent of industrial employment.

Even if the basis of comparison between countries is not strictly the same there is a remarkable similarity in the problems of money and management which small businesses have to face. This is ground which has already been covered but it is worth just picking on a few isolated points which show that while the problems and difficulties vary in detail they are basically the same. The fact that small businesses are less attractive customers to banks than large ones, because they cannot offer the same security and the smallness of their loans involves the banks in higher administrative costs, is sometimes reflected in the terms they obtain.

If, as a small businessman in Japan, you wanted a bank loan in the spring of 1971 the average rate of interest you would have paid would have been 8·03 per cent compared with 7·68 per cent for a big company. In Switzerland as a small businessman one of your major problems, especially if you were running an hotel or restaurant, would have been caused by the labour shortage, and your heavy dependence, for example, on foreign workers from Italy. As a small businessman in a vast country like Canada your particular problem might have been the physical distance your business was from major consuming centres with the disadvantage it brings in additional transport costs for raw materials and for the finished products which you dispatch. There should be food for thought in this for any small British businessman who imagines Britain's entry into the Common Market will produce an automatic panacea for his sagging sales. Certainly the Community will offer great opportunities but the farthest corners of it are going to be expensive to reach and exploit.

Even the travelling journalist, on nodding acquaintance with small business in places as far apart as Madeira and Minneapolis, is provoked to the realisation that it is a sector which is international in its motivations, in its approaches and in its attitudes. International in a sense which is diametrically opposite to the giant international corporations, the activities of which transcend frontiers and oceans. What small businesses everywhere are doing is shifting, adjusting and accommodating themselves in order that they thrive and survive and meet their problems.

Local circumstances and conditions provide their own flavour but the manoeuvring possesses a marked similitude. Local geography has dictated that the dairy industry in Madeira is highly fragmented, archaic and, compared with its modern British counterpart, bears about as much resemblance as chalk to cheese. Small farmers keep their dairy cows confined in small thatched huts all over the island since it is so precipitous they fear the animals will fall down a ravine and injure themselves. The milk, which takes a long time to get to a town like Funchal, suffers in quality because of the heat and the journey. It is not the most economic or healthy way to run a dairy industry, but already there are signs of change which should provide small business opportunities for bright island entrepreneurs. Government experts are trying to introduce a bit more science and technology into the business with stock improvement, milk-cooling plants and a processing factory. The first step is the building of communal cow houses which will take twenty to thirty cows from a neighbourhood instead of them being scattered in individual huts. All this must eventually have an impact on the distinctive milkmen of Funchal who walk the steep, crowded streets blowing whistles to announce their presence, dispensing milk from large cans carried in shoulder yokes.

Surely it will not be long before some smart lad realises that when the production end of the industry is sorted out, the answer to the peripatetic milkman will be a neighbourhood milk parlour full of automatic milk-vending machines where the populace will come and take their own milk, cooled and hygienically sealed in wax cartons or plastic bottles?

In Minneapolis as winter approaches the yacht chandlers and the small boat yards out on the lakes no longer find the bottom dropping out of their business. Because of the growing popularity of the snowmobile—a motor-cycle engine-powered machine on runners which is capable of speeds up to 90mph on snow and ice—they now have year-round sales to sustain them. The snowmobiles and the sledges which they trail behind them take the showroom space previously occupied by sailing dinghies and speedboats. Even local golf courses, under several feet of frozen snow in winter with not a green in sight, change themselves into snowmobile courses for the winter months and charge for it.

If small business is the last repository of the entrepreneurial gut feeling which makes a man get up from whatever it is that he is doing and have a go, then there is many a partisan party who will tell you that it is a small wonder that such men haven't been stifled in the wave of interventionist policies which have characterised the economic thinking of the 1960s and from which the Heath administration has offered some promise of disengagement. Throughout the decade successive British governments were obsessed with establishing targets for economic growth but their hopes of achieving them were invariably short-lived. The economic problems which characterised this difficult period—recurring balance of payments crises, inflation, sagging growth rates—produced more and more government measures designed to resolve them. Massive doses of deflation damped down demand, unemployment started to rise, profits were reduced and the number of business failures mounted. Small firms like Caterpillar Products were hard hit, lost work and were forced to lay-off workpeople.

None of the policies designed to tackle these problems, to achieve the growth which both governments and people believe desirable, were specifically anti-small business, but were concerned more with restructuring the industrial system. They brought intense economic planning and government-backed agencies such as the now disbanded Industrial Reorganisation Corporation to serve as catalysts of change. The latter quite obviously had little direct relevance for the host of small, independent firms in this country, whose disenchantment stems from official indifference and disinterest; from the conviction that politicians and economic planners were too concerned with the needs of large organisations to care about the aspirations of the small man. They felt they were in danger of becoming second-class industrial citizens. When you get down to cases, you cannot help noticing that what the small businessman is really griping about is injustice, the dislike of what he sees as discrimination against him, the offence to his dignity and business beliefs.

There are occasions when you are bound to wonder whether the spirit of disenchantment is not greater than the adversity from which it springs. Until recently there was so little known about the effects on small business of particular government policies, so little sound, independent research on the subject, so little comprehensive statistical information available about small business that it was impossible to pronounce on it with any degree of conclusivity. (And if the Bolton Committee had not managed to meticulously chart some of these unknown depths then it would have been a gross waste of the taxpayers' money.) The point is worth making again because you cannot blink away the fact that while the spokesmen of small business are making pronouncements understandably suited to its own ends, painting grey if not black pictures of its plight, there are a great many small businesses which manage to keep clear from emotive and political argument on the subject and just get on with doing what they do best, being small, well run, and meeting the difficulties with verve, with confidence in their own ability and with enjoyment.

The matter is one of perspective. There are handicaps and difficulties peculiar to small business. There are policies which have militated against it. There are circumstances which have been unhelpful to it. But in the argument about big and little, the fundamental point has to be made that if you are attempting to draw up some sort of national balance sheet of the strengths and weaknesses of large and small business they are in many ways opposite sides of the same coin. One writer, an American, has stated the position like this. 'A set of economic circumstances can be specified in which the attributes of large business will have a substantial advantage. On the other hand, an opposite set of economic circumstances provides a significant advantage for small business. It is, therefore, the fundamental characteristics of the economic environment that determine what the relative positions of what small business and large business will be in the economy. The devil theory of the pernicious encroachment of the octopus-like tentacles of large firms squeezing out of existence the small enterprise is a fantasy that fails to look at the realities characteristic of the economic environment.'[1]

This may well be so but you can still come across instances which look suspiciously like big brother trying to lean—not always successfully—on his smaller one. The following is an extract from the 'Men and Matters' column of the *Financial Times* of 15 September 1971.

'On September 29 the four year legal wrangle between the giant Pillsbury food company and the tiny Forest Laboratories will culminate in an appearance before the American Court of Appeal. The last round of the case, which involves the "misappropriation of Forest's trade secrets by the Pillsbury company" according to Forest, went to Forest with an award of $90,000. But despite a trial which went on for some two weeks, neither side were satisfied —Pillsbury because it thought the damages were too large, and Forest because it thought they were too small. Even if Forest's award were to be substantially increased, Mr Hans Lowey, chairman of Forest, admits that it is unlikely to cover the cost of the battle. "We are not only fighting for money, we are talking about a point of principle. We want to set a precedent to prove that small companies can fight the large corporations and win." '

Small firms can also win at times of rapid scientific and technical advance, at times when the economy is growing, when everyone is becoming better off. The small firm is then able to bask in the warmth of the work opportunities open to it. In such circumstances it finds itself being able to take advantage of those opportunities, and indeed to establish itself on the basis of them, largely because there are so many good chances around that existing firms can't corner them all, nor prevent new ones from getting a piece of the action. This is more true at a time of rapid technological change, when inventions and their application, when new developments in areas like electronics and telecommunications are proceeding at such a pace that there is something new coming up which is exploitable practically every other week. By the same token it is what makes established companies, whose prosperity is based on a single technological innovation unique to them, so nervous about the bright talented newcomers who might come up with something which could put them out of business overnight. Anyone who doubts this ought to see the rush there is every Wednesday morning at the Patent Office in London when the week's batch of patents granted is published—usually about 800 of them—and the professional patents searchers who are keeping watching briefs for various industrial concerns spend their morning flicking through the pages.

The early days of the establishment of new industries also provide untold opportunities for the small firms who are alert and alive to what is happening around them. A vivid example of this is provided by the story of Norman Chalk who, until the search and subsequent exploitation of oil and gas deposits off the North Sea coast of the United Kingdom, was a small restaurant owner in Norfolk. Now he is the biggest caterer to the offshore industry in the North Sea. You will meet him in Chapter 12.

Momentum is also given to small business endeavours at a time when growth rates are riding high because there is a greater demand for the specialised, personal services which are traditionally associated with small business. Thus the general economic circumstances help give a boost to industries where small business is prevalent and where a high level of incomes allows the services of a specialised firm, for example, to come in and plan and fit a new modern kitchen for the housewife rather than her husband undertaking the task on a do-it-yourself basis.

Almost all these conditions in which small firms tend to proliferate and prosper have been present to a greater or lesser extent in the post-war economic history of both Western Europe and America. It is only in much more recent times that what people thought of as impregnable economies, possessing almost unassailable strength, have begun to creak and cause some doubts as to whether the economic climate is now as favourable and beneficial to small business as it has been in the past. For the American small businessman in Europe on holiday in August 1971 the fact that the old economic order of things had changed was brought home to him in a highly personal fashion when he discovered that American Express dollar travellers cheques were not as desirable in the eyes of Europeans as he might have supposed. Back home the Nixon administration was attempting to fend off the worst excesses of the balance-of-payments crunch by imposing import levies and our small US businessman must have wondered, as he read the European newspapers, what was coming to pass in the land of enterprise, opportunity and the mighty dollar.

If there has been a time and place par excellence when conditions seemed propitious for small business, it must have been in Europe in the twenty years following World War II. The story of European economic growth has been dramatised and commented upon more in the context of the German Economic Miracle than any other, but impressive though the commentators of the time made it sound, it was not unique to that country. Despite ups and downs and many changes of gear, the overall European experience, save for the United Kingdom, was one of a high rate of growth, sustained and boosted at various times by projects and events like the Marshall Plan, in which the United States underwrote European economic reconstruction; the Korean War which may have dislocated world trade but which produced its own minor boom; and the formation of NATO and the continuing spending of European governments on arms.

Opportunities were unleashed by the reaction from wartime austerity—in a sense it was this which set Horizon Holidays (see Chapter 10) on the road to becoming one of Britain's major tour operators—and by the ripple movement right across the pool as large lumps of investment were dropped into the middle of it.

Hordes of small businesses rode the resulting waves round the edges. At this time there was also a great shift in employment from the older manufacturing industries to service industries of all kinds, classically the kind of industries which attract the small entrepreneur because the capital required to set up in them is usually minimal. There was also a great surge in technological advance, probably more widespread and rapid than at any other time. The wartime aircraft industry, for example, the enormous advances made in aeronautical engineering, the invention of the jet engine, the use of jet airliners from the early 1950s onwards for the large-scale transportation of civilian passengers, had a multiplicity of rub-offs for small business. These ranged from small companies extruding plastic trays for airline meals to a company called Perdisan which produces a very modern version of the old chemical toilet, so modern that it has been chosen as a standard item in the Concorde supersonic airliner.

It was a time when the lay public gradually became aware of

the new, rapidly growing industry of electronics. Small electronics companies operated all over the place, often specialising in some narrow and esoteric area of instrumentation or computerology. The greatest asset of these companies was the boss's high-level technical expertise. It was precisely these kinds of men, often with academic backgrounds, and their feet firmly planted in university research laboratories, who suddenly went commercial and set up technological companies of their own to exploit their research findings.

In America this development was especially marked, and its roots go back to before the war. In California at Stanford University, and on the so-called Route 128 which girdles the city of Boston, small technology companies, based on the work and researches of their principals within the University of Stanford and within the laboratories of the Massachusetts Institute of Technology, have grown thick upon the ground. On the campus of Stanford University, the Stanford Industrial Park, owned, administered, leased and landscaped by the University, has industrial enterprise inextricably intermingled with intellect. When I was last there roadside advertisement hoardings announced that 3,500 PhDs lived in Santa Clara County and many of the young vigorous companies in the area which started from backyard beginnings were launched by a new breed of small businessman, the scientist-entrepreneur.

Some of these small companies are now far from small and are blue chip names in the world of electronics. In 1937 a young physicist, Russell Varian, working in the University's laboratories, invented the klystron tube. It was an event which was as basic to the development of the microwave industry as he was basic to the founding of a famous company called Varian Associates.

A year later two Stanford engineering graduates, William Hewlett and David Packard, founded the Hewlett-Packard Company, one of the world's largest producers of electronic measuring devices, on a capital of only a little over $500. World War II, America's huge space programme and government-financed research have all combined to give substantial impetus to the growth and development of these science-based firms and others like them, but at the time of writing, with federal funds for research being cut back and the de-escalation of the war in Viet Nam, the chilly wind of contraction has started to blow.

For small business the central question now is whether, with the continuing restructuring and concentration of industry proceeding at a smart clip almost everywhere, the golden era is over and spent, no longer a fertile seedbed for independent, risk-taking, small business pioneering. There is some evidence to suggest that this might be so. The OECD report on Small and Medium-Sized Businesses concluded that in some countries such as Denmark, Italy and Canada, the number of small firms in manufacturing was declining in absolute terms, while in others, like Norway and Switzerland, their relative position has declined in terms of employment. Expert projections in Belgium suggest that small businesses are now expected to develop more slowly than the economy as a whole. In the United States it is reported that in general they are maintaining their position.

In the United Kingdom the numerical importance of small manufacturing firms has been falling slightly in recent years. In 1958, 86 per cent of all manufacturing establishments employed less than 500 people whereas in 1963 the figure was 83 per cent. A comparison of figures for firms employing less than 200 persons in the 1958 and the 1963 censuses shows that the number of establishments fell by 3,319 from 79,748 to 76,429. The total numbers employed by firms in this category remained pretty static at between 2·3 and 2·4 million, but in this five-year period there was a hefty drop in the net output of these firms from £4,908 million to £2,869 million.

Thirty years ago small establishments were more important than they are today.[2] Between 1935 and 1958 employment in small places of work with 10 or fewer workers declined from 9·5 per cent to 2·2 per cent of the total employed in manufacturing industry. Between 1935 and 1961 small establishments (11–99 workers) and medium-sized ones (100–499 workers) provided a diminishing share of total employment, dropping from 25·6 per cent to 20·1 per cent and 39·1 per cent to 31·2 per cent respectively. During these years the number of places with 10 workpeople or fewer was estimated at between 130,000 and 140,000 compared with nearly 31,000 in 1963.

It is not helpful to measure the importance of small firms in terms of statistics alone. It may not commend itself to the spirit of scientific inquiry but at one level it is instructive to make a rough and ready assessment of its vital role by relating it to your personal, everyday domestic life. Small business is with you from the cradle to the grave in a range of services, professional and others (doctor, solicitor, accountant, dentist, painter and decorator, electrician, undertaker), as well as the small independent butcher, baker and table-lamp maker. For all the emphasis on chain stores and supermarkets, if you were to walk down your village or suburban high street and subtract its small owner-managed businesses it would leave a local retailing panorama which was full of holes.

Furthermore, if you think of all the tiers of economic activity, each dependent to a great or lesser extent on the other, where small firms play their part in keeping the wheels of the large ones turning, supplying a plethora of products and services from refrigeration engineers to stationery supplies, you are talking of a small business population of rich variety and range.

But if there were one single event which occurred while writing this book which spotlighted both the nature and the hazards of being one of these small service concerns, it was the largest industrial bankruptcy the United Kingdom has seen since World War II: the collapse of Rolls-Royce. In the heat and excitement of the moment, in the trauma of the failure of a blue chip name, which, because of its special position in the world of international engineering, had taken on the mantle of an institution, the acute and scarifying repercussions on the Derby and Ilkeston Window Cleaning Company were largely overshadowed. This company, employing 28 men, had been cleaning Rolls-Royce factory, warehouse and office windows for twenty-five years. The contract brought in £3,000 a month, and it was virtually the mainstay of Derby and Ilkeston's business.

Thus while the crisis which hit Rolls-Royce was an unpleasant blow for many of its traditional suppliers, firms like Joseph Lucas, for Derby and Ilkeston it was shattering. Window cleaning suddenly became a luxury Rolls-Royce could no longer afford, and the window-cleaning company found itself owed £16,000. It had a £3,000 overdraft at the bank and every one of its employees, some of whom had been with it for seventeen years, had to go on the dole. Taken in isolation its misfortunes were of no great moment compared to those which befell Rolls-Royce, and the threat which hung over its future until plans were announced for its reconstitution and the contract and price problems with Lockheed were resolved, thus assuring a future for the RB 211 engine. The window-cleaning company was equally vulnerable because of its dependence on one contract. It is the sort of circumstance which small firms sometimes have to live with and overcome, and as it happened Rolls-Royce started having its windows cleaned again. None the less firms which don't learn from such a lesson are not usually around for the chance to learn it a second time.

For an amalgam of reasons small businesses and small businessmen do go bust and in 1970 they excelled themselves. The rate of failure among small businesses has always been extraordinarily high but in 1970 the numbers were the highest for the previous ten years. The figure for bankruptcies was an alarming 4,600 of which about two-thirds were pure trading failures, compared with about 2,000 bankruptcies a year at the beginning of the 1960s. During the past ten years company liquidation both compulsory and voluntary has increased too. Voluntary liquidations in Great Britain rose from 3,971 to 7,759, compulsory ones from 535 to 1,208.

It is perfectly true that in the last couple of years the spectacular failures like Rolls-Royce and Lines Brothers, the big Triang, Meccano and Dinky toy firm, have hogged the headlines, but the bulk of bankruptcies are among smaller businesses. In the 4,600 which were bankrupt in 1970 only in 57 cases were the liabilities over £40,000. Unofficial estimates suggest that about 50 per cent of individuals and businesses which go bankrupt do so for liabilities of under £500. On this basis it becomes easy to understand why the bankruptcy league table is headed by small builders followed by retailers, restaurants, and cafés, garages, motor dealers and filling stations and farmers.

The question now is whether the alarming and mounting level of business failures over the past decade have reached their peak. Or is there worse to come? In facing up to the 1970s are small businesses as adaptable and resilient as people believe them to be? Or is it inevitable that as a group they are destined to fall into a further decline? After the passing of a hair-raising decade, what does small business look like and what shape is it in to face the problems and challenges of the next?

NOTES

1 Page 39. Irving Pfeffer, editor. *The Financing of Small Business.* J. Fred Weston, 'The Position of Small Business in the American Economy'. Collier-Macmillan (1967).
2 Page 44. G. C. Allen. *The Structure of Industry in Britain.* Longmans, 3rd edition (1969).

Chapter 3

The anatomy of small business

> The firm as a functional, legal and asset-owning unit. Its organic nature. New firms, old firms, specialist firms. From little businesses big businesses grow. Milestones of growth for small firms, and the problems. What small businesses do best at. The spread of small business by industry. The topography of small business. Small business quarters. The classic strongholds of small business—farmers and craftsmen. The rich variety of small business.

THE quick, easy answer to how important is small business, is that from small businesses big ones grow, although not all of them are success stories like Clubman's Club, one of the more brilliant entrepreneurial ideas of the 1960s. It started on a capital of a mere £150 and catapulted into the big league in the space of five years, making millionaires of its co-owners when it went public. Clubman's Club was launched by Peter Whitfield and Robert Tanner, who had read economics together at Oxford. They were casting around for a formula which would allow them to succeed in business without having much capital.

Like all good ideas, theirs was a gem of simplicity. It was to form a club which carried membership to a lot of other clubs without the bother of having to pay individual membership fees. The idea caught on from the start. Apart from the convenience factor for the club-goer, the clubs themselves liked the idea because they didn't have to pay any commissions, and the marginal customer which Clubman's Club brought through their doors was, with their fixed overheads, very profitable for them.

In their first year Whitfield and Tanner signed up thirty London clubs, but soon they were numbered in their hundreds, all over the country. In its first year Clubman's Club made a profit of £3,000. When it went public profits were £113,000. Later it was sold to Mecca, the big catering and entertainment group. So, as a result of an imaginative and uncomplicated idea in which there was a clear benefit for both club-goers and club-owners, the two ex-Oxford men made sizeable fortunes for themselves comparatively early in life. Taxes or no taxes there will always be men like them who are quick, lively and intelligent and who come flocking in like perky starlings to forage wherever the best opportunities are.

Many small firms, like people, lack the drive and ambition which create the outstanding business success stories and opt instead for a comfortable canter on a quiet horse, rather than a rip-roaring ride on a tiger. But whatever the size and whatever point of growth a business has reached, whether it is Caterpillar Products in Flaunden or Imperial Chemical Industries, with its headquarters in London and a great spread of chemical plants and factories throughout Britain, it exists as a complete entity.

The notion of small business is more an economic than legalistic concept. It derives from regarding a business as an asset-owning entity which has at its disposal buildings, machines, stocks of goods, money in the bank and trade investments; assets of performance like profits and sales; human assets such as owners, managers and workpeople; and a block of intangible assets like expertise and know-how.

A business is also a functional unit which reflects what it does, and the nature of its product or service. Thus many small businesses are small, remain small, and will not aspire to anything larger because the world in which they function is suited to small-scale operations, not large ones. Take the handmade concertina industry, for example. The Crabbs, father and son (who tell their story on p 67), carry on their business in a small workshop in London's Islington; the one and only handmade concertina business in the world. Because their operations are unsuited to large-scale methods of production and highly geared national marketing campaigns, they will of necessity always remain small.

A business as a legal entity is also important, and becomes even more so at times when it is growing rapidly. Because as a general rule the benefits and advantages to be obtained from growth can be better achieved by enclosing a business in certain legal forms appropriate to its needs. Equally the pressures and problems of a growing business may be more easily and efficiently resolved if it is contained in one legal framework rather than another. Thus a company which is showing a healthy rate of growth each year may find that its existence as a private limited company is too constraining when it considers the potential it has under its belt. By inviting the public to subscribe for its shares and becoming a publicly quoted company, it can raise a large slab of money which will help it finance the expansion of which it believes it is capable. In a personal context the change of legal status from a private limited company to a public one may give its previous owners and shareholders the reward for their past ingenuity and hard work, making them, as in the case of the two men who founded Clubman's Club, into millionaires, even if only paper ones.

This does not mean that it is a matter of compulsion that a private company shall go public to assist its growth. There are still a number of outstanding examples of private companies, most of them family-owned, which are constantly on stage, open to public acclaim or disapproval, and which are by no means playing small parts. To the housewife one of the most familiar is Sainsbury's. In electrical engineering Ferranti stands out, in engineering the David Brown Organisation, in footwear C. & J. Clarke. While even though Pilkington Bros, the glass firm which was once Britain's largest private company, has gone public, only some 10 per cent of its shares have been floated and it is still under firm family control.

The form in which a business trades, the manner in which it is constituted, ranges in Britain from the individual owning a firm and trading on his own account to the giant public corporation where ownership is extremely diverse, and is spread over thousands of individual shareholders. The owner-trader, or proprietor, is a familiar part of the landscape in the high street and is thick on the ground among the nation's shopkeepers. He is very much a legacy of the last century, where in the normal run of things retailing renewed itself in a time-honoured and accepted fashion. A man was apprenticed to a grocer or haberdasher, often lived on the premises, nursing the ambition of one day nailing up his own shingle and opening up in trade for himself.

Another business entity which the law recognises is the partnership. This is much favoured by the professions, by accountants, solicitors, doctors and is a form of business in which the arrangements tend to stand for the working lifetime of those involved. It is not normally regarded as a legal stage in the growing process. The patent agent, or consulting engineer, whose practice thrives, prospers and increases in size will take on more partners rather than aim at becoming a public company. Partnerships, of course, are not confined to the professions. They are found both in the manufacturing service industries and are often family based. There is more likelihood of these commercial partnerships progressing to company status than the professional ones.

Before the 1967 Companies Act there were three different categories of non-quoted company: the non-quoted public company, the private exempt company and the private non-exempt company. Broadly speaking all companies had to lodge annual returns with the Registrar of Companies. But the exempt private company got its name because it could get exemption from filing its accounts, and this it was able to do up and until January 1968. The exemption, however, did not apply in cases where the private company had another company as a shareholder. The idea of this was to plug a loophole which allowed public companies to assign certain of their operations to a private one and therefore not have to submit accounts. Now there is no such animal as a private exempt company and all private company accounts have to be filed at Companies House in London where they are available for scrutiny. This is one of the reasons why many people today find the partnership an attractive legal form in which to conduct their business because exemption from filing accounts is still applicable to it.

It was this new company legislation which produced some curious to-ing and fro-ing of businesses as legal entities towards the end of 1967. A lot of small private companies didn't like the idea of filing information which basically disclosed their trading position. These disclosure requirements raised a considerable furore at the time and it was widely held that they made small firms much more vulnerable than they were previously. This belief remains, although there is little conclusive evidence to back it.

The firms argue that having to place their turnover and profit figures on file at Companies House, where for a small fee anyone can go and search them out, gives valuable clues to competitors about a company's share of the market and the level of profitability of particular products or services. This is all the more acute if it happens to be a one-product company. Suddenly instead of getting on producing its product quietly and unobtrusively, information which it considers very much in the category of trade secrets is being splashed about all over the place.

Such were the fears of small companies on this score that a number of them, like the Bell Woodworking Company of Leicester, changed their legal status, reverting from private companies to partnerships or own account traders which they were previously, neither of which are required to file accounts. Bell Woodworking is Europe's premier boat kit manufacturer and machines the kits for the extraordinarily successful *Daily Mirror* dinghy which you see on every creek and beach these days. It changed specifically because it didn't like the disclosure provisions.

Another circumstance which in recent years caused some companies to change their status was the introduction of corporation tax. When it was first mooted, tax experts worked away with their slide rules far into the night calculating the maximum benefits which would accrue in easing a company's tax burden in relation to the legal status.

Considerations of this sort are important if you are planning to start a business, something which it is comparatively easy to do. There are plenty of books on the library shelves which tell you how to go about it and it is not the province of this book to travel over such well sign-posted country, except to say there are a minimum of forms and documents to cope with. The basic requirements are to establish what the company is and the nature of the business it proposes to carry on. For the necessary forms all you need do is pop into a law stationers'.

In fact you don't even need to have a lawyer form a company for you, because you can buy a ready made one off the peg, just like a suit from Burtons, and make of it what you will. Here you are buying a legal framework, not a going commercial concern of the sort you see advertised in a publication like *Dalton's Weekly* (a classic market place for small businesses—especially retail ones). If nothing else, this is a quick and easy way of getting a business off the ground legally. It may seem bizarre, but there are establishments which offer this service in London and into which you can walk and buy a company just like any other commodity. Thomas Herbert runs one of them and what he does and how he does it has been amusingly described by Paul Ferris in his book on *The City*.

Buying a ready made company over the counter, or forming one, is probably the only point in its life where you could describe it with any degree of accuracy and precision, knowing the description would not radically alter at least until it actually started producing and trading.

The temptation for a writer, when he walks through the door of a business, starts talking to its owners and directors and attempts to make an assessment of it, is to freeze it, rather like a quick snapshot at a given moment of time. But companies are like people, for ever on the move, changing from one foot to another, relaxing, twitching a bit, falling sick, being doctored, recovering, feeling on top of the world, running in a race or ambling along. Businesses grow and shrink, change their shape, lose their fat and become overweight. They are essentially organic. The challenge and creative satisfaction which comes from running them derives in a large measure from meeting, coping with, controlling and exploiting all these component elements.

Like people, companies inhabit a world of enormous complexity and diversity. The point has been strongly made[1] that in the main the structure of industry in Western countries has been created by competition and the forces of the market, and that there are large numbers of separate companies of varying size operating together through an intricate web of price relationships. While the broader lineaments of the system appear to remain constant for long periods, it is in fact dynamic in the sense that the survival of every company depends upon its efforts to accommodate itself to a constantly changing environment. The same inquiry goes on to say that even where broad patterns of size, distribution and degrees of integration seem to persist, adjustments in other ways are going on unceasingly behind what might at first appear to be an unchanging facade.

Again, like people, a business varies in complexion and character. It may be a new firm which has established itself in a new industry, rather like a small company called Underwater and Marine Equipment, which is run by an ex-diver named Mike Borrow, his wife and a staff of eight who spend their time designing, developing and manufacturing a fantastic range of underwater electronic gadgets which helps the new North Sea offshore oil industry with all sorts of problems. These range from locating 'lost' well heads which have been capped off and left for a time, to developing special underwater stereo-cameras which make it possible to construct accurate maps of the seabed, showing hills and valleys in sharp relief.

Borrow saw his opportunity when he realised that the offshore exploration industry did not have access to all the sophisticated aids it would have liked, so he decided to set to and make them. His precision pinger, for example, is a 26in long cylinder full of electronic gadgetry which, suspended in the sea, pings back not only information about depth, but temperatures too. It is accurate to within 3ft in 30,000 and, used with other techniques, has made it possible for the first time to measure accurately the depth of the ocean floor through layers of mud.

UMEL is the sort of company which will tackle anything, and everything it makes is tailor-made to do a particular job. It started over twelve years ago when Borrow and his wife set up business in their home at Fleet in Hampshire. Today it has a turnover of about £70,000 a year and a solid reputation as an underwater trouble-shooting outfit. A firm like this, in a new and expanding industry into which money is being heavily invested, and where the big oil and drilling companies have need of a host of small ones to service them in a variety of ways, offers substantial opportunities for growth.

Another group of companies with a very different complexion are those established in trades and industries which are easy to enter because there is only a minimum of qualification or expertise needed. A case in point is retailing. The technological requirements, both in knowledge and equipment, for opening a small drapery business or a newsagent are virtually non-existent. Nor is managerial experience regarded as important by those entering such trades. There is an element of truth in this, but it really only applied in the days when supermarkets did not exist and the competition was not so intense; before the motor car changed household shopping patterns and the small man could at least rely on the prop of resale price maintenance.

Industries which are easy to enter are one of the key problem areas for small business, for in addition to the minimal needs mentioned above, the stake you need to start is usually within the grasp of most people. They can either save it or borrow from the family, and in any case in many areas of retailing, trade credit terms are pretty good. This ease of entry eventually takes its own harsh toll. Hopeful entrants come into the business in considerable numbers when trading conditions are buoyant, but as soon as there are signs of recession, those with the fewest skills and resources find themselves at best having to struggle through some sticky patches, at worst going bankrupt.

This is not to say that companies which establish themselves in new areas of activity are all business deadbeats. There are examples of smaller firms cheekily challenging the giants and turning the tables on the competition. Wilkinson's challenged Gillette in razor blades and Weetabix took a large chunk of the breakfast food market, once very much dominated by the giant Kellogg Company of America.

Another category of small business which is highly characteristic of the technological age in which we live is one which sets out to exploit a very specialised bit of an industry which in itself is technologically complex. This is typical of medical and scientific equipment, instrumentation and electronic control equipment. It is an area which attracted Bernard Hunn, a former big company professional manager with a highly technical and scientific background. He is running a very young company called Revenue Systems from an old disused pub in Luton, producing something which is likely to have a revolutionary effect on the way we buy goods in a shop or make transactions at the bank.

When you visit him Bernard shows you a small plastic card which looks for all the world like a credit card. In fact it is much more, because on it is stored a 'bank' of electronic pulses, and when the card is fed into a terminal, say a special cash register at a supermarket checkout, the machine subtracts a number of pulses from the card to the value of goods bought. In short, what Hunn has created is electronic money. He has every hope that it will make a fortune for him of the common or garden variety.

One of the reasons why companies like Revenue Systems can get established and exist side by side with large-scale industry is that they are on the road to becoming large themselves. There is no copper-bottomed way of guaranteeing that Revenue Systems will eventually assume the shape and trappings of a large corporation, but there are many inherent strengths about it which not all small firms enjoy; a product based upon a piece of clever innovation and a market which is potentially enormous, and international. It has management which is both technologically and managerially skilled, and no less a body than the government-backed National Research Development Corporation and Technical Development Capital (an offshoot of the Industrial and Commercial Finance Corporation) also seem to rate its prospects, because they have put their money in it.

Men like Bernard Hunn, who are managerially educated and technologically equipped and who apply their talents to the right sort of small business, may well produce faster growth and greater profitability than a finer quality of management applied to a far larger enterprise.

The natural progression of business success is to move from being small to being large. But like most things it has the kind of inevitable drawbacks which can put a stop to any kind of progress. On the one hand the efficient small businessman who builds a business and sees it grow will have to face the competition of larger companies above him. They will reserve a special eye and extra sales efforts especially for him as he starts to take an increasing proportion of their business. On the other hand, smaller, aggressive competitors, like he was three or four years earlier, will start darting in and nibbling away at his cake. Meanwhile he is up to his eyes in the problems of being a large company—maintaining his growth and satisfying shareholders. He gradually loses the qualities of flexibility, speed of action and swift application of new ideas because of the commitment to huge investment, geared to large-scale operations, which demands such a high degree of intensity in its day-to-day management.

The inescapable fact is that good small companies are not always content to rest with that label round their necks and as they look about them they can observe plenty of precedents which show there is no reason why they should.

The generation of sizeable British businesses which have grown from smaller ones is a well-documented subject. Marks and Spencer, Plessey, Tesco, Thorn, Lesney and Letraset have all risen from unpretentious beginnings, to become household words, attaining positions of commercial influence and power.

In the study of any firm there are numerous milestones in its growth, markers which reflect its inherent organic nature. It is noticeable that when you talk to the owners of small businesses about these they are apt to isolate purely commercial, financial or physical features which highlight their company's progress. It may be the winning of a particular contract which was a turning point. Or a year when sales topped the £½ million. Or the day when the firm moved out of its old back-street premises into a new factory on a trading estate. Equally, the sheer metabolism of their businesses, the vital process of business nutrition, is perceived in terms of fairly traditional and obvious business procedures; the extending of an overdraft by the bank to tide them through a particularly difficult patch, or the advantageous sale of a piece of land which financed some new machinery. Rarely do they seem to equate the growth of their business with the shift in emphasis of their own functions, with the importation of management help, with the delegation of their own authority. Perhaps this is because so many of them cannot bring themselves to believe that other people will do jobs as well as they can.

For many of them delegation is an anxious and painful business. Having given birth to the baby and lavished care and attention upon it in infancy and childhood, they see it come to manhood and maturity. By then others have arrived on the scene to take a share of the responsibility for it, as well as the kudos which attaches to it. The owner of the business knows full well that the size and growth of the firm demands a more formal and organised management structure. Nevertheless he resents the change and if there is one tell-tale sign of this resentment it is that he continues to perform a task or function which traditionally he undertook in the early and exciting days of the firm's infancy. A task which was important then and which has now acquired an historical importance. Yet it is of no great matter in present conditions and circumstances, and it could equally well be discharged by a junior member of the staff.

Years ago this question of growing was far less complicated than it is today. It was less swift too. Transportation and communications were less efficient than now. Markets were smaller and competition was nowhere near as fierce. In those days a man who started a firm and progressed from half a dozen employees to several hundred could still run a substantial enterprise in much the same way as he ran a small one. The complexities of modern business which today place a premium on making use of management techniques, however rudimentary, were not present. You could run a small business as a one man managerial band. You could run a big one like it too.

To make the comparison let's backtrack over 200 years. In 1759 Josiah Wedgwood, at the age of twenty-nine, founded his celebrated pottery firm on a capital of a few pounds and in a factory which he rented for £10 a year. When he died thirty-six years later he left a fortune estimated at £250,000 and the name of Wedgwood was famous throughout the world. Roger Falk uses the Wedgwood story as a case history in his Pelican, *The Business of Management*. According to Falk, Wedgwood's flair for management was far beyond his time and he says it is doubtful whether, with the exception of the manager of his London showroom, he ever enjoyed the services of competent managers, and must have undertaken a prodigious amount of executive work himself. Yet for all his skill in management it is doubtful whether Josiah Wedgwood would appear quite so head and shoulders above the rest now, as he did in the second half of the eighteenth century.

Today the situation is in sharp contrast. The small man is up against the competition of trained professional managers in larger firms. They bring a comprehensive portfolio of management skills to bear on their task, skills which he has had to acquire in a rag-bag fashion, pragmatically and by trial and error. There is nothing intrinsically wrong in this except when the size and shape of his business outgrows his ability to sustain it using intuition and unorthodoxy. The great watershed in the affairs of a small business which is growing into a large one is the critical point it reaches when one man on his own starts to lose his grip and becomes engulfed in everyday detail. Obviously the point at which this happens varies according to the man, the nature of the business and the market it is in, but as a broad generalisation it does seem to happen earlier and earlier these days.

When this point is reached it is a matter of prophetic certainty that control will fly out of the window unless steps are taken to augment his highly personal role and stewardship of the company with the use of some sort of formal management systems. They are, after all, aids to a more efficient and, therefore, more agreeable and less demanding business life.

There is no more vivid symptom of the changing state of a business than the day when its managers look back dispassionately on the original idea or product which led to its foundation and realise that they have to make decisions, in the interest of the firm's continuing survival, which may well mean ditching it, merging with another company, reaching a reciprocal trading agreement with an overseas company, diversifying into a new product range, building a new plant or going public.

The understanding of what is then happening requires a flexible and adaptable mind from the small businessman. His strength is when he learns to adjust to and accept that these modern management techniques take so much of the informal and opportunist element out of running a business. The adjustment must be all the harder, because these are the qualities he originally built upon. The new techniques and the new functionaries to administer them will inevitably produce a welter of advice, sometimes conflicting views, recommendations and diametrically opposed courses of action. Again, this is where the highly organic nature of a firm asserts itself. Instead of now dispensing a highly personalised rule the function of the owner has shifted. Faced with a plethora of conflicting expert advice it is his task to listen, to observe and ultimately to decide upon the right course to steer through it all. It is frequently the point at which both the businessman and his business become adult.

This, then, is the picture of small business as a living organism, but what of the environment in which small business typically lives and grows? In its prime and oldest form its situation is a matter of geography, of being located in and serving a local market, the way most business was circumscribed before the great and revolutionary developments in transport when steamships, railways, motor vehicles and aircraft opened up markets far beyond the borders of its own parish or the neighbouring one.

Small business still exists to serve local markets, and there is still an ample supply of local markets to be served; but there have been a number of developments in recent years which have blunted the special advantages which local markets bestowed. The yellow-coloured lemonade which is made by Benjamin Shaw in Huddersfield, and which is a peculiarly Huddersfield taste, was historically distributed in the area by a man with a horse and cart. The limits of the distribution were drawn by the distance the horse could travel outwards and back in one day. The yellow lemonade is still very much made to meet a local demand but now it has to face the competition of national brands of fizziness like Corona or the Colas.

The real importance of local consumer markets lies in things like fresh foods, bread, garden plants, but even the importance of these and the reliance of the consumer upon them has been steadily eroded over the years by the emergence of such men as Clarence Birdseye, who discovered how to freeze fresh vegetables over forty years ago. There is nothing local about the packets of Birds Eye Fish Fingers which fill the frozen food cabinets of any shop now. Even the local nurseryman faces brisk competition from the substantial mail order business in plants and garden products. You only have to look at the gardening advertisement pages of a paper like the *Sunday Times* in spring to see what is happening.

But even with forces of this sort eating away at the local market, the movement is not all one way. Every now and then the local character of a market reasserts itself. In the 1950s the big bakery combines swept through the high streets, mopping up small, independent bakery businesses left, right and centre and selling their standardised factory-baked loaves and cakes. But it left a vacuum, a demand for home-baked products from a clientele who were ready to pay premium prices in return for high quality; the knowledge that all baking was done on the premises, and only fresh eggs and best butter were used in the cakes.

Not all businesses catering for the needs of local markets are based on food. A host of firms offer personalised services to local business communities which range from the printing of visiting cards and house stationery to signwriting and shopfitting. In areas where incomes are high and there is more time for leisure, small service industries, such as restaurants, interior decorators and television repairers flourish.

The engineering industry, in its national context, is one of the keystones of the economy, employing a large proportion of the working population, covering every sort of work from heavy drop forgings to the making of delicate scientific instruments. It extends to every-sized firm, from a giant like Guest Keen and Nettlefold to the small jobbing engineer with a dozen men, which is heavily dependent on local demand for its products. In the metal goods trade small firms employing less than 100 people are thick on the ground. The amount of capital needed to start up a firm on a second-hand lathe and a milling machine is still small enough to attract the man who is possibly already working for a larger local firm, and has gained an insight into the variety and quantity of work available in his area.

As they progress some of these small jobbing businesses gradually move away from dependence on local markets and become small components manufacturers for larger concerns, specialising in producing a particular piece of equipment. Most of the small engineering firms which sprout up all over the place in the Midlands are serving a car industry which, although a national industry, happens to be locally based. Without the smooth and reliable operation of these specialist concerns, assembly work in a car plant might easily come to a standstill for the sake of something as simple, cheap and small as the clip which holds the metal rod which props up a car bonnet when it is opened.

The Industrial Midlands, possibly more than any other area of the country, has come to be associated in people's minds as a breeding ground of small business. The image is not always a totally complimentary one. In their Pelican book, *Britain on Borrowed Time*, Glyn Jones and Michael Barnes paint a picture which would do justice to any macabre, industrial horror film. 'No visitor to some of the hundreds of small firms in the Midlands supplying components to the motor industry, for example, can help but be struck by the feeling that he is back in the middle of the nineteenth century,' the authors write. 'Americans who are taken to visit these belt-drive anachronisms, usually ill-lit and filthy, express astonished disbelief. Not only is much of the machinery up to 60 or 100 years old: organisation and methods are unheard of; workers look—and are—defeated by their wretched surroundings; managers, so far from keeping up with the reading they should be doing, look and sound as though they are incapable of reading anything at all. Rule is usually autocratic; workpeople are assumed to have no interest in the progress of the firm, which is usually downhill, and if any workman does inquire about company progress, or the chance of training or retraining, or job promotion, it is regarded as insolence towards the boss or betrayal of comrades. The North and Midlands are sprinkled with black holes of this kind, as though the smuts of the industrial revolution have yet to blow away.'

Of course, Jones and Barnes were very much out to make a case—as the title of their book suggests. To them the firms they described in that passage were menacing Britain's chances of growth and economic development. Certainly for me their description throws up a number of instantly recognisable signals which span a period of nearly twenty years, when I started working as a young reporter in Sheffield, to the present day when I still occasionally stumble across the kind of workshop which you might think was an overblown figment of Dickens's imagination. None the less the picture calls for some counterpoise.

The basic reason why so many of these small firms exist physically in the close juxtaposition that they do is because they are part and parcel of an incredibly complicated web of industrial production in which a piece of metal may go through a succession of processes, each one adding to it in shape and value, until it emerges somewhere as a finished engineering product. Even then it is likely to be used as a part in the assembly of something else. The smaller the firm in numbers employed, the more specialised it tends to be and the higher the proportion of skilled men in it, and it is not difficult to see why this is so. Its existence depends on winning work where skill is at a premium and this is why so many small firms go to such pains to keep their skilled men. This is brought out very clearly in the story of J. Taylor and Son in Chapter 6. Consequently they often pay them over the rate for the job, and make sure there are plenty of opportunities for overtime to keep the wage levels well above those which are the basic minimum for the industry. Obviously this does not excuse the filthy conditions in which some of them operate, but it is quite wrong to lump them all together as outdated industrial anachronisms. They are very far from being anachronisms, but fulfil an essential function and perform specialised tasks for large companies which they can execute much more efficiently and cheaply than the large concerns could do for themselves.

Toolmaking, for example, is one of those small-firm industries in the Midlands where the levels of skill demanded are of a high order. The skilled man who starts up on his own in toolmaking will be intelligent, ambitious and far removed from old and archaic attitudes. It is an industry which very much expresses the independent spirit of the Midlands engineering workers, and it is one which is rich in examples of a couple of men who worked side by side at a factory bench getting together and building up a thriving business, with their first orders usually coming from larger firms which cannot cope with what they have on hand. It is difficult to generalise about the size of these small concerns but, measured on the basis of numbers employed, they are small enough to count the workforce on the fingers of two hands. Running them is not just a matter of possessing a high order of engineering skill and a reputation for quality of work, although both of these factors count, but also the ability to withstand and meet very intense competition. They not only have to do better than the tool room of a big company and do the job more cheaply, but they also have to win their own livelihood in competition with many similar small concerns, and it follows that prices are very keen. But once established in it, toolmaking is one of those industries where small firms depend to a large extent on their past performance and the goodwill they enjoy. They are highly personal firms. Because numbers are few, communication between workers and management is easy and swift, and they are united in the bond of craftsmanship, with the owner often providing the high-level skill at the top end of the scale for highly specialist operations.

As long as manufacturing concerns find it increasingly expensive to maintain their own tool rooms and increasingly difficult to get the maximum efficiency from them, the small concerns, with more personal job identification among the workers, with less difficulty in controlling output and probably greater productivity per head, will flourish on the work farmed out to them.

There is a danger of talking about the Midlands as though it were solely a small business landscape. It isn't, of course. Small business is not something which is tight and well-defined geographically. It embraces dispersed and far-flung areas. It is highly diverse and fragmented in its function. To draw a distribution map of small business in Britain would, you imagine, be a near impossible task. Except in the sparsely populated regions you would never have room to get all the distribution dots in. There are, however, a number of areas where on balance small businesses occupy a greater share of the business activity than larger ones. In many towns and cities there are streets and districts which have come to be associated for historic, geographic and sociological reasons with activities which are typically those possessing a small business ethos. Street markets, such as London's Petticoat Lane or Leather Lane, are one example. There, the business as an asset-owning, economic unit is fairly easy to define: one stall or barrow, assorted stock, one or two stallholders and a loud, compelling and crowd-drawing voice. As small business quarters go they are colourful, positive to identify and still seem to survive in an age when supermarkets are papering their plate glass windows with the large-scale typography of the week's loss leader. It is sometimes forgotten that street traders were using their stentorian voices to announce loss leaders long before the word supermarket was in current usage.

There are numerous other quarters in which small business is concentrated, ranging from the Lanes of Brighton, where antique shops jostle each other, to colonies of packing and forwarding agents clustered in the vicinity of London's Heathrow Airport. Birmingham's jewellery quarter is centred on a few streets and London's Hatton Garden has small gem-cutting and polishing firms flourishing in every other passageway and on every other landing. Sometimes you imagine more business must be done over the salt beef and latkas of a small Jewish restaurant called The Nosherie, just off the Garden, where sellers extract gemstones from their pockets in little tufts of screwed up tissue paper, than in the surrounding offices. In Sheffield the 'little mesters' of the cutlery trade still tend to cluster together in small workshops. In London's Whitechapel few streets are without some small tailoring establishments.

There are a few isolated examples of areas where the balance of business is small rather than large precisely because efforts have been and are being made which foster the establishment and growth of small business. For a long time now the Highlands and

Islands Development Board has been encouraging the establishment of industry in various parts of Scotland in order to help arrest the trend of depopulation. Small business, with its modest demand for labour, is well suited to the bulk of the developments which it backs. This is an example of the particular importance of the social and economic role of small business in a regional economy where there are very specific and difficult problems.

In the Fenlands of England, one of the country's most fertile kitchen gardens, where the richness of the soil is only equalled by the price it fetches per acre when it comes up for sale, there is an established population of small growers who cultivate smallholdings. Sometimes these are no more than a couple of big glasshouses in a back garden which are worked intensively. There is often a crop of daffodils before Christmas, tulips until March, then tomatoes followed by daffodils again, and it is not unusual for a man to earn over £3,000 a year from them.

The farm and smallholding has long been a stronghold of the individual entrepreneur. It can justifiably claim to be one of the oldest and earliest units of small business. Like manufacturing it has its specialist products and it is often located in areas given over almost entirely to the product in question. In a wedge of country between Leeds and Wakefield which is bisected by the M1, more than 90 per cent of the British crop of forced rhubarb (about 7,000 tons of it worth about £1·25 million a year) is grown by 200 individual growers. Forced rhubarb has been grown there, so the story goes, ever since the pollution from factories was so severe that the crop was naturally retarded and delicate. Now the growers simulate the old conditions in huge, dark sheds where the gloom makes the stalk red and succulent and the leaf small and lime green. It is harvested by workers who toil by candlelight to preserve the delicacy of the crop.

Like the smallholding or farm the other long-established fastness of the small business has been the craftsman's workshop. For in this age when income levels are high and the twin notions of discrimination and consumer choice are increasingly prevalent the craftsman can make a comfortable, if not lavish, living for himself. He may produce handmade furniture from genuine Scottish woods the way Peter Byrne does in Inverness. Or he may be a potter, or a weaver, or a worker of wrought iron. For me the flavour, the style, the problems and the sheer satisfaction of being in a highly individual craft business is summed up in a piece I wrote about an engaging pair of craftsmen in the *Sunday Times* for 13 December 1970. This is it:

'The handmade concertina industry has an acute production problem. Concertinas are back in vogue, and the cardboard box where the industry files its orders is overflowing. To be precise it has enough work to last it for the next 25 years, which is why its labour force, Henry Crabb and his son Neville, feels a trifle pressed.

'The centre of the industry is the Crabb's three-storey Victorian shop and workshop in London's Islington. The upper floors are occupied by 150 old and ailing concertinas which haven't a squeeze left in them, and lengths of maturing sycamore wood—some bits have been busy ageing for 40 years—from which they make parts for new ones.

'Underneath is their workshop. Here, working flat out it is possible to roll one new concertina off the production line every fortnight. But in practice the Crabbs don't make more than 20 to 30 a year, costing from £56 to £200 each.

'This is because the concertina repair side of the business is so large—1,000 or more in 12 months. Why, there's hardly a Salvation Army issue concertina which hasn't been through their hands at one time or another. It brings a steady stream of joy and gladness to the concertina business, does the Sally Ann.

'Until a few years ago the Crabbs had just enough work to keep them going nicely without any panics. Then all the trendy folk singers started looking for a new sort of sound and lighted on the concertina, which is about the only musical instrument to be invented by an Englishman, Sir Charles Wheatstone, who patented it in 1829.

'Actually Henry's grandfather originally worked for Wheatstone but left him to found his own firm. Through the years his business enjoyed its ups and suffered some downs. By 1910, for example, the concertina was being squeezed out by the improved continental accordion, a nasty nine letter word which the Crabbs prefer not to have bandied about on their premises.

'Now, in terms of the squeeze box cycle, 1970 is definitely one of the ups. The Crabbs can scarcely cope with the work, and apparently there's no one else who can. "As far as we know we are the only people in the world making handmade concertinas in quantity," says Henry. But what he means by quantity is not what others mean. They can't seem to grasp the problems of a two man craft business serving a world market.

'There's a chap in New York who orders concertinas in batches of 500. Henry has written to explain that they would take between 15 and 25 years to complete. He's even sent a tape recording outlining the situation. But the American still keeps ordering.

'The Crabbs say there's no real money in concertinas. They run their business more as a hobby really, because they like concertinas, and get a deep and abiding satisfaction from making them. "You make one and when you hear the music come out it's a joy," says Henry.

'Last year turnover was £4,000. Outgoings, says Neville, wrinkling his calculating machine for a minute or two, were £2,000. As a matter of fact the Crabbs sometimes adopt a Robin Hood approach to repair charges—high for those who can afford it, but when an old age pensioner comes in with a battered concertina they have a good think and try and come up with a nice low figure.

'They are partners, father and son, and sit at their benches all day using concertina making tools made by Crabb forebears. Henry makes the difficult parts, the board with all the complicated reed work which go at each end of the bellows, while Neville does the rest. With only two of them it's the nearest they can get to division of labour.

'There used to be 1,500 handmade parts in one of their concertinas. But now there's only 1,499, because they've found a small engineering shop which turns the finger keys for them. They are contracting out a bit of work making leather concertina cases, too. "But the old chap who does them is in the same boat as we are," says Neville. "It takes him a fortnight just to make one."

'You can see that the Crabbs are a whole guild of craftsmen

rolled into one—wood, metal and leather workers. Toolmakers too. And they tune and play the things.

'Naturally enough Crabb concertinas are built to last, and sometimes Henry gets his Dad's and Granddad's work in for repair when it's a 100 years old or more. They regard foreign, factory made concertinas with polite scorn. To them an £18 German job on the market is a mere toy.

'The main reason why they can't expand output is that you just can't get concertina makers by going to the Labour Exchange. Not long ago a firm with over £80,000 it wanted to invest said would the Crabbs like their own small factory and Henry could gradually train up a workforce of about 20. But somehow it seemed an awful lot of money, just for making concertinas, and to be honest the amount frightened them off.

'So it seems the world will have to patiently wait for its concertinas. Although, as Henry says, if someone could come with a reed which would play both ways instead of one, it would cut the fiddling reed process by half. Alas, concertina technology just hasn't got that far.'

For those in search of the unique and the fascinating—and sometimes the improbable, the bizarre and the eccentric too—all geared to the pursuit of profit and winning a livelihood, small business provides a veritable feast. Its variety and individuality is a source of refreshment. It enhances the business landscape with erratic, unexpected and lively profiles which stand out all the more in a time when super scientific management techniques and economies of scale are the factors devoted to producing nice, smooth upward sloping gradients of performance. In Herefordshire Cliff Hickling will make and sell you a replica of a sixteenth-century cannon which can actually be fired. In Somerset a splendid lady named Primrose Peacock is one of the liveliest of Britain's second-hand button entrepreneurs, exporting all that is best in old British buttons to button lovers everywhere. There is a tropical fish wholesaler who has a computer in his bungalow near Colchester to help with his stock problems. There's a small firm which operates a long-distance lorry service from England to Afghanistan from above a greengrocers' shop in Kent.

A few pages ago I said if you were trying to draw a distribution map of small business in the United Kingdom there would be some areas in which you could never accommodate all the dots. There would also be some where you could drop them in with ease. Places like Sanday, an Orkney island of 600-odd souls and no trees. If it is manufacturing industry you are talking about, Sanday has just one dot. It stands for a firm called Sykes-Robertson Electronics which must surely be the only electronics company to be found north of Wick? When you see it, located in an old school, standing on its own beside a 2 mile crescent of perfectly white sandy beach where the only interlopers are quarrelling seabirds, you could be forgiven for thinking it was the *only* company north of Wick. There are, of course, others in the Orkneys but Sykes-Robertson Electronics is singularly important because on Sanday its seven-strong workforce makes it the largest single employer of labour after Orkney County Council.

Sanday is 700 miles from London, two or three hours by boat from Kirkwall or a short flight in an aeroplane which sometimes resembles an aerial cowpat. This is because your Orkney farmer likes to make the most of what he has and will often graze his cattle on the small grass airstrips of the island at night, driving them off again in the morning. There are occasions when you can hardly see the next airstrip through the windows of the plane for the coating of 'sharn'—that's the local word for it—from the previous one.

The firm had its beginnings when Jack Sykes, a freelance designer, came to live there in semi-retirement. He started making some simple electronic instruments for a former client, mostly out of interest rather than as a serious attempt to build a business. Local people saw what he was up to and asked if he would start a small factory on the island to provide work for young people who would otherwise have to leave and seek jobs on the mainland. Sanday is no different from the other Orkney islands in that its main problems are depopulation and unemployment. As such it was thought that the Highlands and Islands Development Board might provide backing, but after making encouraging noises, it took it two years to say no.

In the meantime Sykes had been joined by George Robertson, a senior development engineer with Ferranti in Edinburgh, who had read of what Sykes was trying to do. He was fed up with urban living and gave up a well-paid pensionable job, sold his home and moved with his wife and four children to Sanday, investing his savings in what was clearly a risky enterprise. Even the withdrawal of the Highlands and Islands Development Board's blessing didn't make him change his mind when there was time to.

To start with two sixteen-year-old girls were trained to solder and wire components. Being daughters of the croft they could turn their hands to almost anything, from sweeping the floor and making tea to papering and painting the premises. They said they would build a dyke if necessary. Sanday is not a place where people worry about job demarcation. In the evenings the girls went home to milk the cows, drive tractors and plough fields.

Ironically, in the two years between 1966 and 1968, while waiting for the Board's decision at least twenty young people, all potential employees, left the island and it suddenly became clear the company would not be swamped with applications for employment. Anyway, two youths were taken on and several married women accepted part-time jobs. A young farmer took a correspondence course in electronics and became a tower of strength. He engaged his brother to run his farm while he and his wife worked a sixty-hour week building and testing morse trainers. Within a year the workforce was up to a dozen, but it was impossible to increase it beyond that. Young women got married and left to run their homes and farms, and interesting employment close at hand didn't quench the young men's spirit of adventure and the desire to go and work in the big cities on the mainland. Nor did Sykes wish it to be quenched, but the result did severely handicap the company. It became apparent that there was really little need for what started as a source of employment for young school-leavers. The unemployment was among the middle-aged and elderly, normally involved in farming or fishing. By the beginning of 1971 the company's workforce had fallen to seven, when, with the work in hand, it needed three or four times that number. This has held back its growth and limited its ability to take on more work. Robertson found himself putting in a steady sixty-hour week and both he and Sykes have had to take cuts in salary. Sykes has moved to Yorkshire to be in a better position to get new business because in dealing with the home market Sanday's location is a disadvantage. Contracts need a lot of pre-consultation and anyway companies find it hard to believe there is an electronics plant on Sanday.

This is why in the beginning the firm concentrated on export jobs. Yet another irony is that it has been so successful at this, supplying equipment, electronic training devices, and language laboratories to such unlikely places as Surinam, Borneo, Iraq and Tanzania, that the Highlands and Islands Development Board has now made it a £2,000 grant plus a low interest loan of £1,500 repayable over seven years. In 1971 turnover was £20,000 to £25,000 and the company was expecting to break even.

The range of equipment produced has been greatly extended and now includes things like simple data transfer systems. Probably its most valuable stock in trade is not only to design and build communications training equipment, but to tackle the kind of one-off electronics problem which larger firms will not handle. Which is the reason why it is the only electronics company in the Orkneys to know anything about giraffes. It was once asked to design and build a small transmitter which could be fixed to a giraffe and which would work on a battery for six months without recharging. The giraffe turned out to be more of a problem than the electronics. It's such a streamlined animal that it has few places to which you can easily attach anything. Unhappily, in the midst of an analysis of the giraffe's anatomy, the game conservation agency in Kenya which wanted the equipment decided it would be too expensive. Building and experimenting with such devices offers an explanation of why one bitter winter's day Robertson was slipping and sliding all over an ice-covered road emitting, to the mild astonishment of a chilly cross section of local wild life, bleep noises from under one of his arms. He was testing a miniscule transmitter designed to fit in the base of a tranquillising dart so that whoever fired it could eventually find the animal he had put to sleep.

Sykes and Robertson, and the other small businessmen I have mentioned, stand out like beacons because of small business individuality. The small firms they own and run are as much part of Britain's industrial structure as Marks and Spencer, Wimpey and the British Steel Corporation. The diversity in size and form of the separate units which make up modern industry is extraordinary and within its own span, small business is equally diverse. Because this happens to be a book concerned with small business, what it is, how it works, and what makes it tick, it might be tempting to gather it together, label it and tie it up in one neat package, as though it were something which stood apart, functioned on its own, in a separate, self-contained manner. So before we look at what it is which makes people run a business, what their motives are for starting one, what contributes to the driving compulsion to continue with it, it is as well to remember that small business is a part and not the whole of the intricate tapestry of our economic life. The cult of smallness has no more relevance to the country's economic and industrial problems than the cult of size and concentration.

In the end what really counts is the best balance of firms of different size and shape which best satisfies our needs and desires for goods and services and which keeps alive the flame of competition. In advanced industrial societies like the United States, Germany, Japan and the United Kingdom, there is a notable mix of size in business. According to the authors of the Industrial Policy Group paper on *The Structure and Efficiency of British Industry,* the vital point is the optimum distribution of the size of firms in industry which will make for the most efficient structure. 'Just as in a rugby football team there is no optimum size of player,' they say. 'Players of different physique are needed for different functions.' Sykes-Robertson Electronics is as much an important member of the team as Imperial Chemical Industries. It is just that the two concerns do different jobs, in different ways, on a different scale.

NOTES

1 Page 53. Industrial Policy Group. 'The Structure and Efficiency of British Industry'. Paper Number 6 (July 1970).

Chapter 4

The compulsion of small business

The motives for starting a business. Why Ben Jones and Christian Brann did it. The satisfactions of running one. Independence, the urge to achieve. Goals and objectives. The level of risk. Hazarding personal relationships. The wife in the business and outside it. The husband in the wife's business. Effect on family life. The social profit and loss of building a firm. The courage to fail and the will to succeed. The relentless commitment to continue.

THE motives a man has for starting a business, the risks he takes, and what it costs him and his family are all profoundly personal considerations which go to the roots of any story about a newly established small firm. They are factors which on the whole seem to have been neglected by sociologists, offering as they do rich prospects for inquiry. Yet the intensity of the motive, the level of risk a man is prepared to carry and the degree of pressure and strain he will allow himself, his wife and family to bear throughout the all-demanding period of initial struggle to make the business viable are germane to the rate at which new businesses are established and sustained.

These factors, together with that other powerful circumstance in the birth and regeneration of new enterprises, the opportunities which exist for a new service or product, have a substantial bearing on the amount of new entrepreneurial blood coming forward at any moment of time. While the prevailing economic climate may blunt or sharpen the risk, for instance in the ease or difficulty of raising funds to start up, the opportunities are usually closely entangled with the motives.

Thus a man may spot a gap in the kitchen gadget market, dream up a bright idea to fill it and decide to launch a new business to produce and market the product. This is one pattern but by no means the only one. The reason Ben Jones went into business for himself was because as an employee of someone else he felt frustrated at not prospering as well as he thought he should.

So he gave up being something in the City to be something in the country. He was just over forty, in mid-career, holding down a senior manager's job in a London ship-broking firm. After twenty years of hard work and effort he had reasonable expectations—indeed promises—of a directorship with his firm. The day arrived, however, when he found promises were not enough. 'There comes a point,' he says, 'where you realise the donkey is never going to catch up with the carrot.' The trouble was that he was working for a nice company with nice people, so it took a long time to escape from its agreeable tentacles. 'Ben didn't want any more promises that he would be a director, he wanted to know *when* he would be, and he couldn't get an answer,' says his wife Anne. 'The firm said he was too ambitious—and used the word in a derogatory sense. This was the end. He had always worked as hard for them as he does for himself now.'

Ben gave three months notice and went off in search of a carrot he *could* catch up with. He forsook commuting to London (which was no hardship) and set up in business at Campion Hill, the comfortable, sunny, Queen Anne style house in the countryside near the Suffolk village of Nayland in which he had lived for the last ten years. The view from his new office was delightful, the sense of freedom must have been exquisite. There was, however, a problem: he did not precisely know how he was going to make a living. In the event he decided to do what he had spent years in the City and on the floor of the Baltic Exchange doing—chartering ships. For the first year that is what the Jones's lived on.

If you think it odd to be operating a shipbroking business down a country lane, so did a lot of Ben's friends and business acquaintances. 'Some people in London either felt sorry for me or were plain patronising,' says Ben. But when you stand on the threshold of Campion Hill and hear the telex machine chattering inside, the cuckoo calling far away, and the bees murmuring through the flower beds, it all seems to make eminent good sense. 'Anyway, living in a field gives you time to think,' says Anne. 'You can go and hack at a hedge and think out a problem at the same time.' It also demonstrates, according to Ben, that there are so many pre-conceived notions about setting up in business which no one really questions, and which don't really hold water . . . you must have an office in every place you operate straight away, you must have staff in it, you must go up to the City each day.

Another pre-conceived notion a man has starting on his own concerns finance. Ben thought that having had a personal account with the same bank in the City ever since he had worked there it would help in raising money to get his new business off the ground. This was a notion of which he was quickly disabused. He wanted £5,000 for two years. After that he was convinced he could pay his way. But the bank turned him down, and he got caught up in successive financial squeezes (he launched out on his own in 1966), so in the end he had to cash his pension rights and make do on the £1,500 which this realised. It was tight, but at the end of the first two years he had made a little profit. 'I suppose life is just as insecure as it ever was,' says Ben. 'There is no prospect of a pension and no retiring age . . . but then I have seen what has happened to people with all of these things . . .'

As for the initial problems in getting going on your own, Ben reckons the key factor is having absolute confidence in yourself and convincing other people of your ability to do the job. One haulier who in the early days proved difficult to deal with later told Anne, 'You see, I didn't know how long you would stick at it.' As Anne says, 'It's not just a question of building confidence by paying your bills promptly, but you have to *prove* your money is as good as someone else's.'

Most of the first year's chartering business had little directly to do with the muddy creeks, ragged estuaries and small ports of East Anglia. At first, Ben was chartering vessels for an American company with offices in Switzerland. Then, bit by bit, he began to add other activities, like ships' agency work, to his enterprise. 'It seemed to me that the East Anglian ports—Colchester,

Ipswich, Felixstowe—were all developing and there was a living to be made from them,' he says. But he didn't want to be committed to one port so he bought a caravan and used it as a mobile office, and had a radio-telephone fitted in his car. Since those days the business has grown. Ben now has offices in the local ports, employs two part-time office helpers at home and is producing a revenue of £50,000 a year. Less than a third of this comes from ships' agency work which is a job they wouldn't do if they could avoid it because it is fairly demanding of time and not all that profitable. So these days he is increasingly moving into organising the movement of bulk cargoes on a door-to-door basis. This means offering a complete service—chartering the ship, organising land transport and the stevedoring. He already employs his own permanent crane driver for work in East Anglia.

He is still a member of the Baltic Exchange. This is vitally important for the business it brings. Some of it comes from his old firm. 'I couldn't exist without the Baltic,' he says. 'And it wasn't vanity which made me set up in East Anglia under my own name,' he says. 'On the Baltic I was always called Ben Jones and I kept the name for my business when I set up here so people would know where I had got to and who I was.'

It was a move which paid because the word got around that Ben was on the spot in East Anglia and if you wanted a job done you didn't get some whipper-snapper of a clerk sent out, but the boss himself handled it. If it was a tricky, off-beat job so much the better.

There was a time when a ship's officer loaded 4,000 tons of maize and soya beans in his ship in such a way that when it arrived at the new bulk grain terminal at Tilbury it couldn't be handled. Ben was called in to arrange the transfer of the cargo within the ship so it could be unloaded in the usual way. The job was first mooted on his car radio-telephone somewhere in mid-Suffolk just two and a half working days before it was due to start. The success of this job saved the enormous expense of sending the vessel to Rotterdam to be unloaded.

Another of these difficult, off-beat jobs lasted from the autumn of 1968 until February 1971. This was virtually a seven day a week job ensuring awkward, large and heavy construction materials reached the radio research station which was being built at Orfordness, virtually an island off the cost of Suffolk. Bad weather and difficult seas meant little could be shipped in by landing craft on the exposed seaward side of the building site. Road transport through Orford to a short ferry crossing produced all sorts of road and traffic hazards. So Ben chartered a small fleet of old East Coast barges and shipped the heavy gear and materials from Snape Quay, 21 miles from the sea, to a jetty near the construction site. Snape, which as ports go is just about the smallest you can get, saw more tonnage go through it in those couple of years than in the whole of its history.

Ben got the Orfordness job because he was able to make a quick decision. 'Two larger firms were to have shared the risk with us, but in the absence of their managing directors, neither could join us in a firm quotation,' says Ben. The site engineer gave Ben a deadline, and he had to go it alone. By the time the job was completed he had shipped 12,500 tons of assorted materials and engineering equipment from Snape.

Not only do the Jones's undertake odd and difficult jobs, but they also compete for, and get, run-of-the-mill ones by bidding for them at the oddest times. The day I arrived at Campion Hill they were looking for a ship to move a 300 ton cargo of rock talc lying in a barge at Rotterdam to a Worcestershire destination. 'I can put out the inquiry on the telex on Sunday night and it will be on the ship owners' desks first thing in the morning, while in London other brokers will just be arriving at their offices,' explains Ben. 'You beat everyone else in getting the inquiry there.' What the ship owners do not know is that Ben is sitting comfortably in his own house, in his pyjamas, in the heart of the country doing it.

To an ambitious imaginative man driven by the need to achieve, rather than sit back and not give a damn, the frustration of being an employee in a situation where your ideas, suggestions, and initiatives are either ignored, shrugged off or patronisingly batted back to where they came from is almost impossible medicine to swallow. Even more so when as an employee he sees new ways of drumming up and expanding business, suggests them and finds they are ignored. Then both motive and opportunity are irresistibly twinned.

This is what happened to a young Londoner, Dudley Simms, who was working for an old-established firm of shipping and forwarding agents, and whose ideas for bringing in new business fell on stony ground. So he left, and with three partners started a £25 company, handling the shipping arrangements on export quota cars for foreign visitors who had purchased them in the UK and wanted them shipped home. Later, looking round for other business, the partners observed that there was a thriving export trade in British caravans, but as far as they could see companies were pretty disorganised when it came to shipping them. So they stepped in and built themselves a reputation for keeping the caravans moving even during dock and seamen's strikes.

In emergencies this sometimes meant taking them across the Channel behind their own cars. Now they ship caravans all over Europe and North America and the growth of the company has been more akin to the speed of a Grand Prix racing car than the statutory towing speed for a caravan. In three years the turnover of the company—it's called Individual Shipments—has rocketed from £6,000 to £250,000.

The partners' business philosophy is uncomplicated: work round the clock, make yourself unassailable experts in the job you do, and plough back your profits to make more. They certainly don't go in for lavish offices. When I first ran them to ground it was in an old bookie's office over an estate agent's in London's East End. The bookie's name, not theirs, was still on the door, the office furniture consisted of an old dining-room suite, sideboard and table, and the telex machine was next to the kitchen sink, clattering out its international messages while the girls washed up the teacups. The lads made a great point of telling me how they kept a tight fist on unnecessary overheads. They didn't even go in for lavish directors' lunches. Mostly they ate in the corner 'caff' a couple of doors away.

There's a newish company in Hull, with eight directors who take it in turns to be chairman, which was emphatically born out of frustration. The frustration of a bunch of blokes all working in the same firm, some for as long as twenty years, who felt they could not get their ideas through to management, and who couldn't face the thought that they would be stuck in that position for the rest of their lives.

As a result Humber Construction (Successors) Ltd, which started life in April 1970, had by its first birthday clocked up £100,000 worth of business, a good order book and the satisfaction of knowing it had financed its own growth as it went along. Ostensibly the company is involved in steel structural engineering, but in many ways it is more an object lesson in a matey, democratic, egalitarian form of management where everyone falls over themselves to see everyone else knows what is happening. If you wonder how they do any work at all, with eight of them all having their say, it is because they are used to working together as a team, which is precisely what they did before they set up in business together.

It is sometimes said that a high level of unemployment will spark off a flood of new enterprises. This may happen more frequently now that redundancy payments are a statutory requirement and provide a modest stake with which to get started, especially in those activities like shopkeeping which are comparatively easy to get into. This does not only apply to workers but to redundant executives as well, whose golden handshakes at least help finance the early stages of getting a business of their own off the ground. This kind of external influence is often instrumental in creating new businesses. Michael Pickard decided to run a hire shop (see Chapter 9). Bernard Hunn used his golden handshake to start Revenue Systems (see Chapter 13) and George Dawson set course on his impressive small business (see Chapter 15) after a difference with his employers which resulted in him jacking in his job.

For some owner-managers developing their small firms into big ones, possibly with the object of one day going public, is not a consideration which weighs heavily. Their motive is to enjoy an independent, reasonably quiet life and make a comfortable living for themselves and their families. In the jargon of their business, psychologists might say they are a bit low on 'achievement motivation', something which is supposed to ooze out of the real entrepreneur who decides on a course of action, carries it through and knows whether he has been a success or not by seeing whether he has become a millionaire or a bankrupt. It is this facility to have a concrete accounting at the end which is supposed to make entrepreneurial life so attractive to those people who have this burning urge to achieve.

Nevertheless the authors of a research report on Attitude and Motivation which was commissioned by the Bolton Committee to assist it arrive at *its* own conclusion[1] summarised the underlying motivation of the businessmen with whom they had discussions as the need to attain and preserve independence. The report says:

'This need for independence sums up a wide range of highly personal gratifications provided by working for oneself and not for anybody else. It embraces many small satisfactions which running a small business provided—the personal supervision and control of staff, direct contact with customers, the opportunity to develop one's own ideas, a strong feeling of personal challenge and an almost egotistical sense of personal achievement and pride—psychological satisfactions which appeared to be much more powerful motivators than money or the possibility of large financial gains.

'The powerful underlying need to maintain and preserve independence and the strong feelings of personal satisfaction derived from one's own achievement go a long way to explaining the attitudes of respondents in this study, particularly their attitudes to outside help and assistance. Government assistance was seen as leading to Government intervention; using more sophisticated assistance than that provided by the local bank manager would lead to a loss of independence because the organisation giving the assistance would want some measure of control over the firm. Having rejected "the boss" respondents didn't want to suffer the paternalism of Government or anyone else for that matter. Because the sense of satisfaction derived from personal achievement was so important, many of these respondents appeared almost to turn a deaf ear to any outside source of advice or help. They neither knew or wished to know about it.

'Moreover, respondents' attitudes to growth were considerably influenced by this need for preserving independence. In fact attitudes to growth and expansion were highly ambivalent. Many of these owners of small businesses appeared to be torn on the one hand by the desire to remain small and so retain their independence and its concomitant personal satisfactions and, on the other hand, by the need, as businessmen, to conform to the idea of growth—almost as a moral imperative. In the majority of cases, the need for preserving the more personal satisfaction of independence won out and there was a clear preference to maintain the business at its existing level of activity—and to pay only lip service to growth and expansion.'

This theme of independence pervades small business. It will appear time and again in the following pages. It was Norman Chalk (see Chapter 12) who stated it so succinctly in his down to earth Norfolk way when he said running his own business gave him the freedom to drop his own clangers.

It was a prospect which Christian Brann found irresistible too. After twenty-five years of business life spent working for large firms, Brann found that the urge to be free and independent was so strong that, whatever the risk, he decided to go it alone. This was despite the considerable temptation of a new, challenging and highly paid offer to start a new business for a public company in London. All this happened over four years ago and today Christian Brann works in a pleasant and agreeable part of the world, living in the heart of the country, 4 miles away from his office in Cirencester. The firm which bears his name is a classic service company which undertakes direct mail marketing, advertising, print design and production.

He built it up on a stake of £3,000, his wife's and his own life savings, plus an initial £2,000 overdraft from the bank. In its first year turnover was £15,000, in its fourth over £100,000. It has plenty of potential to grow and one day he expects to go public or sell out. Meanwhile he is the envy of people who come down on business from London to see him and his wife Mary Rose. Her considerable involvement in the business with him, quite different from the separate lives they previously led, has given a new meaning and dimension to their marriage.

Striking out on their own was not a particularly easy decision to take because in the first place, with four children at fee-paying schools and a total annual school bill of £2,500 after tax, a secure job with no risk and a high salary needed thinking about. So did the switch from being a big company executive to a small businessman. As an executive in a larger company there were the considerable advantages in having large amounts of capital to play with without major personal risk. There were also the perquisites of being a senior manager; expensive cars, plush offices, high salary, expensive entertaining and overseas visits. 'A small undercapitalised company involves considerable re-orientation and tightening of personal belts,' says Christian. 'From the financial and security angle disaster is never very far away.'

But in making the switch there is the deep satisfaction of making it work and, as Christian says, 'Hard work never seems quite so bad when one is doing it for oneself and one's family, with the hope of building something permanent and really worth having in the long run. This applies especially in the case of someone who is by nature an entrepreneur and has, in terms of taking responsibility seriously, always looked upon the business he was running as though it were his own. Yet the ultimate satisfaction of ownership was never his.'

Christian's first foray into independent business was an unqualified disaster. He and his wife decided to sell ski clothes on a direct mail basis, but the costs of launching the scheme, designing catalogues and holding a stock of clothes were too high in a market which was simply not big enough. 'We quickly decided the only way out was to become a service company,' he says. 'In this way we required little additional capital and were assured of an immediate income.' So Christian became a consultant. Large companies he had previously worked for were glad to pay fees for the right to pick his brains, and he soon had three or four of them paying him fees which in total were much higher than when he worked for a single employer.

From this followed the next stage; the hire of designers, photographers, printers to provide services which followed from his overall advice. Since those very early days the firm has grown substantially. It employs thirty people full-time, about a hundred part-time and has ploughed back its money, not into plush offices or luxuries (the rent and rates for 8,000sq ft of office space are £1,000 a year) but on modern machinery, including an envelope-enclosing machine which cost £4,000 and which is capable of filling 7,000 envelopes an hour with four enclosures using only two operators.

Christian has a very clear idea where his bread and butter is. It is an established principle that the firm does not try to compete with companies which are bigger and more experienced by undercutting them. It sells its services on quality, speed and sheer ingenuity. 'At any one time we may be producing a major direct mail marketing campaign for one of the big oil companies, and a leaflet promoting the conference facilities of a local hotel,' says Christian. 'There is a great fund of creative talent and technical facilities available for large national companies spending from £100,000 to £200,000 a year with big advertising agencies, but the small, often local agencies, who try to look after smaller advertisers, generally lack talent and technical know-how. This, I believe, is where we have found our great opportunity. We apply big company thinking, experience and promotion skills to small and medium-sized concerns.'

Inevitably there have been problems and headaches and Christian has lost a good deal of sleep over many of them. Money has been a major one, especially as the company's rapid period of initial growth coincided with a major credit squeeze. Also the greater part of its turnover is in printing and merchant banks are not keen about investing in this sector which has a poor profit record. 'The company has therefore had to be financed out of retained profits and this has certainly held back expansion,' says Christian. 'At the end of each year we as directors have voted ourselves salaries which we have never been able to draw and on which we will have to pay income tax.'

The greatest problem which faces the company in the light of its continuing growth is that it depends too much for its contacts, its overall creative direction and its entrepreneurial top-level management on Christian personally. The problem of management is that it is very much interwoven into what Christian sees as his goals and objectives for the company. 'My personal ambition is that the company should grow in size and greatly improve its quality. Above all it should grow to a point where it is independent of me personally. I look upon it rather like the bringing up of a child. At first you have to spoon-feed it and perform even the most primitive functions. Eventually you just take a pride in its achievements.'

But while the company has a sound layer of second line management, and while a fund of almost unlimited mutual goodwill exists between all members of the management and staff, which means most difficulties are either avoided or ironed out, the great danger is that the recruitment of a senior manager above the head of the present willing team might act as a discouragement to the loyal second row. But with a new factory planned in the next eighteen months and the decision to develop products—for example, there are plans to go into book publishing—this is a nettle which needs to be grasped. In the next five to ten years Christian thinks the company will grow to five times its present size. By then its value might be in the region of £500,000 and this is when he would either sell out, or go public and expect to stay as managing director for a further ten years before his retirement.

Both Ben Jones and Christian Brann make clear statements about why they started their own businesses and the risks they took. Risk by its nature is a highly personal matter, and it is also a relative matter because it is related to physical resources and human relationships, especially family ones. There came a point in the early days of building his company where Norman Chalk says he became a bear of a person to live with. It got so bad his wife read the riot act to him and told him if he didn't get a grip of himself they had better part. Michael Pickard took his son away from a fee-paying school where he was doing well. George Dawson's reluctance to raise a mortgage on his home (see Chapter 15) was because he had presumably made the decision this was a risk greater than he could afford to take.

One way of measuring the intensity of entrepreneurship in a person might be by assessing the level of risk he is prepared to take with his own resources. Obviously personal circumstances affect judgement about risk. If you are single, don't possess much more in physical assets than a motor scooter, and only have £15 in the Post Office savings bank, you are risking very much less than Christian Brann did.

The chaps who got together and started a company called Phase Separations (see Chapter 12) were all working lads with no capital to call on. Quite literally all they had to finance the company was a total of £100. Nevertheless they succeeded and developed a simple gas chromatograph machine for making rapid analyses in the laboratory. It filled a gap in the market, providing a much less costly model than those being sold by other firms. During the formative years additional capital was indirectly put in, by paying for petrol for sales trips and lunches for potential clients out of their own pockets. 'Every year of the company's existence, without exception, excluding the last two months, has been hostile in money terms but luckily we have had an exceedingly sympathetic and interested bank manager, but even he could not obtain unsecured loans,' says Ken Jones, the chairman of Phase Separations and one of the founder directors. 'We all had mortgaged homes with good equities due to house cost inflation and these with contents secured the loans. It is no exaggeration that if we had gone broke we would have lost everything, a risk which few of our acquaintances remember. Instead when the little, green-eyed monster gets to work they complain of our comparatively higher living standards. In fact none of them would have had the nerve to take such a risk at any stage in life, let alone at ours, situated as we were with young families.'

In the long run the risk involved in hazarding personal relationships is probably more scarifying than losing a few thousand pounds. 'It is not easy to strike a balance between family and a small business,' says David Thorpe, of Richmond Marine. 'Failure to do so was summed up by our storemen who relishing the idea of his first two-day weekend for six months said, "Maybe my dog won't bite me when I get home." '

David has created a successful business out of a hobby, yet its success is largely due to the fact that he did not fall into the trap of producing boats for the established fraternity of dinghy sailors. Had he done so he would have just added another dinghy to the growing number of classes on the market which would have been bought and sailed by a number of devotees, and unless he had been fortunate enough to produce a really big seller that would have been that.

He started from basic principles, from spotting a gap in the market which offered the opportunity to build and sell boats to a whole new class of sailing people who had never sailed before, who wanted something simple and easy to handle. A boat which they could use to have fun with from the beach rather than the yacht club slipway. The fact that he had been sailing since he was sixteen (he crossed the Atlantic with Captain Alan Villiers on *Mayflower II* and was seasick for the first sixteen days) did not prevent him from looking at the sailing scene with a fresh eye. Working in America in 1958 he noticed that a boat called the Sunfish, in essence a surfboard with a sail on it, was selling in thousands. David thought it would be a good idea to have a Sunfish in England and that was how his first boat, the Minisail, was born. It was designed by the celebrated dinghy designer and David's friend, Ian Proctor.

At the time David was working for the General Electric Company in its power plant division so he sold the Minisail at weekends and in the evenings. In 1963 Richmond Marine developed a glass-fibre version of it and David had to decide whether to carry on being an engineer or to devote his total energies to building and marketing boats. As it happened he became three-quarters boat builder and one-quarter journalist, for when Ian Proctor decided to retire from being the *Daily Telegraph*'s yachting correspondent David took on the job.

This was important, because watching people sail provided the company with its market research from which it produced in 1968 a boat called the Skipper. This was completely different from anything else available. It was designed to appeal not to the racing sailor, whose tastes largely dictate the design trends in the small-boat market, but to the family sailor in general, and to the family who had not previously owned a boat in particular. In the Skipper the old idea of a damp behind being an essential mark of the dinghy sailor was discounted. Comfort and dry stowage was integral to the design. The leaflets on the Skipper were not just an attempt to sell boats but provided the newcomer to boating with information and reassurance, even to the point of showing photographically where he and his family would sit.

The Skipper 14, launched in 1969, was an instant success and 1,000 boats were sold in the first year. It became the forerunner of a range of family Skippers. The smallest, the Skipper 12, can be carried on top of a Mini and now there is the larger Skipper 17, the company's first boat with a cabin, which was launched in 1971. In four years Richmond Marine's turnover has rocketed from £80,000 to £400,000.

Obviously it hasn't happened without a lot of pressure on family life. For anyone on the sidelines watching a man building a firm, not just the boss's wife but the families of employees caught up in it too, there has to be some loss. There is the loneliness waiting for husbands to come home, the frustration when the dinner gets cold and the tensions at home caused by difficulties at work. 'It is the exceptional wife who can balance these against the satisfaction her husband feels,' says David. 'Being an entrepreneur is a selfish activity and one has much for which to thank one's wife and family and the wives and families of one's partners and employees.'

One answer is to take the wives into the business, make them part of the process, committed to it and heavily involved with it. Actually there are cases where the reverse happens, where wives take their husbands into the businesses. If, like a lot of other women, Beryl Kempner had not so heartily disliked housework it's on the cards that her husband, Richard, would still be in the toy trade. As it is he is now, according to Beryl, the real business brain in the enterprise she started towards the end of the 1950s.

Beryl, who found dusting, polishing and washing-up singularly unrewarding, sat down one day and had a long hard think about doing some spare-time work from home so that she could afford to pay a daily help. She decided to run a knitting outwork business, and recruited a band of women to knit garments to her own design on knitting machines in their homes. It couldn't have been a worse time to start because the market was suddenly flooded with cheap Italian knitted goods.

Under such an assault her small hobby business did not stand a chance, and there she was with a pile of garments and designs which no one wanted. At first she tried to interest some of the women's magazines in them, but they told her to forget about machine knitting. Could she write patterns for their hand-knitting readers? Apparently there is a great population of knitters in Britain whose hunger for acres of knit one, purl one is never totally assuaged. Anyway they knit their way through nearly £40 million worth of wool a year, a phenomenon which has caused Beryl not only to become involved in the wool-spinning business but in publishing as well.

The Kempners now run a highly successful firm called Lyric Pattern Services with a turnover of £120,000 a year which designs garments, writes patterns, and publishes them in over two million leaflets a year. It also produced the Woolworth's *Knitting Magazine* which has sales of 400,000 and a book of Twiggy-sponsored machine-knitting patterns.

The business revolves round Beryl and Richard, a team of permanent designers and 200 compulsive knitters, who have their knitting needles performing a never ending fandango, as they knit away for 22½p an ounce, test beds for every sort of Lyric pattern and every sort of yarn it can be knitted with.

Lyric has done well because it managed to do what so many small businesses are good at doing. The Kempners spotted a gap in the market which no one else was bothering about. For while big wool-spinners like Patons and Baldwins, Sirdar, Lister and Emu produce their own patterns, there are many small spinners who can neither afford the cost, nor want to be bothered to produce their own. This is where the Kempners score. They can sell their service because they make sure that the original design is suitable for all the standard ranges of wools produced by the different firms. This means the spinners can have the name of their own yarn overprinted on the basic pattern, and their house name on the cover as well. If the requirement is very small they can use the

Kempners' own Harmony pattern label. From this you can see the operation is splendidly economical with the Kempners getting maximum utilisation from each pattern they produce.

Much the same thing happened to Stanley Cowan as to Richard Kempner. One moment he was company secretary of one of Tesco's subsidiary companies and the next thing he knew he was surrounded by other people's children. It happened because his wife, Carole, runs one of the biggest, if not *the* biggest, chain of private enterprise kindergartens in Britain, serving the needs of mothers in suburban areas and in industry as well. Beck Kindergartens started almost by accident. If Carole Cowan had not had two children under five and a spare room, then the twenty-four nurseries she has today would not have come about. 'When my two children were three and four years of age I looked round for a suitable kindergarten to leave them in for a few hours a day, but could find nothing,' says Carole. 'So I decided to draw out my savings, just over £30, and set about starting a first-class kindergarten of my own.'

She decorated a room leading on to the garden of her home in Rectory Road, Beckenham, brightened it with coloured benches and small chairs and opened for business in October 1959. She swiftly filled the nursery with its quota of twelve children, found she had to extend her opening hours to afternoons as well as mornings, was then faced with a mounting waiting list and hired her first hall. The urgent need for nurseries which she found in Beckenham must, she felt, apply in other areas as well, and after she got used to running two nurseries she thought why not a chain of them?

By the middle of 1971 Carole and Stanley Cowan were running nineteen Beck nurseries and five Kindergartens for Commerce stretching from Basildon in Essex across Greater London to Epsom in Surrey. The company's first earnings of a few pounds a week had jumped to £60,000 a year and pre-tax profits of about £12,000, and the staff list had grown from Carole on her own to 100 people, including supervisors and clerical staff. And, of course, husband Stanley.

There was a time in the mid-60s when Carole was becoming

increasingly downhearted at the obstacles which faced her. Many of the halls she used were not really suitable, their rents were rising month by month, and local authorities were insisting on regulations which prevented the venture from being economically viable. She and Stanley talked over these difficulties and decided that the only way to grow was to get industry to realise the need for nurseries. 'Many women were leaving their children with us so they could get to work,' says Carole. 'We thought the next logical step was to put the nursery where they were actually working.' At the time there was a shortage of female workers and the Cowans argued that nurseries on industrial premises would help firms solve this problem.

This was how they came to launch a company called Kindergartens for Commerce. 'To run it properly I realised I must have suitable help and this is when Stanley decided to pack up his responsible position with Tesco and together we would take a chance,' says Carole. Stanley now looks after forward planning, the financial side of the business, general administration, seeks new outlets and meets potential clients while Carole deals with planning and organisation, staff and the general day-to-day routine as well as designing nurseries and nursery equipment and investigating new toys.

In the comparisons which are made between the professional manager in a large firm and the owner-manager of a small one, in the way they function, and in the characteristic skills each possesses, the point is rarely made that for most chief executives of public companies it would be unthinkable to have their wives working in the business. To the small businessman it is frequently the reverse, and he is apt to hold board meetings in bed with his wife late at night or over the early morning tea. What happens when the firm grows and more directors come on to the board, heaven knows!

The part played by the wife in a business can vary from supplying a couple of hours of part-time help each day to playing a full-time part in the affairs of the firm at an executive level. Usually there is the additional burden of running the home too. The publishers of this book are a very successful husband and wife team. David St John Thomas is chief executive of David and Charles, his wife Pamela is editorial director. She is able to edit a book on a subject like the Victorian Celebration of Death and darn socks with equal facility. I know because I have seen her. Indeed she asked me to have the goodness not to put my large feet over some photographs she was choosing for the book which were spread all over the floor of her office.

For many wives of small businessmen the period of their marriage when their husbands are trying to bring the firm on is a lonely and depressing time. They feel their husbands are more wedded to the company than to them. They feel isolated and cut off, seeing their husbands at their worst, at the end of a long, demanding day, perhaps when irritability and tension command the evening rather than a cheerful, easy relaxation. Pamela's involvement in the business has prevented this. They have tended to weather the stormy patches together, and this clearly helps. None the less it would be daft to pretend there have not been times when the demands of running a business impose inordinate strains on a marriage. There are moments charged with volcanic possibilities. 'You see, if we are at work and he says, "No, you can't do this or that," and doesn't explain why because three people are waiting to see him, and two telephones are ringing, then I just have to gulp back what I feel. Fortunately by the time the evening has come, and we get home, I've cooled off,' says Pamela.

Her office and David's are only a short distance apart, with David's overlooking some railway lines, and Pam's overlooking some public gardens; near enough to quickly discuss crucial issues like: 'Are we taking up the option on that American book?' or 'What do you fancy for dinner tonight?'

Ken Jones of Phase Separations echoes the benefits of having wives involved in the business. 'We were careful to include our wives in the company's operations. In the early days all were excellent part-time secretaries, and are still involved as the occasion demands. As a consequence they appreciate the problems and demands and are still tolerant of the time spent away and the long working hours.'

In the early days when Ben Jones was starting his business his wife Anne had contemplated returning to teaching French to fortify the domestic budget. But on the advice of their bank manager she stayed at home to answer the phone and help in the business. She now knows so much about shipping that she can easily take Ben's place when he is not there. The only thing she does not tackle is the fixing of a charter. Nayland is not too far from Colchester so this tends to be very much her own area of operation, especially on the ship's agency side. When a ship docks at Colchester's Hythe Quay, Anne meets it, deals with requirements of the master and passes on instructions to him from the owners. At first she carried a small, pocket-sized written brief itemising all the points she had to cover from advising the port pilots, arranging stevedoring, organising a laundry service, and possibly medical and nursing attention in an emergency. Now she doesn't need a written brief any more.

Anne had learned a lot about shipping over the twenty years Ben had been in the City, but not in a very specific sense. It was certainly not the intention that she would get involved at the grass roots level she has, when they first branched out on their own in Suffolk. 'It's something I enjoy and sometimes the language helps when you go aboard a foreign ship,' says Anne. One worry was the effect working from home was having on the children. 'Because Anne was involved and because the office was in the house we tended to be talking business problems in front of them all the time,' says Ben. Their two boys, David and Robin, and daughter Sarah, are now away at boarding school, while Tim is at home. Having built a successful business Ben is able to assure them of a first-class education. 'I think that is the main extra which we might not have been able to afford before,' he says. They can also afford help for Anne in the house.

It is not only in helping with the running of a business that a wife can play an important role, but her encouragement and influence in making a man decide to cast off the yoke of an employer and work for himself instead may be decisive. When Christian Brann was teetering between starting on his own or accepting the lucrative job he had been offered he decided to leave the final decision to his wife. He put the case for either course to her as fairly as he could. 'I suppose I shall never know whether it was supreme courage or ignorance of the enormous risk and difficulties involved which made her choose the harder course, but it was she who said, "There is no choice. You have always wanted a business of your own and if you don't start it now, you never will." So we did.'

Their children were away at school, work at home had greatly diminished so she decided to throw her weight into the business and do whatever work she could. At first it was running the office, keeping the books (she had some lessons from the firm's accountant) until the company was big enough to have a proper book-keeper. But it is the moral support which wives can give which is of incalculable value. Christian well remembers the time when he was talking to a client who was having difficulty getting some letters printed at short notice. 'With my optimism and enthusiasm I promised my own organisation would do it overnight,' he says. 'The client was impressed, and said there must be a lot of printing you could do for me if you can give a wonderful service like that.' So that night, between 7pm and the early hours of the next morning, he printed the letters himself on a small printing machine he had acquired from his landlord.

'My wife stood beside me, helped to stack and pack them and comforted me when I was close to despair,' he says.

Having his wife in the business with him he regards as an enormous bonus. Previously they had lived separate lives, she responsible for the home and children while he went to the office. But as the children grew up and became less dependent on her, the new family business gave her the chance to escape from being a household drudge, and she soon found she had a talent for business. She also fulfils an important function in providing a bridge between Christian who, after his experience of larger companies, tends to be a little too demanding and sometimes impatient, and the relatively less experienced staff of a small company. 'Because she too is less experienced, she is able to appreciate the point of view of the rest of the staff,' he says.

Christian's own words describe very well the climate of family life which has resulted from having his own business, and having his wife by his side in it. 'The new association between myself and my wife has given a new meaning and a new dimension to our marriage.

'While a marriage and the children are still young there is, of course, a very powerful link between husband and wife. When the children grow up a great gap and a vacuum can often develop. The business which we own together has entirely filled this gap. We are completely partners once more. Yet we have had to work much harder than we had ever worked before. I have less assistance than I was used to in larger companies. I have to do many small chores myself. I have to work longer hours each day and frequently at weekends as well. My wife still has her home to run apart from a very demanding job in the office. Whereas previously my business worries were only something she was vaguely aware of, she now has to share them, not only at the office but at home.

'Even the children get involved. Previously they thought of their father as someone who had a remote job which always seemed to bring in a fair amount of money and quite a few luxuries, but did not really concern them. They now hear the business and its problems discussed much more at home and occasionally they get a little frightened about the possibility of a failure. They also resent to some extent the fact that their mother is no longer quite as available, especially during the holidays. But even they have benefited in the long run. They have become more self-reliant and helpful. Because their help was needed they rose to the challenge.

'During the holidays they now clean the house and cook the lunch ready for us to come home to. They have learned a good deal more about the facts of economic life than they would ever have done in previous days. On occasions they have come to the office and helped with some of the work themselves. Although none of them at present contemplate coming into the business, they all have a kind of proprietory interest.'

Naturally for every benefit which accrues it is possible to think of a drawback or a personal sacrifice which has been made and which are important entries when you draw up the social profit and loss account of having your own business. 'There is no denying that our business life has assumed a much greater importance and has largely pushed our private life into a corner,' says Christian. 'Gone are the days of long weekends, of the occasional week's holiday or taking a day off when it suited us. We are no longer in it just to make a living, we are in it, committed with our whole lives.'

From the point of view of personal earnings the Branns are probably fractionally better off than when he was a senior executive, but because they are not keen on becoming immensely rich to the exclusion of everything else, they are agreed that any surplus cash above their personal needs will in future be spent on additional highly qualified help, which will relieve the strain on them personally and give the company a securer, broader management base.

David Thomas says starting and running David and Charles has made Pamela and he far poorer than they would otherwise have been until recently. He was talking just after the Barber budget of 1971, which at least did something, on both a corporate and a personal level, to making small businessmen feel they were no longer second-class financial citizens. 'I now probably have a larger personal income than if I had not got my own firm,' says David. 'But it has been tough for some years having to lead the life of an executive on the pay of an underling.

'I remember talking to the Devon Federation of Women's Institutions where I was accused of being a wealthy publisher. I told them that if I died my will would say I was wealthy, but you tie everything up in your sole asset, and unless you sell it, you really do lack coppers and wonder if you can afford a bar of chocolate. Bless them, they sent a thank you letter, and with it three bars of chocolate! They may have thought I was putting it on, but three years ago I really did sometimes go without a bar of chocolate in order to save coppers.

'I have always used reasonable hotels to help while under the strain of working, but hobbies and pastimes have been curtailed through cash shortage. It always seemed more important to put the money into the business. This has changed now, but the

, while it lasted—and it was seven years—was very real
n.'

seems that the personal qualities needed to start a business a. not merely those which constitute a driving will to succeed, nor the sheer animal energy to carry on. It is not a matter which entrepreneurs care to spend much time contemplating, but somewhere there has to be a reserve of courage to cope with failure in business. Failure means there is a shattered pride which needs reassembling. Failure means humiliation at a creditor's meeting, sitting by the liquidator, having to face people to whom you owe money, some of them perhaps more than business acquaintances, but friends. A person has to be devoid of both a sense of responsibility and sensitivity not to find failure a harrowing experience. It may take a certain ineptitude to fail, but it often takes a special courage too. Perhaps this is the reason why so many owners of small businesses fight on to the bitter end when failure is staring them in the face. For although a business is many things, it is, after all, a relentless commitment to continue. There are commitments to people and promises made to them. There are premises and overdrafts, machines on the HP. Lastly there is pride and the worry of what your friends will say about you if you do not carry on.

NOTES

1 Page 82. C. W. Golby and G. Johns. *Attitude and Motivation.* Research Report No 7. Committee of Inquiry on Small Firms. HM Stationery Office (1971).

Chapter 5

What do small businessmen look like?

The part played by luck and timing. Recognising and exploiting it. The difference between working hard and working intelligently. Victor Balding—a portrait of an industrial beaver. What does the managing director of a small business do? The ability and the will to manage a growing firm. The small man as a self-opinionated mini-God. Small firm empathy and big firm emotional blindness. Small business and big business management skills compared. Working days, working styles, leisure and health.

IN the last resort, when everything else has been assessed and quantified, success or failure largely depends on the quality of the man and on those wayward and fickle business companions, luck and timing. In business, as in love, there is a time when circumstances are more propitious and a time when they are less so; a time when luck walks hand in hand with her favourite or dances tantalisingly out of reach.

Having the right product or service at the wrong time, before the market is ready for it, before a market has even been created for it, is a stern combination of ill-luck and ill-timing which has caused many a small business to founder, often to the acute chagrin and incomprehension of its owner when later someone else steps in and makes the same thing work. From such experiences springs the business philosophy which says let others do the pioneering and expend the money and effort creating a receptive consumer climate before you put your own two feet in.

Christian Brann thinks that if you took an accountant, a business consultant and a lawyer and asked them to formulate a perfect plan for starting a new business with virtually no capital, with a founder and his wife who needed an income of £5,000 a year to pay their children's school bills, they would undoubtedly prove conclusively that the task was impossible. Yet he and his wife have done it. 'I don't claim that this is due to our own brilliance or even our own industry,' he says. 'I am afraid that at the end I have to admit it is just by the grace of God.'

Grace of God, luck, call it what you will.

The crucial thing about luck in business is a man's ability to see it when it arrives, his ability to seize hold of it and the nerve and courage to exploit it. There are people who, even if they know their luck, see it laced with perturbing and off-putting unknowns. Norman Chalk remembers the time when all the paraphernalia of North Sea oil exploration first came to Great Yarmouth, and opportunities to make money were popping all over the place. Some local businessmen were asking, but what happens if the rigs pack up and go away?

'They find gold nuggets washed up on the beach and the first thing they worry about is what happens when the supply dries up,' says Norman.

For Cyril Lucas luck could not have come dressed in a more fluky fashion. The American Hardshell Clam, the staple of the American clambake, was unknown in European waters until it was discovered breeding in Southampton Water. In the normal run of events the Water is too cold for clams, but nowadays it is considerably warmed up from the outfalls of the Central Electricity Generating Board's Marchwood Power Station. How the clams got there in the first place is a mystery but the most popular theory is that a clutch of them, excess to requirements, were chucked overboard by the chef on a passenger liner. This is a feasible theory because clams, employing the quality from which they get their name, can live refrigerated for weeks, excluding the cold air from their shells.

Anyway, clams breed there and Lucas has a small army of diggers collecting them for him. Once gathered he matures them in what were his old oyster layings in the Newtown River, on the Isle of Wight. As a result Britain has a new, small shellfish industry and in 1970 Lucas sold £14,000 worth of clams, mostly to France. For him the providential arrival of the clams could not have been better timed, since the fierce winter of 1963–4 had been disastrous for him, killing off 99·5 per cent of his oysters on which he depended for a living. If this is not an extraordinary piece of luck allied to a providential piece of timing, you cannot help wondering what it is. The important point is Lucas recognised it for what it was and had the wit to do something about it.

One of the best expositions of the part played by luck in the building of a large business has been given by Lord Thomson of Fleet. Writing in *The Director*, in February 1970, he outlined the main points of the philosophy which has served him well. These were that for any man a fair share of lucky breaks will arise throughout the course of his life; that he must not only be able to recognise them but also be in a position to seize them; that having got this far he must consolidate and press on, and not sit back and wait for events to pass him by again; and that almost anything can be accomplished if you want it badly enough, and are prepared to work hard enough for it.

It was luck which led to him being offered *The Scotsman* newspaper at a time when he was able to leave Canada; but, as he says, it was not luck which had given him a management team in Toronto to whom he could leave the conduct of his North American affairs while he came to Britain. 'Nor did I leave *The Scotsman*'s subsequent future to luck—an enormous amount of very hard work went into converting it from an almost moribund operation into a viable and profitable enterprise. So that when the next lucky break occurred—the opportunity to tender for the Scottish Television contract—I was in a position to seize it.' He cites other instances of lucky breaks which have had a profound bearing on the creation of his business enterprises in Britain, the timing of the offer to sell the Kemsley newspaper empire to him, for example, but he makes the basic observation that although he believes in luck he does not believe in being dependent on it. 'When the breaks are running against you, you simply have to work harder, and use greater skills,' he says.

Hard work, sheer diligence, the long sustained application to the affairs of a business is taken for granted by most small businessmen. Those determined to make something of their opportunities are prepared to work incredibly hard to do it. Unfortunately some of them think hard work is a substitute for good management—and, of course, it is not. There is a man called Alan Brush in Essex who is a local sand and gravel tycoon. When he first started in business he was unable to read or write, due to an interrupted and foreshortened schooling. But he used to work like a Trojan and then one day his manager said to him, 'You know, Alan, you are working hard, but you may be digging that stuff out for nothing—you haven't even written down your costings.' For all his unorthodoxy this remark stopped him in his tracks. From then on he taught himself to read and write, and to produce a set of costings as well as the next man. Having started in business with £70 and a battered lorry, by the end of 1971 he was selling nearly £1 million worth of sand and gravel a year, with the prospects of even larger business as he opened up new pits to serve two of the biggest construction projects in Britain: the new London Airport at Foulness and the redevelopment of 5,000 acres of London's East End. By then Brush had long since learned that hard work is one thing, working hard intelligently quite another.

For a portrait of an intelligent and hard-working entrepreneur you could not do better than Victor Balding, who, like the beaver, is a diligent and energetic creature, always building. For him the beaver has proved an exciting, profitable and romantic inspiration. Balding makes machine tools with the Beaver brand name in a factory he built himself called Beaver Works. In the rare moments he takes time off from emulating the beaver, he likes to take a dip in the swimming pool he mostly built himself, in the garden of Beaver's Wood, the house he also designed and built himself just outside Norwich.

Life was not always as comfortable as this and in fact Balding has survived an extraordinarily difficult half-dozen years in an industry which has seen other small firms either go to the wall or get swallowed up. The monument—though he wouldn't approve of the word—to his success is a modern, airy, clean, almost show-place factory on the outskirts of Norwich. It is flanked by flowering cherry trees, green fields and young saplings which he digs up from the copse in his own garden. If it burned down today the factory would cost him £2 million to replace. He has two other factories—one in Great Yarmouth, another in Fakenham.

Last year he manufactured and sold £1·5 million worth of machine tools and he travelled prodigiously doing it. Sixty-five per cent of his production goes overseas. America is his biggest market, taking 30 per cent of his output. It is in this highly competitive market that Victor has achieved something of a record. Over the last few years he claims to have sold between 60 and 70 per cent of *all* the British milling machines which go to the United States.

By 1972–3 Victor estimates he will be selling £2 million worth of machine tools annually. He has just signed with a New Zealand company which is to produce them under licence. Negotiations for licensing agreements in three other countries are also in hand. About a year ago he set up a sales and service company in America and now he is studying setting up a production unit there. He expects to publicly float Balding Engineering in two or three years time.

His charming wife, delightful home, two yellow labradors called Jason and Sally, a son in the business, who has been through Loughborough University and who will one day run the firm, are all a source of immense enjoyment to him. Fortune may have smiled upon Victor Balding, but it did not come easily. He has worked enormously hard for it, but he has always been possessed with fanatical energy and unswerving persistence.

Specifically it was by listening very hard to what the customer wanted that he has built up the solid export business he has. This was how he learned there was a gap in the American market for a milling machine which had more capacity and capability than those already being sold. It was a time when the plastics industry was really beginning to take off, and Balding swiftly saw there was good money in it for his company. His turret milling machines are very much the mould-maker's master tool, and there is a ready market for them from machine shop operators who make the moulds which, in turn, are used to produce thousands of varying plastic components.

Victor started life on someone else's shop floor in Norwich, and soon demonstrated that there was more to him than just the ability to operate a machine. It was not long before he was works manager of a small engineering company in East Anglia. It was here that he began to acquire his management expertise. But even before that Balding had been struck by the idea of being in business for himself. This was during the war when small engineering shops mushroomed in garages, lock-up shops and garden sheds all over the country. He had a small hobbies lathe in the conservatory at the back of his house, but he needed a larger one to undertake more ambitious jobs. Lathes were in short supply. So Victor sat down at his kitchen table, designed his own machine and then proceeded to build it bit by bit on the hobbies lathe. To set up on his own in 1951, he sold his house and with some money advanced from the bank, £7,000 in all, established his first factory in an old tramways electricity generating plant in Norwich.

'In those early days I suppose I must have been very lonely—I had no employees—so I used to take my dog to work with me,' he recalls. Even then, both struggling and enjoying the fun of building a business, he was developing a commercial philosophy with which he is still obsessed today—ploughing back his money into machines and men.

The first man he ever put his money on was Fred Christman, a burly down-to-earth engineer who is still working on the shop floor of Balding Engineering today. 'I just advertised and Fred arrived,' he recalls. 'I used to go round on my motor cycle and side car picking up and delivering the work, while Fred was in the shop doing it.' At that time Victor was living with his wife in a caravan on £2.50 a week. 'We had so little money I used to go shooting rabbits to sell.' He did this from his motor cycle with a 12 bore shotgun. 'Wild West style,' he grins, 'steering with one hand, shooting with the other.'

He started to build a bungalow on the site of his caravan. Bricks were stacked all round it. But he was still short of money, and as his small business grew he was ploughing back every penny he could afford into buying more machines and paying the wages of more men. The bungalow was second priority. It got built bit by bit as money became available. Sometimes everything had to stop. 'There was a stage when the shell was up and it stood there without any floors inside for a long time,' he says.

Turnover at the end of his first year was precisely £3,739. As each year passed he measured his growth from the orders he was clinching, and the machines he was buying. But he also remembers a touching, homely yardstick to his early progress . . . a washing machine, his wife's first, a Christmas present from him. 'I went home, put it into the hall, went into the kitchen and said, "What's all this in the hall then?" The look on her face when she saw it was worth millions to me.'

In the first three years business was slow and steady. In 1954 his sales were just over £5,000. The following year, as his reputation for good work at the right price and on time grew, his business leapfrogged to over £20,000. By then he was employing about thirty men. Business was growing and he had to take larger premises. A new factory was built in Norwich. Victor laid bricks, moved timber, erected steelwork with the help of his own men and outside contractors. But he outgrew his second premises almost as fast as he built them. Again he set about building a third factory—directing operations himself and prefabricating much of the structure in his existing plant.

Today the inside of that plant is full of machines, including the very latest automated ones, which he has bought from all over the world. A huge slogan on the walls cries out: 'Think and *Work Smarter* not Harder—our customer will not pay for your wasted effort.' Victor, who always wears a blue nylon overall, whether he is sitting in the office or walking through the factory, talks with pride about his men and machines. Some of them are shareholders in the company. He gives them blocks of shares at various levels of long service. 'When I go public

I want them to make some real money,' he says, remembering the days when he had very little himself.

Obviously the details in the picture of Victor Balding are specific to him, his business, his drives and his personal satisfactions. In any general portrait of the average small businessman there will be immense variations in particulars and in texture. None the less it is possible to produce a broad likeness of him as a breed, based on the responsibilities he carries, on the style of his working life, and in the characteristic skills he exercises.

This is how John Davies, Minister for Industry, sees the managing director of a small company. His remarks are an extract from a speech he made to the British Federation of Master Printers, in June 1968, when he was Director-General of the Confederation of British Industry.

'The managing director of the smaller concern is a man involved specifically and in detail in every part of his company's activity. It is he that sees the bank manager on the subject of financial resources. It is he that makes the investment appraisal and the decision to invest in every substantial purchase. It is he that decides the nature of the product and the changes required in it from time to time. It is he that hires and fires. It is he that organises the selling effort. It is he that fixes the prices. It is he that grants credit. It is he that negotiates wage rates. It is he who does a thousand and one other things, including meeting the growing burden of form filling and question answering. In larger businesses the principles of delegation are carefully studied and can be effectively fulfilled. In the small business there is, of course, delegation too, but the duty of decision in practically every department of the concern concentrates upon an individual. Of course, this is not to say that the managing director has no faithful and able supporters. In most cases he will have beside him an immediate colleague concerned with the factory; another concerned with the selling effort; and in many cases another looking after the whole of the administrative side of the business. Very often this whole team will have grown up together over a very long period of time and will be intensely knowledgeable of the particular circumstances affecting their own business, whilst having little broad experience in wider industrial and commercial fields. They will be capable of replacing one another during absence to an extent quite undreamed of in larger organisations. Their experience being derived almost wholly from training on the job, they will find particular difficulty in handling new problems thrust upon them from outside and demanding a professional ability in management techniques which they do not pretend to possess. The characteristic decision-making process in the larger organisation, of resolving to get somebody to do something about a given issue, is one which is wholly strange to them; they are accustomed either to doing things themselves or not having them done at all.'

The basic shift in attitude on the part of the small man which takes him from doing something himself to getting someone else to do it for him is one of the more fascinating, and difficult, trends to chart in the development of a small firm. It does require a major shift because in the circumstances surrounding the founding of his business the entrepreneur is both able and willing to do the job himself, and do it well, but he is temperamentally not suited to getting it done by others. This point does represent a milestone in the affairs of a company because there is a world of difference between wanting to start a business and seeing it gathering pace from your own efforts, and going on to manage it, taking responsibility for the work of others and getting satisfaction from the achievements of subordinates.

These days there is a tremendous amount of talk about how to manage a company, the techniques you employ to do it, but little is said about the will to manage, which is, after all, what makes the art of delegation easy rather than painful. David Thomas says there is nothing which gives him greater satisfaction than just being able to put his initial on something one of his editors has proposed, especially when he sees the man has extended himself and given the proposition a dimension that even David had not thought of.

Anyone who has a power complex, who gets his satisfaction from exercising his authority over others is not likely to want to share much of it with lower level managers. The small business is not the best arena for power games, and the man who runs one depends not on politics but on the ownership of it for his authority and also on his own knowledge, skill and the strength of his personality. To David Thomas, for instance, old-fashioned, forelock-touching, employer-employee relations are an anathema. 'Employee mentality is a company joke,' he says. But the fact is that even in this day and age there are companies which would find a lack of forelock-touching less than humorous. These are usually the companies where the excesses of one man management are regarded as the norm. They exist on one man's inalienable belief in his own infallibility. He is self-opinionated to the last degree and sees himself as a sort of god. He is difficult to advise and believes the decisions he makes are right, largely because there is no one prepared to tell him they are wrong. At best he is paternalistic, at worst autocratic and dictatorial. Now these words don't really belong to me, but to a man who has spent much of his professional life—and still does—involved with small businessmen.

He serves on the boards of some small companies in an honorary capacity, sometimes as chairman. In these small companies he says there are often two or three contenders for the top job and the strongest comes to the top and the others either accede or leave, very often with bad blood. On these sort of boards my informant sees his job very clearly. 'My task is to prevent the strongest personality cutting the others' throats,' he says.

Well, there's one man's view. The small businessman might translate the words differently as tough, determined, self-reliant and sturdily independent. If these are the flags which fly proudly over small businesses there should, perhaps, be added to them another which proclaims the empathy which exists in a small company, its ability to cope with people's emotional reactions which may seem to outsiders small, slight and silly.

It is a quality which is apt to get lost along the corridors of the hierarchy in a large firm, but in a small concern it is crucial in gaining the willing co-operation of the workpeople. Brilliant men with first-class honour degrees from universities, or impressive diplomas from business schools, often fail as managers because the one thing they cannot be taught is one of the most important subjects of all—coping with human emotions.

J. Sterling Livingston, Professor of Business Administration at the Harvard Business School, has described these people as 'emotion blind', and says that when they get their first job in industry they undergo a rude shock because they resent the human emotions which make a company untidy. Sometimes the strength of this emotional climate in a small firm can be staggering. The last accusation which could be levelled at the people who run Danbury Conversions, for example (see Chapter 15), is that they suffer the defects of Livingston's managers.

The distinguishing marks of the small businessman who owns and runs his own concern are thrown into sharp relief when you compare him as a species with the professional manager in the large company. There is a fairly broad popular image of both of them. The small firm owner is identified with individuality, flair, enterprise and opportunism, while the professional manager conjures up a picture of organisation, planning and grey flannel suit professionalism. But the differences go deeper than this—in function, in business philosophy, that is in the attitudes and manner of doing business which have developed in a firm over a period of time, and in the characteristic skills which each employs. One of the most lucid and interesting analysis of these differences appeared in an article on the Owner Manager in the June 1970 issue of *Industrial and Commercial Training*. In it the author, J. S. Deeks, research officer of the Furniture and Timber Industry Training Board, succinctly summarised the differences in entrepreneurial and managerial skills between the two breeds. This is how he sees them:

Entrepreneurial and Managerial Skills

	Small Firm Entrepreneur	*Large Firm Manager*
Source of Authority	(a) tradition (ownership) (b) personal	(a) expertise (b) office

Entrepreneurial and Managerial Skills

	Small Firm Entrepreneur	*Large Firm Manager*
Basis of Philosophy	(a) no diffusion between ownership and control (b) no conflict between personal and company objectives (c) no distinction between person and role (d) integration of work and social values (e) not subservient to economic goals	(a) control without ownership (b) conflict between individual and organisational goals (c) very clear distinction between the individual and the office he fills (d) values of the workplace divorced from both individual and social values (e) economic 'performance' as ultimate criterion
Characteristic skills	(a) adoptive (b) diagnostic (c) exploitation of change: opportunism (d) tactical facility (e) pragmatic use of techniques as aid to problem solving (f) social skills applied on a personal basis (g) consequence-mitigating decision-making	(a) predictive (b) prognostic (c) control of change (d) strategic facility (e) co-ordination and control of specialists (f) manipulative skills applied largely on an impersonal basis (g) event-shaping decision-making

Organisation	(a) informal relationships (b) no divorce between the planners and the doers (c) appointment and promotion often on basis of birth or personal friendship (d) everyone prepared to muck-in as required (e) open system of communications	(a) formal relationships (b) divorce of planning from doing (c) technical qualifications as basis of appointment and promotion (d) precise definition of rights and obligations, duties and responsibilities (e) structured communications system

While this identifies some of the distinguishing features which are singular to the entrepreneur it tells you little about the style and manner in which he conducts his personal and working life. In the early stages of developing a company personal sacrifices of outside interests seem to be an inevitable price which has to be paid. Christian Brann has already described the adjustment which was necessary when someone like himself, a manager in a large company, switched so to speak from the right- to the left-hand column of the table. But in addition there is the sort of deprivation which is caused by the business continually demanding the presence of the person who owns it.

Yet the long hours can be tempered by the circumstances in which they are worked. 'One of the great benefits of our business is that we have established it within 4 miles of our home which is a pleasant house in the heart of the country,' says Brann. 'It takes us less than ten minutes to get to the office, we have somewhere easy to park the car, and we can get home for lunch when the children are home during the holidays. Under these conditions working on a Saturday morning, and sometimes going in on a Sunday for an hour or two, is no great hardship.' He and his wife start at 8am before their staff arrive at 8.30 and leave the office last in the evening. They, therefore, believe their staff realise that they do not expect more of them than they are willing to deliver themselves. 'I believe this is one of the greatest factors in our success,' says Christian.

According to Ken Jones of Phase Separations, the early days of the business provided him and his colleagues with the longest working hours, and yet with the greatest stimulation. 'Each of us, directors and managers, are undoubtedly much better businessmen for the experience,' he says. David Thorpe, of Richmond Marine, regards running a small business as particularly taxing in the speed with which you have to learn, and the control you have to exercise in order that the business can grow. 'There is no avoiding, for an extended period, a heavy personal work load,' he says. 'My working day quite often starts at 7.30am and finishes at 2am the next morning, if I am under pressure.

'In these circumstances I might miss both breakfast and lunch. Abroad I tend to cram far too much mileage into a trip and far too many visits, working and travelling sixteen hours a day for three weeks. During years of this type of schedule until last autumn, when I deliberately slackened off, getting home at 7pm and not working at weekends, a seventy-hour week was the norm. I never take work home in the evening but I do have to make phone calls from home.'

Richard Lamb, of Adcola (see Chapter 7) works from 8am to 5.30pm, has a working lunch, usually sandwiches in the office, or half a pint with one of his staff in the local pub. Most evenings he does a couple of hours work at home and also works on the occasional Saturday morning. Basil Crofts of R. J. Fullwood and Bland, a firm which makes milking machines, keeps normal office hours from 9.15am to 5.15pm but says in addition there is a certain amount of social entertainment with foreign visitors. 'I make a point of very seldom taking work home in the evening or at weekends,' he says. 'I feel I work at quite intense concentration during office hours and that work should not be taken home unless absolutely unavoidable.'

Home for him is a twenty-five minute drive away in his 3·5 litre Rover (not a company car, but his own, which he changes every three years) through pleasant country lanes, to the converted windmill where he lives. Home for Arthur Wilkin of Wilkin and Sons (see Chapter 14) is old Tiptree Hall, a few minutes' bicycle ride across the well-made roads which cut across the jam factory's farm lands and orchards. That's if it is fine. If the weather is bad he drives his Rover 2000. Home for David and Pamela Thomas is a pleasant house in a Devon village, quite a short drive from their office. Home for Donald Hagenbach (see Chapter 13) is a house in Wroxham exuding history in every brick, where he entertains his visitors with lavish hospitality, filling them with good whisky and his own home cooking behind mullioned windows and timbers which have lasted longer even than the rugged boats he builds.

The only Rolls-Royce in this book belongs to Vladimir Raitz of Horizon Holidays who used to be a Jaguar man. He also has an old 1960 Ford Zephyr which he keeps in France for when he goes there on holiday. The Rolls perhaps is one of his few directorial luxuries. Lavish eating certainly is not. Unless he has a business lunch he usually eats in his own office, drinks water with his meal and never has coffee or tea breaks. Of course choice of holidays is not a great problem for him—he has the whole of the Horizon Holidays brochure to choose from. All he needs is the time to go on them.

But for the smaller firms holidays are a problem, especially where both husband and wife are active in the business and staff are thin at the top. Then it is doubly inconvenient for both to be away at the same time. 'Yet we are so attached to one another and our family life is so strong that it would be unthinkable for us to go on holiday separately,' says Christian Brann. 'Last year we found a fair compromise. I went down to the South of France with my wife and children by camping car and spent the first week of the holidays with them. Then I flew back to England, had another week in the office and rejoined them for the third week. The week in the middle was short enough for me to remain relaxed and in a peculiar way I still felt I had enjoyed three weeks holidays.'

If someone running a business like Christian Brann is only too aware of the therapeutic value of a holiday, so are those for whom the health of businessmen is something dear to their professional hearts. Dr Beric Wright, director of the Institute of Director's Medical Centre, is the arch proponent of care for the businessman in body and mind. He produces telling statistics to show why. According to him between 20 and 30 per cent of business executives die before the age of sixty, and they should therefore make an attempt to improve their health early in their careers. He thinks that at the age of forty the businessman should ask himself whether he really is destined to be outstandingly successful, or whether he is placing too great a burden on his own talents. And at the age of forty-five he should ask himself whether his success was really worth it. The good doctor also offers a word of warning about another disease which sometimes destroys businessmen—the wife whose ambitions are greater than her husband's ability. The delusion of indispensability is another occupational hazard, suffered by the man who never takes a holiday and who delegates nothing, which threatens life in the boardroom. There are times when worry at work flows over into home life, and the home life of a businessman has a direct impact on his health and his performance at work. 'The two principal requirements for any potential entrepreneur are a very tolerant wife and the ability not to worry, to turn off the problem whenever required,' says Ken Jones of Phase Separations. 'If these criteria are not inherent in you, either an early death, a divorce or an ulcer will ensue. No business is worth any of these.'

Most of those who profess to know seem to think that it is important that a businessman should develop outside interests and pastimes. Views and practices among the people in this book vary widely in this respect. David and Pamela Thomas take no part in social activities outside the home. They try to keep Saturdays free for family life, but apart from that the affairs of the publishing company take up most of their time. By contrast Christian Brann is actively involved with the affairs of his locality —fund raising and charitable work, the production of literature for local clubs and societies and committee work for the parochial church council, the British Legion and local educational institutions. 'One of the purposes of owning your own business is that you feel free to use your company's facilities to help you in all this semi-social, semi-charitable work. One makes many friends and contacts in these activities which are of some help in one's work as well.'

No one I talked to followed a rigid office routine, although they did like to get the post out of the way as soon as they could. In the course of running the company Arthur Wilkin likes to walk through the jam factory each morning and see how the previous day's batch has gone. Vladimir Raitz spends much of his day reading reports and seeing a lot of people who come knocking at his door, most of them with development propositions of one sort or another. Predictably office surroundings range from the archaic to the modern and functional. In Donald Hagenbach's office papers, books and files seem to ebb and flow with the very slight tide on the river outside. Vladimir's is uncluttered and functional. To find Harry and Rene Chandler (Chapter 14) in the attic office of their home you have to run round a vast billiard table first.

These observations are by no means offered as a comprehensive survey of the life style of small businessmen. As details of workaday actions and surroundings they are of no great moment. But what they do reflect is the differences which exist because a man can make his own decisions about how, when, and in what circumstances he will conduct his business life. The details are different and personalised precisely because small businessmen are not managers in big companies where these things are so often ordered and organised with such scrupulous regard to men of equal status that they end up with identical offices, secretaries and even houses.

Our daily trivia belongs to men of independence and individuality. There is one particular quotation from a small businessman in the Bolton Committee Research report on Attitude and Motivation about the satisfaction of running your own business which sticks in the mind. 'I've got complete freedom of spirit, haven't I? If I want to tell anybody to go to hell I can tell them to go to hell. I can do it as I want, when I want, I can develop it in a personal sort of way . . . you stamp your own personality on it. You have to be a bit of an independent.'

Chapter 6

Some firms are more family than others

The family firm has long been part of the business landscape. It has a distinct and particular character and flavour of its own. J. Taylor and Sons is an engineering firm where 25 per cent of the management and workforce are related, a fact which not only brings benefits, but peculiar stresses and strains too. Four brothers own it and the way the firm is run is both extraordinary and fascinating. It may lack the management methods of many firms but it always has a full order book and it has not lost a skilled man yet.

SOME family firms are more family than others, but J. Taylor and Son is positively tribal. When Joseph Taylor, a highly skilled engineering blacksmith, died in 1954, he left behind not only a family, but a workforce too. Of the forty-four people who earn their living working for J. Taylor and Son, eleven of them are kith and kin and those who are not feel they are, for it is a benevolent firm and it has never lost a skilled man yet. It has a lot in common with many other small family companies which you find scattered about, especially in rural areas, well known in their own bit of the country, and not usually working more than 70 miles from home, so that the men can get home at night. It is a versatile concern whose engineers can turn their hands to almost anything: piggeries, barns, cowsheds for farmers, warehouses, factory and brewery extensions, putting up all the structural steelwork and the sheet cladding which goes on the outside of the buildings. And while the men are doing it, they will often mend a farm gate or fence, and not charge for it. The Taylors are very good at mending things. It goes back to when their father started in business for himself after World War II with a small smithy, some hand bellows, three 14lb hammers and not much else. He had to root round for what work he could get, and it was mostly repairs of farm machinery.

Today they still get a farmer out of trouble when he has broken his plough. But as well as mending, they make. In their work bays in the village of Abberton, in Essex, they undertake sizeable fabrication jobs; water filtering screens for power stations in Malaya, or the canopies for the power units of some big container cranes which the New York port authority recently installed. The firm got the job because no other firm either wanted or seemed capable of doing it. It seems odd that a tiny local concern with its small works built in a field overlooking a great stretch of lonely Essex marshes should be knocking up jobs for the mighty port of New York.

The family makes much of the quality of the jobs it does. This goes back to the brothers' early training, the seven-year family apprenticeship each of them, except one, served with their father. Their father was a man who believed in engineering excellence, and who broke his heart, and his body, working all the hours God gave him to achieve it. On every J. Taylor and Son building job the firm puts up a big board with blue lettering on a white background. It says quite simply 'Taylor made'. It is a proclamation of quality, of a job well done, done on time and personally supervised by a member of the Taylor clan. It is also an enduring memorial to Joseph Taylor the craftsman, and to the craftsmanship he believed in.

As a man he indubitably believed in large families. He and his wife, Martha Taylor, who is still alive and lives with one of her daughters, had eleven children; nine boys and two girls. One boy died when he was eight, but of the rest, except for two who chose their own path and are engineers in the North of England, all are either in the family business or linked with it. There are four brothers who are equal partners. Charlie is the administrator who negotiates contracts, fixes prices, meets the customers and runs the office. Fred looks after the heavy fabrications side. Bill is in charge of the small works which does general repairs, and Arthur is the boss on outside steel structural work. There are two more brothers, Stanley and George, highly skilled craftsmen, who work on the fabrications, and who are employees of the firm. Partner Fred has two sons in the firm, Fred junior, who supervises the outside sheeting and cladding work, and Cyril, who also goes on site work. Cyril was the firm's first employee. He joined straight from school in April 1953. There is a brother-in-law in the business, too. Edgar Rumney is married to sister Olive. They look after old Mrs Taylor, and also have a son, Edgar junior, in the firm. Then there's Barbara Clay, a niece of the six brothers and daughter of sister Maggie. Barbara does the secretarial work, and makes a good cup of tea.

Now the way the firm is run, and who runs it, takes a bit of unravelling. It is tangled up with family history, with who did what, and when. Charlie sits at the table in his office which serves as a desk and looks out of the window, across the yard to where lengths of steel are stacked, to where the big bays of the main works blot out the line of Mersea Island and the Essex coast beyond. He remembers the time it was green fields. To his right there's an old asbestos and corrugated iron building where the smithy used to be. When his father first worked there on his own he had to get his wife to hold the metal bar he was fashioning with one hand (she had baby sister Olive on the other arm) while he hit it. Later when Charlie left the RAF, came home and worked with him all day, banging away with a 14lb hammer, his Dad used to say, 'You lift it boy, God will let it come down.'

In the evenings and at weekends Charlie employed his aching arms on the paper work. It had been Charlie's ambition to stay in the RAF, where he had been flying Mitchell bombers, and take a peacetime commission, but he came home on leave and found his father struggling to make a living. 'He just worked and worked,' says Charlie, 'but he didn't bother about the paper work, about getting his bills out and everything was in a mess.' His father, who had been trained in the Midlands motor industry, was basically a craftsman, not a businessman. Before the war he had been used to earning what was then big money, as much as £25 a week on the large public works construction projects.

This was how he came to Abberton when the big reservoir was built there. Charlie remembers they had their own house and his father had a gang of about 200 men working under him. But with the war people were directed by the Ministry of Labour into essential jobs and Joseph Taylor was sent to work at a small shipyard in nearby Rowhedge.

By 1945 he had had his fill of being directed, told where to go and what to do, and yearned for independence. So he started his small smithy at Abberton. The war had scattered the family. Arthur and Stanley were working in agricultural engineering in Colchester. Brother Bill was in Liverpool, converting Sherman tanks to be used on the ill-fated ground-nut scheme in Africa. It took Charlie several months to get out of the RAF, but he had a month's leave in which time he managed to get things at home on a more organised footing. He wrote to Bill and asked him to come home.

'So in 1946 there was father, Bill and me,' says Charlie. 'Arthur and Stanley used to help in the evenings. We struggled along for five years, doing farm repairs, and taking on heavy forging jobs which no one else would touch, big plough blades for the ground-nut scheme, 1½cwt each, and we forged those by hand, without any modern equipment to help us. They didn't turn out profitable and we lost money on them. At that time the whole household was running on only £15 a week, and we were getting £2 a week each.'

In a way the Taylors were hoist by their own hand forgings. They built a name for them, building their own jig and tools as they went along, because they couldn't afford to buy them. But the forgings did not really make money. 'It took us seven to eight years to get out of that rut,' recalls Charlie. Gradually the scope and spread of the work they tackled increased. They started making water screens for power stations, for example. One by one the brothers started to return home. First Fred, who had been on power stations with civil engineering firms. Then Arthur, the baby of the family. All of them, save for Charlie who had joined the RAF when he was seventeen, had served their time with father whether they liked it or not, and they had all worked with him on various reservoir building projects before the war.

'During those early days we stuck it through thick and thin,' says Charlie. 'Father used to start work at 4.30am in the morning and call us at 7.30am. Then he would work through to 8.30 or 9pm at night. We all used to put in a couple of hours after tea which we didn't get paid for. It was just money which went into the family.' Later Fred's son Cyril joined the firm and then sister Olive's husband Edgar Rumney. 'Our first employees got £11 a week which was four or five times as much as the four partners,' says Charlie.

The year 1954 was a notable one, both for the family and the firm. The Taylors decided to put up a big building, a new works in effect, which would enable them to jack up the size of jobs they could undertake and help improve their profits. At this point the business was scarcely roaring away. Turnover for the previous year was £6,235, net profits £770. Predictably they set to and built the new bays themselves for £1,000 instead of the £2,000 contractors wanted for the job. An essential bit of the new development was an overhead travelling crane capable of lifting 5 tons at a time. To the Taylors the crane was infinitely more than just a piece of equipment. It was a landmark in the growth of the business. It was to take them away from handcraft into heavy fabrications. For their father too, now seriously ill in a private hospital ward, it was an important and exciting event. Sadly, the night before the bearers, on which the new crane ran, were due to be put in, Joseph Taylor, the highly skilled engineering blacksmith, father of ten, and the largest single employer of labour in the village of Abberton, died. The last thing he said to his sons was, 'Leave me to put those bearers in, won't you?'

His private ward had been a family decision, but he had been in it for six months and it cost money. The family and the firm were in a fair amount of debt. The bank manager told them they needed an accountant more than a bank manager. So they got one, and a solicitor, and they have been with the firm ever since.

From that point the story of J. Taylor and Son is very much one of riding from debt to glory. For a firm which does not have a proper managing director, which has no reps or sales people and which would view anyone who talked about market research with grave suspicion, it has put up a worthy performance. Between 1954 and 1967 it increased its turnover twenty-fold, from over £8,000 to over £161,000. In the same period its net profit jumped from over £700 to over £24,000, a thirty-four-fold increase. Then, in 1968, it suffered a jolt. Both turnover and profits dropped. Charlie had a quick eight-month audit because he wanted to know what was going to happen in 1969. The picture which the figures threw up was not much of an improvement, and Charlie could see some swift action was needed.

'We were getting all the work we wanted so the first thing we did was to increase our prices,' says Charlie. 'We were doing building at 7s 6d to 8s a square foot so we went to 8s 6d, and for the jobs we didn't want to 9s per square foot. At 9s per square foot the orders still flowed in. Obviously we had been working too cheap.' Secondly, all the relatives were called together and told to pull their fingers out. As Charlie puts it, 'They were informed that J. Taylor and Sons was no longer a built-in gold mine for the benefit of them.' Thirdly, a bonus scheme was started for the employees who were relatives, but this did not really work, so they went on to a high hourly rate plus overtime. The result of all this was that by 1970 both turnover and profits were up again to over £226,000 and over £25,000 respectively.

In print the diagnosis and the treatment of the problem seem sensible, but in a small family firm such a situation is liable to produce a variety of peculiar undercurrents. If there is not an old adage which says 'never mix money and relatives', perhaps there ought to be. Charlie says until big money is involved there are no problems. But when it is, watch out. When I spoke to him he talked darkly of one of the wives who wanted the firm's books for an independent audit. It is part of the passion that family businesses seem to engender. The personalities of the relatives, their relationship with each other and towards the firm and what they get out of it, their small jealousies and imagined injustices, are all inextricably mixed up with invoices, order forms and jobs-in-hand. If these emotions were all tabulated, laid bare and made the subject of personal confrontation in such a consanguineous environment, half the family firms in Britain would shatter into tiny fragments. Perhaps it pays to just let them be, scarcely the accepted agents for keeping the machinery oiled, but strange to say, helping do it none the less.

You sense the undercurrents are there because of the way the firm has come to be run. It is easy to say this happens by everyone having their say, in an admirable, democratic way, and then deferring to Charlie in times of dispute. But this is only the half of it. There may not be many arguments, but there is a funny old groundswell compounded of loyalty, resentment, approval, indifference, gratitude and envy. Charlie is the nearest thing the firm has got to a management structure. He says he and the other partners hardly ever discuss things with each other, do not have any meetings or get togethers to decide common policy, or anything like that. Charlie is not even sure whether the other three partners see the balance sheet. 'I used to send them a copy each . . . they are very good at reading blueprints, but balance sheets . . .' So the way it seems to work is that Charlie does what he thinks is best. Sometimes his decisions are not popular, and he gets to hear they aren't through Barbara. The relatives tell her what they think, knowing she'll tell Charlie. As management techniques go it is quite extraordinary, but it works.

When you are in the middle of it, it can make life difficult. In a large firm the privileges or, if you like, the perks of being the boss seem to be more generally accepted, and, in any case, are a lot less obtrusive. But in J. Taylor and Sons everyone knows the partners in the firm get free petrol. 'Then the next thing you know is the nephews want it, then everyone wants it, but it would be too big an operation to lock up the pump and get keys for everyone entitled,' says Charlie.

The style of J. Taylor and Sons is very much that each partner gets on with running his own bit of the operation. So when a spot of trouble brews up, a question, perhaps, of shifting employees from one brother's patch to another's, because production is getting behind, there is at least one brother who is going to be upset about it. Understandably there have been times when one or the other of the partners have felt like pulling out. But the way the company is structured, the money involved and tax considerations, all conspire to make this something which is much more easily said than done. In any event the firm gives them a good living. They get £35 a week each, but draw on loan accounts much more than that, and what with the houses and bungalows the firm has built they are probably living at a rate of £5,000 a year. Charlie cheerfully admits he takes more out than the others because he runs a small shoot.

The red hot issue, so hot no one talks about it, is one of succession. For the partners in the business it produces an unnerving array of interrogatives. Who is there? Who could do it? Would they be suitable? Why wouldn't they be suitable? Would the others accept? Who is capable of becoming another partner? In Charlie's mind it is complicated by the fact that some members of the family in the business are more loyal and hardworking than others. He says there is at least one person he would have sacked if circumstances had been different, but because he is family you can't. If they tried to bring in a new partner on a time-serving basis they would be in difficulties, because the candidate is in his sixties. He recognises their weakness and improvidence in this respect, but makes the valid point that when the nephews could have been groomed for management, there was nothing much to groom them for. The ultimate answer in Charlie's eyes is to bring in a top man from outside, someone who would run the whole show, and to whom the family would defer.

These are some of the more awkward messy problems which underlay the business. When these have been taken into account there still remains the other side of the coin. J. Taylor and Sons has just as many, if not more, virtues and strengths because it is a family firm. One of the reasons it wins orders for jobs, which on the face of it might be beyond such a modest-sized business, is because there is a strong sense of family. It means as a firm the people in it are prepared to put themselves out, to stay on the job longer, and to work harder than in firms lacking this personal identification.

The other important factor is that customers feel that their job is getting personal supervision from someone in the family who cares. Ever since the days they learned their craft from their father, the brothers have been obsessive about quality. Charlie says the quality control is automatically built into their products as they go along. Often if they are on a farm building job they will undertake a couple of repairs and not charge for them. It all makes for good relations with the customers. The firm does advertise a little in the local paper, but most of its business comes from recommendations and people who have used them before. 'We have never had to knock on a door and sell yet, and we are always invited to tender for jobs so we are one up on everyone in the market to start with,' says Charlie. The other thing is that when Charlie goes out on a site, and gives a price and a time for a job, he knows damn well it can be done. It is not like someone in a bigger firm, remote from the production side, committing them to dates and prices for the sake of the order.

Charlie reckons it also helps, the firm being non-union. Nor does it suffer upsets and crises through losing its highly skilled workforce. Even the people who are not in the family tend to stay with the firm. One thing it seems to be particularly good at is keeping its skilled men. Charlie boasts it has never lost one of them. All of them are on BUPA schemes and the men have a non-contributary pension scheme which gives them a £2,000 lump sum and £5 a week when they retire. Since they do not contribute towards this, if they were to up sticks and leave they would lose it all. This is to keep the quality and to keep the skill, which after all is the most important part of the firm's stock-in-trade. It also holds a Saturday morning welding school and even pays its trainees at time and a half to attend.

As in many other family firms there is the spectre of estate duty lurking in the background. They have had various experts looking at this problem, trying to sort out the best course of action in making provision for it. But, as Charlie says, no two people in the City seem to agree on it, so the partnership continues in its present form. 'If two of us were to die at the same time the other two would really be in queer street,' says Charlie.

At present there are more immediate priorities. The business is still growing and suffering the growing pains that businesses do. Space is one of them. 'Ideally we ought to build another bay on our big workshop.' If the firm does it itself it will cost about £10,000 whereas an outside contractor might charge as much as £15,000. The answer looks obvious, except that if the family workforce undertakes the job they cannot be in two places at once, working on contracts for other people, and keeping the cash flowing in. It does tend to come in slowly. 'We have nearly always got £40,000 to £50,000 owing to us,' says Charlie. 'Sometimes it is almost impossible to get it in. We had to wait for nearly nine months before a bill for £5,000 was paid.' But then like a lot of small companies J. Taylor and Son frequently finds itself acting as unofficial banker to its customers.

There is one way out of the problem. It is a course which would also help solve the problems of death duties. The British tax structure being what it is, the firm wouldn't be the first to sell out, making a small fortune for its owners, a course which is far easier to cope with in tax terms than having assets in a company. There have been nibbles from interested parties. They like the look of it because of its expertise, because at Abberton it has room for expansion, and because there is hardworking labour available in a rural area, which can be successfully retrained. 'We have even done the sums and the figure comes out something like £750,000 with a service contract for us to stay on,' says Charlie. 'But if we don't get the right offer we'll just keep soldiering on.'

There are other firms which are as pronouncedly family as J. Taylor and Son. A small brewery and wine merchants in Halstead in north Essex called G. E. Cook and Sons is also run by four brothers who are directors; between them they have three sons in the business and another three brothers who are employees of the firm. The firm owns a few off-licences but it does not have any pubs. It sells its beer on a 'milk round' basis with fifteen vans making regular calls at houses and cottages in the country districts throughout Essex and Suffolk (the customers even leave the empties out on the doorstep), and before they covered the rounds with motor vans, the Cooks did them with a horse and cart. Like the Taylors, the Cooks perform a highly useful role in the economy. Their importance as a small, family-owned concern is that they do not fear to tread where large concerns do. They supply a market where the economies of large-scale production just would not be sufficient to attract the big concern and outweigh the costs of being big. You would not, for example, find Allied Breweries messing around with a van fleet just to cover the scattered and isolated rural communities of parts of East Anglia. In such circumstances the most efficient unit of activity is the smaller company.

In this context if it is a family company so much the better. It enjoys an edge over large concerns because its particular business requires local independence and initiative. It is so often a question of knowing your customers, being on nodding terms with them as you walk down the High Street, and of knowing your ground too. Engineering, for example, in all its diversity is a highly fragmented industry, and the Taylor's sector of it no less so. Their business comes in bits and bobs from all over the locality. To handle it well calls for independent, local management, not a man sitting in a large office a couple of hundred miles away, impersonal and remote.

These small family firms perform an admirable function filling the gaps on the industrial map. No matter how good a large company is, with its national distribution and selling networks, there is always space for the little man, and scope for him to serve the needs of the community in a wealth of ways under conditions and circumstances which deter big companies. In any case the presence of the small family company alongside chain stores, or a string of big company subsidiaries, is a constant reminder that they are an important vehicle of competition, a means of keeping consumer choice at its widest. They are not public, their shares cannot be mopped up on the Stock Exchange, and they cannot be bought all that easily. And although there is a certain type of family company which presents an antediluvian horror story of low calibre management, ageing and breaking machines and misanthropic workers, there are others where the quintessential kith-and-kin flavour is allied to a strong team spirit and a sense of adventure which produces new ideas, products and services. Often the small family concern is a platform for innovation of the sort which would become stifled in a large, highly structured business.

Sometimes from the outward trappings, you would be forgiven for thinking that a new idea would cause grandfather's picture to fall off the wall. A visit to the chairman's office of Benjamin Shaw and Sons, soft drinks manufacturers of Huddersfield, is a bit like this, except that there are three generations of sepia-toned Shaws above the fireplace where a coal fire blazes in winter. Along one wall there is a tall, rich brown Dickensian counting-house desk, from the drawers of which the company's chairman, Michael Shaw, is apt to fish out old almanacs dating from the 1890s. Some of them contain old Benjamin Shaw's very personal advertisements. In recommending soda-water and sarsaparilla, horehound beer and botanic porter, he exhorted potential customers thus: 'Benjamin Shaw would ask that portion of the public who are in the habit of purchasing high priced mineral waters, imported from long distances under the impression there is some superiority attaching to them, to test them against his, under conditions which will ensure fair play to both.' Well, that was one way of gently getting at competitors' products, a sort of late nineteenth-century can-you-tell-the-difference-between-butter-and-margarine? technique, but it also shows that Benjamin Shaw and Sons is very much part of British soft drinks history.

It came into being at a time when the idea of nationally distributed fizziness such as Tizer, Corona, Canada Dry, Pepsi and Coca-Cola had not entered men's minds, and soft drinks were locally made imitations of imported mineral waters like potassia, lithia and selzer and were sold within one day's horse-and-cart delivery distance of where they were made. It was in 1871 that Michael Shaw's great-grandfather, Benjamin, trundled a handcart into Huddersfield market and sold his first batch of non-alcoholic home brew as befitting a staunch member of the Methodist temperance movement. Now, from all this you might feel that Shaw's sense of history is something which has overwhelmed its sense of business, but emphatically it has not. Although there are four great-grandsons of the founder and one son of one of the company's earliest employees on the board of directors today, they exhibit none of the third-generation management wishy-washiness which old family firms sometimes display. As for new products and ideas, and letting much bigger and stronger competitors feel the edge of their competition, they cannot be faulted. Nor apparently can they be acquired, judging by the hard cash offers which have been turned down from the bigger bubbles in the industry. While they stay as they are they help stave off the day when alcohol-free fizziness will be a near monopoly in the hands of just two or three giants.

At the beginning of 1971, when Tizer suffered a setback and their profits were disappearing in a mist of carbonated water, Shaws just carried on bottling the seventy lines of soft drinks—from the vivid, yellow-coloured lemonade which Huddersfield likes to the sarsaparilla which Lancashire insists upon. Included in the product list were bottles of a new drink called Space Special, designed as an impulse purchase for children, which the Shaws came up with after a lot of hard work in their research and development department. Perhaps one of the reasons why Shaw's went marching on while Tizer suffered is that they have a business philosophy which, in the £140 million a year soft drinks market, is by no means so soft as its name suggests and has served them well. It is that they always like to have a go at new things, to try out, for instance, the green fizziness of Space Special which, if it had failed, they would have withdrawn.

In one specific development the British soft drinks industry owes Benjamin Shaw a great deal, for the company was the first in the country, even the first outside America, to put soft drinks in cans. This was in 1959. The step was taken, a calculated risk really, without any clear idea of the sales potential. But like the company's decision to sell soft drinks in quart bottles at a price only 50 per cent higher than the pint bottle in the 1930s, the can has proved to be a runaway success. It was also one of the first companies to sell drinks in one-trip, non-returnable bottles in shrink-wrap packs. Nowadays, of course, canned drinks are a very high volume sales line in every sort of outlet from supermarkets to off-licences. It is through their canned drinks that Benjamin Shaw, although strongly entrenched in its North of England market, finds itself in the curious position of not being a nationally known brand name in the United Kingdom, yet successfully selling its brands internationally. The company started to do good business with ship's stores and airlines because the 6oz cans were easy to handle and store. Then the business extended from ship's stores to overseas export markets, which is how the company's canned drinks come to be quenching the thirst of the Portuguese Army in Portuguese Guinea and the French Army in French Somaliland.

Michael Shaw sums up clearly why it is that a family firm in the difficult soft drinks industry can more than hold its own. 'It is important that a constant watch should be kept on changing trends in the market place, both in regards to types of drink and types of container. The company is extremely flexible and has usually been ready to take advantage of such changes much more quickly than a larger company would be able to. For example, a period of only a few months elapsed between the decision to produce soft drinks in cans and the actual production and sale of the first canned drinks. Also because of its flexibility the company is well placed to carry out test markets on drinks and withdraw them quickly if they don't succeed.' This is the voice of a provincial, family-owned firm whose pioneer innovating has led us to radically changing the way we all buy our soft drinks.

Chapter 7
Following in father's footsteps

The problems of family firms, large and small, are singular: questions of succession, ticklishly complicated by family relationships, and death duties which can threaten a company's continuing existence. Passing the business from father to son is the way such firms perpetuate themselves, but the divine right to manage has driven many a promising firm into the ground. Yet it can and does work, though the sons tend to make it do so in ways different to dad, as the stories in this chapter show.

OF all the special characteristics of the small family firm, the most outstanding is that it produces a distinctive style of business, a form of kith-and-kin involvement in which business decisions and objectives are inevitably complicated by personal relationships. While there are firms where members of the family peacefully co-exist, and run the enterprise in amiable concert, there are others where family rifts and differences usually mean that the question of succession is solved in uneasy compromise. Instead of following the sensible course and bringing a strong, professional manager from outside to whom the members of the family will defer, the firm is saddled with management leadership which, because of the circumstances of its election, is likely to be weak and over-accommodating to family factions.

There is a temptation always to look at this from the viewpoint of the present holder of office. Succession is seen as a problem for him and the firm. The difficulties and pressures facing the man who does take over tend to be forgotten. Becoming the new boss in the prickly, sensitive arena, where family feelings are constantly on show, is no bed of roses. The least painful and commonest form of succession in a family business is the straightforward one of father to son. Here family complications are minimal. Even so such succession is not always achieved without anguish. The sudden death of a father who is running the firm can precipitate a son into a position where he is responsible for the destiny of the family company. Sometimes he has not acquired the experience and maturity to undertake the job without misgivings. It can be an unnerving prospect.

It happened to Richard Lamb when he was twenty-six. His father died suddenly and the main responsibility for Adcola Products, a small London firm of about 100 employees producing high-quality electrical soldering instruments, fell on his shoulders. 'Four years later another director died and the whole of the concern was left to my tender mercies,' says Richard. 'I took over the business thinking I knew it all. How sadly mistaken I was, but at least I did have the sense to sit on the wall and look and learn. Although I had the privilege of working with my father for a number of years, there were many things he did, and many things he knew, which he couldn't possibly have passed on in such a short period. So I had to look. I had to learn. And I had to study.'

It was during this period that the Labour Government started to reduce spending on arms. Adcola Products lost not only its direct government contracts but many of its customers, who were also suppliers to the government, suffered as well. The net result was a considerable reduction in the use of soldering irons. It was scarcely a welcoming gesture to a son facing both the day-to-day business pressures and the psychological and emotional ones of taking his father's place. The compulsion to carry on was sharpened all the more because of the circumstances in which the firm was started. Richard's father had been retired from the Post Office, where he was an engineer, at the age of forty-six with a heart condition. He had been advised to take things easy for the rest of his life, but he did not. In the early days the tools were made in backrooms, attics and sheds by home workers. 'The assembly and the actual business of the company was conducted in our flat at Streatham,' recalls Richard. One of the major problems then was credit from suppliers. There was a time when his father could buy carton containers only in quantities of 10,000. Because the outer cartons they came in were valued at 25p each they had to be immediately unpacked and returned in order to recoup this outlay. 'My father couldn't afford to have this credit hanging round his neck, so the front room of our small flat was completely filled from floor to ceiling with containers,' says Richard.

These modest beginnings, and successive moves to larger premises as the business grew, have a recognisable familiarity about them. They echo scores of other accounts of how small businesses have struggled and grown. When Richard's father died the firm's sales were running at just over £190,000. But over the next two or three years there was a substantial fall in business. 'Sales slowly started to climb back to the peak they were at at the time of my father's death, but they still have not achieved this happy situation. Much of this can be attributed to my own ignorance, and to a certain amount of ignorance on the part of the management generally,' admits Richard. 'It takes a long time to learn the ways of business, to educate staff in new ways of thinking, and to adjust to the conditions in the modern and fast-moving world of commerce. Many of the staff were inherited. Some have been with the company fifteen years or more. To a young man with new ideas and wishing to apply modern methods it is difficult to command the respect of people considerably older than oneself; to get them to work on new ideas, and to change what to them has become a tradition. I am most grateful for the loyalty of the existing staff but we have to keep up with modern methods and how does a man of thirty tell a sixty-year-old that his accounting system is wrong? Or tell a works manager, old enough to be his father, that his method of production control is incorrect?'

In sharp contrast the succession of Peter Carroll to running the family company was less traumatic but no less interesting, because as a consultant with the PA Management Group he was supposed to know exactly how businesses tick over and what to do about it if they didn't. Peter left PA Management to run the family company when his father was taken ill and told to ease up. The company, Panavista, imports door knobs. Peter's arrival offered splendid opportunities for merry quips. 'You must be the best run door knob company in the country,' people said. As a matter of fact Peter did know a bit about the business before he left PA Management because he sometimes lent a hand on Saturday mornings, but that was not so much solving management problems as doing up parcels of door knobs. It is, of course, a very small company, nowhere as big as the corporations in which Peter did his stuff as a consultant. Just to give you an idea, the year he took over, Panavista was importing £150,000 worth of door knobs annually; enough knobs for one million doors.

What was it like coming into a small family business after several years in consultancy? 'My first feeling was that both the company and I were on a sort of mutual trial,' says Peter. 'I remember my father saying when I arrived on the first day, "Don't just sit there, start management consulting!" There was certainly a little apprehension, with people remembering stories they had heard of the consultant or axe man turning companies inside out. For my part it was a complete change of environment and scale, and I wondered how I was going to make out. At the back of my mind there was the knowledge that many people hold the view that "those that can, do; and those that can't, teach." Teaching in this instance being consulting.

'Certainly the two worlds are very different, but some of the differences between the small company and the vast industrial complex can be exploited. Some of the large companies' systems and techniques can be adapted and used in a much more informal way in the smaller unit. Personal contacts made in the old consultant days can be retained and often prove useful. A snag may be that if one is asking for advice, the advice given may be the best available for a giant corporation but entirely inappropriate for a tiny business.'

Peter found the biggest change came from being a specialist in one field, and concentrating in depth on it, to having to turn his hand to anything from mundane details to long-range planning. But he feels this is one of the main compensations for giving up his job with PA Management. 'It is very satisfying to know all the important things that are going on and to be largely in control of them,' he says. 'There is a great deal of satisfaction to be gained by applying oneself to every size and shape of problem and having a go at solving it.'

'In a small business the results of one's decisions come quickly but one is more involved in the long-term effects which is probably a good thing. It is also good to be able not only to formulate an idea or policy, but also to play a large part in carrying it out.'

Peter says the widely based training and experience he had with PA stands him in very good stead. 'I get the impression there is very little formal training around in small businesses and most people have worked in the family firm since a boy,' he says. 'In general I am very happy with the change over and life in many ways is much busier, with more day-to-day details to cope with. I find that I am much more reluctant to switch off at 5.30pm than I was as a consultant, and this puts more pressure on home life. On the other hand family involvement is much greater in this sort of business and the piles of work lying around the house are not viewed as impersonal papers, but rather as details of "Old so and so's knotty problem about prices". All in all, I feel it is a better arrangement.'

Succession is important to most family firms because it is after all what determines they will continue to be family firms. In any case the feeling that a man has in building up a business and working hard because he wants something to pass on to his son is not entirely dead, despite the spectre of estate duty which looms so menacingly over it. If there is a pervasive thread of fatalism running through the story of J. Taylor and Son, it is because of the twin inevitabilities of death and the tax burden which springs from it. The character of the firm is such that there seems little the brothers can do to stave off and avoid the worst excesses. It is a classic case of the growing success of a small firm contributing to its ultimate and greatest weakness. As yet the crisis hasn't occurred. All the brothers are alive and well, and while they are—and having taken professional advice which was of little help—the best they can hope for is a lucrative sale while the going is good. Otherwise all they are left with is the hope that somehow the problem will go away of its own accord. But the current arithmetic of tax gathering makes this unlikely. The fact is that wealth taxes in Britain—estate duty, capital gains tax, stamp duty and so on—yielded an estimated £840 million in 1970–71, and the chief of these is estate duty, the top rate of which is 80 per cent. Stamp duty was abolished in August 1971.

It seems ironic that the threat to the continued existence of the company comes not from some fierce and tough competitor in the next village, nor from some amazing new advance in technology, nor from changing market conditions, but from the nature of the British tax system. For some family firms one way round the problem is to go public. For that you need a sustained profit record better than the one fielded by the Taylors. In any case it is highly questionable whether the firm, still essentially craft based, with its unusual pattern of management, could command the necessary rating for public flotation. Its strength is its independent, local nature. Sustaining in public the promise foreseen in a private performance is not always an easy matter. Capabilities apart, there is the question of whether the Taylors want to go public and lose some of their sovereignty. There are plenty of people who feel it is improper that small firms should be hounded on to the Stock Exchange, or into liquidation, and in doing so they say the government is thwarting one of the most dynamic forces in the economy. The whole question is an emotive and complex one, and we will return to the subject of the small company and its tax burden in Chapter 16.

But it is worth bearing in mind that you are just as vulnerable, just as likely to find yourself in a difficult predicament over estate duty if you are a large family company. In December 1970, Bulmers, the family-owned cider firm, went public, floating off the minimum number of shares enabling it to get a Stock Exchange quote. Bulmers made it clear that the sale of shares was to meet estate duty liabilities faced by the Bulmer family following the deaths of two of its members.

Earlier the same year, Pilkington Bros, the largest privately owned company in Britain and the originators of the revolutionary 'float glass' process (which did away with the long and expensive business of grinding sheet glass on both sides), had to put 10 per cent of their equity on to the open market for the very private reason that the family had been finding it increasingly difficult to raise enough money to buy the shares of shareholders who, for death duties or other reasons, had been forced to sell. To do this some members of the family had already borrowed heavily and, as Lord Pilkington put it, had 'more than all their eggs in one basket'. The position was exacerbated by the introduction of tighter tax laws on interest on loans, on children's income and on trust incomes. The deaths of three substantial shareholders in the eighteen months prior to going public meant that family resources were getting near to their limits.

Under the circumstances many people find it surprising that a family firm like Pilkingtons has been able to provide both the money and much of the management for the fourth biggest flat glass company in the world for so long; ever since, indeed, the present Lord Pilkington's great-grandfather, William, got involved in glass, in 1826, more as a side line than anything else. The cash has been forthcoming largely because of the family's frugal, non-conformist tradition of ploughing back almost all the profits into the business. This, combined with a long record of success in technical innovation, has meant that the company has rarely needed to raise money. Eventually it had to, and in doing so Britain's largest private company has become Britain's most private public company, with 90 per cent of its shares still held by 300 of the prolific Pilkingtons.

But prolific though it is, there are now signs that the Pilkington family is running short of men as well as money. There are only a few members of the younger generation in the firm and, although totally dissimilar in scale and ethos, J. Taylor and Son also faces a similar problem. It is not purely a matter of numbers, but more a question of who, in terms of succession, is both available and acceptable to the rest of the family. With family feelings involved it can prove a messy, untidy and awkward problem.

David Watt is a man with succession very much in mind. He is managing director of a small company called Spearhead Chemicals which he started from nothing from the sitting room of his house in 1965. By the time you read this his sales will be over £150,000 a year. He comes from Tyneside, where his father was a shipyard worker, and he is now happily married and living with his wife, his nine-year-old daughter and seven-year-old son in Oxshott, Surrey. The reason he gives for starting Spearhead is essentially simple.

'I want to pass on something to my son,' he says. 'I'm a working-class chap and I got my chance by winning a scholarship to university. The reason I want to build a business is because I can expect nothing to be handed on to me. There are a lot of people like me, who want to create something in the form of a living business to hand on.' Because of this drive, this compulsion, David has been very cautious about any proposition which smacked of his losing control of the business. He is concerned above all in creating, making and growing a family concern. His is the highly personal motivation which spawns new family businesses, his is the fervour which makes them grow, but whether his son will possess the qualities to build on those foundations is another matter.

If he does take over from his father at some future date, it is likely that their business styles will be as different as chalk and cheese. Each generation makes its own contribution to a family firm and with the spread of management education, a greater awareness of business skills, a more outward looking view of the commercial world, there is no reason why the running of a business should be a carbon copy operation of the way the man before did it. This may be suitable for primitive patriarchal societies, but it is scarcely appropriate in the fluid, competitive commercial society of the modern world.

Derek Lawson Hill, for example, runs a small family firm called Watercraft which has its headquarters on the River Thames near Hampton Court. Watercraft is a lively company and enjoys an international prestige and reputation out of all relation to its actual size. Furthermore its expertise is such that it has been able to conclude licensing agreements, which are still producing revenue for it today, with such large companies as Blohm and Voss in Germany and similar-sized shipbuilding concerns in Spain, France and Italy. For the thing at which Watercraft is so superbly good is building ships' lifeboats, £1 million worth of them a year, of which 70 per cent is export business.

Watercraft's lifeboats are to be found on the major passenger ships of the world including the QE2, on giant-sized oil tankers, on new modern container ships, and there is scarcely a shipbuilder or a shipping line of any substance which is not among its long list of customers. Small though it is, it is a company which has innovated and developed all along the line. It was one of the first companies to build ships' lifeboats in glass fibre and it has developed easily manoeuvrable jet-propelled lifeboats which can be manned, lowered and got clear of a ship as rapidly as possible in an emergency. It also produces a highly sophisticated closed-in lifeboat with built-in water sprays, designed for service on tankers, which will bring crews safely through oil fires at sea.

Derek says the story of Watercraft is very much that of his father, Joseph Hill, who at the age of sixty-six is now semi-retired due to ill health. 'I now run the company and am at the stage of consolidating his work to prepare for the next move forward,' says Derek. 'It is the classic change-over from his authoritarian drive and intuitive flair, with perhaps more explosive ups and downs, to my quieter, but I hope more planned and orderly, scheme of things. The business has always been run informally by word of mouth, although compared with my father's one man rule we now work more as an informal committee with my own decision as final. Running the business the way my father did is very time consuming and excludes almost all outside interests. Business always came first, and I am anxious not to follow his example in this respect and leave myself without other interests.

'There are certain people, my father and myself among them,

who could not work for anyone else. We have a busy atmosphere and, I think, a happy one. We like to think there is a sense of family. The workforce is very stable and loyal at all levels. Newcomers either leave in a few weeks or stay for good.'

It is an image of a family firm which many people will readily identify. Pictures of family firms always seem to be painted in extremes. At one end of the spectrum there is the solid, enduring business where management passes, as the accepted order of things, from one generation to another, where there is a sense of responsibility to workpeople and community which manifests itself in good works and benevolence. There is an immensely strong sense of continuity too. It is enshrined in the old employee who knew your dad when he was a little lad. It comes too, not from archives and faded records, but in the homelier situation where the affairs of the business are discussed between father and son over the breakfast table. It comes in a family firm largely because the dividing line between office and home is blurred. Many a director of a family business has been involved with it from early childhood, with the assumption he would enter the business, even though the assumption is often implicit rather than explicit. 'On balance it is probably an advantage to have one's business and personal and family life integrated,' says Michael Shaw. 'Family companies are, or have been, common in the Huddersfield district and many of one's friends and acquaintances are themselves owners or directors of their own businesses, so the whole social climate tends to reflect this.'

However, there still remains a whiff of the squirearchy about some of these lasting family firms and in the twentieth century it is this bit of their image which appears incongruous and worn. The dangers of placing what some might describe as an excessive degree of dependence on the family firm as a source of livelihood, well-being and knowledgeable omnipotence was amply demonstrated in the spring of 1970 when the town of St Helens in Lancashire, home of Pilkingtons, was torn by a long and bitter strike which was as much about the paternalistic relationship between the company and the town, as it was about the glass-workers' wage packet.

This sort of benevolence, paternalism, call it what you will, is an undeniable hallmark of older family companies. Nor is it the sole prerogative of large family companies though it is not so overt in the smaller ones. You can find it in the story of J. Taylor and Son of Abberton just as much as in C. and J. Clark, the big shoe people of Street, in Somerset, who have put an indelible family and company stamp on the town. C. and J. Clark is the town's one and only industry. You cannot help feeling that over the years the Clark family has had a hand in every development of importance in the community—schools, swimming pool, theatre, even contributing to the cost of a new by-pass. The scale and intensity of their involvement is clearly larger than that of J. Taylor and Son in Abberton—but the seeds of benevolence are present in the smaller company just the same.

There is another picture of the family firm. It is one which the critics paint in dark strokes, producing a grim still-life where the dynastic tradition of family takes overwhelming precedence over the business affairs of the company; where the owners treat it as a prolific milch cow, ever ready and available to be milked. In such firms management is a matter of divine right. They encapsulate all the defects of third and fourth generations, where the thickness of the blood and the tilt of the nose, not ability and expertise, are the yardsticks which are applied. The quality of management is weakened and diluted, and it does not even possess the saving grace of benevolence. The firm's future may be committed into the hands of someone singularly ill-suited to the task, who comes to a position of leadership without the taste or urge for it. In these circumstances what passes for management may be nothing more than an exercise in bravado, a 'By heck I'll show Pa if it kills me' philosophy which is more likely to kill off the firm than the philosopher. This attitude will be the fruit of a previously autocratic and egocentric rule where little thought was given—and indeed crushing disbelief expressed in the idea of—anyone else, let alone the son of the house, running the firm successfully.

Equally ineffective is the notion of stewardship, the temptation to conduct the business within the confines of an ultra-cautious, riskless policy, so that what is passed on to the next generation will not be anything less than what was passed on to the present management. Sometimes there are disinterested female relatives lurking in the background, who are unlikely to make the most exacting shareholders; nor are they the stuff that ginger groups are made of. Indeed their presence as family shareholders, and their dependence on income from their shareholdings, may mean that the management of the company is more concerned with security, with preserving the half-yearly dividends, than with investing money in new plant or on developing new markets overseas. This doesn't make for a lively, growing business, but is a splendid recipe for producing a moribund one.

In practice, the violent extremes of family firms are rare, and the mass of them fall somewhere between the entrenched and ingrowing and the progressive and outward looking. These are the members of the great legion of firms which soldier on, conscientiously trying to do their best, not very good at management, nor at having the requisite information to hand on which to base their decisions. They belong to a family of firms which are so busy getting on with their business, attending to the day-to-day details, that they never have time to give much thought to where they are going or why. Above all they could do with some modest help from outsiders, a bit more management education for their directors, but the trouble is that they are either too pressed or busy to contemplate it, or they don't want to know.

Their biggest single domestic weakness is dependence on one man, an owner-manager with his finger in every pie, whose involvement with every detail, in every corner of the firm, may well be blocking and discouraging initiative lower down the ladder, as managers become disinclined to back their own judgement and make their own decisions, since the boss is always popping up to look over their shoulders. It is one of the classic family firm syndromes—too much power in the hands of a man at the top who is afraid to delegate.

One reason why the death knell has sounded for so many long established family firms is because of their inability to adapt what exists in the business to fit circumstances which were undreamed of in the last century. Firms wallowing in the nostalgia of great-grandfather's past commercial glories are seldom adept at exploiting changing conditions to their advantage. In an old and rooted family firm, adaptation is always more difficult than starting again.

Richard Atkinson and Company of Belfast is an old family firm which has put up a notable performance in this respect, by taking the assets and reputation bequeathed to it by its Victorian forebears and tailoring them to suit business conditions of the 1970s. It is an example where the lines are sharply drawn since the product is a quality one produced by hand. So is the material from which it is made, produced on handlooms which are older than the company's oldest employee. David Nicholson, Atkinson's young chairman, explains the firm's philosophy neatly: 'Because it is a craft, it doesn't have to be archaic,' he says.

The firm makes ties, mostly striped ones, from a material called Royal Irish Poplin. It has been weaving the poplin for 150 years, but making the ties only since sometime in the 1880s. Royal Irish Poplin depends on the diligent activities of the mulberry silk moth of China. The fibre it produces, allied to wool from the fleeces of Australian Merino sheep, produces a cloth which is resilient, durable, takes well to rich crisp colours and produces an opulent sheen. In short it is splendid stuff for making ties. It is upon this cloth that Richard Atkinson and Company has pinned its hopes and fortunes for so long. And it has done very well out of it. In the last ten years sales have increased by 80 per cent, net profit by 140 per cent. Towards the end of the 1960s it sold over 250,000 Irish Poplin ties. By 1970, 60 per cent of the firm's sales were to customers who ran classy, fashionable men's shops in cities like San Francisco, Hamburg, Copenhagen, Vancouver and Rotterdam. It sold energetically, developing home and overseas markets, designing a complete new collection every two months, and producing modern, colourful designs which were more and more in demand as the menswear industry became more fashion conscious. Long before David's father, Alex Nicholson, died, he had tackled the problem of providing for proper and trained succession by sending David, who is the company's designer as well as chairman, to the famous textile engineering school at Krefeld, traditional home of the German silk industry, for three years.

Thus Richard Atkinson displays all the outward signs of a wide-awake firm intent on going out and winning business, rather than contenting itself with sitting on its reputation for the quality of its product and waiting for business to come in. Yet for all this, five years ago it gave the appearance of having one foot planted firmly in the twentieth century while the other was stuck in the nineteenth. It had been making a song and dance about its ties to such effect that sales increased, business mounted and greater and greater pressure was being put on the firm's production capacity. But at the same time its production lines relied on handlooms, and hand manufacturing methods of yesteryear. Faced with this problem Atkinsons demonstrated that you can use old, traditional methods and still be modern minded. A firm of management consultants was called in to address themselves, surely with some mild astonishment, to the problem of getting more productivity from rows of wooden handlooms with the patina of age all over their well-worn timbers.

The last thing anyone wanted was an automated production line which would have lost the quality and personal care a weaver puts into her cloth. So probably, for the first time anywhere, handloom weaving was subjected to a modern work study analysis. The resulting productivity scheme produced an impressive increase in output. In applying this modern technique to an old handcraft the company changed a pattern of payment to weavers which had applied since the Dublin silk trade rates were formulated in the eighteenth century. 'We didn't want to break the tradition overnight,' explains David Nicholson. 'It was a system built up by craftsmen who knew the work, so to replace it we had to employ work study engineers to go back to basics and reassess the work content in the job. The job was exactly the same but it was broken down and assessed in the light of modern practice.'

The parallel problem was ensuring an adequate supply of labour. Skilled handloom weavers are not two a penny, and to replace those lost through natural wastage the company set up a training scheme. Again this was based on the findings of the work study analysis, and it produced a qualified handloom weaver in six months against the traditional twelve to eighteen months accepted previously. The basic skills in the trade had been retained but this modern, analytical look at it killed off a lot of restrictive old wives' attitudes and practices which had been current for donkey's years. Richard Atkinson and Company could so easily have become a fusty, ailing, out-dated anachronism. Instead it took its encapsulated experience of the past and is now using it in a modern manner as a potent commercial weapon. It is something you might like to think about next time you knot an Atkinson Irish Poplin tie round your neck. You might also like to remember that there are nearly 560,000 companies registered in Great Britain and the great majority of them, some 542,000, are private companies which are either family-owned, or which owe their beginnings to the family.

Chapter 8

The decline and rise of a village store

Roys of Wroxham used to boast it was the biggest village store in the world. But all the time it was boasting of the fact, it was also ailing and falling into a decline. Now this extraordinary village emporium has successfully transformed itself into something more in keeping with modern shopping trends. However, it was an achievement not lacking in traumatic episodes. The story of the fight to retrieve the company from the almost unbelievable predicament in which it found itself highlights all the passions and problems that can lurk behind the plate-glass windows of a family shop.

In Norfolk all roads lead to Roys. Well, perhaps not all, but the ones from Norwich, Coltishall, Stalham and Horning do. They meet, the four of them, at a junction in the centre of Wroxham, an oversized village on the upper reaches of the River Bure which has served as a gateway to the Norfolk Broads for as long as people have been going there on holiday. There is a fifth road, more of a lane really, which spokes into the junction, and which leads to some boatyards and to some public conveniences which, until 1953, were a piece of splendid private enterprise. Like nearly everything else in Wroxham they were owned by Roys, a firm which is a shiningly individual landmark in the topography of British retailing. At first glance it also seems a bit of a mess, but it isn't anything like the mess it was, and as reorganised messes go it is a nice profitable one. The Ladies and Gents, by the way, are now the responsibility of the local rural district council. Their change of ownership is not particularly important in itself, but it just happens to be one of those bizarre details about this extraordinary firm which stick in the mind when you have forgotten a lot of other things about it.

At the road junction end of 'Loo Lane' there's a home freezer and frozen food shop on one corner and a furniture store on the other. On three other of the junction's corner sites sit a chemist's shop, a combined supermarket-coffee-tobacconist-clothes-wine and spirits shop, and on the third, a modern two-storey, L-shaped brick building. Here the ground floor is taken up with hardware and garden sundries, and in the short leg of the L, Barclays have a bank. The first floor houses fashions and clothes, the registered offices of Roys (Wroxham) Ltd and Frederick Roy, chairman and managing director, son of the late Alfred Roy, and nephew of the late and flamboyant Arnold Roy, co-founders in 1895 of this incomparable shop.

Frederick Roy, a sturdy figure in his early fifties, makes you feel he is very pleased to meet you. He also makes you feel he is quite pleased with himself, not arrogantly, but in an honest sense. His cheeks have a tinge of the outdoors; if he were not a shopkeeper, he might be a Norfolk reed cutter. In fact, he learned his shopkeeping with the Kettering Co-operative Society as a young man, but the war interrupted and he found himself serving in the artillery with Mr Edward Heath. He laughs quite a lot in a small, sharp interrogatory fashion and his accent is unmistakably Norfolk, though not so pronounced that it is a caricature. When he asks a question it is rather to the point. 'Mr Clarke,' he says, 'is all this talking with you going to do my sales any good, eh?'

The window of Frederick Roy's office is large and overlooks the road junction. From it, rather like a baron of old, commanding a strategic pass, he notes the cars as they pass. Cars are the very stuff of business to Frederick Roy and he has spent a lot of time, money and energy providing for them. Each one which turns off into one of his two car parks (one takes 100 vehicles, another 50) has arrived in the epicentre of a small commercial kingdom. Stand in the middle of it, swivel round a full 360 degrees and the facia of every shop on each of the five corners carries the name Roy. The remarkable thing is that this village conglomerate not only dominates the shopping habits of the population of Wroxham and nearby villages, but its influence goes even beyond, as far afield as Norwich, Caister and Great Yarmouth.

Nor is the reputation of Roys confined to its own neck of Norfolk. Successive generations of holidaymakers, hiring cruisers and yachts locally, have filled their galleys with delicacies from Roys, and have taken the name of the store home with them, far beyond the borders of Norfolk. If you ask Frederick Roy who his competitors are he tends to ignore the string of small shops which Roys do not own lining the Norwich Road between his junction and the hump-back bridge over the Bure, and mentions instead Marks and Spencer, Sainsbury's and Tesco in Norwich. He knows in no time at all what their loss leaders are for the week, whether they have upped the price of salmon, or whether 2oz tins of Nescafé are on special offer.

To describe Roys merely as a shop tells you little, and does it a disservice. It was, and still is, a conglomeration of shops, and it came to be like it because as business grew in the 1920s and 1930s so did Roys, in a higgledy-piggledy fashion. It has always put great emphasis on the variety of goods it stocks and the quality of its service. In 1930 Arnold Roy told the world quite specifically where he saw Roys going. He intended to build Harrods in Wroxham, he said. He didn't quite manage it, but in the 1930s Roys of Wroxham was the next best thing Norfolk had to that inimitable shopping institution in London's Knightsbridge. Even today, despite all the changes which have been wrought on the face of Roys, it still provides a choice of twenty-nine different marmalades on its supermarket shelves and keeps unheard of brands of Tennessee whisky in its wine shop.

In the thirties Roys enjoyed a heyday of sorts, though with hindsight its present chairman would almost certainly arrive at a different judgement now. The style of Roys then was the style of its colourful managing director, Arnold Roy. People still remember him as a great card, a man possessed of a restless and driving nature, an unpredictable temperament and a vanity for showmanship, for which, it has to be said, he had enormous flair. The character of the business was stamped by this, by salesmanship, by a quality of exclusive magnificence and by outward beneficence. A fleet of limousines were used to bring valued customers in from outlying villages. When he sold a suit Arnold tucked a packet of free cigarettes into the pocket. He appeared on the memorable BBC radio programme *In Town Tonight* billed as the owner of the world's largest village store. Roys was Wroxham and Wroxham was Roys. Half the village population seemed to be in its employ.

Reading between the lines there is a feeling of division and difficulty based on the differing temperaments of the two brothers. 'As a family the two branches were really miles apart,' explains Frederick Roy. Arnold was always too busy selling to get involved in even quite elementary management techniques. Too busy embracing the village of Wroxham in a warm, paternalistic hug. When broadcasting first began Arnold had loudspeakers set up in the streets so everyone could listen. The street lamps were his too, and on dark, winter nights the village streets were lit with flickering gas lamps supplied by courtesy of Roys. What the local council didn't undertake, Roys did. The lavatories down the lane were another facet of the firm's bounty.

In those days the firm's hold on local business was much tighter than it is now. In addition to grocery, fashion, furniture and hardware stores it owned a fish shop, a garage, a bicycle shop, a fishing-tackle shop, an antiques shop and a restaurant. If it were not a local monopoly, it was a fair imitation of it. It was all wrapped in a large, ungainly package; part department store, part emporium, part little shop on the corner, making a whole which, in the words of *In Town Tonight* and the slogan on the give-away postcards, showing an artist's impression of Royland in all its diverse facets, was the world's largest village store.

It was a slogan which sustained it in business for a long time, but modern pressures have replaced it. Roys has been reorganised and it now trades as Roys Out of Town Shopping Centre, which you might think odd, since it is not out of town but right in the centre of the village. The description, however, is largely directed at towns and villages other than Wroxham. In 1970, out of town shopping brought in for Roys sales of £874,000; by the beginning of 1972 Frederick Roy expects to be hitting the £1 million mark.

The figures slip off the typewriter easily, but when you start to scratch around behind the plate-glass windows and get to grips with the modern business story of Roys, you find it has been through some hard and difficult times. If ever a firm suffered a hair-raising succession of years, Roys did in the 1950s.

To start with, the British tax structure and estate duty being what it is, and families being what they are, sometimes behaving in peculiar and unpredictable ways, the Roys very nearly lost control of the business to outsiders. In addition the company's trading problems, though both acute and supposedly separate, inevitably became tangled in the family ones and so all during the time the family, Frederick Roy, his brother Peter, and his sister Elizabeth, were trying to keep hold of the business, it was teetering on the edge of a financial abyss, with overdrafts round its neck and the spectre of liquidation round the corner. It was threatened with break-up, or outright sale, to meet the death duties on the estates of its two founders, Arnold and Alfred Roy, both of whom died in the early 1950s within three years of each other. This was the legacy bequeathed to Frederick Roy, though bequeathed is scarcely the word for it when he set about extricating Roys from an almost unbelievable predicament. The nub of the problem was that there had been no real provision for succession. It did not follow in the family in an ordained and prescribed manner. You could almost say the succession at Roys had to be seized.

When Frederick came out of the army at the end of the war he returned to the firm's Coltishall branch and helped his ageing father run it. His father died in 1951. In the meantime Arnold Roy continued to run Wroxham, but the company was floundering. A lot of the steam had gone from the elderly Arnold. 'There was no real policy and there was no one really in charge,' recalls Frederick Roy. 'It was the old story of a family company where the shareholders are old, and the people they trusted as supports were not much younger.'

In March 1953 Frederick Roy, his brothers, sister and mother took a joint decision that he should leave Coltishall and install himself at Wroxham to protect the family interests (one of the brothers later emigrated to Canada because he could see no future for the firm). Frederick was not exactly welcomed with open arms. The store was being run by a manager, to whom Arnold, now a sick man, had given his trust. 'At first I was not even offered an office, so I gave myself the job of getting in outstanding debts,' says Frederick Roy. It was a course which Arnold approved, and it helped Frederick Roy to get a little closer to his uncle. However, he had only been there a month when Arnold died and left his half of the business and a £30,000 loan due to him from the company, not to the family, but to his store manager. For the Roys the picture was one of unremitting black. 'In effect the Roy family had lost control of the business,' says Frederick Roy; 'what business there was, was going down, overdrafts were going up, net profit didn't exist and the company was on the point of bankruptcy.'

The manager who now held half the shares was all for selling out. The Roys were against this, even though a firm of consultants, which they called in, had come down in favour of a sale to solve the problem of meeting death duties. But Frederick Roy felt that whoever bought it would reorganise the firm and turn it into a profitable concern; so why shouldn't it be the Roy family? In any case, there was a considerable pull against selling out because of the loyalty of the staff, many of whom had worked for Roys for thirty to forty years. It is one of those firms where those with twenty years service are reckoned to have just joined. So Frederick decided against selling, spent the next couple of years negotiating with the store manager, who later retired, and who finally agreed to being bought out.

Where the money was to come from was quite another matter. The coffers of the company were not overflowing, even though throughout all this traumatic period Frederick Roy had been taking steps to reduce the firm's overdraft at the bank. He bought it down from £48,000 in 1953, the year he arrived at Wroxham, to £18,000 in 1955. Ultimately the overdraft was translated into a credit, but this didn't happen in time to resolve the problem of where to get the money to buy out the former manager, himself faced with £20,000 duty on Arnold's estate. Eventually the money was raised by selling some property, the antique shop and the fish shop, and by obtaining £30,000 on a twenty-year debenture on company property from the Eagle Star Insurance Company.

With this money, part of the outstanding loan due to the estate of Arnold Roy was paid out. This in turn helped the former store manager settle the estate duties and by the autumn of 1955, after several excruciating years, the decks were cleared for action. Frederick Roy brought new management into the company, especially on the accounting side; the company itself was restructured and on Thursday, 18 December 1955, the first meeting of a new board of directors was held under the chairmanship of Frederick Roy. It was a small board, made up of two close professional advisers, a lawyer and an accountant. Later it was enlarged until it included five directors who were Roys either by birth or marriage—Frederick himself, his brother Peter, Frederick's wife Anne, his sister Elizabeth, his sister-in-law Margaret and another director who was as good as one of the family since he had started with the firm as a sixteen-year-old grocer's boy. Once again the Roy family was firmly back in the saddle with a near 100 per cent shareholding in the business.

All that remained to do was to take Roys as a retail trading concern into the twentieth century. The supermarkets were coming and although retailers did not know it in the mid 1950s, those early supermarkets, quite small by today's standards, were to be the forerunners of a radical change in the way which people were to do their shopping. Now the trade is brimming over with ideas for jumbo-sized supermarkets, the so-called 'hypermarkets' of the seventies, and out of town shopping at big centres. In some areas these are already a reality and there is ample promise of more to come. People talk about these changes, the 'retail revolution', as though the nation's shopping habits had altered only in the last fifteen years. The truth is that the industry which now accounts for about one third of the gross domestic product, which is how economists measure goods and services available to the country, and which in 1969 enjoyed sales of £11,000 million, has been in a state of considerable change for the last 100 years.

When Frederick Roy's father and uncle started in business in 1895 they would have been as much entitled to talk of a retail revolution as we do now. Victorian England was, of course, the domain of the independent tradesman, but in the latter years of Victoria's reign both the shops and the shopkeepers began to change. The small man was still as entrenched as ever, but department stores were opening, co-ops began to flourish and chains of multiple shops started to appear. After World War I the multiples sprung up even faster, offering standardised products, often heavily advertised. Boots, Marks and Spencer, Home and Colonial, W. H. Smith . . . these were the names of which the shopping public became increasingly aware. Many of these businesses grew and prospered from humble and unpretentious beginnings. W. H. Smith's roots are in a small shop which opened in the London of the 1890s. Marks and Spencer sprang from a stall in Leeds market.

Sainsbury's, a household name for quality and excellence in food lines, began in a small and unremarkable way. Sainsbury's first shop opened at 169 Drury Lane, London, in 1869, just over twenty-five years before the Roy brothers set up in Coltishall. The shop sold butter, milk, eggs and later cheese. From the outset, the young J. J. Sainsbury and his wife Anne prospered. Their spur to growth, initially anyway, was to have a branch for each of the sons born into the family, but by the time their boys could run a shop there were not enough of them to go round all the branches! On these modest foundations four generations of the Sainsbury family have built. In 1969, when the firm celebrated its centenary, it had 242 branches of which 120 were supermarkets. Its sales were £165 million a year, it employed 30,000 people and the average turnover in one of its supermarkets was £24,000 a week.

Roys had not prospered quite so dramatically; indeed, when Frederick Roy finally turned his back on the crisis of the early fifties, he found himself in charge of a firm that was still rooted to the turn of the century in the relationship between it and its customers, to the days when they drove to the Coltishall shop in carriages, and sat comfortably, while they gave their orders over the counter. In those days most of the grocery items—currants, sugar, soda, dried peas—arrived in bulk and had to be weighed and cleaned when required; the currants, in particular, had to be washed before being put on sale. Four of the staff made boots and shoes to customers' requirements, and up-to-date fashion was provided by sending two buyers to London twice a year. The chemist's department existed for the most part on the sale of Beechams Pills.

The staff lived in, and the business was run very much like a large family. The shops' postal department was dominated by a large bell, which rang in the staff dormitory each morning when the mail arrived, and a member of the staff was obliged to leave his bed to go downstairs and receive it.

There was another anachronistic link with the past. For years the firm had served surrounding communities with van rounds which had always provided a large lump of the business, and which had come to occupy in many of the staff's mind an importance out of all relation to what they earned for the company. They caused the firm to be left behind when frozen foods started to come in; a time when the business was wallowing, with no firm hand at the helm and the feeling about frozen foods was simply that if people stocked their fridges with them, to last over several days, this would hit the 'rounds' which, it was argued, were the backbone of the business. They *were*, just prior to World War II, when there were sixteen vans on the road, bringing in sales of £200,000 a year out of a total turnover of just under £500,000. But after the war there were only a dozen left doing the rounds, and before Roys stopped them, as a matter of deliberate policy, there were only six. Naturally there was a small outcry from people for whom Roys roundsman calling regularly was part of their lives, but for the business it was a realistic decision. 'The rounds were losing 10 per cent a year in sales, and although we tried to make them go, they were getting less and less profitable,' says Frederick Roy. The cost of keeping the vans on the road, petrol, insurance, tyres, maintenance and wages, were increasing all the time. The last year in which they operated, the van sales were just over £120,000.

The rounds had produced other problems too. Some of the roundsmen were earning more than the store's senior buyers, which very much illuminated the need for a proper salary structure. More worrying was the absence of any effective stock control. No one really knew what the roundsmen took out with them and what they brought back. Opportunities for fiddling the company were rife, and the situation was not peculiar to the rounds alone. 'The system was based not on proper receipts but on honesty, on the idea that unemployment in the 1930s being what it was, no one would risk their job by pilfering,' says Frederick. When he took over he estimates pilferage was costing the company £10,000 a year. 'Quite apart from anything else the premises had far too many doors,' he says. 'You didn't know what was going in and out of them, so one of the first things I did was to block a lot of them up.'

Even though the profitability of the rounds was falling, it was still a sizeable slab of business to give up overnight. So at first the frequency of the rounds was reduced, amalgamating them where possible with the shop's delivery service. By the time they were stopped in 1967 Roys new, modern, shopping centre had been built and trading for three years, and in that year the increased business being generated by it more than equalled the loss of sales from the rounds.

Another major departure was the killing off of the special provision service for yachts. Holidaymakers had long been used to sending in their grocery list a week or so before picking up their hired boat from one of the yards, with the expectation of finding the cornflakes and kippers waiting in the galley when they arrived. It was not big business, but nor was it to be sniffed at. In 1961 it produced sales of £25,000 a year. Before it was closed down in 1971 it was bringing in £12,000 a year. It was a decision which at the time caused a few old timers in the firm to indulge in a quiet tut-tut because this was, after all, the trade which Roys of Wroxham grew up on before World War I when Alfred and Arnold heard that visitors who were coming to the Broads to take month-long trips on the traditional Norfolk wherries were alighting from trains at Wroxham Station loaded with cases of food and hampers. The Roys thought it would be a good idea if they supplied the food instead, and they did, undertaking to take back unused cases of canned goods at the end of the voyage and refund the money. They were on to a singularly good thing and knew it; there was no shop in the nearby villages of Ludham and Horning, and in Wroxham itself only a few old buildings, a mill and a pub. Beyond that the prospect was one of marsh and open fields. (Frederick Roy still remembers when the site on which his grocery supermarket now sits was a field with a five-bar gate.)

In the interwar years, as sailing on the Broads became an organised holiday industry, the yacht provisions service thrived and it still did after the war, when people came by train and hadn't got room to bring their own food with them. Later when they began arriving in Wroxham in large numbers in their cars, they came loaded with food. 'The trouble was that we were dear—our prices were high because they reflected the expense of running the delivery service to the yachts,' says Frederick Roy. So it was the motor car which finally spelled the end of the service, cutting one of the last links with the early history of Roys.

In business there are often considerable virtues in what appear at first sight to be disasters. Again increased sales from Roys new shopping centre, much of them attributable to motorist shoppers driving in from a radius of 15 to 20 miles, more than balanced the disappearance of the yacht trade. In the first quarter of 1971 they equalled the total sales of provisions to yachts for the whole of the previous year.

In 1960 Frederick Roy commenced his courtship of the motor car in earnest. He visited America, Canada and Australia and saw for himself how big out of town shopping centres were catering for the car-borne shopper. He also saw how the same principles could be applied to his shops in Wroxham, though there had to be a degree of compromise, because on physical grounds alone it was obviously not possible to build a modern American-style shopping centre consolidated under one roof. Over the years Roys real estate had been acquired piecemeal; translating it into a 2½ acre, £60,000 development with a £6,000 car park took seven years, before even any building work was started. It involved steady application and persuasive presentations to planners and local authorities; it involved a deal with Barclays Bank which required an exchange of land; it involved knocking down old buildings which had been a familiar part of the Wroxham landscape and it also involved the closure and diversion of quite an important road. When you compare it with big redevelopment schemes in large cities it was a tiddler, but for Wroxham it was a major upheaval, although by the time you read this another largish piece of redevelopment will have taken place in the village. This is the new Riverside Centre with a supermarket, eight shops, offices, and a hotel and restaurant, boat moorings and parking for 100 cars. It will provide Roys with their first major competition and Frederick Roy welcomes it. 'It will bring even more shoppers into Wroxham,' he says.

Meanwhile Roys redevelopment has, and is, giving a substantial fillip to the company's fortunes. In what was once a seasonal trading area, with the harvest in the summer months, the firm now takes as much in winter as it used to in summer. In 1970 the company's turnover showed an increase of 19 per cent on the previous year and stood at £874,000, and gross profit was 23 per cent of turnover. All of which is a world away from the time when, in Frederick Roy's words, 'We had bugger all to sell, a whopping overdraft and no profits.' In business textbook terms what he has done would surely rate as a classic rescue and company reconstruction, taking what was essentially a village shop bedevilled with self-exalting idiosyncrasies, unprofitable eccentricities and wasteful practices, pitching it headlong into the 1970s, and making it catch up so fast on lost ground that it is now in the van of retail revolution.

Furthermore, he has demonstrated that family companies don't have to be fuddy-duddy, inward looking and ingrown in their attitudes, and can bestir themselves into positively electric action when threatened. Ask Frederick Roy why he did it and he says, 'I suppose it was family pride and a sense of achievement.' Think hard about how he did it, and it comes down to the simple view that if you are a shopkeeper in the age of the motor car, you need to serve the vehicle before you can sell to its occupants. Easy, isn't it?

Chapter 9

Shops and shopkeepers

Nowhere has the world of small business suffered more radical change than in the high street. The retail revolution—supermarkets, out of town shopping centres, discount trading—and the abolition of resale price maintenance have had a huge impact on the small shopkeeper. Some have succumbed, others have survived the assault, and are still alive and imaginatively kicking—either by making shopping a pageant, giving a personal corner shop service which supermarkets cannot do, or by embracing voluntary trading groups and techniques like franchising which gives the best of both worlds, independent ownership plus big business backing.

For the small retailer, the 1970s are likely to prove even more confusing than the previous decade, when on the one hand he was gratified to feel the benefit of a major campaign on commercial television speedily turning a new, unknown detergent into a commonplace household word within a week, and on the other, worried and vulnerable as the protective shield of resale price maintenance was stripped from him. Little that is happening on the retail stage at this moment (larger and larger supermarkets with own-label brands, the advent of the so-called hypermarkets, out of town shopping centres, higher rents and escalating property values) gives him much cause for optimism. Accordingly the ability to effectively compete with big groups becomes more and more difficult. But it can and is being done; by catering to specific needs or by employing new commercial techniques (such as franchising, which we shall look at later in the chapter).

Undoubtedly one of the foremost problems of today's shopkeepers is to meet the needs of the motoring shopper. Frederick Roy is by no means the only retailer in Britain who has learned to live with the motor car. There are others, like Charles Robertson in Cornwall and Archie Smith in Essex, whose relationship with it is less a matter of passion, more a question of commercial perception, the perception that in business it is sometimes necessary to forgo personal preferences and subdue likes and dislikes in favour of what is convenient, expedient and sensible at the time. Roys catered for the specific needs of the motoring shopper as a matter of deliberate policy. Archie Smith found himself forced to cater for them: either that or lose a lot of business. Charles Robertson went the whole hog and told his customers they could be certain of space to park their cars at his shop, and when they did, they would not only get some bargains, but have some fun as well. If the 1970s appear to be the appropriate age in which to woo the motor car, then it can be fairly said that the Roys, the Smiths and the Robertsons, representatives of the legions of small men with which retailing is so densely populated, have their noses ahead of the pack.

It is impossible to say how many Archie Smiths there are scattered over the land. Or how many shops like his, the classic little corner shop, where every customer is known by name, which stays open late when everything else is shut, and does so simply in order to survive. None the less late opening is one of the specific services it can give (with mum, dad and sometimes the kids, serving behind the counter), which a big supermarket cannot. Shops like Archie Smith's have long been a part of Britain's urban and village scene. They sell sweets, tobacco, groceries, bread, milk and a score of other odds and ends. For the most part they are run by amateurs who started them on demob gratuities, golden handshakes, pensions, or hard accumulated savings. They have to learn on the job, and often they do not learn very much.

'Frequently they mistake hard work for good management, working incredibly long hours and achieving little,' says Bryan Sutton, Vice-Principal of the Bournemouth College of Technology. Sutton learned his practical retailing as a Marks and

Spencer trainee, switching later to education, and becoming heavily involved in courses for retailers in various colleges throughout the country. (The Bournemouth College has launched some interesting and unique courses for retailers which you can read more about in Chapter 17.) 'Several times I have been asked to look at the accounts of a small shop and have had to tell the shopkeeper he would do better to sell up and get a job,' says Sutton. He paints a picture of small retailers as a very prickly section of the community, prickly about what they call unfair competition from the multiples and the supermarkets. 'They have been brought up on a diet of resale price maintenance and very much resent the fact that they have not got it any more,' he says. 'But the good small shopkeepers stand out head and shoulders above the indifferent ones, and often they stand out because the indifferent ones have gone to the wall.'

Yet small corner shops, in spite of the enormous growth of multiples, still fulfil a social function and cater to a real need. No less a person than Sir John Cohen, founder and life president of Tesco, a firm which over the last ten years has grown at a prodigious rate and which now has over 800 supermarkets, sales of over £238 million and pre-tax profits of £12·5 million, makes this observation about the place of the small man in Greville Havenhand's book, *Nation of Shopkeepers*. 'The small man will always be there,' says Cohen. 'If you want to buy a box of chocolates for your girl friend, you aren't going to go round one of our stores and through the checkout. You are going to go and buy one over a counter. Also we can't stay open late or open on a Sunday morning. The small man will always make a living; he gives his own labour. They love us, you know. We've shown them how to be efficient, to use self-service themselves, to get together. No, there's always a place for the small man, I'm sure. Some people don't like supermarkets. My wife wouldn't shop in a supermarket.'

Certainly the successive assaults of co-ops and supermarkets with dividends, loss leaders, trading stamps and special offers have depleted the ranks of the small shop but not put it under. It has faced up to the high street giants by putting emphasis on personal service, by keeping round the clock hours, and by banding with other small men in organisations like Spar which is one of the little man's bulk-buying organisations. In this way instead of succumbing to commercial pressures, or just scraping a hair-raising living, there is many a small corner shop which has thrived, prospered and grown, though as Archie Smith says: 'It still isn't as easy as it looks.'

Archie Smith's shop is at 15 Queen's Corner, West Mersea, Essex. Archie, who is fifty-four, has been in business there for the past eighteen years. It is an unpretentious, red-brick place and stands opposite a pub where the main road from Colchester sweeps into West Mersea. The shop and the living-quarters attached to it have stood there for fifty-odd years. Archie was brought up there and his mother still lives there. In its time the shop has seen many different goods on its shelves. Before the war Archie's mother sold sweets and home-made cakes. After the war Archie used it as a centre for repairing children's toys and it became the local doll's hospital. But for frequent and long periods it stood empty. 'For as long as I can remember it had been a liability,' says Archie. Yet today, the same diminutive shop, neither extended, enlarged nor basically altered, with no posh modern facade, but certainly a bit brighter inside than it has ever been before, is what a lot of the villagers swear is 'a little goldmine'. It has a turnover of £1,100 a week, and in the summer months when visitors flood into the local yachting centre and beach, the shop's average revenue goes up to £1,500 a week.

By village standards this is impressive but it is unlikely that the true cost of building up the business will ever appear in any balance sheet. 'We open all day and every day, from 8am to 8pm on weekdays and from 9am to 8pm on Sundays,' says Archie. 'We used to open on Christmas Day and Boxing Day because we couldn't afford not to, though we haven't done so for the past two or three years.'

At one time Archie had a second shop on the opposite corner where he sold wet fish and delicatessen. Its turnover was about £150 a week, much smaller than the main shop, but it showed a higher profit margin, about 15 per cent. Archie found it difficult to increase business by introducing other lines because most of them he already carried in his main shop on the opposite corner. But he has given up the wet fish shop now and taken over a small food supermarket farther down the road, which he has been running since August 1970. The previous owners seemed unable to make a go of it, but already Archie is making profits on his £800 a week turnover. He had to buy it freehold and go to a finance company to raise the money. 'It is a struggle but if you are a small man in this business everything is a struggle,' he says. Not only does he sell food (he moved the fish and delicatessen to the new shop), he has a licence for wines and spirits as well. One of the reasons he bought it was to protect his trading position. He did not like the idea of someone else taking it and threatening his existing business. 'I couldn't just watch it go to someone else, could I?' he says. The new shop keeps normal hours, but his old corner shop still stays open late. This is where he has had his confrontation with the motor car, or more correctly with double yellow no-parking lines, painted on the kerb in front of his shop.

The effect on Archie's business was bad. He lost a lot of his summer weekend trade from passing motorists and reckons it was costing him £200 a week in turnover. At first he put up a sign outside his shop saying, 'Please Drive on to the Forecourt', but this meant driving over the pavement, which is illegal. In any case there was only space for a couple of cars. So now Archie has built a small car park at the back of his shop which has cost him £200. He built it himself, otherwise it would have cost a lot more. 'When you are a small man you have to do something to hold on to the trade you have,' he says. Well, he did, and for him providing space for six or seven cars has made all the difference, winning back the business he was losing.

When Charles Robertson became involved with the motor car he had no lost business to win back. Cars and parking places were the last thing in his mind when he bought a stretch of sea trout and salmon river at Twowatersfoot in a tranquil valley in the heart of Cornwall. He and his wife Pamela liked fishing, but this half-mile stretch of the River Fowey, between Bodmin and

Liskeard, cost so much more than they could reasonably justify as a hobby that they had to turn it into some sort of business, and settled on the idea of building a pleasant fly fisherman's holiday centre. The planning authorities turned it down on the grounds that cars leaving and entering at the main road would create a hazard. Robertson found this peculiar, to say the least, since Trago Mills had been an explosives factory since before the Napoleonic Wars, and in more recent years had been in continual use, attracting numerous heavy vehicles. So piqued at the iniquities of what he calls darkly 'The Planning', he decided to take action and demonstrate his commercial user rights on the site.

He did this, in his characteristically unorthodox way, by spending his last £2,000 on the stock of a bankrupt builders' merchant, adding on 10 per cent and advertising it in local newspapers. The line of the advertisement he wrote was certainly original. It was at a time when there had been some local fuss from the planners about the colour people could paint their doors. Robertson suggested customers might like to buy the paint, in a line of rather dreadful colours, and use it on their houses specially for the benefit of the said planners. 'To our surprise we sold the lot in under a week and therefore started looking for and buying bankrupt parcels of all kinds,' he recalls.

This was the start of his out of town shopping centre, a business which prospers on the three-pronged proposition that a morning or afternoon spent shopping should be both a spectacle, a pageant and an entertainment for the family; that shoppers will gladly drive 30 to 40 miles in the family saloon to enjoy it so long as there is adequate free parking (and by this Robertson means space enough on his Trago Mills Trading Estate to cope with an average of 1,200 cars a day); and that, contrary to the old maxim, business and politics *do* mix! For every week Robertson spends £800 in full- and half-page advertisements in fourteen West Country newspapers, ranging from *The Independent* at Plymouth to the *South Devon Times*. In these, not only does he offer his bargains to the populace with all the razzmataz of a market trader, save that he uses the printed rather than the shouted word, but also his own particular message on matters of the moment. All of which has made him one of the most trenchant, outspoken, and extraordinary newspaper 'columnists' in the South West of England. He takes it very seriously, often staying up to 3am pounding away on his typewriter, like a reporter in a hurry.

The chief ingredients of his messages are a plague on Socialist Governments, down with bureaucrats and bumbledom, stand up to the planners, reform the tax system and don't touch the Common Market with a barge pole. All this is laced into an ocean of words offering the prospect of untold and staggering bargains, the like of which have never been seen before. There are galvanised dustbins, Chinese carpets, one lorry load of rough sawn timber, divan beds, toothbrushes, terrazo tiles, typewriters, miniskirts, kitchen equipment, trout rods and engagement rings. There are small gems of homely advice for the readers too; one memorable one was when he told them how to claim tax relief for their dogs.

All of this has created excitement and interest, and, as Robertson himself wrote in yet another of his advertisements, 'If you are strangers in Cornwall you will probably wonder what the blazes are the Trago Mills? The easiest way to find out is to ask any local who will probably tell you that despite being a trifle cranky, and having a thing about bureaucracy, we have succeeded in reducing retail prices on a very wide range of goods by 20 to 50 per cent against average cost.' He achieves this by buying in bulk with payment on delivery, and accordingly has managed to keep his prices never less than 20 per cent below retail, with the all round average nearer 33⅓ per cent. The clearance of bankrupt stock now accounts for less than 10 per cent of his turnover, and on the Trago Mills site this is over £1·1 million a year. Robertson says his advertising style is not just a commercial gimmick, but that he sincerely believes what he writes. 'Every week we have a bash at some form of official bumbledom and I suspect that the majority who read our adverts do so less for what we advertise than for what we are having to say on controversial matters.'

Obviously the customers love it and Trago Mills has become a place for a day out and a bargain. Some have made it a place for a two- or three-day outing. One man came all the way from Newcastle-upon-Tyne to buy equipment for a new bungalow he was having built. To do it he fitted a tow bar to his car, hired a trailer and drove to Trago Mills to buy a fitted kitchen, carpeting, and a pile of other bits and pieces. His costing allowed for two nights' accommodation, meals, petrol, wear and tear on his car and trailer hire, and even then he says he saved over £80 on Newcastle prices.

Yet it is not all bargain basement. Trago Mills is set in 30 acres of woods and has wild rabbits lolloping about which are tame enough to feed from your hand. There are a string of artificial lakes noisy with every sort of waterfowl, from hissing geese to ducklings, and to see someone staggering out to their car, loaded up to their eyes, nearly tripping over a peacock which then sounds off with one of its unnerving, metallic cries, is a sight that cannot be enjoyed in the average High Street.

To further enhance the spectacle, and the aura of individualistic self-sufficiency which attaches to Robertson, it is worth recording that Trago Mills has its own quarry, its own fire brigade, and a lovely red fire engine. Fire drills with members of the staff acting as firemen are held once a week. It generates its own electricity and pumps its own water supply using its own waterwheels. Robertson sums up the theatricality of his enterprise by saying: 'I think shopping can be made the occasion of a family outing, and the provision of park-like surroundings, lakes, waterfowl, is a considerable attraction to city and suburban dwellers, who see so little of the country.' Because of the success of this, he has devoted more than 40 acres to the development of a park, with 5 to 6 acres of lake, woodland, winding paths and park benches at a new shopping centre near Newton Abbot. On this site there will also be a children's crèche, for which mothers will pay a nominal charge, and a play area for older children. It took him a four-year battle with the planning authorities before he could get approval for the development. (In this he is not alone, because complaints are mounting from big concerns about the planning authorities' reluctance to grant approval for out of town shopping facilities, because they feel this may contribute to the decay of town centres.)

Although low prices and showmanship are the main planks of his success, Robertson very fairly makes the point that one of the more important factors is the loyalty and hard work of the staff who are given a wide degree of trust and responsibility. When selective employment tax was first imposed, Robertson responded by calling a meeting of the eighty people who were then working for him. After some discussion, and a vote, they all became self-employed, thus reducing the burden of the tax on the business. The present staff of 140 are still all self-employed, have no union, a multiplicity of skills and earn well above the average for their kind of work in Cornwall. 'With productivity bonuses, plus long-term service and year-end bonuses, the men are averaging close on £35 a week, and the older women around £19 a week, earnings which are very nearly double the West Country average,' says Robertson. In addition they have up to three weeks' sick pay a year, five days' paid holiday a year and a 15 per cent discount on all goods. Robertson maintains that the relationship between him, his staff and the business is unique, and could never be achieved on a traditional employer-employee basis; he has certainly used some fairly unorthodox methods to build it up, methods which must have given the staff the measure of the man they worked for. On one occasion there was disagreement about the way the bonuses were being shared out, so Robertson put £300 in 10s notes in a bucket, and told them to sort the money out among themselves. 'They were still arguing about it at 9 o'clock that night.'

Robertson says running Trago Mills has given him the most exciting years of his life and profits too. They have risen from over £12,500 before tax in 1966 to over £57,700 in 1969. As for the excellent fly fishing, in the river which runs alongside the customers' car park you can scarcely put a price on it. What a way to make management decisions, in thigh boots, casting away, listening to the melody of a fast-running river, as the money comes rolling in!

The Royal Navy gave Alfred Harper the most exciting years of his life, though what he does now is not without its moments, such as when a manager made off with £500, or when customers mix salt with the soft sugar, squirt tomato sauce up the walls and order one bottle of coca-cola and seven straws. Commander Alfred Harper, RN (Retd), is a 'hamburg basher'. At least this is what he told His Royal Highness, Prince Philip, Duke of Edinburgh, when, a few years ago, he received a royal inquiry as to what he was up to now that he had left the navy. Harper, a career naval officer with twenty-five years service, once commanded the frigate HMS *Magpie*. When he handed over command it was to Prince Philip.

What the Duke may not have realised was that Harper was cashing in on a rapidly expanding commercial technique called franchising. The protagonists of franchising claim that it offers new horizons to independent businessmen, that it gives them new economic power and a greatly enhanced chance of survival in the business rat race. Certainly it is growing fast, and having a marked impact on the small business scene in the United Kingdom, but nothing like the impact it has made in the United States. Franchising in the UK is reckoned to be worth £25 million a year. In its 18 April 1969 issue, *Time* magazine reported that America's 500,000 franchise operators enjoyed a $90 billion a year business, accounting for 10 per cent of the total US output of goods and services, a remarkable 28 per cent of retail sales, and the business was expanding at about 15 per cent a year. Franchises in the US range from the more obvious, fast-moving food lines to the We Sit Better baby-sitting agencies and, incredibly, even a franchise deal for the cure of bed wetting.

It so happens that Harper, with his five Wimpy bars, is participating in one of the more successful and well-run franchise schemes in the United Kingdom, which was started by J. Lyons & Co, the big catering concern, in 1954. Wimpy International is its fully owned subsidiary. When Harper first started he scarcely knew what a Wimpy was. Now this curiously named snack, a pure beef hamburger patty in a toasted bread bun, enjoys not only a national name, but is beginning to get an international one too. The story goes that the name Wimpy comes from the old Popeye cartoons in which a character named J. Wellington Wimpy used to consume huge hamburgers. This is why the British Wellington Bomber of World War II was known as a 'Wimpy'. Certainly in these days you can find Wimpy bars in Europe and as far away as Japan. There are over 500 in the United Kingdom and new ones are opening at the rate of one a week. Many people still think Wimpy bars belong to a big chain, and don't realise that the man or woman working at the griddle are more than likely the owners. This goes right to the heart of what a Wimpy franchise, or any other franchise, is all about.

But let us look at how Harper, a retired naval officer with little knowledge of catering and business, managed in the space of ten years to build up a solid business bringing in sales of £113,000 a year. He came out of the navy early because he could see it was a shrinking service, and did not fancy a desk job. He was offered the first job he applied for. On this basis he could plainly see he was a valuable commodity and therefore, in justice to himself, ought to pick and choose a bit. From that point on he was never offered another job. So he decided to work for himself and started by opening a Wimpy bar in Southampton in 1960. 'Fancy a naval officer being in the Wimpy business,' said some people, but Harper paid no heed and carried on working eighteen hours a day, staying open until 2am and then getting back on the job scrubbing out the bar at 7.30am. At first he intended going into partnership with a Jewish friend, but then they thought about it a bit, and Harper said, 'Look, I'm a Yorkshireman and you're a Jew and I don't think it will work,' so they had a laugh about it and Harper went solo.

The bar cost him £3,500; he put in £1,000 of his own savings, borrowed the rest from the bank, didn't take any wages himself but lived on his naval pension, and by the end of the first year his sales were £23,000 with profits of nearly £5,000. He had more than recouped his investment. Harper always thought that when he had built up a bit of capital, he would move on to something more stimulating and intellectual than the Wimpy. But he is still waiting to do so and meanwhile he goes on expanding his small chain of Wimpy bars, moving nearer to his main objective which is to sell out, making a handsome capital gain, buy a boat and go back to sea. Only this time it will be in order to sail round the world with another ex-RN officer friend of his if he can persuade him to come; if not, he will go single-handed.

Today he owns and runs five Wimpy bars on the south coast with pre-tax profits of £11,500. He has a total of ninety staff working two shifts, and keeps his bars open from 9am to 11.30pm. 'You have to go for as long a day as possible,' he says. 'If you merely opened from 9am to 5pm you would be hard put to make a profit.' In some locations Wimpy bars do trade profitably on a daily basis, but they are not in the same league as Alfred Harper's.

He still makes a point of personally giving a face lift to his bars, redecorating and altering them himself, undertaking the plumbing, and mending refrigerators, griddles and toasters when they go wrong. This is one of the reasons for Harper's success, the fact that he has worked incredibly hard himself and not been too proud to roll up his sleeves and get stuck into the most menial tasks. He has also applied a lot of good Yorkshire and naval common sense to his business problems. But another reason is that franchising, this characteristically twentieth-century technique for conducting a business, has given him the best of both worlds: the independence and incentive of the small man working for himself plus the backing and expertise of big business, a corporate image or brand name, technical skills, marketing knowledge, and a streamlined and highly developed catering system all wrapped up in one neat package.

Wimpy in the United Kingdom happens to be one of the longest established, most obvious and reputable examples of franchising. There are others which have a surprising influence on our lives and which offer a small businessman the opportunity to trade in a wide range of goods and services, mostly services. Hertz and Budget Rent a Car, Five Minute Car Wash, Dyno Rod Drain Cleaning, Manpower Employment Bureau, Kentucky Fried Chicken, Toni Bell Ice Cream, Arnold Palmer Putting Greens, Pit Stop Exhaust Repair Fitting Centres, Piggy Back Trailer Rentals and a host of laundry operations are all franchises.

The laundrette franchises provided, perhaps, the outstanding small business successes of the 1950s (and some harsh disappointments in the 1960s as the market became overcrowded), offering a means by which retired professionals and servicemen could invest their savings and satisfy their untrained entrepreneurial talents.

Franchise agreements tend to vary in detail, but in basic essentials are usually the same. A businessman rents or leases the name, the product and the operating method and style of a large company, and he is normally granted the exclusive right to it in a particular geographical area. For this he makes a lump sum down-payment as well as paying a continuing percentage of the profits. This is by no means an absolute rule because Wimpy, for example, only ask for a modest down-payment of £300. The franchisee also has to undertake to buy the product he is selling from the company which is granting the franchise. This is the part of the operation where the parent company expects to make its money. Beyond this there are many variations, and good franchises can be distinguished from bad ones by the continuing relationship between the parties.

There are bad ones, and there are plenty of crooks who have blatantly jumped on the franchise bandwagon intent on doing little other than separating investors and their savings. The trouble is that franchising is eminently promotable. Virtually anything which is called a franchise can be sold to someone or other. This, probably more than anything else, is what has made franchising a dirty eleven-letter word in many people's eyes. The *Sunday Times* has been investigating and warning the public of crooked franchises for over three years, but people still get taken in. This newspaper believes there should be an official franchise register which would approve, monitor and regulate all franchise operations, and it has published a ten-point charter, specifying the requirements to make franchising respectable. At the time of writing nothing like this has been established, so I cannot spell out too strongly that anyone planning to put hard cash into a franchise should investigate and check it out in great detail. It is easy for a franchisor to spend *your* money, and any franchise which does not stand up to a searching inquiry is best forgotten.

One of the best check list of questions to guide a potential franchisee in doing this is contained in *The Guide to Franchising* by M. Mendelsohn published by Pergamon Press.

Disenchantment with franchising does not spring from the activities of charlatans alone. In the last analysis it is the quality of the franchise and the confidence which exists between the company granting it and the individual taking it up which counts. Harper makes the point that the success of Wimpy is very much due to the friendships and loyalties which have developed over the years between the executives in the company and the Wimpy bar owners. Certainly Wimpy International expends time and energy fostering the matey, 'brotherhood-of-Wimpy-bar-proprietors' feeling, with get-togethers and a bright and breezy quarterly house magazine called the *Wimpy Times*.

In purely commercial terms Harper says the Wimpy franchise is of more value to him now than when he was starting, when there were fewer bars than there are now. One of the problems of a franchise is that to be successful in a national sense it needs to be got off the ground quickly, and a specific identity based on a product firmly established.

'It is this effort to produce this packaged appearance which is what franchising is all about,' says David Taube, managing director of the Zockoll Group. 'When the effort is successful you have a true franchise. When it is not, though the legal definitions have been met, you do not have a true franchising system.' The Zockoll Group started in the United Kingdom in 1963 with its Dyno Rod Drain Cleaning service which was based on the fact that expansion in housebuilding and increased numbers of older properties created a demand for this service which could not be met by conventional plumbing means. The essence of Dyno Rod is that it combines sophisticated equipment, trained technicians and a nationwide twenty-four hour emergency service.

If the packaged appearance to which Taube refers is not established swiftly, the result can be a source of acute disappointment to existing franchisees. If the enthusiasm and drive of a franchising company slackens, if there is a change of management less keen on the idea, if there is a change of policy and gradual disengagement from franchising, or, if in the belief of the franchisee the technique does not work as well as he feels it should, this can only mean frustration and difficulty for the small man who has committed himself, his family and his money. Michael Pickard once found himself in this position.

He had been a professional management man all his life but wanted to find out if he had any entrepreneurial skill. In 1966 he read an article which said that SGB, the public company best known for its scaffolding, was planning to start a franchised Hire Shop operation: it already owned several. The idea was to franchise individuals to run their own businesses with SGB backing and know-how, in return for a down-payment licence fee and a percentage of all hire revenues.

Pickard sold his five-bedroomed house in Ewell, Surrey, scraped together every penny of cash he possessed and raised his starting stake of £8,500. But even then money was short and he had to take his eldest son away from a school where he was doing particularly well. 'That was a terrible thing to have to do and I don't think my wife will ever quite forgive me for it—her stipulation was that it would never happen again.' The Pickards went to live in a flat over the shop, and had to give up many of the things they used to do, like sailing.

The legend across the front of the shop in Station Square, Petts Wood, Kent, says: 'Here You Can Hire Almost Anything.' This claim is the bedrock of Pickard's business, and it is certainly not an idle one. Standing together in the window you might see a silver punch bowl and a timber winch, or a bread basket and a bow saw. On the shelves at the back of the shop, in the yard behind it, and in two lock-up garages a couple of minutes walk away, is stored a multiplicity of goods. There are ladders, cameras, carry cots, electric hammers, wheelbarrows, bedpans, sleeping-bags, wheelchairs, wallpaper pasting tables: anything a householder, or a contractor or an industrial firm might conceivably want in the way of light equipment for a day, a week, a month or even a year.

The Hire Shop has a big catchment area but even so some of its equipment wanders surprisingly far from Petts Wood.

While all the well-to-do folk in nearby Chislehurst are hiring Pickard's sherry glasses for their weekend parties, there may be an industrial space heater of his as far away as Nuneaton. Hiring things out is a classless business. Pickard has an inflexible rule that everyone must be called 'sir', and as his wife Ruth, who works in the business with him, points out: 'Before we took on this business Mick hadn't called anyone that for years.' Experience has taught Pickard not to make judgements about people by the clothes they wear. A man with half a building site on his clothes is usually a labourer, but sometimes he is the boss of a big building company. Certainly Pickard is no longer surprised when one day a man comes into the shop to hire a saw, and the next day his chauffeur returns it.

What keeps them coming in is that Pickard stocks—or can very quickly get—precisely what they want. A hedge-trimmer is immediately available. A harpsichord takes a trifle longer. Secondly they know the equipment will be 100 per cent reliable. 'If it is not we change it and never argue,' says Pickard. 'After all, what we are really hiring out is mechanical excellence.' But as well as hiring out top-quality equipment Pickard is offering reassurance and solving customers' problems. He has to be very much the friendly, neighbourhood jack-of-all-trades. He needs a feeling for do-it-yourself, a knowledge of things mechanical and the ability to communicate, whether it involves talking to a contractor at a professional level, or a householder at an amateur one.

In spite of the encouraging way the business grew there were strains upon it. Pickard says: 'I'm not sure, if we had known what a tough struggle it was going to be, whether we would have undertaken it.' According to him things did not work out as forecast in the franchisor's original proposition, and in fact Pickard was for a long time involved in a dispute with SGB, because he wanted to sever connections with them. 'It was my judgement to go into business on this basis in the first place, but my advice to anyone taking up any sort of franchise is—*don't*,' he says sourly. This apart, Pickard's faith in the hire business itself is unshaken. He has learned the hard way where the growth is and which are its most profitable sectors. 'It took me eighteen months before I realised the full potential of the contract hiring side of the business,' he says. When he started the shop his customers were 100 per cent domestic users. Now 50 per cent of them are contractors. It is this side, hiring out light plant, everything from wheelbarrows to power tools, which looks most promising.

Like many small businessmen Pickard's most difficult problem has been finance. His vital need was to plough more and more money into equipment, but the sort of industrial plant which gives him a 200 per cent return on its first year is expensive. Space heaters cost about £60 each, an electric hammer £150, a generator £200. 'Put another £5,000 into equipment and this business would really swing,' he says. This was another reason why he wanted to disentangle himself from SGB. No one else would be interested in putting money into the business until that happened. Meanwhile the bank was pressing Pickard to reduce his overdraft. At one stage he sat down and wrote to his bank manager in much the same terms as hundreds of other small businessmen throughout the country have found themselves doing during the squeeze years.

'As far as liquidity is concerned I am beset by the problem which is plaguing most small service concerns,' he wrote. 'My industrial debtors are taking longer and longer to settle their accounts, while at the same time my creditors are pressing for payment. Our turnover is expanding rapidly and to meet the demand for extra stock I am having to finance through hire purchase at up to 15 per cent interest.' None the less Pickard was determined to carry on. 'It's the only thing I can do, but to be honest I suppose what I wanted was the best of both worlds—my own business plus resources of £20,000 to call on,' he said. It was a sentiment which must be familiar to every man running a business which has the potential to really go places.

The story demonstrates that like most other business operations, franchising is subject to stresses and strains at grass roots level; it has defects and virtues. It is not an automatic passport to untold fortunes, nor is it a totally cunning and villainous system devised by big business to exploit its smaller brethren.

It has, after all, benefited many people with aspirations towards owning a small business.

At the headquarters of Wimpy International in Chiswick High Road in West London, they can wheel out Wimpy success stories one after the other. The man who puts his money into a Wimpy bar must expect to cough up between £5,000 and £25,000 depending on size, type and locality. After business expenses have been met Wimpy International reckons an average bar with a turnover of £400 a week can turn in a net profit before tax and depreciation of £62 to £86. Failures are reckoned to be few and far between, and in Wimpy's case, over the whole period in which they have been operating, the drop-outs account for about 2 per cent of Wimpy franchisees. They make the valid point that Wimpy bars have to be a success, and that they move heaven and earth in their partnership with owners to make them so, because if they were not, Wimpy International would be out of business. Wimpy International's most outstanding success story to date concerns a Cypriot named Ali Salih. When he arrived in London from Cyprus fifteen years ago he got a job as a £4.50 a week kitchen porter in Lyons Corner House in London, but his ambitions went beyond washing up dirty plates and dishes. He was soon promoted to the Wimpy griddle where he spent hour after hour cooking the sizzling beef hamburgers. As he flipped them over he dreamed of the day when he would own his own Wimpy bar. By dint of working hard and saving hard he accumulated enough capital, about £2,000, to buy a half share in one. Since then Ali has never looked back. He now owns nineteen Wimpy bars, a chain of Texas Pancake Houses and Aberdeen Steak Houses and a Rolls-Royce. Two of the Wimpy bars are the largest in the world, both 300 seaters, one in London's Coventry Street, the other in Catford in south-east London. When it works well it seems that franchising works very well indeed.

Chapter 10

To grow or not to grow—that is the question

In 1950 Vladimir Raitz pioneered a new style of holiday—the inclusive air tour. Although he did not know it, it was the start of a multi-million pound industry. Twenty-one years later his company, Horizon Holidays, one of the big five tour operators and the only independent among them, was on the threshold of going public. It arrived at this point because one day Raitz decided there was no future in being just another small business. He decided to grow—and has, remarkably, without having to go outside for financial backing.

IT was the evening of Wednesday, 28 April 1971. Halfway to Palma de Majorca from Gatwick a frisson of disquiet was detected on British Caledonian charter flight BR 315. It occurred when the paying customers on the BAC One Eleven, extracting their pack-away dinners from inside the back of the seat in front of them, discovered they were not being supplied with a quarter of chicken and a spike or two of asparagus as they might have expected. Indeed, there was no dinner on a plastic tray at all, but fruit cake and biscuits instead. Someone back at Gatwick had boobed. The chief stewardess clearly felt bad about it, and chatted to the passengers so winningly that they remained jolly and tolerant, and did not get into a frazzle. There was one, though, about whom she was a trifle more concerned than the rest. He was my travelling companion, sitting in the facing seat, a tallish man in his late forties, black haired, wearing spectacles, casually dressed and very relaxed. He was not displaying outward signs of being in a lather either, but he did look like a man mentally composing a strongly worded complaint for someone back at base, way, way above the unfortunate who erred.

As customers go he was emphatically the biggest aboard. Only a few weeks earlier he had bought over £11 million worth of flying time with the airline. 'This must be Adam Thomson's work,' he joked, holding up the fruit cake and naming the chairman of British Caledonian. 'We negotiated such a keen deal with him, he's got to make some profit somewhere.' Vladimir Raitz, owner, chairman, and governing director of one of Britain's big travel and tour operating firms, Horizon Holidays, was taking one of his own charter flights to Palma.

In the travel industry the incident of the fruit cake is the sort of detail you do sometimes get involved with, no matter who you are. Management consultants might throw up their hands in horror, and say it is like the chairman of the British Steel Corporation concerning himself with one batch of strip out of one of his rolling mills; but then, as Vladimir Raitz observed on one occasion, 'Travel is a messy, pernickety, personalised business, more akin to the entertainment industry than anything else.' For over the past twenty years Raitz has been using the whole of the Mediterranean as an arena for staging his successful and profitable shows, and if it were not for his grandmother, on his mother's side, large stretches of the Mediterranean shore would not look the way they do now: extraordinarily overcrowded.

When his grandmother died, she left Vladimir £2,000 with which he began his tourist revolution by starting IT. IT stands for inclusive tour, by air, which may not seem very remarkable now, but in 1949 in the world of travel it was the epitome of daring and adventure; or perhaps foolhardiness. For there were those who shook their heads and said little good would come of it. Among them was the grand panjandrum of the travel business, Thomas Cook and Son, and it went on nodding its head so long and setting its face against the idea of air charter holidays so firmly, that when it did eventually enter the market years later it had no hope of catching up. In those days the travel business in the United Kingdom was dominated by Cooks, its arch competitor, the Polytechnic Touring Association and a few others like Sir Henry Lunn and the Workers Travel Association. Cooks Tours and Poly houseparties were the order of the day and the Swiss lakes and mountains were one of the main destinations. The Costa Brava was a name known only to a discriminating few, and not to the holidays masses bound for the Continent who met under the clock at Victoria Station, London, and were put on chartered trains. If you wanted to fly anywhere on holiday you had to go on a regular scheduled service and the State had a virtual monopoly on these in the shape of British European Airways.

It was into this established and ordered scene that Vladimir quietly arrived, standing in the wings, an amateur among the professionals, unnoticed, unremarked, knowing no one in the business, nothing about it and totally uninfluenced by its traditions. Had he been constrained by the pecking order, by rooted techniques, by preconceived notions of what was, and what was not possible, it is almost certain he would have never pioneered a new means of offering austerity-ridden Britain a cheap and cheerful holiday package. The ingredients consisted of magic carpet transport (even if it was in an old Dakota), plus bed and board in the hot Mediterranean sunshine, a meat dish guaranteed twice a day and the aromatic scent of the maquis in their nostrils.

What he started was quite as astonishing as Old Thomas Cook hitting on the bright idea of organising a cheap day excursion by rail from Leicester to Loughborough in July 1841. It was the birth of the inclusive air tour industry, an industry which created completely new, privately owned airlines, which were largely, and sometimes totally committed to inclusive tour flying, and at a later date it even brought the State-owned airlines, British European Airways and British Overseas Airways Corporation, into the inclusive tour air charter business. It paved the way for a new style of mass, low cost tourism and it attracted large, powerful companies into what had been very much a cottage industry. It also helped finance, particularly in Spain, an astonishing hotel-building boom and played a significant part in pepping up the economy of what was once one of Europe's most economically backward nations.

By the beginning of the 1970s, 5·75 million Britons were taking their holidays abroad, their spending, including fares, totalling £460 million. Over half of them went on inclusive air tours, flying in fast, modern, luxurious jets (not ageing wartime work-horses like the Dakota), which were contracted to tour operators on a time charter basis, a whole season at a time. It was from the headquarters of Horizon Holidays in London's Hanover Street that Vladimir Raitz announced in March 1971 that he had signed the company's largest ever time-charter contract, three years of flying worth more than £11 million, with the United Kingdom's leading independent airline, Caledonian/BUA, now known as British Caledonian Airways. His company was then carrying over 300,000 passengers a year, had a turnover in excess of £18 million and pre-tax profits of around £500,000. Vladimir was driving back and forth from his ten-roomed house in fashionable Chelsea Square in a new Rolls-Royce Silver Shadow, and was finding it increasingly difficult to find time to spend at his own holiday villa on the Costa Brava.

Then forty-nine years old, he occupied a unique position in a roaring growth industry. Horizon was one of the United Kingdom's 'big five' travel companies, the last of the privately owned independents amongst a pack of strong and vigorous competitors. These included Clarksons, a subsidiary of Shipping and Industrial Holdings; Thomson Skytours, part of the Thomson Organisation; Cosmos, with Swiss money behind it; and Global, the travel offshoot of Sir Isaac Wolfson's Great Universal Stores. From small and inauspicious beginnings Horizon has survived, endured and grown over a period of twenty rumbustious and exciting years. Survived in an industry notorious for the sudden and spectacular nature of its business collapses, usually induced by companies trying to run with the giants on the financial resources of a flea.

But in the early days, being undercapitalised was not the besetting sin it is now, and Horizon, which was no different from many others in the beginning, was one of the companies which managed to grow large without financial backing from outside, but purely on its own endeavours and resources. Its profit record was good, though a trifle erratic, and it was Vladimir's ambition and avowed intention to go public. He still ran his company with a sense of adventure and vitality, with the entrepreneurial flair which had got it off the ground in the first place, and he had managed to sustain it in that most crucial phase that every developing company passes through, the graduation from one-man bandism to professional management. There was one other thing which added a certain dimension to Vladimir's achievements. The government had put Thomas Cook up for sale, and he was trying to buy it. Very ironic, because as he says himself, 'When I started years earlier I never understood why Cooks didn't squash me like a fly.'

All this had come to pass in the space of twenty-one years. In the very early years the ratio of luck to judgement was weighted in favour of the former. To start with, when he organised his first holiday he did not realise he was getting into a growth industry. Nor did he know that when he started he was to have the inclusive air holiday virtually to himself for a few years before the competition woke up to what was happening. By then he had a reasonable foothold in the business, and when he was hit by his first real competition, although it gave him and his company a notable jolt, he reacted swiftly by cutting his prices, maintaining his quality image, going hard for the middle-class market which he saw as his strength, and aiming for volume business.

This was a watershed in the affairs of Horizon, because it was a major shift from a position where a lot of luck plus a seller's market had to be replaced with more judgement, skill, nerve and professionalism in a business which was now far less beneficent to its favoured firstcomer. 'In other words it sorted the men from the boys,' says Vladimir. Moreover, with the existing turmoil in the travel business, with the sharpness of the competition, and with the ample resources of sizeable groups backing their own travel companies, a privately owned concern like Horizon needed to become more sophisticated, to have a much clearer idea of where it was going, and how it was going to get there. At this point Horizon changed from being just another small business to one dedicated to the idea of growing into a larger one. Certainly Vladimir was blessed with getting his timing right at the outset, which was a matter of providence more than anything else. Where he has been so adept since is in never relinquishing his initial advantage for lack of expertise or energy, for lack of the will to grow; or by striking an easy and comfortable posture.

For with a nice home and money in the bank, why bother to grow when it leads to stresses and strains and starts to erode the advantages of being small? It is a question many businessmen have asked themselves many times. For growth is accompanied by growing pains. Fruit cake and biscuits instead of dinner on a charter flight; upset clients; administrative clog ups; hotels overbooked; a fine, imposed by a Magistrates' Court for breaches of the Trade Description Act because a hotel didn't measure up to the attractions promised in the brochure. These are some of the pinpricks of expansion. The body blows come when a firm starts to outgrow its staff, its premises and its own financial resources.

For the well-being of the nation as a whole it is fortunate that there are people like Vladimir who are either forced to sit down, or do so of their own accord, and consciously take the decisions which lead to growth. In his case he knew if he were to compete effectively he had to. There are, after all, only three courses you can opt for in business: to grow, to stand still, or fall into a decline. Since businesses, like people, are organic bodies, standing still is about the most difficult manoeuvre of the three, and in a number of respects it is an invitation to fall into a decline. There are several arguments against the non-growth school of thought. It is a philosophy which makes a firm vulnerable because it encourages competitors to overtake it with new and improved products. It invites management to turn a blind eye to changing trends, tastes and fashion, and it commits employees to a stultifying working life which pays little heed to their personal worth, which holds out little prospect of advancement and which leaves little room for nurturing the spirit of opportunity. It means that a company, and the man who runs it, has in effect said, 'There's no further contribution I can make to my industry, there are no opportunities any more.' In short it takes the adventure and excitement out of business and runs counter to one of man's most insistent drives, the urge to achieve.

Yet, when all this has been said, growth, as experience shows, is an elusive commodity, hard to come by. For as long as I have been writing about business, politicians and economic pundits have been preoccupied with the rate of growth, ever ready to latch on to inter-country comparisons to illustrate just how badly the United Kingdom has performed in this respect against many other European countries. It is precisely the prospect of growth offered by Britain's entry into the Common Market which has been one of thc pro-marketeers' main planks in the argument for entry. Sometimes all this tends to obscure the fact that grass roots growth depends on the decisions and actions of individual businessmen, like Vladimir Raitz. Whether the national output of all goods and services is growing or not depends in a very specific sense upon them, on the efficiency of their management and on the productivity they win from the resources they have available.

It has been said before, and it no doubt will be said again, that owners and managers in Britain are not sufficiently excited by the idea of growth, by the attraction of material prosperity, to want to make the effort to promote it. It is a revolving argument because the businessmen blame what they regard as a penal tax system for lack of incentive (especially the smaller, family concerns which have long felt discriminated against) while their critics blame the lack of professional management. Probably the best statement of the why's and wherefores of growth at the level of the individual form is contained in *Attitudes in British Management, A PEP Report*, published by Penguin Books, which itemises the main thrusting and sleepy characteristics of companies, contrasting those which opted for a quiet, comfortable life with those which were growth oriented. One of the report's main conclusions is that the most important determinant of a firm's potential for growth and improved efficiency is the ability of its management to learn about its environment and systematically adapt their policies to take advantage of it. Vladimir Raitz's Horizon Holidays by no means possesses every characteristic of a thrusting company. It would have swallowed up the whole of the travel industry by now if it had.

None the less, it is imbued with enough of them, and has demonstrated the essential attribute of adaptability, to have made the company into what is unquestionably one of the better small business success stories of the last two decades.

Vladimir Raitz was born in Moscow in 1922. His mother was the daughter of wealthy parents who, prior to the Russian Revolution, owned breweries and had other business interests in the capital. His father was a doctor. In 1928, when Vladimir was five years old, his mother left Moscow and took Vladimir with her to Berlin. His father stayed behind. Subsequently the parents were divorced and his mother remarried, to another doctor, in Warsaw. Vladimir continued his interrupted education at the French Lycée in the Polish capital, but he was not very happy there, and in 1936 his stepfather and mother sent him to boarding school in England, to Mill Hill. He already had two uncles in this country, but he arrived speaking not a word of English, and the first conversation he had with his deputy house master was conducted in French. After leaving school his uncle had some idea that he should join his hosiery business in Nottingham, but it was not an idea which appealed to Vladimir so he sent himself to the London School of Economics to read Economic History. The school was then in its wartime premises in Cambridge. His Polish stepfather and mother had some money in England and he used to receive £20 a month plus his school fees.

At Cambridge he lived in a first-floor room at 3 Mill Road. Gordon Brunton, now managing director of the Thomson Organisation, had a room on the ground floor. Years later Brunton talked with Vladimir about the growing travel business and tried to persuade him to sell, but Raitz rejected the idea and suggested to Brunton he might try a young and fast-growing travel company called Skytours. Brunton did. This was the beginning of the Thomson Organisation's large-scale involvement in Britain's travel industry. It was a decision which strengthened the picture of Vladimir as a loner, a man intent on driving his own company forward and not taking quick financial advantages and comfort from the resources of a big group. From his schooldays, being sent alone to England, he was very much his own man. 'I was delighted to be on my own, even though I love my mother dearly, but I was always wanting to make my own decisions and this was not easy in the over-protective environment of being an only child,' he says. 'So from the age of fourteen I was basically alone.' He didn't stay at Cambridge to take his degree but came to London to work for United Press and Reuters. He got a job with them on his facility for languages, spent his time monitoring the French, Russian and German radio, and then writing reports on the broadcasts. He was still a Soviet citizen, and had not been called up by the British authorities, but the day after Germany invaded Russia, Vladimir indulged in what he now regards as a somewhat quixotic act, and took himself to the Soviet Embassy to volunteer for armed service. At the time there was a fair amount of confusion and the Embassy told him to go away. 'Thank goodness they didn't take me up on it,' he says. He became a naturalised Briton in 1949.

In 1944 he decided he ought to go back to Cambridge and finish his degree, so he took three months off to study, lodged in the Garden House Hotel for the final month, and got himself a second-class honours degree in economic history. He returned to Reuters and spent the next four to five years with the news agency, working as a sub-editor on foreign news, but really yearning for the job of a foreign correspondent. His frustration over this mounted. So did the realisation that journalism would not make him rich.

In the August of 1949 Vladimir went on holiday to Calvi in Corsica, where he met some Russian friends from Paris, who were planning to run a small holiday camp at Calvi called the Club Olympique and were keen to have clients from the United Kingdom. Why didn't Vladimir send them some? To travel by train and boat from London took thirty-six hours, which seemed appalling to him, but there was an old airstrip at Calvi which had been built by the Americans. Because of runway restrictions the type of aircraft which could be used was limited, but he started to make inquiries when he returned to London and discovered that a Dakota would be ideal. Furthermore the aircraft could do the journey in five and a half hours, including a half hour stop at

Lyon. Air Transport Charter, a Channel Island company, had two thirty-two seater Dakotas and this firm quoted him a return trip rate of £305, which by the standard of regular air fares prevailing at the time was absurdly low.

Unfortunately there was a major obstacle to be overcome—permission to fly the service. 'BEA has the monopoly and it is virtually impossible to get permission,' the Air Transport Charter told him. At the time there was no formal licensing machinery and Vladimir had to visit the Ministry of Civil Aviation to try and obtain a permit. In the first instance he was turned down, but he continued trying for three months and in the end the Ministry relented, and he finally got his permit to start the service at Easter 1950.

There was one important condition. The tour could only be sold to specified closed groups; students and teachers. So he set to work on a duplicating machine and produced his first simple brochure: 'Holidaymakers live in large tents fitted with beds and mattresses, two to a tent . . . the best sanitation . . . meals are taken out of doors . . . English visitors will be pleased to find they are served twice daily with a meat dish . . . departures every Friday by Douglas airliner . . . cost of this unique holiday is £35.10s.' To get the brochure you either had to be a reader of *The Nursing Mirror*, *Teachers' World* or the *New Statesman*. The advertisements in these publications made the point that this special air holiday to Corsica was for bona fide students and teachers only.

Because of the delays in getting the permit the holiday was advertised late, and it did not take the holidaymaking public totally by storm. Only 300 people booked and Vladimir learned sharply and expensively one of the most pertinent lessons of the tour operating business: namely, that you do not stay in business long unless you manage to get break-even passenger loads for your aeroplanes. He needed 400 passengers for the whole season to cover his costs. On one departure he had only four clients on the aircraft. He missed the target by 100 passengers and finished the season with a loss of £3,000. He gave serious consideration to packing up, but by then he had the beginnings, small though they were, of an organisation: himself, his secretary Connie Kirby (she is still his secretary today) and a one-room office in Fleet Street. Discouraging as his first venture had turned out, Vladimir's instinct told him there was nothing inherently wrong with the principle of chartering aircraft and providing people with fast travel and holidays in the sunshine. He decided to give it a try for another year.

He financed himself on an overdraft from the Westminster Bank, and used the holiday deposits paid by his clients. 'You cannot do that today,' says Vladimir. 'It would give everyone in the Tour Operators' Study Group the shudders.' TOSG has a bonding scheme where its members have to deposit a bond equal to 5 per cent of their turnover which is money to be used to save the holidays of their clients in the event of financial collapse. The scheme arose because there had been cases of badly under-capitalised tour operators overstretching themselves and then going bust, with unpleasant and unhappy repercussions on holidaymakers already abroad, and those still to go suffering the loss of their deposits. In his second season he was still handicapped by being able to sell only to bona fide students, but he was able to time his advertising more efficiently and he got the required number of clients, just over 400 of them, which took him past break-even point. There was even a very small profit, and Horizon Holidays was beginning to grow, if that is the word to describe another girl being taken on in the office, and an old friend from Vladimir's student days looking after Horizon clients in Calvi on a three-month summer job.

For the next four to five years Raitz had the inclusive air tour business substantially to himself, though a company called Whitehall Travel, offering group charters and drawing its clientele very much from the Civil Service, was hot on his heels. In the early 1950s the whole business of inclusive air travel, its prospects and its potential, was given a hefty push by two events. The first was the establishment by the government of a fully fledged route licensing agency, the Air Transport Advisory Council, which many people felt was a change for the better in the climate for private enterprise flying. The second was the building of an airport at Palma, an event which was to have an electrifying effect on the growth of the island of Majorca, transforming it, in the space of two decades, into Europe's most frequented resort area. Vladimir had visited Majorca in 1949 and had seen the tremendous tourist potential of the island. The fact that it was an island had, until then, militated against its development, but now this geographical fact became part of the lure. For the rest it was made up of the Mediterranean trinity of sun, sea and sand, plus inexpensive hotels and cheap wine.

Vladimir was quick to get an application in to the new Air Transport Advisory Council. At the time there was no direct air service to the island from the United Kingdom, and if you made the trip by air it involved flying to Barcelona and then taking a Spanish domestic flight to Palma. British European Airways opposed the application but lost, and in the 1952 summer season Vladimir was able to add Majorca to his brochure. This he regards as a really significant breakthrough, and from then on he added new Mediterranean destinations to his programme virtually each successive year. It was a highly successful year for Horizon, with the aircraft flying with 90 per cent loads, and since the holidays were costed on a break-even load of 66⅔ per cent, the operation was gratifyingly profitable. In 1953 Horizon was still serving the same destinations, Corsica and Palma, but had extended the size of the operations in both places by adding hotels. In 1955 Vladimir discovered that Spain's Costa Brava could be served by air much better from Perpignan in France than from Barcelona. Using this airport turned out to be a winner and the rapid rise in Horizon's carryings in the second half of the 1950s was largely due to the opening up of the Costa Brava.

Thereafter, year after year, Horizon followed a deliberate policy of adding new destinations to its programme. People looked forward to the Horizon brochure because they expected something new in it. Thus repeat business ran at a high level and this coupled with opening up new areas of the Mediterranean to the inclusive air tour kept Horizon growing. The company also began to acquire a solidly middle-class market, and in the minds of the customers it possessed a quality image. Vladimir says he did not set out deliberately to cater for the well-to-do middle class but aimed more at choosing destinations, like Corsica and Corfu, which seemed to him to be slightly more interesting and unusual than the Costa Brava. 'I was marketing the kind of holiday which I would have liked to have gone on myself,' he says. Increasingly his holiday advertisements were addressed to a public who read papers like the *Sunday Times* and the *Observer*, and his passenger lists were dotted more and more with politicians, professional people and business executives. One of the main points of the Horizon sales pitch was that their holidays gave not only full value for money but maximum freedom as well. 'We treat our clients as individuals, not just numbers in a crowd. On a Horizon holiday it is the arrangements that are planned, not the holidaymaker.' Thus the Horizon brochures offered a message of reassurance to a middle-class clientele increasingly driven into the embrace of the tour operators by economic circumstances and small travel allowances. It also appealed to other holidaymakers who, as their affluence increased, graduated to a Horizon holiday from lower down the market scale. With this kind of client very much in mind, Horizon set out to buy hotels which were a bit better than other people's, and to do the same with their aircraft.

The arrival on the scene of the new Viscount in 1957 added another piece of solid brickwork to the pillar of quality upon which Horizon was basing its business. Vladimir recalls that for the first time, as charter operators, the firm was able to offer a really first-class aeroplane; for at this time there were still many ageing and near obsolete aircraft flying holidaymakers to and from the continental sunshine. Some years later it was the first tour operating company to employ the new BAC 1-11. The policy of paying a little more for up-to-date equipment paid off, especially since at best long delays, and at worst disasters, occurring to older planes, began to build up a bad image of the air charter industry in the public's mind. At one sales conference for retail agents Vladimir told his audience, 'Horizon has always appealed to, and will continue to appeal to, the most stable market in travel—professional people, businessmen, in fact the solid middle class whose position is secure and who take foreign holidays as an integral part of their standard of living.' This is a well-defined lump of the travel business which many others cast covetous eyes upon. For as long as the British middle class continues to thrive, so it seems will Horizon.

By the mid-1950s the company was carrying 3,800 passengers, had a turnover of £160,000 and its profits were £9,000. Its staff had grown to twelve and it was still operating from offices in Fleet Street. Among the new faces was Leonard Koven, an American advertising man who was an old friend who Vladimir had met in Paris in 1949. Koven, who had studied in Paris under the GI Bill of Rights, desperately wanted to paint, took himself to the Costa Brava to do so, and earned the groceries while he was there by acting as a representative for Horizon. The following season Vladimir asked him to come to help in London. The two have been solid friends and business associates ever since. Koven is now chief executive director of the company, has no stake in it, but takes a percentage of the profits, which must make him one of the highest paid travel executives in the country. Vladimir pays himself between £7,000 and £8,000 a year, and has never taken any money out of the company apart from his salary.

In the early days Vladimir used to look after air charter and the hotels, while Koven, with his advertising agency background, concentrated more on producing the brochure and the advertising. Life was less frenetic then because the yearly cycle fell into distinct phrases: making arrangements with hoteliers and airlines in September and October, producing and dispatching the brochure just after Christmas, selling from Christmas to April, and operations from May to the autumn. 'We did quite a lot of travelling ourselves, but when we were in the office the hours were quite reasonable, from about 9.30am to 6.30pm,' recalls Vladimir. 'I can't say I killed myself with work, developed an ulcer, or anything like that, though the business and its problems was never out of my mind. Now with the growth of cheap winter holidays, the extension of the summer holiday season and many more destinations, the old well defined cycle of the year's work is not as well defined as it was, and all the various types of activity are taking place year round. Certainly it is more demanding, but for me the business is still like a hobby or a game, a difficult game perhaps, but never a chore. I still look forward to going to the office on Monday mornings.'

Unusually for a small, growing business finance was one of the least of Horizon's problems. The company was able to operate on trade credit, and on the cash flow provided by clients when they paid deposits on the holidays. Aircraft charter, advertisements and brochure printing bills did not have to be paid until sometime after. Problems were minimal and the competition was still not of the calibre to worry Vladimir. The main difficulties were concerned with getting licences. There were odd, unexpected problems, like getting one of the reps out of an area very fast. 'He was one of our men in Sardinia and he got a local girl into trouble—we had to get him out before her family killed him,' says Vladimir.

Then, in a very short space of time, the situation changed radically. In the late 1950s he found himself facing the first real competition since he started out in business seven years earlier, when he suddenly discovered he was being undersold on price by a new up-and-coming tour firm called Skytours. 'Previously it had been OK to pitch your prices below the cost at which people could organise exactly the same holiday for themselves. About £15 less than this and you were in business, but Skytours changed all this, and we had to take a very hard look at our prices,' says Vladimir. 'We had acquired a good reputation, but were now too expensive. So for one year we were caught napping, and since others had come into the field, the public no longer ceased to marvel at our prices compared with scheduled air fares. They now had a different basis of comparison.'

His reaction was to go hard to win back Horizon's position, and he made 10, 15 and 20 per cent cuts in the price of his air holidays. By 1961 the company had recovered its traffic, and had increased the volume of its business, but its profits started to shrink. Vladimir realised he could never become fully competitive with opposition like Skytours, which had its own airline, Britannia Airways, while he was paying what he was for seasonal charter of his aircraft. He couldn't bring that price down until he had an even greater number of passengers travelling. 'It was at this point we saw we could not stay small with this kind of competition. We had to be big in order to get a good aircraft rate. To time charter an aircraft you need at least 50,000 or 60,000 passengers, and in 1960 Horizon was carrying 15,500,' says Vladimir. It also became clear that he had to spread his overheads over a much larger number of bookings. Two years earlier the company had moved from its offices in Fleet Street to new premises in Hanover Street. It moved in time for the 1958 season which turned out to be a fantastic year. 'There were queues yards long outside in the street waiting to book on Saturday mornings, and in one year our numbers of passengers carried jumped by 100 per cent,' he says.

To get this kind of business in the early 1960s you had to fight hard. The market and the firms serving it was already starting to change. Prior to moving to Hanover Street, Horizon was still very much aloof from the rest of the industry, and had few contacts in it, and was still running things in its own sweet way. It was still selling its holidays direct to the public, and not through retail travel agents. Later the competition became even fiercer as Clarksons, backed by the publicly quoted Shipping and Industrial Holdings, came into the market and swiftly embarked on a policy of aggressive, mass marketing which in a very short space of time took them to a position where the company dominated the trade in terms of numbers of passengers carried. At this period there was an even greater demand for financial resources, because in the scramble to secure hotel beds at new hotels the big groups were putting down deposits with hoteliers, paying out large sums of money in advance, and this was something which, until the arrival of Skytours in the business, had been unheard of.

Suddenly the tour operator changed from a man who assembled bits and pieces of other people's services to one who was involved as a principal. A new style of mass tourism forged a new industrial structure, with big business owning or having a strong lien on hotels, airlines, ships and even the coaches which transferred clients from airport to hotel. It was a business environment in which a small, independent concern like Horizon could have been excused for an attack of faint heartedness. Instead it directed its attention to holding on to what it had, and winning more wherever it could.

While the market as a whole had been evolving, so had Horizon's response to it. Throughout the 1950s nearly all the company's air tour departures were from London, but in the 1960s provincial airports and departures from them became more important, and to tap and cultivate this rich and valuable market Horizon set up subsidiary companies, with their own offices and staff, which became firmly identified as local tour operators. Horizon's Birmingham company, for example, is very successful and profitable, carried 70,000 passengers in 1970 and made £100,000 profit. To emphasise the local identification, even the charter aircraft which flies from Birmingham Airport is named City of Birmingham. The company has also ventured into the lower end of the mass travel market with a new company, 4S Travel, which has been set up with separate management in separate offices. Vladimir is not anxious to repeat the mistake of a few years ago when Horizon ventured into the lower end of the market with a company called Streamline Tours. This was run by Horizon people, from the Horizon offices and it was consequently accorded very much second priority. It didn't work and Vladimir concedes it was a bad mistake.

Obviously the growth and development of Horizon has made demands on its management strength, and it has met this either by growing its own managers, or by acquiring a ready made team, as it did in the case of 4S Travel. It is the sort of growth which has demanded the establishment of an organisational structure, and which has caused Vladimir to graduate from the man who once had his finger in all the firm's pies to someone who lets others get on with the day-to-day running of the company, while he looks a little farther ahead than the rest, having time to clarify his objectives and knowing what he wants to happen to the company. Thus he is involved with forward projects, with talking to people and examining propositions for new hotel developments, new destinations, new types of holidays. 'At first the delegation this demanded was difficult but it was inevitable,' he says. 'None the less you still feel you can do any job in your company, from opening letters to chartering aircraft, better than anyone else. It is your company and you feel for it more, but in the end you know that you must accept the job will not be done as well, so you resign yourself to it, and either forget about it or grumble . . .'

All the important decisions are taken by himself and Leonard Koven. The two men lunch together in the office most days. Sometimes they even take a couple of hours off on a Saturday and go to one of the early cinema matinees before the crowds start to arrive. On Fridays all the directors lunch together. Only five years ago there were no management meetings of any sort at all. But now the old, matey word-of-mouth way of doing things is gradually being replaced by memo writing. 'You have to watch this, though, because you cannot afford to fossilise into a bureaucracy,' says Vladimir. 'In the travel business you have to be a pusher. You can't just administrate. You need ideas and drive as well as administration if you are to stay ahead in this business.' In his book, staying ahead means Horizon being one of the three or four companies which will dominate the trade. It means being able to look up Horizon's share price in the *Financial Times*.

Why does he want to go public? It is not as if Horizon, with its profit record, especially the bonanza year of 1969 when it made £600,000 pre-tax profits, desperately needs the money to expand. It has always been in the fortunate position, even though a close company, of being able to convince the tax man that it was vital it should not be forced to distribute 60 per cent of its profits, but, because of the peculiar nature of the travel business, to retain them. This is one explanation of why he wants to go public. He recognises a built-in hazard here, and the dispensation which the company has in this respect may not last for ever. 'If we are a public company instead of a close one there will not be any problem,' he says. The second reason for public flotation is a predictable one. The position his heirs would find themselves in if he were suddenly to die tomorrow. He says there is little doubt that the company would have to be sold in order to pay the estate duties. 'Lastly I suppose it is vanity,' he says. 'You have

N

built a company up, it has satisfied your urge to build something, and going public sets a seal on it.'

As a company Horizon has done well, but in over two decades of trading it still has not grown at the rate of some of the younger entrants on the travel scene. 'I was the first and I should have grown faster,' he says. 'But the snag was that I would have had to bring others in, and this is often difficult to do without surrendering your sovereignty. In any case I have never fancied justifying my decisions to a board of directors.'

When a man chooses to stay independent and continue to build he has to be very confident that his entrepreneurial vitality and flair has not dimmed. He has to be equally sure that he can ally it to good, professional management, which is essential if the momentum of growth is to be maintained. Many businessmen fail to recognise that growth *per se*, the headlong rush into expansion, has as many inherent dangers as sitting back and letting someone else take the bread from your mouth. If you grow too fast there is the likelihood of a sharp attack of the corporate burps, a dose of industrial indigestion which can have a detrimental effect on the functioning of a company, disrupting its production and marketing, eating into its profits.

On the other side of the coin is a level of growth well below the potential of the company, which means opportunities are being missed and rivals are mopping them up; which means staff become frustrated and leave; which means new products and services are not introduced as fast as they should be. For every company there has to be an ideal rate of growth which is balanced, sustained and repeated from year to year. It is a gradient of growth which is infinitely preferable to sudden explosive success followed by rapid fall offs, but it is extraordinarily difficult to achieve. A growing company requires from its owner an even acuter commercial sixth sense, a greater sensitivity to what threatens its business and an even swifter response in offsetting it, than it did when he was just getting it off the ground. One of the reasons why Vladimir Raitz is so interested in Thomas Cook and Son, a company whose poor profit record tends to be overshadowed by its tremendous reputation, is because he would be very reluctant to see such a potentially valuable prize fall into the hands of one of his rivals.

There is, of course, no statutory regulation which lays down that you have to run a business with growth in mind, that you cannot keep it ticking over on the basis of earning a living and no more. Thousands do exactly that, shopkeepers, plumbers, painters and decorators, but there comes a point where it is impossible to continue following what is essentially a sterile course, and a man has to move to protect his interests, or be prepared to go under. In a business growth offers the prospect of reaching a size which helps stabilise commercial results, which assists in ironing-out the uncertainties and the vicissitudes of a day-to-day, hand-to-mouth business existence. On a personal level it is still, in this day and age, the only way a man can really make a fortune for himself, more than he ever would working as a highly paid executive for someone else. In spite of our tax system there is still an appealing arithmetic of wealth which springs from building up a business and, then, either selling out, or going public. It springs from the comfortable feeling that the capital gain which has accrued from fifteen to twenty years hard work and dedication has more than handsomely countered inflation.

Yet this is rarely the sole motive for growing. Frequently business goals are compounded of a variety of highly personal considerations. Vladimir Raitz started a business because he wanted to make more money than he was getting when employed by someone else. It is not the reason, as we have seen, that he continues to run it now. Firms such as his, by their nature and record, by their style and vitality, by the intelligence, originality and drive of the men who head them, are those which offer themselves ready-made to anyone asked to compile a list of companies which would still be growing and prospering in ten years time.

Chapter 11

The fastest publisher in the west

This is the story of the firm which published this book. David & Charles started as a hobby and is now one of the fastest growing publishing houses in Britain. It has progressed from garden shed beginnings to merchant bank backing. The ingredients of its success are many: but one of the main ones is named David St John Thomas, a man who gave rein to a deep urge to run and manage a business of his own, and who, at first unknown in publishing and knowing next to nothing about it, has made this traditional and circumscribed world sit up.

MORE authors pass through the ticket barrier of Newton Abbot railway station in the course of a year than any other single barrier in the 12,459 miles of the British Rail network which is open to traffic. The authority for this astonishing assertion is me, and anyone wishing to challenge it may make their own private surveys at all the other barriers. The inescapable fact is that, as railway stations go, Newton Abbot is more bookish than most, and while you are there, you are never very far from a good read . . . *Bloody Versicles*, the *Field Service Pocket Book 1914*, *Archery for All*, the *Sublimations of Leonardo da Vinci*, *Victorian Sentimental Jewellery*, *The Snakes of Europe*, *A Treatise on the Steam Engine*, *The Bird Table Book*, *Yesterday's Shopping*, and, appropriately, a plethora of books on railways. This is as nice a sample from a publisher's list as anyone with catholic tastes could wish for, and it makes Newton Abbot railway station eminently worth a place in a book about small business. It is where the book you are now reading was appraised, pondered over and finally published.

David St John Thomas, a tall, eager, chuckling fellow, is the man who has made this station a force to be reckoned with in British publishing. When you walk through the ticket barrier you are confronted with a sign which says:

Welcome to Newton Abbot
Home of one of Britain's most enterprising
Publishing Houses
David & Charles

The firm's front door is no more than half a dozen steps from the barrier where the ticket collector sometimes finds himself acting as unofficial commissionaire to the only publishing house in the United Kingdom with a railway station in its address. It is probably the only publishing house with an old Great Western Railways gas meter on its premises too. The offices of David & Charles are over the booking hall, and used to be the old locomotive headquarters for the whole of the west of England from Taunton to Penzance. David St John Thomas's own office overlooks the main up-line from Penzance to Paddington and he runs his office with the precision of a railway timetable. The employees come to work as the Leeds train departs from platform 5, and a Plymouth train on platform 4. A little later a Plymouth–Paddington express thunders by on the Up Through, halting David St John Thomas's dictation for 30 seconds (33 if there are 12 coaches instead of the usual 10). They hear the Up-*Cornish Riviera* roaring through if they are back early from lunch, and the day ends with the *Mayflower*.

Apart from the firm's own showroom, the nearest outlet stocking David & Charles books is the Menzies station bookstall and from his office window David can see parcels of his books on the platform, waiting to be dispatched by various trains. In his office he sits beneath a sign on the wall which says 'ENGINES MUST NOT PASS THIS BOARD' (a birthday present from his staff), throwing off ideas for books on the one hand, watching the finished product being dispatched by Express Parcels on the other, a piece of unparalleled management control if ever there was one. The suspicion may be forming in your mind that he is some sort of railway nut. He certainly used to spot trains at Newton Abbot as a boy and claims he learned his management by telling British Rail how it ought to be run; and his early publications were biased towards railways and transportation. But he says he is trying to play the railway thing down a bit now. In any case, when you have had all the fun about Newton Abbot railway station, there still remains one significant fact about the old railway offices. It is the rent; £1,300 a year. 'Where else would I get this sort of space for that sort of money?' asks David.

If there is a key word which is in the David & Charles sign on the station wall it is 'enterprising'. It may seem precocious but it is this quality which brings the authors through the barrier, manuscripts through the post and orders through the bookshops. Authors like the way David & Charles publish their books, even if they are not overwhelmed with huge advances. But as publishers, they actually seem to care what happens to an author's efforts. After all, writing a book is a bit like a long pregnancy which reaches its climax when the book is published—a sort of parturition in print confined in hard covers. At a time like that you need a little pre-natal encouragement and cosseting every now and again. The point is they make a writer feel important and they take immense pains to turn his work into a good, well-produced book. Their attitude to writers is not a sycophantic indulgence. It is damn good business sense. It is how you assure a continuing supply of raw materials for your business. In a young, growing publishing house you have to build up your list of titles fairly rapidly if you are to compete effectively. You need authors to come to you. You need their goodwill and interest. The skill comes in sustaining these ephemeral qualities and from them formulating the sort of books which David & Charles are so good at publishing. Books which are apparently limited in appeal, serving minority interests yet which surprise your interest, because they are often on subjects you wouldn't dream of buying—until you see the book. Then you feel you would like to handle it, read it and have it. Titles like *Rabbits and Their History*, *The Comic Postcard in English Life*, *Newspapers of the First World War*, *The Fairground Organ*. Now this is what I call an unlikely book: yet it has been a gratifying success. As it happens, David plays the organ a bit himself and has a small one in the corner of his sitting-room at home, but the organs in this book are in quite another league. 'There could only ever be one book on a subject like this, so we had to make it a really good one,' he explains. 'Not everybody will buy and restore a steam organ, but our book is absolutely vital to those who do.'

Booksellers are discovering that David & Charles books are very often vital to someone who is doing this or that. Furthermore they like the way the company dispatches books almost as soon as it gets the order. The house believes there are very few others who equal it in swiftness in this regard. It counts for a lot because it so happens that getting a book to a customer quickly is something which much of the British publishing industry apparently feels is infra dig, taking as it does anything from a fortnight to seven weeks to accomplish this simple job. When the Booksellers Association last published a delivery league table showing the promptness with which fifty-four publishers swung into action when they received an order, David & Charles came second. It is from such minutiae that reputations are ultimately made.

The reputation of David & Charles has even caused august London bankers like Hambros to flick the dust from their lapels and sally forth to Newton Abbot. I wish I could say they came by train too, but in the stylish way they do things in the City, they opted for a helicopter instead. What Hambros like about David St John Thomas is his track record; short but very impressive. He makes profits almost as fast as he publishes books and it is not an easy business to do it in. They can probably see him going public in the not too distant future, and indeed, so can he. 'I like the idea of outside participators in many ways—it prevents you becoming stuffy,' he says. Anyway this is one of the reasons why merchant banks will put money into a private company to help it grow even more. Funnily enough, at the time Hambros was looking David & Charles over, one of their men happened to be in a bookshop when he heard the bookseller tell a customer, 'Oh, you'll get that book quickly. It's from David & Charles, and they send by return of post if they can.' It made the Hambros man feel quite perky. There's nothing bankers like more, after they have done their sums, looked at the colour of their prospect's socks, and given him a full-scale once over at a lunch with the board, than getting an omen like that drop in their laps.

There are some who come through the ticket barrier because they have decided that David & Charles is the kind of firm they want to work for. They like what they have heard about it, and when they have been there for a while they will tell you they like it even more, because it is a personal, friendly place, because there are no politics or infighting, because the management operates an open door policy, is passionately interested in everything going on, and you can get quick decisions from them. Since it is a growing firm it offers the excitement of things happening, new challenges and prospects of getting on for those who work in it. And it is plain that people find a lot of fun and job satisfaction working there. Chris White had been with the company eighteen months when I talked with him. He is a chartered accountant who is production executive. The decision to put a chartered accountant into the job instead of a traditional print buyer is based on the simple premise that this is the one area of the business where really large sums of money are spent so it seems sensible to have a highly numerate person looking after it who can learn the print side as he goes along.

Chris White well remembers a fragment of the letter David wrote to him after White had put an advertisement in the *Western Morning News* saying he was an accountant looking for a job in the West Country. David wrote in reply, 'We are a small, growing publishing company here in the West Country and we are located here because I happen to like it.' So do most of the others who work there. The company secretary, Ken Davis, another accountant who was at one time company secretary of Harris Bacon, came to Devon originally because he wanted to start a practice of his own. Somewhere along the line he did some work for David and the next thing he knew he was in Newton Abbot railway station, costing books like mad, with the notion of his own practice rapidly disappearing down the track.

There are three ex-managing directors of London publishing

houses working for the firm and freelance editors, authors and academics tend to turn up out of the blue from far horizons—like the professor from a South African university who arrived while I was there saying he would like to take on some freelance editing because he would be retiring soon. Most of the people employed by the firm have had no previous experience of publishing. Like David himself, who knew very little about it when he started, they have progressed from amateur status to a professionalism which has helped in the dramatic growth of the company.

One obvious advantage of the company's location has been that labour is available in Newton Abbot at cheaper rates than London. Another is that being 200 miles from the capital, the traditional publishing centre, there was no one to whom David could turn in the early days of the business when he had a problem, no chums round the corner whom he could telephone and pick their brains on the old boy network. It forced him and the company to think through all problems at rock bottom levels. It made them make their own mistakes, it taught them not to be frightened of making mistakes, and it showed them how not to make the same mistakes again.

The other advantage—and I know David sets great store by it—is that there is no compulsion to tackle things in the old traditional way in which, say, a family-controlled, three-generation publishing house might. There are no inhibitions, no hide-bound practices to slow up growth. Moreover the company has not picked up what David calls the bad habits of the industry. It has not always been nervously looking over its shoulders to see what the others are up to. It has just got on with publishing good books, the sort of books its own staff like and enjoy, in its own way. Curiously, in a world as gregarious, agreeable and intimate as publishing, it has stood apart, and that isolation in many respects is one of its great strengths.

The roots of this attitude are to be found in its beginning. David started his career as a reporter on West Country newspapers, later became a freelance, and earned a very tolerable living from it, making about £3,500 a year working under contract to the *Western Morning News*, writing books and doing radio and television work. It is the fact that he has written books which makes him see himself very much as the authors' friend. He knows what it's all about. This is not to say that he lets them do as they like. The firm's obsession with quality, with getting a first-rate, definitive book on a subject, means authors often find themselves being driven hard. They do not have much sympathy or time for idiosyncratic authors at David & Charles; like the man who put up a synopsis for a book on the history of Bath. There was no mention of the Romans in it anywhere. Odd, thought the people at David & Charles, there must be a chapter missing, and queried it. 'Not at all,' said the author, 'it's merely that the Romans do not interest me in the least.' He may be writing the history of Bath for some other publisher sans Romans, but certainly not for David & Charles.

Of course there are some books which David and his wife Pamela, who is editorial director of the company, look back on with the shudders. But then everyone has to start somewhere. David started at his home in the village of Ipplepen where at one time he had made a brief excursion into fruit farming, when he and a colleague named Charles Hadfield (the Charles in the company title) wanted to publish some small booklets for which they thought there would be a demand but which London publishers with their overheads would not touch. The partnership started on April Fool's Day, 1960, and in the first three months they produced three booklets, all very much on a hobby basis. Their big success was a topical booklet on the 1960 Devon floods which sold 21,000 copies in six weeks. David has memories of working incredibly long hours during this period, physically handling and invoicing the 21,000 copies himself, and trying to keep it all as quiet as possible from the newspapers, with whom he had freelance contracts. The turnover for the year was the princely sum of £1,600, and the profit must have really rocked them down in Ipplepen. It was £6, an unsensational 3 per cent return on the £200 capital employed. But then, it was only a hobby; or was it? Well, it was a hobby which was starting to grow. In the second year David & Charles produced a few more booklets. David was still freelancing in order to buy the groceries, but the book publishing was demanding more and more attention and the employment of staff. It was a time Pamela remembers because she got a bit fed up with people tramping in and out of the house and the telephone ringing at all hours. So David & Charles, publishers, moved into a wooden hut in the garden. The toilets were in the packing shed nearby. The period of the wooden hut did not last long, about nine months, because the success of several books meant the firm grew more rapidly than expected. All that is left inside the hut today is an old, faded David & Charles advertisement from the bookseller, curling at the edges, pinned to the wall. The children's guinea pigs have taken over, which is about the only sort of take-over that David is likely to accept. He has had plenty of interested parties knocking on his door since, but the idea of selling out is anathema to him. 'I shall not and I will not,' he says. 'I reject take-over overtures without inquiry and I don't believe publishing mergers usually work either.'

The wooden hut period, and just prior to it, was an era more of problems than achievements. David was still writing, but had to break off to supervise staff during his working time. The fact that he and his partner lived 125 miles apart did not help either. This was the period Pamela disliked, particularly, she says, for what it did to David. The demands on him were heavy, trying to lift the company from its old hobby, cottage industry base and place it on a proper business footing. Differences in temperament between the partners led to other differences. It is not an unfamiliar story in business. The upshot was that David bought out Charles Hadfield, but their association still continues since Hadfield works for the company as an author and editor. Pamela says the strain of all this made David physically ill. 'He just didn't bubble any more, he just wasn't his old self,' she says. Talk to them about those days, and they are not really all that long ago, and they are divided as to whether they would do the same again. David says you cannot really answer the question because the circumstances would not be the same. They certainly do not nostalgically hanker for the old days and they consider the present is the really enjoyable part of their company history. Life is more fun than it used to be and Pamela certainly would not want to go through all those early years again. David, she reckons, has the happy facility of being able to anaesthetise the bit of his mind where unpleasant past memories are stored.

The move from the wooden hut in Ipplepen to the Newton Abbot railway station took place on 1 February 1965. The staff consisted of three people. The main problem now facing the business, and it is the bedrock one which faces anyone now in publishing, was the building up of the title list, getting authors and manuscripts flowing in. David says money problems were secondary to this. Friends became authors and he will always feel very grateful to them for their support. Later in the year he took over a guide-book firm called Raleigh Press (its imprint has now been dropped) and it helped to create turnover and support the company's first full-time sales rep. Obviously with expansion the question of money became more pressing. It was the crucial point at which many a small business has foundered because the qualities called for in a person to get a business off the ground and then to make it flourish are often lacking in one and the same person. David expresses it succinctly. 'It is easy enough to start publishing, and with a bit of helpful publicity to get some good sales after a couple of years, but the problem comes when you begin being a business and start incurring overheads.

Pamela's family helped financially, injecting money into the business in several instalments to the tune of £10,000 to £15,000, as the first pressures on liquidity built up. Equally important, they guaranteed loans from the bank, and from the Export Credit Guarantee Department. Money has never been a major consideration, not in the sense of accumulating a fortune, though David is the first to recognise its usefulness: it was a long time before he took any out of the business, largely because it seemed to him more important to keep it in. His aim is not to be the richest publisher in Britain, but the most creatively satisfied and fulfilled. There is little point stockpiling money for its own sake and this is why he tells his staff that money is fuel. 'Certainly we make sure our tank is never empty, but we wouldn't store cans of petrol in our homes, would we?' He changed banks not because he thought the one he was with was not in funds but largely because of its attitude. If people are involved with his business, in the course of their business, he reckons they should show some sort of feeling for what is going on and try to drum up a modicum of rapport. One day when he was paying in a cheque for £3,000 the bank manager said to him, 'Do people *really* spend that sort of money on books?' 'The more I thought about what he said, the more I thought, what an absolutely daft thing for a bank manager to say to a customer,' he says. He still sees the old manager around the town—when he's on his way to the bank he changed to, Lloyds.

When he did need to raise money he decided to shop around for it and contacted four merchant banks. The reception he got, the way in which he was treated and the way he felt about it is probably pretty typical of the experiences of many other small men in search of funds to develop their businesses, and it more properly belongs to Chapter 16. The outside money was essential if the company were to take its next big stride forward into publishing, and in the end it was Hambros Bank with whom he did a deal early in 1970.

A great deal had been achieved but the company had now reached the point at which it was just not possible to finance further expansion from its own resources. Remember 1965 was the year in which it became less of a cottage industry and more of a business. It was the year in which book sales jumped from £16,000 to £56,000, yet it was still a small company run by one man and two assistants, a company where a few staff worked like dervishes to cope, but where the size of the business was not really sufficient to justify an organisation with a proper management structure. Management structures are not all that meaningful when there are only three of you in a business. But during the next five years turnover nearly doubled each successive year. By 1970 sales were nudging £500,000 and pre-tax profits were £59,000. David knew that unless he grew quickly he would be trapped as far as outside money raising was concerned. After you have passed the £250,000 sales mark you have to go like hell to interest the institutions. This is so often the point at which a business, if left to its own resources, plateaus out and finds it hard to progress. The importance of the newly injected Hambros money was that it enabled the company to continue at the pace it had been going, rather than slow down.

On its past performance forecasts of a turnover of £1 million in 1973 look feasible, although, as everyone knows the best-made forecasts can shatter into pieces right under your nose. Also, as the man from Hambros says, while the company still has a lot of steam in it (shades of the railway station again), it cannot go on growing at the rate it is for ever, otherwise it will swallow the whole of the British publishing industry. Actually, on my arithmetic that will be in 1980! What was not in the least fanciful about 1970 was that the firm produced 200 new titles and in 1971 over 225. It also has a backlist of 500, sales of which are high, and it is David's boast that he has never remaindered a book (that is sold it at a reduced price) since the firm started.

In the end the whole story comes back to books. How a small company tackled an established and entrenched book publishing industry, profited from the inertia of others, grasping opportunities which had previously gone unrecognised. David still thinks publishers are waiting for business to be lifted from them. There has been no real revolution in the book trade since Penguin and its paperbacks, and third or fourth generation publishers often seem to me more concerned with their social position in the publishing industry than with their books and businesses. 'Publishing was once classically a gentleman's occupation,' says David. 'Often authors, editors and publishers are all great chums and as a result books come out late, longer and more expensive than they should be.'

An important landmark, an indication of a firm's maturity as it changes from a cottage to a serious business base, is its attitude to risk. 'Any fool can publish cheap booklets involving no risk and therefore requiring no judgement, but we found the more adventurous we were the better we did,' says David. 'If flair in publishing means judgement then we proudly say this is one of the chief factors in the growth of the company. There's no point in being coy about it. We honestly believe we will outjudge any competitor.'

'We back our judgement, some people won't,' says David. 'We try not to get involved with outside opinions on books. If we did we would never publish enough of them. It is quite normal for one of our editors to sort out, fix and sign about twelve contracts in a month. We had one chap who came for an editor's job who told us that he had been hard pushed in his previous post, and he didn't want to do more than three. He didn't go down at all well.'

Ideas for books are the lifeblood of the firm. On the back of the David & Charles catalogue it says, 'If you have a book of our type in you, please write.' But a lot of ideas emanate from within the company, from reading newspapers, from discussions, from travelling about the country, even from relaxing in the proverbial bath. This was where David got an idea for a book called *Your Second Income*. So in the sparking and trading of ideas he and Pam are always on duty, even in the middle of a domestic discussion at home or on holiday.

In so far as they can escape the pressures of the business, Ipplepen, 5 miles from Newton Abbot, is where they do it. They love country life and try to keep Saturdays absolutely free to enjoy it, but by the time Sunday evening arrives they are back on the David & Charles wavelength again. During the week they tend to bring work home with them since there are always manuscripts to be read and book blurbs to be written. And those ideas keep insistently popping up all the time. I do not particularly want to parade my problems in the writing of this book, but just consider what happened. I took a train to Newton Abbot to write a bit in the *Sunday Times* about David. The next thing I knew I found myself in the close embrace of a book about small business which, in spite of its subject, turned out to be a bigger project than I had ever imagined. I found myself researching, interviewing, checking, cross-checking, even taking my typewriter on holiday with me. All because David had an idea. He really is a very persuasive and enthusing chap. The fact that there is a large lump in this book about him and his company is not in deference to his vanity, but more to my laziness having covered the ground already, and to the recognition that the story of David & Charles, from its wooden hut beginnings in Ipplepen to a company which will one day go public, is a classic of small business achievement.

Anyway his life is a turmoil of ideas, and there is scarcely a fragment of it which does not have a book in it somewhere. When he tells you of his ideas he sits in his office chair, hooking a leg over the arm, subsiding into a strange, sideways, half-keeled-over position, with a distinctive way of bringing his arm up in a half circle, resting his finger tips on his head. At home he extends his long limbs from the depths of an easy chair and rests his feet with unerring skill on the corner of the fireplace. I can report with understanding on this phenomenon because we elongated people have to arrange our bodies to best fit the corporate and domestic topography. But I bet David gets a book from someone out of this, something like a tall man's travelling companion, written by a tall man, for tall men, about tall men's trials and tribulations.

His life is also a turmoil of decision and action and David & Charles goes about its business at a sharp trot. The year 1970 provides a number of cases in point. It was the year the company ceased to be dependent on other publishers' distribution networks and set up its own. It also opened an office and bookshop in London, bought a south Devon printing works, and with it a local weekly newspaper, the *Dawlish Gazette*, which the ex-journalist twitching in the long fingers of David would have loved to have played with, except that his priority was running the whole of his show, not a tiny bit of it. It also undertook the distribution of books for the Smithsonian Institute Press in Washington, Augustus M. Kelley of New York and the International Wine and Food Society. It also negotiated a deal with Pan which gives the paperback firm the right to eight David & Charles titles each year.

In 1971 the company went into the book club business, adding a new dimension to its trading, giving it the prospect of growth in an area in which it was not represented, and also affording David not a little satisfaction because the club in question, Readers Union, once had Pamela as one of its subscribers. The company even appointed a part-time secretary in the United States. All told it was displaying definite symptoms of growth, and the intention to grow further. But in which direction is it going to grow? Like a lot of businessmen David finds this a hard question to answer. 'We don't really know ourselves, except for the next eighteen to thirty months. Thus we knew where we would be now two years ago. To promote ourselves with equal success overseas as we have in Britain would be more realistic, perhaps, than trying to grow larger here.' Pamela says that he is restless, has to try new things all the time. 'We don't want to be big for the sake of bigness but when you go on trying new things and being successful it is inevitable.' David says you get used to things changing from year to year. This year's problems will be different from last's. He reckons money is the easiest problem to overcome, keeping staff and customers alert to changing conditions is tougher, while the growing pains caused by pressure on space is the most acute problem of all. Basically it takes so long to either find or build suitable accommodation.

That he is the mainspring of his company is easy to see. He explains his job and reveals his style of management like this. 'We rely heavily on internal memo forms to give editors the authority to commit the firm financially, to tell production how to produce, for routine matters, often some very expensive ones including whether we should spend thousands of pounds on a title. We have a lot of company meetings on general policy and on the difficult books on which it is hard to make up one's mind. We have a lot of private discussions too.

'I regard myself as captain of the ship, and don't like to think I am the owner. Indeed I hate normal employer-employee relationships and employee mentality is a company joke. Many decisions are taken without my knowledge, but it is fairly well known what I care about. Accounting methods don't concern me in the least, but certain invoicing procedures do because they affect the speed of service, the availability of sales information, customer relations and so on. So a new accounts system could be installed without consulting me, while a relatively minor change in invoicing would be brought to me. People get to know what you are concerned with. Many "I propose to do so and so memos, OK?" only need rubber stamping. Where we have real differences of opinion everyone speaks and listens. I don't "win" much more often than others, but do occasionally overrule, having heard all the arguments for and against, but then I feel I have an obligation to explain patiently why I am doing so in considerable detail.

'The thing I often ask myself is what would happen if I were killed and how much does the company depend on me now. The answer I think depends on whether you mean keeping on going or growing. I'd be missed surprisingly little for everyday affairs, and it would grow somewhat by momentum as more and more authors offered manuscripts. There is plenty of skill to handle that. But I would be missed when a major cross-roads loomed ahead since I'm the chap who usually says let's be daring and adventurous. You can't arrange succession in my circumstances, but you can make sure the business wouldn't collapse like a pack of cards without you. It would carry on very happily in the same spirit but it wouldn't conquer so many additional fields.'

In a small firm the managing director's job is frequently a lonely one, especially when it is virtually a one man band. No matter how loyal staff are, there is a point at which you cannot discuss problems with them. When you get larger, have other executives around you, a lot of this loneliness disappears. In David's case he experienced it, but he was insulated from the worse excesses of it by Pamela. Even before their marriage they had this professional rapport. She was a librarian, and they met when David was researching in Plymouth Library. After they married he would often dash off a piece and leave Pamela to polish and tighten it up. Her experience as a librarian helped develop her critical faculties in judging whether a book was good or not. 'People in the library soon brought the bad ones back and complained they didn't tell them this or how to do that.'

David says that is the root reason why David & Charles books are good. Pamela, as editorial director, supplies a built-in quality control. Certainly she goes to inordinate lengths to get the books right editorially, writing long critiques of manuscripts with detailed suggestions on how they should be improved in every respect, from style to content. Books after all are the bricks the firm is built on.

David & Charles solidly base the business on individual books. 'A good book sells itself and this business is about books rather than money,' says David. 'It is fun making money with books on subjects you enjoy and which other people think you can't make money on.' It rather tickles him that he has often been congratulated on subsidising good books which were in fact making a profit. The books themselves may be more expensive than other publishers', but then they are better books, says David. Each one is conceived, nurtured, produced and sold as a thing in its own right. One of the snags is that books, like oysters, take a long time to mature, perhaps two years or more from the time someone sits down to write one until it appears on the booksellers' shelves. Books are a long-term project, and you have to be prepared to wait. It is no good getting impatient for a quick return. To David a successful book is one which does not reduce gross margins, one which will sell out if you price it correctly. A sale of 3,000 to 4,000 covers most David & Charles books, and the policy is to produce books which cover production costs and overheads within a few months rather than years. To expand rapidly the business needs cash and so there has to be a limited time in which money is locked up in a book, because David needs the same lump of money to finance possibly two, or even three, books over a period of ten to twelve months. One of the irritations of life is that he cannot pay out big enough advances to keep his authors going. 'When you are growing quickly you can't do that because of the strain on liquidity.'

Whether a book is financially successful depends first, in David's view, on whether it is editorially a good book, combined with whether or not it has been costed well. The trick is to avoid throwing away potential profits on good books which have not been costed well, which explains why there is a chartered accountant who is the firm's production executive. In a number of publishing houses the price of the book is finally decided by the sales department who price it in relation to the market at the moment, without thinking that in nine months to a year's time inflation will have started to make a nonsense of it. In David & Charles it is estimated by the production department, goes to company secretary Ken Davis who works out his own magical figures and from them tells David what he reckons the selling price should be. Sometimes David gauges they can get more than that for it, and they go for the higher price. They work closely with their suppliers of print and paper and have taken a leaf out of Marks and Spencer's book in the way they exercise quality control over the product. Suppliers are encouraged to query anything they think wrong and curious and in this way mistakes are often picked up before they become too expensive.

As a publishing house they do not have best sellers in the traditional sense of 50,000 sales in hardback. But they do have many books each season which do well at their price level and which often enjoy enduring sales for several years. The individual sales figures of books without considering their prices are not very relevant. 'How do you equate 15,000 copies sold of the paperback *Kings and Queens of England* with 5,500 of *Yesterday's Shopping: the Army and Navy Stores Catalogue for 1907*, the first selling at 45p, the second at £12.60?' he asks. The latter, of course, is a reprint, and in the early days reprints played an important part in bulking out the David & Charles list. But now the firm has substantially dropped publishing them. 'We don't need them as much, and in any case most of the best reprints have been done, and the reprint market is less exciting,' says David. In 1970 one third of the list was reprints. Now at most they account for about 10 per cent.

As an outsider you cannot but help notice how the three directors focus their attention almost solely on the business, giving it their undivided attention, paying scant heed to outside activities or social events. 'Myself, Pam and Ken are not terribly influenced by money and there is no pressure to climb the social ladder which is so expensive of time and energy when you are building a business,' says David. 'We don't go to conferences, none of us are members of any outside organisations, we don't play golf, and we don't wine and dine socially.' He counts it as lucky that publishing is alien to the area in which he operates, so they do not get involved. The local newspaper does not try to sell them advertising space because it just does not think of them as part of the local trading scene. 'This is right, because though we work in this town we are really selling books internationally,' says David. 'For us New York is more important than Newton Abbot.'

For the company it is a happy truth that many people, non-professional authors, write books, because they have something they want to say and for the sheer and intense satisfaction of seeing their work in print. With these money is very much a secondary consideration. It is precisely this band of people, often with expert knowledge of a subject and with an urge to communicate it, who are the foundation of David's list. They far outnumber well-known professional authors.

But should you be thinking about writing a book for David & Charles, on railways, say, for goodness sake do your homework properly, because David seems to be on personal terms with every bit of track from Newton Abbot to Inverness. His formidable expertise can leave untutored souls like me feeling very stupid. When he saw me off at the station the train came in from the opposite direction to which I had been looking. I should have guessed when I saw David St John Thomas peering up the other track. But then I think it has been demonstrated that he has a very considerable skill in making things move in the right direction.

Chapter 12

When opportunity knocks

There are many small business success stories which are not the fruits of long and best laid plans. Quite the opposite. They are much more the result of a wide-awake chap with entrepreneurial blood flowing in his veins getting a sudden whiff of an opportunity and swiftly acting to make the most of it. Norman Chalk's opportunity came when a very big business wanted a little business to do its cooking. Which is how Norman Chalk, who used to spend his evenings producing steak and scampi in a small restaurant he owned, became the largest caterer to Britain's North Sea Oil industry.

So much of business is sheer, rip-roaring opportunism: a matter of luck and happy circumstance, a matter of recognising something promising is happening under your nose and having the energy and drive to do something about it. The way Norman Chalk did when a friend said to him, 'Norman, have you heard about these Yanks who are drilling for oil in the North Sea. There's a big Texan, a nice, friendly fellow, looking for someone to do some catering for him.' It was the mid 1960s and at the time Norman Chalk was owner-manager-chef and chief bottle washer of a small restaurant at Acle Bridge where he spent his evenings cooking steak and scampi for the holidaymakers who came to sail boats on the Norfolk Broads.

Up to 1960 Norman had been a soldier, a boy entrant into the army at fifteen who did well for himself. He was commissioned into the Army Catering Corps but later resigned his captaincy because he found the prospect of another sixteen years, twelve of them at Aldershot, rather daunting. He came out thinking he was

God's gift to catering, expecting to be offered a highly paid job, and found it astonishing that the catering industry did not immediately recognise the incredible talent available to it. So he opened a restaurant for himself, doing moderately well, but by no means causing J. Lyons and Co any shudders of disquiet.

When he heard about the quest for oil in the North Sea he knew nothing about the stuff, other than you put it in your car engine every now and again. He had never seen an oil well, nor an oil rig, and the idea of prospecting for it off the Norfolk coast seemed to him . . . well, he thought, the experts must know what they are doing. They did. Six years later, by the beginning of 1971, North Sea gas was flowing into the national grid in ever increasing quantities; 20 per cent of the householders in the United Kingdom who used gas appliances had fires, refrigerators, cookers and central heating systems converted to take it; there were sixteen offshore rigs either drilling for oil and gas or pumping it ashore; the international oil business had invested millions of pounds in the search, and the old and decaying East Anglian herring fishing port of Great Yarmouth had been given a new lease of life as it became the main base for the industry. In June 1971, it was announced that new concessions were to be put up for auction by the British Government and it was calculated that by the 1980s the North Sea would yield three-quarters of the United Kingdom's oil needs. At the time of the announcement Norman Chalk was already the largest caterer, launderer, cleaner and general dogsbody to the offshore industry in the North Sea. His company, called Chalk Drillcater, had its own catering crews on ten rigs (there was another off the coast of South Africa), was turning over business worth more than a third of a million a year and making profits of £20,000. Norman was driving a splendid old Bentley instead of getting around in a mini-van, and his hair had turned several shades greyer than it had been when I first met him four years previously.

It had not taken him long to pass from what he describes as his 'dead ignorant period' on oil, to one where he saw its potential, and summed it up, with an earthy tinge of Norfolk in his voice, as 'the biggest thing to happen in these parts since thatching'.

Not quite how an economist would phrase it, but it was, and still is, a vivid and pertinent way of summing up an exceptional opportunity for a small businessman.

In business the motives for a man doing what he does cannot always be defined in a precise and measured way. Norman Chalk's opportunism was larded with a couple of other compelling spurs to action. The first was that he had just got married and the second was that the lease on his restaurant at Acle Bridge was due to expire. So he went to meet George Stetson, the big, affable Texan from the International Drilling Company who explained that his company was building a rig called the *North Star* on Clyde Bank, in the famous shipyard of John Brown, builders of the *Queen Mary, Queen Elizabeth* and *QE2*. 'He wanted to know whether I would quote for the catering, and I said, yes I would,' recalls Norman. 'But I was blind ignorant about oil, so I went to Norwich City Library to find out all I could about it.'

Norman was starting from scratch and had no one he could turn to locally for advice. As it was in those early days it looked as though Middlesbrough was to become the big base for North Sea exploration. Two other catering companies were already competing for contracts and one of them, Albert Abela, was part of a big Middle Eastern company which had been serving the needs of the international oil industry for years. Norman could hardly pick up the telephone and ask their people what he should charge per head for catering. There was only one thing he could do: use his common sense.

'I thought that because of the tough and demanding nature of the job, the weather they would be working in, the open air life and the size of the men, that they would all be very hungry when they finished their shifts on the rigs. The question was, how much food would a hungry oil man get through in a day?' Norman undertook a spot of market research, on himself, with his wife Hazel obligingly cooking the steaks, chops, bacon, eggs and vegetables which they considered a famished oil roughneck would devour. The answer came out at a convenient round figure, £1 at wholesale prices. Norman, straining a bit at the waistband, knew the men would have a hard job to eat more. He was, however, still faced with another unknown which in the catering business is a crucial one in terms of the difference between making profits and losses; the problem of wastage. There were even more imponderables. How much would labour cost? What were the rates for chefs and stewards on the rigs? He put an advertisement in the local paper for a chef and received seventy-four replies. As for the cost of cleaning materials, he toured the shops, did some mental arithmetic and finished up making a guess. On this basis he worked out his quotation. It was for £2 12s 6d or $6.30 per head per day.

Norman remembers the quote with great clarity. It was written on the headed notepaper of his restaurant at Acle Bridge and the date was 27 March 1965. 'By pure luck more than anything else it was dead right,' he says. It won him the contract for the *North Star*, and it was profitable. Later on he discovered that his competitors had quoted more, and he has little doubt it was his price that got him in.

For him the contract was a commercial landmark. It was also the start of his hair going grey. The euphoria of winning a £4,000 a month contract wore off and was replaced by worry as he tackled the problems of financing the operation, raising the money for wages and food. Like many a small businessman he soon discovered that having won a contract, it is all the more nerve racking to find yourself being pushed because of a shortage of working capital. Raising money to start something is one thing, to keep it ticking over quite another. When he started his restaurant Norman sold his car for £500 and borrowed £150 from a friend. Now, servicing the rig in John Brown's yard, travelling back and forth between Norfolk and Glasgow, the money was flowing out—and there was none flowing in. 'It just hadn't occurred to me that I would have to wait for my money,' he says. The trouble was that the contract had been signed, and Norman was too worried, too shy and felt he was too small to thump the table at the International Drilling Company's headquarters. So in June and July 1965 he suffered six excruciating weeks waiting for the cheque. His father, a butcher in Norwich, had supplied the meat on credit, £6,000 worth, and there were food bills of £12,000 owing. Each Wednesday Norman robbed the till of his restaurant, took the cash to Glasgow with him, working the men's paypackets out on the way. 'Somehow it always came out just right,' he says. 'But it really was very worrying. It was all hand to mouth. There was no control. I wasn't sleeping and Hazel wasn't getting her housekeeping.'

Eventually Norman sunk his diffidence and asked for his money. 'That's all right,' they said. 'We'll put a cheque in the post.' Norman had never had any real business training, but that was the day he learned a valuable lesson. Always ask for your money. The amount of the cheque sticks in his memory. It was for £6,900. 'What I found so frightening was that my creditors were not shouting or screaming, or putting on pressure, but just said, "Any sign of that cheque yet, Norman?" and when I said, "Afraid not," they just groaned a bit and looked disappointed. If things had gone wrong . . .' Chalk prefers to leave this ghastly thought unfinished.

Not all his problems were money ones. He was not familiar with the American way of eating and soon discovered that for an Englishman there were many esoteric gastronomic mysteries attached to it, far more demanding than straightforward hamburgers and coke. Oddly, the companies employing him would not specify the menus they wanted, so he learned very much the hard way that cooking for predominantly American crews meant keeping stocks of Louisiana hot sauce, and serving corn bread and hot pancakes for breakfast. Luckily Norman is the eager, hustling, zealous sort. There were times when he was to be seen questing about all over the place, even in Woolworths in Norwich, looking for toothpicks.

A few years later, in July 1969, he landed the contract for the catering during the 12,000 mile tow of the world's largest multipurpose barge, the *Choctaw*, when it was taken from Holland to join the gas search in the Bass Strait off Australia. By then he had learned enough about feeding oil crews (not just American ones either) to have 27 tons of stores on board, including hundreds of pounds of T bone steaks, 400 head of poultry, and 10,000 tea bags, in order to satisfy the nationally sensitive palates of Americans, Dutch, English, French and Scandinavians. But without doubt his highest accolade came with a contract to feed an all-French crew on a North Sea rig, using an English chef!

There is not much security of tenure about servicing the rigs. The first contract he signed was for thirty days, and his bank manager and his accountants did not like it. The contracts are still for thirty days, and the bank manager still does not like it. 'It is the sort of business in which it is very hard to borrow,' says Norman. 'Mostly you find yourself trading off your creditors and it is therefore very important that you have their confidence. The banks will not lend much unless you have reasonable assets. All we have is thirty-day contracts and a high-risk business. We are now working on an overdraft of £2,500. If we had more money at our fingertips I feel we could go after more contracts.'

Thus one of the biggest snags of the business is a shortage of working capital. Slow payment is still a problem. 'Of course, we have got to know the oil company accountants, and we can tell them we are a bit pushed, but it is not something you can do too often,' says Norman. So he and his accountants have become adept at juggling with his cash flow, making the tiny, detailed decisions like keeping half of a bill back, until so and so's cheque is in. Events like the postal strike in the early part of 1971 do not help. 'We had two £7,000 cheques stuck in the post, and this was the point when one of the accountants came in and asked me what the hell were we going to do,' says Chalk. 'In the event we went to London and begged for fresh cheques.'

Prospecting for offshore oil is unquestionably a business where the risks run beyond the normal ones you would expect on dry land. Many a hard-handed American oil man thought the North Sea would be a piece of cake. After their first winter there they rapidly changed their minds. It has had its share of violent storms, blow-outs and disaster, of rigs being damaged or lost, and men too. Good luck or bad luck are not entries easily made on a balance sheet to explain profits or losses, but in the oil business they count for a lot. Even when the surveys have been made, the geologists have pronounced, the consortia formed and a great tide of money poured into building rigs and operating them, there is still a large lump of luck in whether you hit oil or gas sufficient to work in commercial quantities. It is one of the reasons why oil men are always is so much of a hustle. Time is money, and if you get good luck you move fast to exploit it; bad luck, and you move even faster to escape it. If, like Norman, you are working for oil men it is a maxim which insinuates itself very rapidly into your business and profoundly influences the style in which you conduct it. The quayside at Great Yarmouth when the supply ships are coming in and going out is not an ideal environment for slow-moving yokels.

For one prospecting company there was ill-luck when a blow-out occurred on its rig, the *Unifor 1*, in February 1969. It was ill-luck for Norman too because it was a profitable contract, and it meant his men were off work for more than a month, which in turn meant there was no money coming in, money which had already been pledged to Norman's suppliers. But overshadowing everything is the constant anxiety of what would happen to his men if things really went wrong on one of the rigs. Fortunately he did not lose any in this particular accident, but when another rig had a blow-out one of his chaps risked his life to go back and get the takings from a small shop which they run on board. 'He came ashore and gave me £33 in wet, soggy notes,' says Norman. 'I said, "You bloody fool," but I could have kissed him.' Large-scale crises like this are not commonplace, but delays and frustration due to bad weather, especially in winter, are much more so. Norman's relief crews may have been standing by since early in the morning to go out to the rigs but have to kick their heels at the heliport because fog has stopped the helicopters flying. The decision has to be made whether to take them out by boat which takes much longer. So they set off, then the fog lifts and the boat is cancelled, and the men are shuttled back to the heliport. Even then the fog may have clamped down again. It is an expensive and irritating way to play ducks and drakes.

There are other snags, but these are bound up with the business itself, just how good the quality of the service is, how well it is run. The quickest way to spread disaffection, trouble, and near mutiny on a rig is by serving bad food. 'You have got to rely on your chef-manager who is out there when you are not,' says Norman. 'Put it another way, your company is only as good as your worst steward. If he doesn't clean, make the beds and tidy the cabins properly you are in trouble. To sort things out when they do go wrong isn't easy. You are operating at arm's length and on the helicopters the rig crews take priority, not the owner of a catering company, intent on bawling out his cook. So you have this big problem of communications. They are not the sort of problems you can resolve over the radio with the whole of the North Sea listening in.'

This is why Norman has done what no other North Sea caterer has. He periodically charters his own helicopter, and visits all the rigs in one day. With him go his base managers for supply and personnel, his financial director and a doctor to make tests on the food in the refrigerators. Even so the tour of each rig is speedy. 'You can't have your chopper sitting there taking up all the heli-deck in case they want to use it urgently,' says Norman.

Each mobile rig normally carries a crew of about fifty, while the production platforms (permanent structures used when a successful well is being commercially exploited, like *Amoco A, B,* and *C* in the North Sea) have fewer men on them. Norman's catering crews vary from eight men aboard the large rigs to two men aboard production platforms. He has always paid his staff more than the other catering companies, and because he has expanded so fast, has been able to offer them some prospect of promotion. He has sixty-eight offshore who work two weeks on, one week off, and about ten onshore. He likes to keep his onshore operation as lean as he can, even sharing a secretary with his fellow directors. Nowadays his offices are a bit more spacious than the room above his restaurant in Acle (not to be confused with the one he used to have at Acle Bridge, from which he operated for a long time). Actually when his partner, who runs the restaurant, goes on holiday, Norman takes his place there every evening, and cooks steak and scampi for the customers just as he did in the old days, and enjoys it. Interestingly, he kept his restaurants going, even though he was heavily committed to oil, because he was prudent enough to want something to fall back on if things had not gone well in the North Sea.

'Remember it was quite a time before they even found gas, and there were times when I thought the whole enterprise would be a short-lived one,' says Norman. 'Then they struck gas, and again, and again, and I began to realise that it was going to be a big business, and as a result neglected my restaurants. At one time he owned five, and they lost him £10,000 over two and a half years. Now he just has the one in Acle. 'Although the rig catering has reached a very comfortable stage, and the companies now come and ask us to tender, rather than we going to them, I still have it at the back of my mind that if everything all fell through, I could sit back and say, I've had an exciting time, worked hard, learned a lot, and then go back to cooking. Though sometimes I think, why do I go on doing this, and I suppose it's because I like being my own boss. I'm not tied to a treadmill routine and I can drop my own clangers.'

Now that the business has grown and he has learned to delegate, something he admits was not easy to do, he still gets a feeling of irritation sometimes that he is losing touch with the detail, getting away from the men who are actually doing the job, especially since he says his executives and staff give him such high-quality backing. He finds out, perhaps, that one of his stewards has had an advance on his wages, hears about it much later, and feels ashamed for not knowing the man needed it. On the other hand, before he acquired the knack of delegating, the strain of the business took its toll both on his staff, on him and his home life. 'I think it has become a happier company and I'm no longer a bear to live with. At one point Hazel told me I had better get a grip on myself or we had better split up,' says Norman. The strain which hazarded both business and marriage has passed and, says Norman, he has now made up his mind not to worry any more. He relaxes by taking two or three days off during mid week once a month, by renovating and restoring old horse carriages and coaches, and by spending time with his two small sons. He is comfortably off, has a nice house and car, but says that money no longer means all that much to him, whereas in the early days he was in it very much for the cash. 'I think I would rather finish this business voluntarily than sell out,' he says. 'My sons are six and four and a half, and, you know, I have not met many rich men's sons who were really happy.'

If he has one short-term ambition it is that he would like to take six months off and visit the United States, but ask where he sees himself going and he says quite honestly, 'I wish you wouldn't ask that, I really don't know.' If he has a precise objective for his company, it is not to be the biggest offshore caterers in the world, but the best. 'I don't think this is impossible, and in many ways it boils down to watching a man eating one of your meals and then hearing him say, "I really enjoyed that." This brings great satisfaction to me.'

Inevitably because of its size, its sophistication and being accustomed to operating on a grand scale, in everything from money to equipment, the oil business imposes sustained pressures on the small company running hard to keep up with it. By its international nature it forces a man like Norman to face up to the decision, sooner or later, of whether he is going to become international too. And it is not easy. Oil companies have the resources, the back up and team operations which make the other side of the world seem like the next parish. Chalk Drillcater does not. So when a rig moves and the rig boss says, 'Norman, we're off to the Far East—you coming to do the chow?' that simple, friendly question throws up all the disadvantages of being small, not having the money to speculate with or the men to second. None the less for a red-blooded opportunist like Norman, as the oil business moves there is a compulsion to move with it. It would be a formidable test for any company, let alone a small one from a small neck of the Norfolk woods. The test really is daunting because for a small business, being in its local market gives it a competitive edge. It gets its supplies and labour locally and it is run locally. But as soon as it moves from its own patch, the specific local advantages are lost and it finds itself operating in a big league, competing in an alien environment against others with all the advantages of working on their home ground. If it survives doing this it deserves to get bigger, but it must have a lot of strengths working for it, other than knowledge of local conditions.

Norman already has subsidiary companies in Holland, Norway and South Africa. When I talked to him early in 1971 he was bidding for a possible contract to supply three linked fixed platforms off the Norwegian coast, a job which would involve feeding nearly 300 men. He was also very tempted by an exciting operation off the coast of North Borneo. The shore basc would be miles from the nearest rail head. Real adventure story, head-hunter country, was how Norman described it. 'But it is going to cost us £1,000 to find out whether it is worth putting a bid in,' he says. It is one thing to serve the best T-bone steaks in the North Sea when you are sitting on the edge of it. It is quite another, and takes a deal more management skill to do it, and do it well and profitably, in the South China Seas.

Among the thousands of men who run small businesses Norman is by no means exceptional in that he has had no formal business training. 'I am very conscious of my own limitations and the fact that I act on impulse and hunch,' he says. 'But having said this, if there is one overridingly important lesson I have learned, it is that you must have some sort of control, some management information system to tell you what is happening when you want to know, not when it is too late to act upon it, and that is why we now have twice-monthly accounting instead of hastily scribbled calculations and surmises on the backs of old envelopes.

'I think perhaps one of my biggest weaknesses is the way I change my policy and ideas with the state of the accounts. If they come out bad, I am all for cutting back, holding things up, consolidating. If they are good I'll say let's go ahead and do this or that. It worries me because I reckon the boys in the offices next door must get thoroughly fed up with me for chopping and changing like that.' It is odd that Norman sees this as one of his weaknesses. There are many who would argue a diametrically opposite case. One of the great strengths of a small business is supposed to be its adaptability, the way it reacts quickly to changing circumstances, how it trims its sails to the changing wind. In the North Sea offshore oil business, where the wind frequently blows unpredictably, Norman seems to me to be a very handy bloke to have at the helm.

At about the same time Norman Chalk was starting to exploit the opportunity which suddenly appeared off the seashores of eastern England, there were a couple of men doing precisely the same on the seashore on the opposite side of the country. Although it is doubtful whether even the most imaginative observer could have reconciled the sight of two men picking up stones on New Brighton beach in the early hours of one bitterly cold winter's morning with a piece of business opportunism. In fact this seemingly eccentric excursion was the beginning of a new business based on serving the needs of science and scientists ranging from sixth formers in school chemistry labs to chemists in giant oil refineries.

The two men, Ken Jones, a research chemist, and Derek Hilton, a one-fifth partner in a laboratory equipment company, wanted stones to make their own ball mill, a device of somewhat greater capacity than a pestle and mortar, but designed to do the same job; to crush materials down to a fine and consistent powder. In their case the powder was made from, among other things, a variety of crushed firebricks and was needed as a 'support' material in an instrument known as a gas chromatograph. It is used in a technique of chemical analysis (invented by two British scientists in 1952) known as 'gas chromatography'. Nowadays, to the delight of Jones and Hilton, gas chromatography is a standard technique in chemical research laboratories throughout the world, and is probably the most widely used of all analytical methods.

It is important because it is accurate, rapid (it can achieve in a day what might have previously taken a week or a month), it is capable of analysing practically any gaseous or liquid sample, and it can be easily automated which is obviously important in its industrial application. Not only can a gas chromatograph tell you what a substance is made from, but it can help determine where it was made and how old it is. One of its most recent and famous (or infamous, depending how you look at it) applications is in the analysis of blood samples taken after breathalyser tests on motorists. It can also be used as a technique in pregnancy testing, though in this instance it cannot tell you where it happened!

In many respects the company Jones and Hilton started, Phase Separations, is almost an archetype of a highly specialised firm which has grown up on the back of a developing area of science. It has men running it who belong very much to a new and growing breed of businessmen, the scientist-entrepreneurs, who, in an age when man has set foot on the moon, are increasingly making their mark in corporate life. But at the time, foraging on the beach, sitting in the garages of their homes, sieving materials till the small hours of the morning until they looked like dusty Rip Van Winkles, it was scarcely the role in which they would have seen themselves cast. Certainly neither of them realised quite what a fast-growing enterprise they were founding.

When the company won its first 17s 6d order its principals were suffering too severely from a dose of euphoria to make any clear-sighted claims about the future. For at the time selling 17s 6d worth of chemicals for a gas chromatograph machine seemed a major marketing triumph. In its first week of business it took £30. In its second £150. At the end of the first six months, with its two founders still running it on a spare-time basis in the evenings and at weekends, it showed a turnover of £2,000. By the end of the first year it had reached £14,000 and then it rocketed upwards—to £52,000 in the second year of operation; £100,000 in the third.

In its fourth year of operation the company deliberately limited sales to £130,000 instead of going for the original target of £180,000. The money it would have cost to achieve the £50,000 extra sales was put into research and development instead. Already it has had to move premises twice since it left the £1 a week lock-up shop it started in and the four men who run it, Jones, Hilton, Peter Bonnett (the sales and marketing director to whom much of the credit for the second year's jump in sales is due), and Derrick King, the technical director, are now moving into areas of new technology based on certain aspects of gas chromatography. With the addition of these new developments they have set themselves a sales target of £1·5 million in 1975. They have made a name for themselves in what is, after all, a somewhat esoteric world and they believe they stand out as a small company which can still give a more personal and motivated service than their competitors.

'We are the supermarket for chromatography supplies. We remain completely updated in technology in our own right without waiting for a customer to request new products and we back it up with probably the most experienced application team in the country,' says Jones. 'The latter would be too expensive to maintain under normal circumstances, but since most company members have been or are currently practising chromatographers, this is not a problem.'

Their initial success was very much due to spotting a gap in the market. When he was studying for his PhD, Jones built a gas chromatograph for himself because they were too expensive to buy. Today the company's standard instrument is under £300, which they reckon is where a large lump of the UK market lies. Not with machines ranging from £500 to £2,000 which is what some of their competitor's products cost.

The effectiveness of the gas chromatograph depends on one expendable component, a separating column of diatomaceous earth, a highly porous, granular, inert material on to which a specific chemical is absorbed, which is packed into metal or glass tubes and through which the gas and sample to be analysed is passed. The complete column usually costs between £3 and £20 depending on its length. While most instrument manufacturers provide a column service for their own instruments, consistency from instrument to instrument, so important in this technique, was lacking. It was the need for a common reference point for supplies which was, for Phase Separations, an exploitable market gap. So the company commenced trading on the basis of weaning the practising chromatographer from established American trade-named materials to its own cheaper, newly developed products, offering them as alternatives to imported raw materials. For a company formed on £100 capital and a £200 overdraft secured on a second mortgage on the founders' homes it was a formidable task.

The directors soon discovered that business success can be accompanied by some agonising stresses. They found themselves in the classic dilemma of a fast-growing company. Business was booming, almost running away with itself. In their anxiety to meet orders they over-ordered on materials and then found they could not get their money in fast enough to meet their liabilities, a familiar enough phenomenon in times of squeeze and freeze. 'I had to go round and tell people we would be out of business if they didn't settle,' says Bonnett. Although most of them were very good about it, the bank finally had to come to the rescue and gave them a £2,000 overdraft in return for a personal surety on their homes. Acutely conscious that they were under-capitalised and without effective stock or cost control systems in operation, they attended a course of evening classes in the winter of 1967–8 which one of their wives had seen advertised in the local paper. 'Business Principles for the Small Company' the advertisement said. They attended the course for one night a week throughout the winter months. 'Every time the lecturer opened his mouth we knew we had made another mistake and nudged each other under the desks,' recalls Hilton. Now they are wiser and have taken steps to see that the flow of management information they need to take decisions is forthcoming. They have their fingers on so many pulses in the business that if they did go bust it would not be for the lack of knowing why.

The unnerving revelations of the evening classes caused each one of them to study intensively a particular area of finance and to become a multi-disciplinarian. 'No matter how good a scientist/engineer/marketing man one is, without a deep knowledge of finance to guide you, separate disciplines become less than useless,' says Jones.

They all learned the lesson of overtrading staggeringly well and think it has contributed a great deal to their present success. They have a daily accountancy system, each director receiving a statement of the day's trading (with cumulative totals), including turnover, gross and net profits, and operating costs and bank balances. Every new employee is quantified in terms of potential profit. Research and development expenditure is monitored weekly and the company's corporate plan, which is vigorously applied, is reviewed quarterly. The firm's debit-credit ratio has been reduced, and still is being reduced, by taking a tough line with companies which will not or cannot pay within the trade credit terms allowed. All this, of course, is time consuming and expensive in man hours but without it the company would not be able to maintain its competitiveness in the market place, which is where it matters most. The firm readily concedes that it has been fortunate in having bankers who have been kind to it. Even so the men who run it are the sort who, when things were going wrong, had the wit and intelligence to go and learn from other people—and then come back and put their house in order. Nor are they the sort content to rest on the one opportunity which got them off the ground. For them the Common Market and the steady build up of the new, technically based anti-pollution 'industry' offers further scope for satisfying exercises in opportunism. Nevertheless it would be wrong to suggest their development is a matter of chance. Phase Separations, as befits the men who run it, is a bit more subtle and scientific than that. What they do is to prepare the ground to make sure they can take advantage of the opportunities when they occur. Which is why in 1970 they spent £19,000 on research and development, a very high percentage from the income of such a small company, and which reduced their profits for that year to about £4,000, but then that is one of the advantages of having no outside shareholders to answer to.

The reasoning behind this high research and development expenditure was simple. To start with the enormous growth in standard gas chromatograph instruments had slowed, and had fallen to about 15 per cent a year. Originally the company had intended to develop its relatively simple instrument to more sophisticated levels. But a spot of market research among customers showed that the existing instruments were perfectly adequate for many analyses; their price was right and, in any case, there was already an adequate choice of instruments at the more expensive and sophisticated level. The company's reputation was centred on providing low-cost products and to have gone up the market would have meant re-educating the customers to more expensive jobs which gave the same quality, reliability and service as the competition's equipment. Clearly this was a more difficult course than exploiting a market gap where no instruments existed before. This, in essence is why the firm spent £19,000 on research in 1970 on the topical subject of pollution analysis. The argument was that patented and exclusive instrumentation, developed within the firm, would allow it to escape from its low-cost reputation and provide sufficient profit to finance the development of further ideas of its own staff as well as the many offered to it by customers.

'We believe the British are still the most inventive nation in the world,' says Jones. 'If we can generate sufficient funds and reputation before the Common Market becomes a reality we will slaughter the opposition.'

At the time of writing Jones and his fellow directors had registered two new companies, Pollution Analysers and Environmental Analysis, which they were rather tickled about because they are generic names, as synonomous with their function, as Hoover is synonomous with vacuum cleaners. The first company will construct the instruments, the second provide the service and applications. Prototypes of the analysers were being field tested, and some pre-production models were almost ready for measuring car and diesel exhaust gases. Others were being developed for measuring water pollution, their advantage being that they took two and a half minutes to make an analysis, could distinguish organic and inorganic pollution and could be fully automated for industrial use. This compares with the present almost universal method of measurement, known as 'biological oxygen demand', which takes about five days for each analysis.

Understandably the directors were excited about their future and relentless about getting where they want to go. It's only a short span of time since Hilton was a £20 a week partner in a laboratory equipment company, Bonnett a salesman with Air Products, Jones still studying for his PhD, and King in the electronics business. That now seems far behind them with a lot of experience in between. Today they can look back on the discomforts of pebble picking with comfortable equanimity. But when it comes to new opportunities, they look forward to those with a wide awake restlessness. For they have demonstrated, like Norman Chalk, that when opportunity knocks, the trick is to answer the door swiftly and invite it into the parlour.

Chapter 13

Try and think of something new

Considering their size small firms have a very good record for invention and innovation. The young science or technology based business is typical of the age in which we live and it demonstrates that it is the application and relevance of invention to business situations and opportunities which is important for the national well-being, rather than just the capacity to invent. This is a point not always grasped by those with a facility for thinking of something new. But in this chapter the people producing a new sort of garden irrigation system, a new sort of boat and a new sort of money all seem to understand it perfectly.

EVERY time you pull out the bath plug and watch the water gurgle down the waste pipe you should think of Sidney Searle, his daughters and his garden irrigation system. Sidney's idea, which was intended to make his garden grow better, is uncomplicated, homely and eminently sensible; but it scarcely ranks with the flashes of visionary insight which have given the world the great and glamorous inventions of penicillin, the jet engine and the hovercraft. Very few inventions do. When you look round our highly scientific and technological world it is plain that revolutionary inventions of the calibre of the steam engine are getting few and far between and, although the overall rate of invention is increasing, it is minor inventions which are becoming more frequent, while major ones are on the decrease.[1] There is still scope, however, for the man with the inventive mind, especially if he devises some highly marketable product, or markedly improves what already exists, or develops a new way of making it more cheaply.

Sidney Searle's idea was to irrigate the garden with his bathwater. It has a large measure of appeal to people like you and me because we can use it to our own benefit, and, on a loftier plane, it enables the ordinary man in his bath to do his bit for conservation. It is a definite improvement on bathwater being allowed to run to waste down the sewers and, more to the point, it has clear commercial possibilities, especially in the more arid areas of the world hard hit by drought and water shortages. In short it is the sort of innovation for which a manufacturer can see a market and some prospect of an ultimate pay off. Which is why one of Britain's leading firms of irrigation engineers, Cameron Irrigation of Littlehampton, Sussex, is marketing an irrigation system based on Sidney's patents.

At first sight the outstanding objection might be that dirty bathwater, laced with Palmolive or Pink Camay, filmy with exotic bath oils, scented with bath salts, might be injurious to the cabbages and the chrysanthemums. But according to Sidney, who has made exhaustive tests in his own garden at Birdham, near Chichester, the same phosphates from soaps and detergents which pollute the seas, which even now are destroying marine life in the lower depths of the Baltic, can be utilised by land plants as essential fertiliser. What better way of spreading it and saving water than his system?

Basically it consists of a link from the bathroom waste outlet to a simple filter box, through which the warm, soapy water passes on its way to a storage tank. A special type of syphon in the tank automatically picks up the water and feeds it to 'trickle' irrigation lines, where the water drips out of nozzles set at intervals along the hose. Sidney's researches show that healthy plants, like grass or trees, fully covering the soil surfaces, remove up to 1in of water from the soil in a week during spring and summer in order to maintain maximum growth. This is equal to $4\frac{1}{2}$ gallons to the square yard, or 100 tons of water to the acre. So even a quite small back garden can benefit from all the waste water a bath can supply. Man benefits because anything which helps green plants grow and provide and maintain the essential oxygen in the atmosphere will help the cause of anti-pollution. Sidney says he got the idea, not in his bath, but because of his daughters' baths. When they were all at home together they seemed to live in the bathroom, and waste water was forever disappearing down the plug hole in a continuous stream. He has even worked out that ideally you need 25 to 30 daughters to the acre in southern England to get the best results!

The trials which he conducted showed that in no case was warm, soapy water harmful to plants, and in a number of cases the plants grew better than those watered with identical quantities of tap water at the same temperature. He argues that this is partly because it contains essential phosphates, and because the action of soap and detergents reduce surface tension in the soil. This is significant since it probably assists the plants to extract moisture from the soil more readily than they might otherwise be able to.

Whether Sidney's small piece of original thinking will do as much for mankind as penicillin is arguable. It may become a raging success and make the name of Sidney Searle known in every corner of the universe where people are accustomed to pulling out bath plugs. On the other hand, like so many innovations it may prove commercially insubstantial and short lived. Great tracts of the inventive landscape are littered with inventions which fall into this category. It is one of the hazards of being an innovator, and one of the risks which firms which back them have to be prepared to take.

None the less the successful application of invention to the commercial world can have an enormous impact on the growth and profits performance of a company. It can take it from kitchen table beginnings to public flotation. It can catapult it into the larger leagues of business, and it can make a fortune for that rarest of birds in business, the successful inventor-entrepreneur. A man like Demetrius Comino, an engineer who had a very simple idea and invented Dexion Slotted Angle, a meccano-like construction system which has had tremendous world-wide success. Or a man like John Davies, a freelance print designer, who developed a form of instant lettering which he called Letraset which also became a world-wide best seller. The sequel to producing such highly original and commercial products is that imitators come on to the market with their version of the product, and it often happens that companies who depend for their fortunes on a single piece of technology which they developed find themselves involved in costly world-wide litigation protecting their patents. This raises the whole question of whether the patent system affords the protection it should. This, however, is part of another long and complicated story. In practice, actions which are fought on the basis of a country's patent laws are all part and parcel of the groundswell of technological change, part of the vitally important process of diffusion by which innovations are adopted and copied and spread across the industrial spectrum. Sometimes the imitators go on to better a product or technique and the pioneers then find themselves lagging behind.

To the nation the importance of invention is quite explicit. Without it technological change would be impossible, and since economic growth depends on technological change, on being able to produce more existing products more efficiently or cheaply and a range of completely new ones as well, the part played by invention in the growing prosperity of a country is crucial. Invention for the sake of invention contributes little to economic growth, and inventions with maximum market and commercial potential are usually those which solve previously unsolved problems. The laser is a brilliant invention, but it is still basically an invention which is seeking markets and worthwhile applications. Original though it is, people have still not found sufficient problems for it to solve.

In the last analysis it is the application of invention to business situations which counts in terms of national well-being rather than the mere capacity to invent. This is what innovation is all about and in Britain it is something at which we have not always been awfully good. According to past experience we are good at invention but poor at exploiting it. Too often the fruits of our native ingenuity have been enjoyed by others rather than ourselves. A notable and historic example of this is the work which the nineteenth-century physicist, Michael Faraday, did on the chemistry and physical properties of optical glass. Because of the dilatoriness of British industry in grasping the importance of it, it was allowed to become the basis for Germany's thriving optical industry. A more recent and traumatic loss in the field of invention which still rankles was the discovery of penicillin by Alexander Fleming. The way in which this was lost to America is a sad and bitter story. The result was that we, as a country, eventually had to pay the Americans thousands of pounds for the licences and know-how to produce the drug here. Disagreeable episodes like this partly explain why there is now in existence a government-backed body like the National Research Development Corporation which is charged with funding, supporting and exploiting the fruits of British invention in the national interest. Much has been done in the last twenty years to foster and encourage a climate conducive to invention, but this does not mean that all that could be done is being done. There is many an inventor who, given half a chance, is liable to grip you by the tie and tell you so.

The outstanding and classic difficulty of an inventor is getting his idea off the ground, of seeing it established in a commercial context. Partly this is the fault of inventors themselves, many of whom are determinedly obsessive about their brainchild but positively childlike in their understanding of its commercial viability, or indeed what it takes to make it commercially viable. The reason why merchant bankers are sometimes observed semaphoring help signals to their colleagues with their eyebrows while in the company of an inventor, is usually because the latter has just not bothered to undertake the elementary business research which launching his product demands. Bankers, on the other hand, have been known to be less than enthusiastic when even reassuringly common-sense inventors have knocked on their doors. If there is a general lesson to be learned from all this it is probably that it is better for an inventor to get his invention off the ground commercially, albeit in quite a modest way and to establish some sort of track record. He will then find the lending institutions more disposed to listen to him than if he were solely hawking an idea. Possibly it is this lack of understanding of each other's problems which produces such markedly unhelpful attitudes in the cause of invention. The key to this question is the creation of the right climate for investment in innovation. 'The classical problem of the inventor is how to get support for his brainchild on any terms, not to get a fairer share of their results,' says William Kingston in *Invention and Monopoly*.[2] 'His classical situation is to have 100 per cent of nothing.' There is a very human reason why businessmen do not fall over backwards at every invention which comes along. Quite simply this is because they are cautious. They know that backing inventions is a risky business. They know the chances of finding a winner are slim. Out of 7,400 fully developed inventions which arose out of government research in the United Kingdom in the seventeen years between 1949 and 1966 less than 5 per cent became established industrial products.

For the inventor, the first foray into the world of finance and business sometimes produces a chastening truth. It is very hard for him to grasp that in commercial terms, vital though his idea may be, it is only a small part of the whole and is of secondary importance to a number of other critical attributes; technical skill, market awareness and commercial ability. All are needed to make an invention into a business. This point is made in a booklet called *Making an Idea into a Business*, published by Technical Development Capital.[3] This also says it is not difficult to see cases where the commercial handling of an outstanding invention has been poor, thus resulting in poor commercial business. 'On the other hand, a second-rate idea well handled can lead to the development of a fine company. And it is companies we are concerned with, not just the brilliance of ideas,' says the author. Technical Development Capital, a subsidiary of the Industrial and Commercial Finance Corporation, is a financing institution whose aims are to ensure that worthwhile technical innovation in the private sector of British industry is commercially developed and exploited, and that its management is not thwarted through lack of financial support.

Despite the difficulties inventors continue to invent, and a good thing for industry that they do. Precisely who the inventors are and where inventiveness is most prevalent in industry is a subject which has fascinated a number of researchers. You might expect that large firms, with substantial research and development budgets, would be a hot house of new ideas and developments but it does not seem to work like that. The larger firms, for a variety of reasons (ranging from the management's reluctance to disrupt an established way of doing things to being answerable to a board of directors for an innovation which did not work) are not therefore the begetters and architects of innovation which many people imagine. Innovation inertia in large companies is by no means an unknown phenomenon. Incredibly there was a time when computers were rejected by IBM, the Polaroid camera by Kodak, and the jet airliner for civilian passengers by the Boeing, Douglas and Lockheed aircraft companies.

Often it is the actions of small firms, darting into the market with a new machine or product, undercutting the large concern and taking sales from it, which forces the industrial giant to bestir itself and react to what is happening. This busy, cheeky gadfly approach possibly contributes more to large companies overcoming inertia in the field of innovation than any self-generated, internal drive. There is mounting evidence to suggest that in the innovative league table it is individuals and small firms which are at the top, especially during a period of rapidly advancing technology. The period when the pace is so fast that large firms, constrained by and committed to huge investments in existing production lines, cannot respond in the flexible manner of the small concern to all the opportunities which present themselves. In such a climate it is not unusual to find small firms excelling in sectors such as instrumentation and electronics, which are rich, demanding and specialised markets. In highly specialist scientific or technological areas the small company is quite often unbeatable. It has a command of expertise, a reputation for advanced thinking, an aptitude for innovation, and a degree of high-level personal contact between it and its customers—often with scientist-owner talking with scientist-manager—which gives it an enormous edge. Doubtless large companies if they set their minds to it could put it out of business, but the market the small company serves may be so small and specialised that it wouldn't interest them anyway, and they have more to gain by allowing it to exist and produce for them or service them far more efficiently than they could themselves.

One authority claims that 80 per cent of the brilliant creative inventions spring from individual inventors or from inventors in small organisations.[4] Others have underlined the theme, arguing that small businesses are responsible for an important portion of the significant inventions and significantly larger percentages than their small investment in research and development would suggest.[5]

To many inventors the idea of even a modest research and development budget is something they would regard as major beneficence. With little or no money both they and their invention soldier on through long, difficult development years. Somehow they survive the despair and disappointments, as prototype follows prototype and backers are impossible to find, and when found, often come in and go out again, with what to the inventor appears unseemly haste. If inventors had any idea of the frustrating time lag between inventing something and seeing it translated into a commercial reality, it is possible they would not have embarked on the course they did. On the same score the time lag between expenditure and money flowing in adds to the delay and frustration. Unless a small undercapitalised company is successful in securing outside backing, the chances of getting its invention off the ground are substantially reduced.

John Cann, an engineer who lives in Axminster, Devon, a long time ago hit upon the idea of a car turntable for private homes. His turntable seemed a viable idea. It opened up new possibilities for architects faced with space problems when designing blocks of flats or houses on small, restricted sites, and for people in existing homes with the same problems, it offered the possibility of building a garage in a position which normally would not allow you to drive your car into it. It was really Cann's discovery that it is illegal to back your car out on to a main road which sparked off the idea for the turntable. In particular, in his own hilly part of the West Country there are many homes with garages cut into steep, hillside locations where this is a specific problem and where, in his view, the car turntable would fulfil a long felt need.

His Axess Turntable is simple, easy to operate, easy to install and is built on the see-saw principle, thus removing the problems of stones and dirt which might get under a disc turntable. It consists of two wide steel runways built on a steel frame which pivots. As the car approaches its front wheels depress the two runways, and the rear wheels run on before the weight of the vehicle makes the end touching the ground see-saw upwards. Once the car is on the turntable, strong coil springs beneath it hold it level. The whole unit revolves on a bearing and is easily turned.

He first thought of the idea for the turntable in 1966. The following year he went to the motor show in London, talked to various exhibitors and outlined his idea to them. They all thought it had potential and told him as far as they knew there were no car turntables on the market for private homes quite like this. Later a patent search confirmed this view. For John and his wife there followed an enormous amount of research and burning of midnight oil in the office and workshop in a shed at the bottom of his garden.

His own engineering drawings for the turntable ran to sheet after sheet as the design was modified, changed and refined. There was a huge pile of work involved in tabulating and collating the specifications of British and foreign cars so that he could be sure the turntable would be suitable for most makes. John had little capital—just a few hundred pounds. A local farmer said he would help financially and Cann built the prototype of the turntable on his farm in 1967. But then the farmer backed out and Cann was left with what he was convinced was a winner, but no money to develop it further. 'I tried everywhere for financial backing. My solicitors who were enormously interested in the idea tried too. All I wanted was £2,000 to buy back the prototype from the farmer and get on with developing it. In industrial terms that's not a huge amount, but in the West Country it was,' he says.

It took him two years before he secured further financial backing from a retired businessman. A partnership was formed, but later the businessman pulled out because there was a limit to his funds. John had no capital and the intention was that he would pay back his partner from future profits. While he was spending time and energy on developing and improving his invention there was, of course, no money coming in, and to support himself and his wife he produced hand-made coffee tables, with county or country maps carved on the top of them. But although they were satisfying to make, the tables were not very profitable as a basis of a small craft business. This is one of the reasons why John has this compulsion to get the turntable into production. 'We have struggled on making coffee tables and it has become a matter of necessity,' he says, and there were periods when the turntable took so much of his time that his wife had to remind him to get on with the tables to bring some money in. John is still working on his invention, still has fervent hopes that one day Axess Turntables will be on sale, but there are times when as an inventor-cum-small businessman he must wonder if it will ever get beyond a pipe dream.

While John Cann's inventiveness has still to be judged in commercial terms, he and other individual inventors like him are cast in important roles in the scenario of invention. Without them and their original thinking, whether directed towards a modest, utilitarian product like a car turntable or a piece of major technology like the jet engine and the hovercraft, the world would be a poorer place. Yet it is important to realise that a large wedge of invention and innovation falls under the general umbrella of improvement, of achieving greater technical excellence and efficiency in a product than before, of being able to make it more cheaply, or being able to make it on a greater scale than hitherto. Sometimes a contemporary innovator comes along and by dint of patience, hard work and lots of faith, puts an entirely new gloss on a half forgotten technique. He develops and perfects it so that it has clear and apparent market advantages, and by the quality of his improvement carves out a specific market for it. And, again, as we have seen so often in this book, the course he follows and the decisions he takes are inextricably tangled with very personal considerations.

Such innovation sometimes comes in strange guises. A persuasive nephew encouraged Donald Hagenbach to take some perfectly ordinary building materials, some commonplace tools and equipment, some traditional craft skills and an idea which was by no stretch of the imagination new, and build a boat. It was not so much a question of innovation as renovation, for the idea had been around for more than 150 years. As it happens Donald has renovated it to such effect that if the world wants to do what he does so successfully, it has to beat a path to his boatyard in Wroxham, Norfolk, and buy a licence and the know-how from him.

His is a very traditional-looking boatyard, an 8 acre jumble of boat houses, mooring basins and building sheds with creosoted wooden walls, green corrugated iron roofs and red brick offices. In one of these offices, one which has its windows overlooking a stretch of water where a fleet of hire cruisers were once moored, papers and files spill out in some disarray over the desk, on to the chairs and the window sill. Here you will find Donald Hagenbach, a bulky, deliberate, courteous man, sixty-one years old, the son of a Swiss father and Scots mother, who once practised as a solicitor in Wakefield, but didn't much care for it. Now he is a boat builder and the craft he builds are not made of wood, fibre glass, or steel as you might expect, but in concrete. Nowadays his small yard is the world centre of this uncommon and surprising craft.

When he started in the early 1960s half the shipwrights in his yard, born and bred to building in wood, to fashioning and shaping craft with traditional boatbuilding tools like the adze, thought he had gone mad. When the first cement mixers started to arrive they were convinced. The other half had what he describes as a touching faith in the 'governor', but outsiders were less than encouraging.

Donald was splendidly philosophical about the reaction. After all it took a long time to convince *him* that it was not a zany, hair-brained excess from the fertile mind of his civil engineer nephew Paul Hagenbach. He can, of course, afford to be philosophical now because there's nothing like starting something new and making it work convincingly both technically and commercially. It has taken time, perhaps longer than Donald originally thought, but when you build small boats you are in an industry where old attitudes die hard, where the old way of doing things are enshrined in men's memories. It takes time and patience to persuade a man working with well tried and tested shipwright's tools to move to mixing machines and trowels. Buyers are cautious too, though it is more than conservatism which explains why Donald's concrete boats did not explode into a major industry overnight. For it happened that at the same time as he was developing concrete boats for the commercial market glass reinforced plastic was making its own competitive revolution.

Glass reinforced plastic, or fibre glass, offered the opportunity for volume production, and product and brand development in boats, which it is hard to achieve with wooden hulls. It has given the small boat building business a great shove, away from its cottage industry roots to something near to industrialisation. In 1960 only 20 per cent of the boats at the London Boat Show were in glass reinforced plastic. Ten years later the figure was over 60 per cent. Now although the bulk of Donald's business is building commercial concrete boats (charter craft, fishing trawlers, pontoons, barges and so on), it is none the less true that glass reinforced plastic has overshadowed much of what has been happening in the boatbuilding business in the last few years. Even so, when you watch Donald's men putting the finishing touches to a 65ft motor yacht, the largest in the world to be built in concrete, with a gang of local plasterers using their skills to put a fine finish on the hull, you begin to wonder if concrete might not change all that.

To you, to me and to them it *is* concrete, but Donald and his technical chaps describe it more properly as marine ferro-cement, or by the apt trade name they have given it, Seacrete. Whatever you call it, it is still made the same way, in a cement mixer, with sand, cement, water and a special additive which gives the cement plasticity and adhesive qualities. The mix is applied to several layers of special steel mesh manufactured to Donald's own specification and it took 14½ tons of Seacrete to make the 65ft motor sailer. (Only five years ago Donald would hardly have dared to tackle a boat of this size: now there are plans for a 90ft fishing vessel.) It all sounds incredibly simple, but it has taken him and his team ten years to arrive at their present point, which, they claim, is far ahead of anyone else in the world in marine ferro-cement technology. For a small firm it has been a courageous and financially demanding piece of innovation. It took a long time to perfect the product, because the scale of research funds which might have been available in a large concern were just not forthcoming from what is still essentially a family boatbuilding business in Norfolk.

Until 1960 Donald's yard, Windboats of Wroxham, was similar to dozens of others on the Norfolk Broads, building boats during the winter months and chartering them out by the week and fortnight in the summer. Donald came to Norfolk from the West Riding of Yorkshire after World War II, and bought the yard because he felt it would be a more agreeable existence for him, his wife and children than living in Wakefield where he was in practice as a solicitor. 'I didn't find the law very congenial or very creative,' he says. He saw the yard advertised in *The Times* one Tuesday and by the following Saturday had bought it. It cost £12,500, and took all of a £5,000 inheritance which he had. The rest he raised from friends and relations. 'So you see this is not really the story of a man who hauled himself up by his bootlaces from nothing,' says Donald. Even if he forgot all about boatbuilding tomorrow the yard is a very handy property investment to have behind him. It has been valued at £150,000.

One of the more curious aspects of starting a business at that particular time (in 1946) was the way in which people used to arrive out of the blue, looking for a sanctuary for ready cash. Presumably these were the proceeds of both lawful and dubious wartime business activities. In some cases, recalls Donald, they were quite unconcerned with earning interest, but wanted a safe repository for a suitcase of £1 notes. It really happened like that. 'One little man arrived, asked if I could do with some cash and opened up a suitcase in which there was £2,000 in used notes,' says Donald. At the time it was rather like manna from heaven, and in this unconventional fashion Donald acquired the working capital he needed, and in a very short time found himself employing £40,000 in a business which he controlled with his £5,000. Imagine the complications of attempting to employ such financial unorthodoxy today!

When he took the business over it was in a sorry state. The previous owner had been a superb boat builder, but was less good at selling them at a profit. In fact, there were no books, no profits and, as Donald discovered when he sent one of his men to Norwich for materials, no credit from suppliers. To make matters worse the yard was ticking over on the tail-end of government wartime contracts, and these, of course, were declining. All in all the prospect was austere, if not daunting. Donald's ambition was to build up a hire fleet. He had twelve men but no hire boats. 'In those days, in order to survive you had to employ a high degree of low cunning,' he says. 'There were four or five motor fishing vessels still under construction, and they were at the stage where the frames had been built. We couldn't get timber to build hire boats, so we dismantled these and built four hire cruisers with the wood.' In those early years his policy was to build three boats and sell two, which helped pay for the third boat he kept. This he put in his string of hire boats, and at this rate was building up his all important fleet at the rate of about one boat a month. This period, when he was steadily making the name Windboats into something to be proud of in Broadland, is one on which Donald looks back with pride and joy. It was a period of great happiness for him.

Not that he was making a fortune. In the first year he drew £500 salary from the business, in his second £600. 'My wife was terrific. She used to scrub out and service the charterboats for the next lot of visitors who would be arriving on the Saturday afternoon. If you used your own men they would be on time-and-a-half, so we used to both roll up our sleeves and pitch in. We lived on the yard and we gave a round the clock service,' says Donald. He saw himself very much as the patron. He used to welcome his clients, and he liked to be there to say goodbye when they left. 'I thought it was a very pleasurable life,' he says. 'It must have been profitable, I don't know. I didn't look at the books. If it hadn't been profitable I suppose I would have looked at them.' The fleet grew to twenty-four cruisers, the customers came year after year, and by this time Donald had paid back the little men who had rolled up with their valises full of notes. Sometimes when the time came to pay them back he persuaded them to buy a boat with the money!

'The money itself didn't really interest me very much,' he says. 'I have often tried to analyse this driving force men have, whether they go on for money, or power or prestige. With me it is prestige. From 1950 to 1960, those ten years, were the heydays of my hire fleet. The acid test was the weeks of bookings for each boat, and ours were always high. We replaced the fleet and kept putting in new craft. I thought we were pre-eminent and this was a great source of gratification to me. As for money, the children were well educated, my wife was well provided for, and we were able to travel a good deal. The business was a way of life, a hobby rather than a business per se. My wife loved it and the children did too. Work isn't hard if it is something you enjoy doing. On Saturdays we worked from early morning to 7 at night with nothing to eat, because there just wasn't time. No one was ordering me to do anything, the drive was in myself, and I can only tell you that I loved it.'

Even so life was not totally idyllic. In 1948 he found himself facing a financial crisis, largely brought about by a contract undertaken by the firm's engineering shop for some textile machines. The firm which placed the order went bust and Donald lost over £8,000. 'I had to go round and see all our important creditors, tell them what the position was, and said we would meet our obligations, but needed at least nine months to get out of the mess,' he says. 'I will always be grateful to one man, our timber merchant. We owed him about £500, and he said you can have the extra credit and go on drawing timber. I thought that was terrific of him. Eventually we solved the problem and paid up our debts by creating about £9,000 worth of preference shares which various people took up.' Donald went on building up his fleet, renewing it, and giving a good service. 'Up until 1960 I think we excelled over all the other yards,' he says.

Then his wife, who had worked with him through all the difficult years of the business, was taken ill. Donald spent more and more time with her. He began to lose interest in the yard. Service standards on the fleet started to deteriorate. 'I brought a man in to run it for me, but I didn't really tell him very much, or how to do it, which wasn't very fair,' he says. In December 1962 Donald's wife died. In such circumstances it is easy to understand why he should think business was not really very important any more, wonder, perhaps, what it was they had worked so hard for. The whole business seemed an anathema: problems, people and customers were just too much trouble. 'I had lost interest; the yard as such certainly didn't provide it for me any more. I didn't know what to do,' he says.

It was about this time that Paul Hagenbach, Donald's nephew, came up with the ferro-cement idea. He was a civil engineer with Ove Arup, the celebrated consulting engineers in London, and the idea of building concrete boats, with all their virtues and advantages, excited him enormously. Donald was by no means sold on the idea. 'At first I had misgivings and was very sceptical. It took time for Paul to convince me. Yet it was a new challenge, a new toy, and I had to do something to get into circulation again.' Concrete boats were not new. The first hull on record using the ferro-cement principle had been built in France in 1840. Others were built at the beginning of the century in Holland and more recently in Italy, where one of the world's leading experts in the design of shell roofs used the technique to demonstrate that 'ferrocemento' was suitable for boats.

The notion intrigued Paul. 'We had the boatbuilding techniques, and he had the engineering knowledge. He was very confident although neither of us had any idea of the difficulties ahead,' says Donald. In the end Paul's enthusiasm and arguments won Donald over, and he agreed to build three boats. 'Looking back, it was the sort of decision which, if I had had to answer to a board of directors, they would have put a stop to straight away,' he says. Paul made voluminous calculations, came down at weekends from London, and eventually watched as the first concrete hull was cast. This hull still stands in a corner of the firm's car park today. It is discoloured and battered, and no wonder. Donald likes to take the unconverted to see it armed with a 7lb hammer with which he beats away at the hull like a man demented. It makes a telling demonstration of the strengths of Seacrete, and it is a nice piece of showmanship.

More telling though are the ten years' experience and over 300 craft built in the material, which ensure that the claims for Seacrete now command a greater measure of belief than they did when Donald built his first three Broads cruisers with it. If there are still doubters he points to the fact that Seacrete is still the only form of marine ferro-cement in the world to receive an unqualified classification 100A1 (their highest accolade) from Lloyds Register of Shipping. Other bodies to have given it the official nod are the United Kingdom White Fish Authority, which has allocated grants to fishermen to have boats built in Seacrete, and the Food and Agricultural Organisation of the World Health Organisation in Rome.

The total cost of a concrete vessel is not much lower than a traditionally built one, but the saving comes in upkeep. The hulls need virtually no maintenance. If they are damaged they can be quickly repaired by unskilled labour, by cementing over a crack, or a hole, using the mix from the special repair kits supplied by the firm. This cement mix, plus a fast-drying agent, will set in three minutes, even if the repair is carried out under water. The maintenance-free aspect has proved an attraction, especially to underdeveloped countries where boats may be hard used, and where traditional repair facilities are likely to be few and far between. Besides this, Seacrete is totally beetle proof. Marine beetles are an immense problem with wooden hulls in many parts of the world, especially the tropics. According to Donald corrosion on steel hulls can account for as much as an $\frac{1}{8}$in loss over four years. Additionally Seacrete can withstand extremes of temperature without deterioration, and although the oldest Seacrete hull has not yet reached the age of majority, the firm says that a realistic estimate for the life of a hull is forty to fifty years, especially since one property of concrete products is that up to a certain point they increase in strength with age. Seacrete is also said to be more highly resistant to abrasion than fibre glass, has the impact resistance of steel, the resilience of wood and greater resistance to fire than other boatbuilding materials.

Setting up a plant to build Seacrete hulls is not all that costly. It takes an investment of about £5,000 and this is an attractive point for underdeveloped countries which want to build their own fishing boats under licence from Seacrete. Nor does the labour to build them have to be all that highly skilled. Donald sends his own men abroad to set up production units and train local labour to do the job. There are now over twenty boatbuilders throughout the world operating the Seacrete process under licence for downpayments of £1,000 to £5,000 a time, plus royalties, which vary from 3 to 5 per cent of the price of each vessel sold. Donald travels widely and has established a close personal relationship with the licensees. The system works on friendship, on a rapport with the personalities involved, which would more than likely collapse overnight if a large company tried to take it over, and run it with a professional manager. It is not the sort of arrangement which would take kindly to that sort of treatment.

One of the snags is that there have been a number of failures in concrete boatbuilding, mostly vessels built in backyards by amateurs without any skill whatsoever. This has not helped the cause of marine ferro-cement, and Seacrete in particular, which Donald is swift to point out has an unblemished record. A lot of data has been published by cement and concrete associations and technical and marine journals, and much of this has, in Donald's belief, produced wild ideas as to the ease of building in ferro-cement and its cheapness, neither of which are valid in the light of experience. Thus failures and disappointment have produced suspicion and mistrust of the method, and this has unfortunately rubbed off on Seacrete. Sales have not come as fast as Donald would have liked, especially when you consider over a decade of research and an investment of £50,000 has gone into the process. His sales are about £100,000 a year of which over a half are in exports. Profits are not huge, about £4,000 to £5,000 a year after tax, but Donald says he is not all that worried about the money. So long as there is enough to embark on world-wide business trips when he wants to and allow him to have a fortnight in the South of France when he fancies it, where he lives aboard one of his own Seacrete houseboats moored in Menton Harbour.

'Even if we did make £20,000 a year profits I would spend them on Seacrete research,' says Donald. This is precisely what he plans to do with the £10,000 a year he estimates the company will be earning from its royalties in 1973. But even if there is still a lot to learn, Donald long ago progressed from a stage where there were misgivings to one of complete confidence in the product. He demonstrated his faith in it in 1965 when he sold the last of his hire cruiser fleet in order to concentrate solely on building Seacrete boats.

Since he made the decision he has committed the business to one product, to one source of revenue, and concedes that in theory this makes it vulnerable. 'But I have always had entire confidence in the product, and if you are getting repeat orders you must be doing something right,' says Donald. The one product he sees as the firm's strength. 'It has given us singleness of purpose and total drive in pursuit of that purpose. There are no side issues. We are building and selling concrete boats, no other. We are not working in timber, glass fibre or steel. We have no hire fleet. Step by step we have knocked all these things off. Our business is concrete boats, and there isn't anyone in the world to touch us in building them.'

As a text for illustrating the importance to the nation of small companies and their contribution to the national stockpile of innovation and inventiveness these last remarks of Donald's could hardly serve better. It is why the Seacretes can beat the ICIs. So often large corporations are committed to product ranges and are constrained by many pressures, ranging from shareholders and management attitude to inbuilt procedures, not to do anything new. Or it may be quite simply that the market for something like concrete boats just is not big enough to interest them. This is where the Donald Hagenbach's of this world score, though sometimes when they have developed their product into a commercial proposition, when the market starts to rapidly grow, they agree to be bought out because they do not possess the capital or management suited to large-scale production and marketing. This, however, is not the path which Donald would choose. 'Why should I sell out?' he says. 'What else would I do? It's part of my life now.'

It is a sentiment which is echoed by many small businessmen. It is an expression of the fact that the course of business is so often determined by individual and private circumstances. Donald Hagenbach became an innovator because he needed to grasp on to something, to be committed to an all consuming interest which would help fill the sad void which had occurred in his life. The story of Seacrete also demonstrates the dogged persistence of a small company which chose to follow the demanding road of innovation, questing all the time for technical excellence in its own special technique and sticking to its objective through thick and thin. Considering its size the course on which the company embarked without recourse to outside resources was both ambitious and hazardous. It was a decision to innovate which, as Donald has already pointed out, would have been promptly thrown out of court by any responsible board of directors—had there been a board to which he was answerable. But there wasn't, and because he was a small, independent businessman, he was able to follow his own nose without let or hindrance from anyone.

Donald Hagenbach and Seacrete illustrate one style of innovative business. But there are others which contrast sharply with it. In innovative entrepreneurship, in this rapidly accelerating technological age, it is possible to identify the characteristic small business which is started by a technical or scientific entrepreneur and which is based on the personal exploitation of research activity with which he was involved, perhaps, in a large company, or, more likely, as a participant in university or government research projects. The main asset of these so called spin-off companies is unquestionably their brain power. As they grow it is vital that there are further supplies of brain power to keep them fuelled, which is why they are often to be found located, like industries of old, on or near coalfields, adjacent to the source of their power supplies, in this case near university or government research laboratories.

The outstanding examples of such small business development are to be found in America where companies have grown up in scientific complexes or research parks. At Palo Alto, in the San Francisco peninsula, the private enterprise industrial research park is actually located on the campus of Stanford University. On the other side of America in Boston, Route 128, which girdles the city, is the home of so many research laboratories and scientific based industries that it has been dubbed 'Think Alley'. The reason they are there is their close proximity to the research labs and buildings of the Massachusetts Institute of Technology.

The British equivalents of these scientific business complexes are not so readily identifiable and well defined. There tends to be a gathering of this kind of industry in and around Cambridge, and in the Scottish Lowlands where there are about eighty electronics firms. Some cities, and their associated universities, have gone out to devise schemes to attract small science-based industries to the area. Lancaster is an example of an area which offers special help and assistance in this respect. The Glenrothes Development Corporation, administrators of the new town of Glenrothes in Fife, Scotland, launched an imaginative scheme at the beginning of 1971 to help individual inventors carry out original work which might develop into a commercial proposition. Details of these schemes are given in Chapter 17.

One of the Glenrothes workshop units, supplied at a nominal rent, might have suited Bernard Hunn if it were not for the fact that he is currently busily innovating in an old pub called the King Harry in Luton, for which he pays a rent of £425 a year. 'I didn't want to put NRDC into real estate for seven to fourteen years,' he says. One of the rather special things about Hunn and his company, Revenue Systems, is that it is being backed both by the government's National Research Development Corporation and the private enterprise organisation, Technical Development Capital.

Bernard Hunn is one of the new breed of businessmen nurtured by the post-war surge in technology. He is a highly qualified and original thinker, his experience as a professional manager in large companies is substantial, and when he decided to give rein to his ambition to set up in business for himself he decided what he proposed to do in the clear, analytical manner which well befits a scientist-entrepreneur. Basically he used the intellectual discipline and training of the boffin to determine the direction he would take as a businessman. At the centre of his thinking was the hypothesis that he should operate in a field in which he had most experience; that if he had any hope of getting to the size and winning the turnover and profitability he wanted, then he had to launch something which had explosive growth potential; and that he needed this in order to make a case for raising money, since, apart from his record as a big company man, the lending institutions had no performance on which to judge him as a businessman running his own show. From this emerged two key points: that he would operate in the field of electronics, and secondly that he would not compete with anyone else, or anything else already on the market, but would produce something quite new. Thus Bernard coolly made the decision that his path to fame and fortune rested on his ability to successfully invent something for which the world would have a need and therefore swiftly apply it.

This is why he chose to make money—electronic money; and why there may well come a day when, in the truly cashless society, your grandchildren will regard the 1p piece you show them as something out of the ark. For by then they will be doing their shopping and making transactions with Bernard Hunn's electronic pulses, stored in convenient form on something like a credit card, without having to search through pockets or purse, or write out a cheque. 'My first thought,' he says, 'was where can you expect to make most money, and the logical answer seemed to me to be where money changes hands most frequently—at the retail end of things. The problem was how to cream off this 100 per cent turnover to my own business advantage?'

Why has Bernard chosen to tinker with something as sacrosanct as money, with the hard, familiar, comforting cash in which people have every confidence that they can buy food, clothing, shelter and the amenities of life? The argument is that you and I are beginning to turn away from traditional money to safer and more convenient methods of payment. At present we make use of two centralised systems to do it, by writing cheques or by presenting our American Express, Diners Club or Barclaycards. The trouble is that as more people do this the central systems start suffering from indigestion as a result of their data handling problems. They demand bigger, better and more costly centralised computers as the numbers of transactions increase, as wealth spreads. In Bernard's view this is like trying to automate the horse when it would be more intelligent to invent the motor car. So he has quite deliberately set out to produce a new medium of exchange, and to convince people that it is sound, practical and economic.

It had to achieve four things: reduce bank costs, reduce cheque trading, reduce cash in circulation and reduce credit card costs. The sensible way to do this, thought Bernard, would be to imbue the new medium of exchange with the quality of weightlessness, so that it could be counted automatically and transmitted at the speed of light. The cash register for this new currency would then contain unstealable cash. It would count it itself, and transfer it to the bank once a day over the telephone. How could this be implemented? This is how Bernard explained it to delegates from bank, credit card and petrol companies at a symposium on electronic money which he held in November 1970.

'The most obvious solution was a portable plastic card encoded with machine readable data for the account number together with a magnetic storage medium carrying cash information which could be modified after each transaction. Because credit card companies seem to be standardising on a given card size, this standard seemed a good one to use. We aimed to make a card which would look like any existing credit card so that in the absence of a terminal "cash register" which automatically subtracts electronic pulses from the card to the value of purchases made, it can also be used in the normal way, across the counter as a conventional credit card. It has embossing and signature as normal but is, in fact, substantially different from a credit card because it carries invisible, machine-read data. We also aimed to have the machine read fixed data in such a form that its presence could not be detected by other than our terminals and that, even when the secret was known, it would be virtually impossible to modify without spending a lot of money and making it obvious that it had been done. So we had to do a bit of inventing.

'Finally, because we were storing money in the form of magnetic pulses on the card, we aimed to make it as difficult as possible both to take it off or put it on. This meant not only protecting the card stripe by a layer of opaque plastic, but also developing magnetic techniques to an order better than anything existing.

'The information on the card is so designed as to be the minimum necessary for the job. It was the desire to cope with the largest market which resulted in the international/national code. We felt that we could not be sure how many trading clubs would use the system throughout the world so why not use the same numbers for each different country? The way to do this was to identify the currency and to establish the rule that terminals would not accept the wrong currency and only international cards could have their currency changed at a bureau de change. Hence, also, the currency identifier. We also felt that whereas the data on the card identified it, one could not be sure that the user belonged to it. So we use a personal code, derived by a trick from the coding, which must be entered to unlock the system.'

What of the future for electronic cash? The employee using his card for clocking-in and payment purposes may go to a slot in the factory wall and take his pay at any time, not just on Friday or the end of the month. He may go from there and pop his card into a slot in any telephone, suitably designed, dial the bank computer, make a deposit of any amount or make a withdrawal on to his card. His wife or children may do the same and the computer can be programmed to determine fund limits for individual members of the family. Then he can go to an unattended petrol station and serve himself petrol and pay automatically. Or he may pay for his goods at the supermarket, buy an airline ticket to anywhere knowing he needs no travellers' cheques and has a plastic passport which is processed through the airline system gates so that he cannot get on the wrong plane or get off at the wrong point. He may go on the Underground and, at the point of departure that fact and the date and time are registered on a reserve magnetic stripe. At the point of exit his card is read and his journey value is computed and subtracted from the balance. The employer loses no hard cash and pays his employees' bills at the end of the month.

What kind of man is it who not only thinks up an idea like this, but then throws up his job in his mid-forties and starts a company to exploit it? Bernard has always been a big company man, and during his career he worked at various times for Shell, Hawker-Siddeley, Vickers, Elliott Automation and Plessey. Somewhere along this impressive career path he remembers someone saying to him (he thinks it was when he was at Vickers), 'Why on earth don't you start your own company?' While it appealed as a notion, he dismissed it as a reality because he felt it was financially impracticable. Anyway at this time of his career he had adopted the deliberate policy of changing jobs every four or five years, with the thought at the back of his mind that by the time he was forty this would give him the right variety of modern technological experience to be a competent manager of a project, and a very powerful background which would enable him to take up anything which interested him. Accordingly, during these years he spread himself over a number of disciplines: aircraft design, guided weapons design, and electronics. He was not doing all this with a precise and clear idea of where he was going, but rather with the feeling that it would stand him in good stead. 'I suppose the long-term objective was one of being a marketable product, and industrial polymath,' says Hunn. 'It seemed to me that if we were getting into the technological era we were, then blokes with experience in all these fields would have a great many assets.' The broad base is something about which Bernard is almost obsessive. 'If you become an expert in something, as you go deeper and deeper into the subject you start to run out of people with whom you can communicate. The more expert you become the more this happens. What the hell is the good of becoming the world authority on something if there is no one with whom you can communicate and exchange ideas?' he asks.

His own career has been very much an exercise in communicating and exchanging ideas with a very wide variety of people. As a Captain in REME during the war he submitted a paper to the War Office proposing a defence system against the V2. As a result he was posted to AA Command Research Workshops, and by the time he was twenty-three he was in charge of research at AA Command headquarters. After the war he went back to King's College, London (not having completed his course), and came down with a first in Mathematics. He joined Shell as an electronic research engineer, went to Hawker Aircraft where he was chief mathematician for four years, during which he wrote five original mathematical research papers, and left to get wider engineering experience. This was as deputy chief designer for guided weapons at Vickers Armstrong. In 1961 he was busy setting up the Airborne Computing Division of Elliott Flight Automation which he built up from six to 600 staff in four years with a turnover of £2·5 million and annual profits in excess of £300,000. On the strength of this performance Bernard was poached by Plessey who gave him the job of establishing their new Traffic Division at Plessey Automation. Some of the contracts it won included those for traffic control in West London, Liverpool, Glasgow; the London Airport Arrivals Indicator Contract; and the first motorway signalling contract. But things did not work out well for him at Plessey, following the failure of the Automation Group as a whole to reach its targets. Bernard quit in September 1968.

It was at this point that he decided he had had enough of big business and would set up for himself. Nearly twenty years involved with large companies had given him an invaluable insight into the things that management textbooks fail to tell you, the considerable art of company politics and the power of survival. It also showed him the conflicts which existed between the Civil Service and industry, and what a particularly nasty morass they presented for the unwary. In Elliotts he became involved in the backwash of the cancelled TSR 2 aircraft project, and had to get rid of 450 people out of the 600 strong team he had recruited. All this helped sow the seeds of independence and served to sharpen his sense of frustration. By the time he did start his own business he was by no means a wide-eyed inventor obsessed with a way-out commercial idea.

Possibly, like others before him, he needed the final shove in order to disengage himself from the embrace of a big company and put him into orbit as a small businessman. The situation at Plessey Automation provided it. 'As head of the traffic division I was called on to achieve a 40 per cent per annum growth. I was assured that all the products were viable and there was plenty of business in the traffic field. To my cost I omitted to check on this,' he recalls. The long and the short of it was that Bernard found himself faced with a sorry succession of trials and tribulations, a legacy of loss-making contracts, and immense frustrations and difficulties. The result was that he achieved the growth in business, but not in profits.

'I took stock of the situation and came to the conclusion there was no future with the Group,' says Bernard, 'and Plessey agreed with me.' He departed with a golden handshake which was enough to make it possible for him to contemplate starting his own company, but it was not big enough to finance it. His experiences over the years had taught him that any worthwhile development project needed up to £250,000 to get it off the ground. He had given up a job which paid him a salary of £5,500 a year, and which included a car, BUPA contributions, bonuses and stock options on shares, all of which he calculates added another 40 per cent to his salary. His golden handshake amounted to a little under £3,000, but it was enough to keep him afloat while he went about raising money for his new venture. It also helped him buy a car, a Zodiac Automatic, with which the company had supplied him originally.

Bernard already knew what he was going to do. His long, hard think had produced the exciting and novel idea of electronic cash. His problem was now to convince other people of its viability, especially the City institutions which he hoped were going to lend him the conventional hard cash which would enable him to make and market the electronic stuff. The case he presented to them had to be good because the bankers had no track record on which to judge him as an independent and individual businessman, and there is a world of difference between running a company on a one-man-band basis, and running it with all the back-up and comforts of a large concern. Accordingly Bernard sat down and wrote out a business plan. 'It was important that both I and the bankers had a clear idea of what I was going to do, and that we knew something about the size of the market, the projected success rate, and what volume of turnover would be sufficient to cover an investment of the kind I had in mind,' he says.

His business plan took him a month and £5 worth of typing. His next move was to look up all the merchant banks in *Kelly's Directory*, and at the same time he was visiting Companies House, the building in London which houses company registrations and accounts, investigating other newish, technology-based companies which he knew about. As he went through the files he noticed the name Technical Development Capital kept cropping up. It offered an alternative to the government-backed National Research Development Corporation.

It was at this stage, while he was knocking on doors in the City of London, that Bernard discovered that his years of big business had not taught him anything about the esoteric mysteries of shares and debentures. To him they were just words tossed back and forth across the table, and he had to jump in at the financial deep end, and learn as he went along. It was a fascinating but nerve-racking period, in which he learned a lot about money-lending institutions, about how they work, and about the people who inhabit them. 'I began to learn that one's status as a member of a big company sprang from the status of the appointment, and not the individual. As soon as you are a private individual you have no status in the City. This is a crucial lesson. It is also a bitter one, especially when you come up against people you have been dealing with before, when you were a big company man,' he says. 'This is when you discover you are no longer persona grata, and that in most circumstances friendship is related to business. It is also when you learn you must stand on your own two feet.'

It is at a time like this that there occur rather ordinary, personal confrontations which none of the textbooks that tell you how to start a business ever mention. 'It was tedious and complicated to explain to people what one was doing, and when you met neighbours out shopping they said, "Sorry to hear about your job," and conversations of this sort were the most tiresome part of the whole thing. Some people who found I was telling the truth seemed to rather resent it,' he says.

'I think my wife's attitude was, "What a quaint idea he's got hold of but I had better let him get it out of his system." Now I think she is rather surprised that I haven't. When you have been used to working in a big company there are things you previously took for granted which you now miss. One day my car engine seized up. With a big company I would have just got another car, but I had to go out and buy one, and in terms of personal finance the net effect of going it alone is that I now have a four-figure personal overdraft and a very patient bank manager.'

For Bernard the few weeks of March and April 1969 were the turning point. This was when the National Research Development Corporation made encouraging noises, but would he hang on a bit longer? As a Plessey man he had previously had some contact with NRDC and therefore harboured a shrewd idea of how long it took to get a project through the machinery. 'In any case if you want to be big you can't do other than be patient and wait. In the same way if you want £250,000 and have only put up £3,500 yourself, you cannot expect 51 per cent of the equity,' says Bernard. Eventually both NRDC and the Technical Development Capital coughed up and backed Revenue Systems on a joint basis. NRDC is the largest shareholder with a 46 per cent stake, while Bernard and his colleagues hold about 30 per cent, TDC 20 per cent and a Dutch company about 4 per cent. Bernard received the first slice of his money in September 1969, and it was at this point he commenced bringing in staff, top graduate engineers from companies like Elliot and Plessey. All told there are twelve of them.

Bernard took the old pub in Luton because it was cheap, and because it was within a 15 mile radius of where he lived at Berkhamsted. He spent the first two months cleaning up the place and making it fit to work in. He decorated his own office and even had to set to work and make the lavatories usable. When I talked to Bernard early in 1971 he was able to say that things had mostly gone according to plan, and the next priority was finishing the job and getting the orders in. He was very conscious that the investors in the company expected to see something which would do the job claimed for it, something which people would buy in the market place and something which would recover their investment. Inevitably, in innovating and launching a new product for which there has never been a market before, the cash flow in the development years is non-existent. Until Bernard actually gets money flowing in, say three months after the first sale, the outgoings will have totalled something like £220,000.

One thing which did not go quite according to plan was that Bernard failed to get the full £250,000 he reckoned he needed. NRDC and TDC decided to put in about £100,000 between them by the end of September 1971, and, at the time of writing, Bernard did not know what shape the company would have in the future, because he regarded it as essential to have further capital and this would not be forthcoming until he had both proved the product and the market.

He was then scheduling the first pilot use of electronic money at a self-service petrol station in Buckingham Palace Road, London.

The plan was to equip it with an experimental unit for taking electronic money. Selected customers were to be issued with it and asked to take part in the experiment. Obviously there will be a lot of people watching this development with more than passing interests. The shareholders in Revenue Systems. The staff in Revenue Systems. And Bernard, the man who started it. All of them have something to lose; money and jobs. But Bernard more than most because he is testing his belief in himself as an entrepreneur, a risk-taker, who has not even the benefit of an established market he can exploit by underselling rivals with a better product. If it were just that, it would be much easier. But he has chosen to cast himself in the riskiest of all roles—an innovator. Not only has he to develop his product, but he also has to develop a market for it. He has no misgivings about the excellence of his technology. What makes him nervous is whether he has got his timing right, whether he can create a new market receptive to his new technology. Bernard believes an entrepreneur is a man who takes a sniff and changes the rules, and the rules he is changing are about something as sacred in a capitalist society as money. He is trying to generate a new medium of exchange which is a psychological problem as much as a technical one. It is a substantial vision. It seems worth noting that it is not Plessey or IBM which is doing it, but a small, independent businessman, with a powerful belief in himself. Such men make hair-raising risk-taking sound as if it is solid assets.

NOTES

1 Page 232. Peter Fairley. *Project X—The Exciting Story of British Invention*. Mayflower Books (1970).
2 Page 237. William Kingston. *Invention and Monopoly*. Woolwich Economic Papers No 15.
3 Page 237. R. F. Morgan. *Making an Idea Into a Business*. Technical Development Capital Ltd.
4 Page 239. Tim Eiloart. 'Fanning the Flame of Innovation', *New Scientist* (11 September 1969).
5 Page 239. P. G. Peterson. *The Climate for Innovation*. Science of Foundation Discussion Paper.

Chapter 14

How to be best without being biggest

Wilkin and Sons Ltd and the Travel Club of Upminster are two firms very different in style, in age and in the product they produce. The first is a jam manufacturer, the second a packager of holidays abroad. What they both share in common as small companies is an ability to survive and hold their own in industries which are dominated by large firms and in which many of their former small firm colleagues have long since gone to the wall. They do this by sticking to what they do well, and by making sure they continue to do it very well indeed. And, of course, they charge a bit more for it.

No one following the industrial and business pages of the newspapers in the 1960s could be unaware that it was a time when both industry and government were conducting a love affair with bigness in business. Government ministers, company chairmen and economic planners were all caught up in the fashionable economic creed which said the way to tackle the inherent weakness of the country's industrial structure was to reorganise into even larger units, the better able to reap the rewards of economies of scale and to compete more effectively in international markets.

In the United Kingdom the Industrial Reorganisation Corporation became the government's chief instrument for getting companies into bed with each other. Now it no longer exists, but while it did it was part of the machinery devoted to creating a business climate in which, to many, it seemed the willingness to be corporately wed was almost a moral imperative. The results of two of the more dramatic interventions of IRC stand today for all to see in the shape of International Computers, with £118 million of assets, and the huge British Leyland Motor Corporation with assets of over £320 million.

Yet while the merging and the marrying was proceeding apace, the great mass of small businesses were getting on with doing what they had always done, carrying on and surviving, and showing a remarkable aptitude for it. To them in 1970, for instance, it was only of passing interest that the number of European companies whose annual turnover topped the £1,000 million mark had risen in twelve months from seventeen to twenty-five, or that giant, multi-national corporations like Shell, IBM, Standard Oil and General Motors were increasing their grip on the economies of the Western world and that there were 100 large companies controlling over half of all the commercial assets and income in Britain and the United States. Most of the small men, like Wilkin and Sons Ltd, had more pressing matters on their minds.

Like getting in the strawberry crop.

Teatime would not be the same without Wilkin and Sons Ltd, jam and marmalade makers to Her Majesty the Queen. Nowadays, any supermarket that knows anything at all about jam stocks a range of Tiptree's. But there was a time right up to World War II when people bought it not over the grocer's counter, but by writing direct to the factory, or sometimes by sending a telegram to 'Preserves Tiptree'. The communications came from the great houses of the land, from shooting lodges in Scotland, from house-party hostesses entertaining during Ascot and Cowes Weeks, and from Royal Houses. The orders were for several cases at a time, and every nanny worth her salt had a Tiptree seedless, or a jelly jam, in the nursery. In those days the mailing list was an amalgam of Debrett, Crockford's *Clerical Directory* and the *Medical Directory*.

Even today, although times have changed and you cannot order it direct by the case any more, you are still left with the feeling that it is the people who matter who partake of Tiptree jams. The Director General of the Ordnance Survey of Great Britain, for example. When you consider the legions of factories, large and great, which dot the landscape, how else do you explain Wilkin and Sons rating the distinction of a mention on the one inch to the mile map? The firm is not mentioned by name, but it is there just the same, just below the village name of Tiptree, which is the firm's registered trade mark anyway. The sheet is number 162, Southend-on-Sea, the map reference 899156. Factory (Jam) is an invitation if ever you saw one (at least to those for whom a Tiptree conserve is a matter of urgent compulsion) to make their own way to the source of all that is best in jams. There is Strawberry Little Scarlet, Quince, Morello Cherry, Damson, Green Gooseberry, Greengage and Raspberry Sweet-Tip: and jellies too, shining and lambent in their jars, Crab Apple, Blackberry, Medlar and Plum. Then there are the country coloured preserves, Green Fig, Peach, Apricot; a trio of chutneys, a sextet of golden honeys, and ten different, assorted marmalades with names like Old Times, Tawny, Crystal and Double One with Tangerine and Double Two with Lime.

Wilkin and Sons' letter heading is a testament to those halcyon days of the ritual afternoon tea, a splendid piece of graphic Victoriana which happily is not yet lost in this telly-ad age. It has the firm's name across the top, the royal coat of arms in red, centred immediately beneath, and on one side of it a scene depicting strawberry picking in the 1880s. On the other side is a view of the Tiptree Jam Factory, with smoke from its old coal-fired furnaces swirling from its chimneys over the surrounding Essex orchards, and a train steaming, yes, *steaming*, out of the factory siding. The first train clanked into the siding on Whit Monday 1904. Fifty-eight years later, in 1962, the line was closed and the track removed, but today the train still goes steaming on in the letter heading. The firm has considered changing the design of its stationery to something a trifle more up to date, but it has made no final decision yet. Wilkin and Sons is not a company that makes radical changes overnight. It is a family concern which pursues a cautious, careful and conservative path in business.

This policy appears to have paid handsomely, for there are many distinctive things which you cannot help noticing about Wilkin and Sons, but the most distinctive of all is its success. Success in an industry in which the total market has been steadily dwindling since World War II. Not only has the business survived, while many of its commercial confreres of a similar size have gone to the wall, merged or sold out, but it has endured, grown, prospered and progressed, pushing up its output and its sales, flying absolutely in the face of the general market trend. During this period, when a firm like St Martins, which once enjoyed a fifth of the market, found itself in the hands of the receiver, when the national sales of jam dropped in the space of one decade alone from 200,000 to 140,000 tons a year, when vicious price cutting was the order of the day, Wilkin and Sons has been steadfastly getting on, in its sturdy, independent, some might say old-fashioned style, with doing the thing it does best: making the high-quality, expensive jams which discriminating jam eaters everywhere insist upon. Like the retired Colonel who once wrote: 'I am glad our home-made jam is finished because I can now eat yours.'

With loyal and stalwart customers like the Colonel, little wonder that Wilkin and Sons has been steadily expanding its business and profits and never really had to worry about competition. In the twenty-five years since the end of World War II the sales graph has been steadily climbing, save for four years only, when a drop in sales produced some small, but irritating kinks which spoiled the nice, smooth climbing curve. Immediately after the war the factory sold a little over £54,000 worth of jam. Five years later the figure almost touched £168,000. Throughout the 1960s Tiptree jam eaters everywhere put up a tremendous performance. Even when Hartley's New Jam came sweeping into the shops in 1963, Tiptree loyalists carried on the good work. They wavered only slightly (to the tune of a £35,000 drop in sales) when seduced by a £110,000 Hartley television advertising campaign, slanted towards the magical word 'New'. It referred to a vacuum-sealed jam-making process which had first been widely used in the United States. It was the biggest thing to have happened in British jam making for years, the last event of note being the discovery that you could preserve fruit with sulphur dioxide. But for Wilkin and Sons recourse to such chemical stratagems was, and still is, unthinkable. (Actually they had tried vacuum processing in the early 1900s, but abandoned it as unsatisfactory.) The following year, 1964, floating jam eaters were still dithering and Wilkin and Sons sales went down another £20,000. Then, as if experiencing a twinge of remorse at their fickleness, Tiptree supporters suddenly rallied, dug deep into their jamjars, spooning it out in larger quantities than ever, and for the rest of the decade sales galloped away. The year 1970, the first year of the new decade, very appropriately produced a record sales figure of over £700,000.

Compared with the big makers, Wilkin and Sons share of the £30 million United Kingdom jam and marmalade market is minute. No one really knows exactly what it is, and no one bothers to find out. It is not that they are complacent or smug, but just terribly busy keeping up with the demand. 'You must understand, Mr Clarke, we are concerned with making the best not the most.' In other words let Robertsons of golliwog fame, and Hartleys, Chivers and Moorhouse, all owned by Cadbury-Schweppes, get on fighting it out to see who will be biggest.

Wilkin and Sons has always made jam in homely batches, 50lb in a boiler at a time. It enables them to keep a very close eye on the quality. In any case, when the boilers were installed years ago, the firm did not foresee itself competing with Chivers or Robertsons, but more with the housewife who made her own. Now housewives rarely seem to make jam any more, at least not in the quantities their mothers and grandmothers did. Other firms make their jam on a mass production basis and would not look at a line unless they could make it in a 50 ton batch. For Wilkin and Sons it is more like 1 ton at a go. The firm has had many inquiries to make larger quantities for special orders, but it could not do it at the price, and keep up the quality. The buyers went away highly puzzled at a small family firm turning down good business like that. If they had possessed any perception they would have realised this is one of the reasons the firm is still in business today. In his advertisement for Tiptree preserves the company's American agent says: 'We're the people who would rather be better than big, the point being that we have not deserted the sturdy British principle which has kept us small, namely—take time to do it right.' In other words it is a company which knows what it can do, and does it well.

This particular credo has not only pushed up home sales; the company exports to twenty-seven different countries as well. The

Americans, West Germans, Canadians, French and Japanese are all great ones for Tiptree jams, according to Arthur Frederick Wilkin, chairman and joint managing director. One of his long-cherished ambitions was to get exports up to 10 per cent of total sales, and he is very happy to tell you that in 1970 he reached this target. He has been looking hard at the export business, not that he is nervous about his home sales, but, as he says, you have to be forward looking, and what with the Common Market coming along . . .

If there is any apprehension it is the fruit-growing side of the business which causes it. Frost or drought can have a severe effect on fruit supplies from the company's farms, a hazard which sometimes means going without or buying in from outside. Certainly the company makes profits. These have climbed from £16,486 before tax in 1965 to £68,779 in 1970, but whether they are up, or whether they go down, depends a good deal on the weather.

From its sales figures you might think the company sales force has been making a tremendous and sustained drive over the years, but with the best will in the world you can hardly describe it quite like that. You see, Wilkin and Sons does not have a great army of reps on the road. Indeed it has no reps at all. It has a sales manager, and a consultant who is the former sales manager, now in semi-retirement, who comes in occasionally. It does not go in for clever, trendy and expensive advertising campaigns either. Indeed it is only now that it is beginning to get used to the idea of calling advertisements advertisements, and not announcements.

The heydays for announcements were the 1930s. In May 1930, for example, the firm sent out by post, direct to its customers, the spring clearance sale offers. The purpose of the sale was honestly explained to potential buyers. Wilkin and Sons wanted to shift stocks of Tiptree Scarlet Strawberry, Tiptree Sweetheart Strawberry and Morello Cherry, of which it had a surplus, in preference to other varieties, of which it was getting short. 'Will't please your honour to taste of these conserves?' exhorted the 1930 Tiptree model girl in the photograph on the order form. By today's standards the prices were truly remarkable: eighteen 2lb glass jars of mixed jams for £1 13s carriage paid; a 7lb stone jar of raspberry and of seedless red gooseberry at 4s 8d; blackcurrant jelly at 6s 11d. On the order form a Miss Mary Salmon, Training College, Swansea, had enclosed her remittance and marked her choice, the Guinea Case of Assorted Specialities, fourteen 1lb jars, for £1 2s, carriage paid in Scotland and Wales. Is Miss Mary Salmon, formerly of the Training College, Swansea, still relishing Tiptree conserves now? I hope so.

These days the firm spends very little on advertising and the most it ever went to was £14,000 in one year. In 1969 it decided to cut its advertising budget by one third. It might as well have cut it completely because all that happened was that its sales of jam went *up* by 7·7 per cent. Now that is the sort of statistic which makes the backroom boys in advertising agencies ditch their slide rules and turn to chicken farming. It does not go in for public relations consultants either; inquisitive journalists used to talk to the old sales manager when he was there, or to Arthur Frederick Wilkin himself. He is the third-generation Wilkin to head the firm since his grandfather started it in 1885. As befits an old family firm he is assisted by a trio of other Wilkins.

There is his brother, Thomas G. Wilkin, who is joint managing director and company secretary. He runs 1,000 acres of company owned farms and grows much of the fruit which goes into the jam. Besides the factory and the farms the company owns four residences, seventy-two houses and flats and a cold store. Another director, Arthur's cousin John S. Wilkin, is factory manager. There is a fourth Wilkin in the business, Arthur's son Peter, who is destined eventually to head the business.

When Arthur Wilkin first took over from his uncle, who ran the company before him, he was not only chairman and managing director, deciding the policies of the firm, but virtually jam production manager too, concerned with the very practical and important details of taste, look and consistency. With the Wilkins, jam making is a matter of artistry, excellence and perfection, so much so that even today Arthur Wilkin himself answers the rare letter of complaint. The thought of chemicals, colourings, or fillers going into their jams instead of pure fruit and sugar would envelop the Wilkins in black despair. Arthur Wilkin still goes round the factory every morning, inspecting the previous day's production and tasting samples.

Arthur Wilkin's whole life has been jam. 'It has been dedicated to making best-quality jam and that consideration is foremost,' one long-serving Wilkin employee told me. Arthur's father, Arthur Swinburne Wilkin, was only in the business for a few years and left to farm elsewhere in Essex. Even so, it seemed young Arthur was destined for the jam factory. 'When I was about six I can remember my grandfather sent me a postcard of an old thatched house in Tiptree and on the back he had written, "How would you like to make jam in this?".' Arthur was sent to school in London, a bad choice for a country boy, he says, and later spent time in an accountant's office there, as well as a year in Covent Market learning the fruit trade. It was all directed towards coming into the family firm where, at first, he was personal assistant to his uncle, learning every aspect of the business from him, everything from jam production to office administration.

Arthur Wilkin is now seventy-one years old, a courteous, polite man, with short greying hair, and a solid build which betrays the Essex farming stock he springs from. On fine days he commutes to work on his bicycle, from Tiptree Hall, over the well-made, narrow, private roads which cut across the Wilkin farm fields to the jam factory. If it rains he drives his Rover 2000. He has been head of the firm since 1942 when his uncle, Charles John Wilkin, died. All told Arthur has been in the business fifty-two years.

When you go to see him, you pass into the factory through tall, green iron gates, park your car in front of an old Georgian house, which used to be his uncle's home and which has now been made into flats for Wilkin workpeople, then walk across the yard to reception. Here you sign the large, heavy visitors' book. On the wall are a collection of fading photographs dated 1886 to 1895, showing bearded and long-past Wilkin employees and a big four-wheeled traction engine, not moving, but in situ, providing the power for some mysterious jam-making process. The roof of the building has been extended to cover it and its smoke stack goes through the roof, just like any normal, self-respecting chimney. Delving into the written history of those nine years you emerge with the fascinating minutiae of what running a family firm was all about. At one point old grandfather Wilkin writes of the financial pressures of 1887. 'The deficit that year was £1,400, but before I had been personally responsible to the bank for above £3,000. It needed a lion's heart to go on!' In 1893 there was a great drought and heavy losses. No dividends were paid. In 1895 the boiling room was rebuilt, chiefly with oak trees from Wilkin's Grove.

Not surprisingly the Wilkins have been in Essex a long time, farming in the county since the 1700s. The family got into jam making because grandfather Wilkin wanted an outlet for his acres of strawberries, other than sending them to the London hotels. The strawberries were picked fresh very early in the morning, taken to Kelvedon railway station, and were in the London hotels in time for breakfast, almost with the dew on them. 'My grandfather started making jam in a converted barn,' says Arthur. 'He delved into a lot of things—farming, canning, jam making and started up at about the same time as John Chivers.' Chivers is still a familiar name in jam today. But it is no longer an old family firm like Wilkin and Sons, but part of Cadbury-Schweppes.

Much of the physical appearance of the Wilkin domain is redolent of the period when John Chivers and grandfather Wilkin were thrusting jam entrepreneurs. It is almost as though you are looking at the physical expression of some of the attributes which the late Victorians held so dear. There is immense order and tidiness everywhere. A place for everything, and everything in its place. Even the farm fields, the orchards with their symmetrical rows of precision-pruned trees, the regimented rows of strawberry beds seem to tell the same story. Wilkin and Sons is a business which is run with propriety, rectitude and a mixture of benevolence and austerity. The chairman's statement for the year 1969 refers to an £11,700 increase in trading profit. 'The increase has provided the opportunity of an allocation of £10,000 to the Employees Pension Fund, wholly funded and guaranteed by the company, to augument the pensions payable to employees on retirement,' it says.

When you visit Arthur Wilkin, his part-time secretary conducts you from the inquiry office, across the yard and up a flight of narrow, wooden stairs to the boardroom which is very ordinary and functional, where not a trace of modernity impinges on the mahogany. 'We're a bit spartan here,' says Arthur Wilkin. 'It's how we've survived.' Along one wall is a bank of heavy wooden drawers, now unused, a repository perhaps of all the secret Wilkin jam recipes in the days before office filing systems were called systems. There are fifteen drawers in all. Each has a small metal frame card-holder on its front, but there are no cards in them save for one which reads Special Resolutions 1910–1921–1936. Just one drawer. To those of a curious disposition those special Wilkin resolutions suddenly become the most desirable reading matter in the room.

On one of the shelves above there is a plaque presented by the employees of Wilkin and Sons to Arthur Wilkin in 1967 to mark a new milestone in the company's history, a record year for sales and production, and in appreciation of his leadership and dedication towards the continuing success of the company. It is a tribute to a modest man who, to tell the truth, would rather not have been mentioned in this account at all. 'It's the company which matters,' he says, 'and I think it can be called a success story due to the teamwork by management and employees as a body.'

The plaque is part of the modern history of the firm which has not yet been written. The official Wilkin archivist got as far as 1922, and you have to quiz Arthur Wilkin himself for the details since then. In that time, to him and to the family, one of the saddest events was the death in 1942 of Charles Wilkin, his uncle and head of the firm. To many a Wilkin employee things would never seem quite the same again. It was a predictable sentiment from those who had given long service and loyalty. There was also much truth in it.

World War II changed many things, not the least the way Wilkin and Sons sold its jam. Jam was rationed. Food manufacturers had to do what they were told by the Ministry of Food, supplies were heavily curtailed, and strict regulations were laid down about the fruit and sugar content of jam. Britain was enduring a siege economy, and austerity became very much the order of the day. However, the Ministry of Food's idea of what constituted good-quality jam was not the same as Arthur Wilkin's. Somehow he managed to get a special dispensation to keep the fruit content of Tiptree jam higher than anyone else's. Grocers and their customers who got a quota never forgot it.

In the years after the war, with food rationing still in force, a lot of their old private customers dead, big houses closing down, big estates being broken up, it became plain that the old pre-war way of selling jam, by the case, direct from the farm, really would not do any more. Meanwhile the grocers were crying out to get their hands on Tiptree jam. It got to the point where they were almost queueing up to buy it. Because the fruit content had been high in the war Wilkin and Sons had charged a higher price, and the grocers were quite accustomed to this premium. 'We gave a lot of thought to the situation, could see that we had built up some good connections and decided to change our policy and supply them instead of direct to our customers,' says Arthur Wilkin.

It was probably the most radical policy decision the company ever made. But having made it, it had to be extended. The old family grocer was a dwindling breed; the assault of the supermarket saw to that. So the next step was to work through the wholesalers. 'This is why we have no real control over where our jams are sold now,' says Arthur Wilkin; 'it is why people sometimes write and complain they can't get our quince or mulberry. The trouble is the big boys' computers only list the popular varieties of jam, and haven't been programmed for the more unusual ones. But if we had stuck to the old ways out of nostalgia we would have been out of business by now.' Other advantages were the savings by selling in bulk, which is less costly than dispatching odd crates all over the land. And, of course, if you sell as much as you make without the expensive overhead of a sales force that helps the profit figures considerably.

Possibly it sounds as though it has all been very easy. But this is a notion to which Arthur Wilkin gives short shrift. 'It's been hard work building up and maintaining the firm. It is not what we have got out of it personally. We could have been better off if we had sold out, instead of keeping our noses to the grindstone. But in a family firm like this, very often decisions are made for the sake of the company and its employees which result in the company benefiting, and not the people who run it. It's a very demanding business. I once said to my uncle, "It seems to me the price of success in this business is eternal vigilance," and he said, "How right you are." In our method of making jam you can't just say to a man there's a load of blackcurrants, see to them, and make them up. You just can't sit back and forget about them. I prefer to work hard for the sake of achievement, to see the business flourish. That has been my ambition, my objective in life. I get my creative satisfaction in seeing it prosper and thrive.'

But upon this particular ambition the British tax structure has imposed a large degree of restraint. Wilkin and Sons is no different from other family firms. It echoes the cri de coeur of so many of them: the heavy burden of tax. In 1968 corporation tax and income tax combined absorbed over 60 per cent of the firm's profit, making it very difficult to improve cash resources at a time when plant renewals were more costly than ever before, and when large sums of money were needed to finance the continuing expansion of the business. A year later in his chairman's statement Arthur Wilkin sounded a warning. 'Substantial inroads are being made each year into our liquid resources, and your directors are of the opinion that probably within four or five years the cash balance may have been expended on capital account for the improvement of housing for employees, also for factory and plant modernisation. No new capital has been raised since 1926. . . . Since then the sixfold expansion of the business has only been possible by the ploughing back of past profits, enabling the company still to be free of debentures, or other charges on its assets.' In this respect the Wilkin story is repetitively familiar, one you find in many small family controlled companies. Cash resources have been steadily depleted as the company was prevented from ploughing back the profits it would like. It has meant that a firm like Wilkin and Sons has had to grow slowly, within the limit of the profits it was allowed to retain, plus overdrafts at the bank. Arthur Wilkin might have gone knocking at doors in the City of London, and borrowed in order to expand more quickly, but the cost, and perhaps even more offputting, the strings attached, like outside participation in the company, is precisely the situation from which many established family firms shrink.

The lack of cash has had quite specific effects. 'We have had to put up with older things, put off building a new department because we had not got the funds,' says Arthur Wilkin. 'Fortunately we sold a farm very advantageously. We sold it because we needed the money, but we didn't need the farm. The problem is that in our business so much money is tied up in stock, and it is only partly turned over once a year. In summer the demands on cash flow are very high. There is a lot of overtime being paid in the factory and casual fruit pickers being employed. And should the company's own red or blackcurrant crop fail, then it has to buy in from other growers and the fruit has to be paid for within fourteen days.'

If you live in or around Tiptree the annual jam cycle is something you cannot help but be aware of. From January to the end of April there are no fresh English native fruits available, so Wilkin and Sons is busy producing its range of marmalades. Marmalade now accounts for about 35 per cent of the firm's sales. With freezing techniques perfected the firm can now make blackcurrant, raspberry and apricot jams from frozen fruits, which helps keep the Tiptree labour force of over 200 in work all the year round. The strawberries for strawberry jam, which is the company's largest single selling line, come in early June and are being brought into the factory until mid July. From July onwards it is the turn of fresh blackcurrants, raspberries, Morello cherries and stone fruits like greengage, plum and damson. Medlars are last of all, beginning in November. For some of their more specialised lines they may reply on the local populace bringing in quinces or mulberries from the trees in their cottage gardens. They do not actually go round asking for fruit, or put small ads in the local paper. People just seem to know instinctively. Sometimes they give the firm a ring on Tiptree 407 before they go foraging through the lanes, frisking the hedgerows for elderberries.

It is all Wilkin country and the jam factory chimney is a landmark for miles around, a monument to three generations of quality jam makers, to whom jam making has been more of a vocation than a way of earning a living. When the employees presented Arthur Wilkin with his plaque in 1967 he told them he meant to keep on as long as he was physically able. It was not the family's intention to sell out, although they had several opportunities presented to them, all of which had been turned down. 'I told them,' says Arthur Wilkin, 'they had helped build the firm up, and we were not going to let them down. In any case Tiptree jam has been my life, and my brother's life, and we know it would have been the wish of our grandfather and our uncle to keep the firm going.'

For Harry Chandler the art of survival in a business world which has been rapidly changing all around him, the ability to endure and hold his place in the face of competition from the giants, is contained, just like Wilkin and Sons, in a basic and unshakeable dedication to producing a product of excellence. Harry's product is not tangible like a jar of jam, and when you tell his story there is no symbolic factory chimney you can point to, although he has raised one or two more contemporary monuments to his success.

Harry is a lively individual, nattily dressed, silvering at the sideboards, and wears an irrepressible air of having succeeded. He drives a motor car which shows he has—a beautiful Jensen, registration number HC 1000. There is a boat in Menton Harbour, but that, says Harry, is now sadly neglected in favour of a villa which Rene, his wife and lifelong business partner, has built in Portugal's Algarve. Harry and Rene enjoy their lives, travel a lot, and have a number of eyries to which they retreat to think, work and relax. There's an eyrie above his office in Upminster, and a large, almost palatial attic eyrie above their house, which you can get to either by outside fire escape, or the more usual internal stairs. They bought the house, a big, spacious place, for £2,000 at the time of the Korean War. They have put a lot of work and money into it, and it must be worth well over £20,000 now. To give you an idea of size they have a full-scale billiard table in their attic and room to dance a jig as well. But as Harry says, 'Who's got time to play billiards?'

They have a penthouse eyrie off Park Lane too. When you ask if they are millionaires, they gaze about in other directions, as though the question is directed at someone else who is not present. What they say is that they are comfortably off, and that they pay themselves very good salaries. Certainly they are now enjoying some of the fruits of past labours. Harry, having got his business, the Travel Club of Upminster, to a particular size which he and Rene can handle, is not interested in becoming a giant.

Harry is a Cockney; he was brought up in Canning Town. Before World War II he used to work as an office boy in a shipping company called Continental Express. In those days cycling was very popular, cycle clubs flourished, and after exhausting Wales, England and the Lake District, Harry started taking his bicycle abroad. He was about sixteen then. The hostels he stayed in were pleasant and inexpensive. So were the small hotels and it struck him that it would be a good idea to fix up holidays for his friends. Some of the very first hotels he used when he started his travel business in 1936 still feature in his holiday programme today, though a hotel like the Karwendelhof, at Seefeld, in the Austrian Tyrol, which used to be a small pension, is now de luxe. There is almost a family connection with some of his hotels because romance reared its sweet head and hotel proprietors' daughters started marrying Harry's couriers. Today one of those couriers is the proprietor of an hotel with which Harry still deals.

One of his first trips in the 1930s was to Fusen in Bavaria where he stayed in a youth hostel. He thinks it was for about 25 pfennigs a night. In the same village was an old post house which the Workers Travel Association was using, so Harry found another hotel in the same place where full pension rates were 6s a day and he came back to London, found out what the rail fares were, and advertised his two weeks holidays.

In those days he was working from his home in Canning Town and thought an Albert Dock phone number on top of his notepaper did not quite measure up in class and prestige to what he would have wished for his headquarters. So he carefully made sure just the exchange initials appeared, ALB, working on the thesis that prospective clients would assume it was something posh like Albemarle. He got three people. 'I and another chap went out on my tandem,' says Harry, 'and they went on the train.' Harry did not know the area, so used to go round on his tandem to reconnoitre so he could take his holidaymakers on a taxi excursion the following day. When he came home he packed up his job, because to act as courier on the first holidays he organised had meant taking two weeks holidays from his job as a shipping clerk.

He decided to name his business the Travel Club, because he believed in a friendly approach and he could see that it would be friends he would be taking. The next year, 1937, he arranged holidays in the Bavarian mountain village of Berchtesgaden and took about 200 people. Berchtesgaden, hitherto unknown, became front page news when German troops marched through it, and later on it was even more infamous as the mountain retreat of Hitler and other Nazi leaders. Then came 1938, the year of the Anschluss in Austria, and he found himself taking only four to five people on each tour instead of the twenty to thirty he had bargained for. Because of it he lost the money he had made the previous year. In 1939 Harry decided to take his holidaymakers to Switzerland. He had a very good year and carried around 300. His charge was £10 for the fortnight, and on that he reckons he made about 50p (10s) gross profit. 'Which proportionally is a damn sight better than now,' he says wryly.

Then came the crisis. On 26 August, the Saturday before Germany invaded Poland, Harry turned up at Victoria to meet his party and saw that Cooks, Frames and WTA had all cancelled their tours. There followed a long discussion with the forty to fifty people in Harry's party, with Harry arguing they should not cancel. But in the end they decided not to go, but to wait and see what happened over the weekend and come back on Monday. 'And they did,' says Harry, 'just three of them.' So he took them, had a hell of a journey and it was not until eight weeks later that Harry got back, having met a chap who was in the RAF (VR) and was trying to get back to Britain. They drove across France, in this man's big Lagonda and kept going all night until they got to Abbeville, and from there to Calais and on a fishing vessel home.

That was the last bit of travel business he transacted until years later, towards the end of the war. He was posted to Singapore in army movements, shipping home PoWs of the Japs. Shrewdly

Harry kept the names and addresses of all the officers he sent home, and when he eventually came out of the army, and started to pick up where he had left off in travel, he wrote to these ex-army men, between 2,000 and 3,000 of them, and suggested that they give themselves and families a nice holiday at Sarnen, in Switzerland. It was a marvellous piece of marketing, although as Harry says, if that is what you had told him it was at the time, he would have looked blank. Anyway he knew they all had some gratuity money and he got a cheap duplicated leaflet out about the holiday. The whole thing was successful and he carried over 500 of them. 'They had been separated from their wives for many years,' says Harry, 'and the result was that the birth rate jumped when they returned home.' Harry is happy to say this new generation provides a large portion of his clients in 1971. His price then for the fortnight was 20gns—virtually double what it had cost before the war.

Harry's Travel Club has advanced a long way from those days. He now carries about 20,000 passengers a year, summer and winter, which notches up to a turnover of about £1·5 million. While Harry sells package holidays like a host of other people, he does not, and never has, sold through retail travel agents, and he does not spend huge sums of money on the annual after-Christmas splurge of holiday advertising either. Both of these bits of business policy have paid handsome dividends, because Harry has always been able to win a high degree of profitability (for the travel business anyway), from not having to pay the normal 10 per cent commission to agents, by not having to service them with brochures, publicity material, free phone booking services and cocktail parties. In addition Harry and Rene did most of the work themselves, had only a small staff, and their overheads were small compared with London-based firms having to pay West End rents.

Until the big travel groups like Clarkson and Thomson entered the business a few years ago, started leasing hotels, taking aircraft on time charter (they depend for as much as 90 per cent of their business on the retail travel agents) and cutting prices to the bone, Harry had been enjoying a pretty unique advantage. But the trouble is he is not big enough to take advantage of things like time charter, and he cannot finance the building of 200 to 300 room hotels, so he has lost a bit of the profitability lead he had, and he keeps the show on the road by aiming up the market—solidly middle class—and running a lean, tight, streamlined operation. He reckons his ratio of staff to passengers carried is the smallest in the business: 1:2,000.

He is barred for practical reasons from using time charter arrangements and therefore enjoying the benefits of scale, because, as a rough and ready guide, you need a minimum of 100,000 passengers per year, and you have to commit yourself to something like £800,000 of flying time a year. A series charter, ie a contract for a given number of flights per season, as opposed to time charter, where you are buying aircraft hours year round with the rate more and more competitive the more hours you fly, which is what Harry uses, means you are having to pay 15 to 20 per cent more. Seven to eight years ago Harry based his programme on series charters breaking even with 75 per cent of the seats taken up. Every booking after that was pure profit. Now with the big firms competing on time charter, he needs 91 per cent occupancy on a series to get a profit per passenger of £1 compared with the £10 it used to be ten years ago.

Harry gave up advertising in the early 1960s. Then he was spending between £5,000 and £8,000 each January, having started years earlier with a 1in personal column announcement in the old *News Chronicle*. But as the years went by, Harry realised more and more that his enterprise depended very heavily, 100 per cent he says, on personal recommendation and repeat business, and so he knocked off advertising. Besides, he found employing professional advertising agents to run his account did not work either. It started with lavish lunches with the top man and declarations of the grand job to be done. But Harry and Rene discovered the agents were sending a mere lad down—and they had to start from scratch and tell him what the business was all about. 'So we ended up teaching them, instead of them teaching us,' says Harry. From that day Harry decided to write and produce his own brochure, and a very well organised, quality product it is too.

Harry's market is solidly middle-class, and he is competing with established tour operators like Cooks, Horizon and Wings. Harry made a definite decision not to expand, not to take the big leap from 20 to 30,000 up to 100,000 plus, which would have pushed up costs and taken large capital resources. In any case being big does not necessarily mean being profitable. The gospel of success according to Harry is to know precisely the market at which you are aiming, and to provide exactly the right number of seats to the right destinations at the right prices, which is difficult because tastes and fashions change but the programme has to be planned a year ahead. 'For these reasons we decided a few years ago that we wanted the minimum of expansion. We aim to perfect the product so all our aircraft seats and hotel beds are full, even though at a slightly higher price. We would rather be the best than the biggest,' he says. He and Rene felt that the business was based on this personal, friendly quality, and though Harry obviously cannot deal with everyone on a personal basis now, the way he did in the old days, he still believes it's a good business philosophy for his market. It seems a cardinal way of surviving in what is a tough business. In the last ten years the Travel Club has never made a loss, and its gross profits have risen from £24,000 to £94,000.

More to the point, having reached a plateau at this particular size, he is able to contain it and handle it with his existing management, and he and Rene can still travel, test the hotels, and handle all the negotiations. The business is not so big that if something starts to go wrong, they personally cannot put it right.

They both used to work a sixteen-hour day, did nothing but work for ten years after the war, and succeeded in building up a sound business which was to find itself, in the sixties, involved in a very different scale of competition to which it had been accustomed. The fact that the Travel Club has survived and endured in an industry which has suffered some notable failures, fiascos and disasters, with tour operators folding up right, left, and centre, is a tribute to Harry and his wife. It is also a tribute to the shrewd way he has operated, and to the policy decision he took to keep up-market, one from which he has not veered since. 'I cater for the market which the big chaps don't cater for,' he says, 'I can't look at an hotel with 200 to 300 beds, I want 30 to 40 and I don't want them in a towering concrete box.'

Harry genuinely does his best to keep faith with his clients. Since he is so heavily dependent on repeat business this is both prudent and sensible. Unlike most other tour operators he has never included inches of small print, and has never carried booking conditions. 'When I started with a bicycle I didn't know what booking conditions were,' he says, 'and I don't see why I should start now.' Interestingly no one has ever questioned the fact that there are no booking conditions. So Harry relies on what he calls common sense from both parties, and Common Law if only absolutely necessary. All this Harry believes helps him produce the perfect product, and, as he says, 'We are the optimum size to do it.' So he looks after the organisational side and Rene, who learned her cost accounting at Fords, sits up in the attic eyrie working wonders with the company's cash flow on her own personal comptometer.

Harry has had several approaches from big companies and airlines, evidently keen on taking him over. He mentions both Forte and BUA. 'But we have always turned our face against it,' says Harry. Obviously his company would be a useful prize for any big group determined to get into travel, and intent perhaps—counter to the practice of the industry—on starting up a serious operation for selling holidays by mail order. Many of the big groups, paying as much as £1 million and more, in commission to retail agents, have doubtless flirted with the idea, but have come to the conclusion they need the agents. Harry is accepted by the industry and never has used them, so no one gets particularly excited about his comparatively small mail order operation.

A man like Harry is the greatest asset his company has, and because of the decision he has taken to expand slowly, broadly holding the company at the size it is, he isn't engulfed, overwhelmed, or subject to the classic stresses which so often beset successful, small companies, driven by one man, when they start to grow and need more men, management and money than their originator and driving force can muster. In short, Harry deliberately keeps, as a matter of considered policy, to the size which he knows he can handle—and is content to leave it there.

Chapter 15

A case of corporate togetherness

Danbury Conversions is a prosperous and profitable firm. In the few years it has been trading it has become something of a legend in its own line, and is the largest converter of Volkswagen commercial vans into motor caravans in the United Kingdom. But it is made up of more than profits, production and sales records, for it is a company which bears detailed testimony to the fact that small businessmen and their working colleagues often place as much importance on independence, creative satisfaction and a close, comradely and affectionate quality of business life, as they do on money.

DANBURY Conversions is a small, successful company which takes Volkswagen motor vans and turns them into motor caravans in a disused gravel pit in Essex. It is run by three working directors, including the managing director who owns it. His name is George Dawson, and he is in business for himself for the somewhat paradoxical reason that when he was selling motor caravans for someone else he did far too well. His bosses said they were going to more than half what he was earning, and he said, then you know what you can do with your sales manager's job, don't you!

George is an opportunist. His whole approach to business is like that. He says he is strictly a pragmatic soul and does not believe in too much jazz or jargon. He would not be found, for example, fiddling with a slide rule working out his return on capital employed. Instead he goes by feel, driving by the seat of his pants. His fellow directors say he is classically the man who makes things happen, and they love him for it. They say that with George they are stretched, enthusiastic and believe in themselves, whereas wherever else they have worked they have just been competent.

They say they are cowards about their jobs, afraid of losing them, not in the sense that most people mean, but because they would be deprived of something very special. This something special is compounded of many things, but its main ingredients seem to be love and respect, and the fact that Danbury Conversions is a way of life. Respect is all right, but love is an unexpected word to be using in a profile about a small business. It is one you hesitate to write down, because you can already hear the cynics nearly busting their sides in the background. Before they do they should read on, for George and his fellow directors have arrived at the substantial truth that profits are perfectly splendid and proper things to have around you, but real people are even better.

George Dawson started his business life as a grocer's boy of twelve. He says his northern upbringing was harsh and down to earth, and he pays little heed to business conventions. He seldom wears a jacket or a suit, although he did contemplate it the day I visited the firm, but decided against it, and put on his Marks and Spencer woolly with the hole in the elbow instead. It goes better with the company image: informality, escapism, the open air and life on the open road.

George's right-hand man is Charles Wilkins, who had worked with him before he set up on his own, and later joined him as production director. He keeps the conversions rolling out so that George can sell them. In 1970 the firm produced 1,186 conversions. It is a figure which has made it something of a legend in the young, up-and-coming motor caravan business. Three years earlier its total was 100. Then it was near the bottom of the converters' league table: today it is the largest Volkswagen converter in the United Kingdom. Its turnover in pure conversion work, that is not counting the basic cost of the vehicle, was £280,000 in 1970. In the last four years, its pre-tax profits have soared: £2,852, £15,603, £30,411 and for 1970, £59,020.

Suddenly the directors find they are being invited to pleasant, civilised lunches by bankers, one of whom stirred his coffee and asked if George would like £250,000 to expand? Charles even had a letter from the bank which started 'Dear Mr Wilkins', but Mr Wilkins had been scored through, and Charles written instead. He laughed about it, since it was not all that long ago the bank scarcely wanted to know them. But George says when you do become successful you cannot go shifting your account just because of a thing like that. You cannot be nasty to people, and to be honest, if he had been in the banker's shoes, and saw this nut strolling in in an old Marks and Spencer cardigan asking for an increase of the firm's overdraft, he would have adopted much the same attitude. Still, George has to admit that the bank disguised its enthusiasm very well. Sometimes this is what Charles has to do, when he acts as unofficial mediator in the company. He is a secure, stable, dependable character who nicely balances the fire, flash and exuberance of the other two. When George and Joy are having one of their theatrical rows it is Charles who puts his head round the office door and tells them not to be silly buggers.

Joy is George's right-hand woman. She has worked for him since she was a chit of a girl who knew nothing. She is determined, headstrong, sometimes a bit wilful, but rather nice with it, and she is also acutely possessive about her job which she says she can do as well, if not better, than any man. She used to be George's secretary when they both worked for Canterbury Industrial Products, the motor caravan firm where he was sales manager, then she joined Danbury Conversions to be his secretary, and general dogsbody, too. Now she is rather grandly known as director in charge of administration. Besides George, Charles and Joy, Danbury Conversions has a workforce of nineteen plus five reps and six secretaries and office girls. The one thing it does not have is a ladies' toilet. When the girls want to go for a 'whisper' (George's word for it), Joy takes them by car to the public conveniences on Danbury village green.

When she joined George in the spring of 1967 the personnel of the firm consisted of George himself, Robert Taylor, one of the two original partners, who was bought out by George later on, and four lads. Not only did she do the secretarial work, pounding away on an old typewriter in an office which was built as a garden hut, with mice making nests underneath, but she also helped convert the vans, fitting cushions and curtains.

George, of course, was off selling; not just conversions, but ideas, propositions and prospects. The first to experience his persuasiveness was the Westminster Bank in Chelmsford. Just how he did it, with no money and nothing more reassuring behind him than his sales records from his previous firm (which, magpie-like, he had kept), is anybody's guess. But he convinced them that it was emphatically not a good idea to put his house into hock (which is what they wanted him to do), but far more sensible for them to increase the company's present overdraft from £2,000 to £4,000 (which they did not want to do). As it turned out this particular overdraft played a critical part in helping to get the company on the road.

To properly understand why, it is necessary to go back to the beginning, to when George parted company with Canterbury Industrial Products. He still has the sales records he clocked up there in his drawer at Danbury, and they show how, in his first year he sold 106 vehicles, in his second 287, in his third 470, in his fourth 525, and in his fifth 550. He went off on holiday feeling rather pleased with the 550, with the commission he was making which was bringing his earnings up to £4,500 a year, and, above all, with the satisfaction of a salesman who knows he is selling well. When he returned from holiday to be told his commission would be cut he felt disenchanted and bitter, but he is not the first man, nor will he be the last, to chuck up his job out of a sense of frustration, anger and injustice, start up for himself in the same line of business, and give his former employers a hard, competitive run for their money.

Selling has always been George's forte. After coming out of the navy he sold cleaners for Hoover. Later he ran a domestic appliance company which was suddenly taken over, leaving him with what he describes as a £500 copper handshake. With it came the realisation that his total lack of formal training and a rag-bag education did not even make him worth £3 a week as an office boy. But then he heard that the Ford dealership, from which he used to buy vans for his domestic appliance company, was starting motor caravan conversions. George's salesman nerve ends began to tingle and he landed a job with the company as sales manager. This was in 1962.

The motor caravan business had started a few years earlier, though who pioneered it is not totally clear. There were two contenders for the title, both now dead. One was an executive of the old Folkestone coach-building firm of Martin Walter, who noticed people coming to the coast at weekends in vans with mattresses spread on the floor, and reckoned his company could improve on that. He dreamed up the phenomenally effective marketing name of Dormobile, now a generally used synonym for motor caravan the way Hoover is for vacuum cleaner, and produced the first two-berther in 1957 at a price of £725. The other man was an inventive electrical engineer named Peter Pitt who started a firm called Pitt Moto Caravans. At one time Charles Wilkins was his production manager, and poor Charles had a lot to contend with, for Pitt would design something one day, tell Charles to go ahead, then come in the following morning, push his glasses up on his forehead, and say, 'Now, I've been thinking . . .' At this point Charles knew that he would have to start all over again.

Pitt always claimed the idea for a motor caravan came to him when he used a Volkswagen van on a photographic safari in Africa and thought how much better it would be if properly fitted for bed and board. Not only did he design and build the fittings for his first motor caravan on his kitchen table, but he fought a long battle with the government, and won it, over purchase tax. The fact that it is not levied on motor caravans, plus the economy, versatility, freedom and excitement the motor caravan gives, are the main reasons for the industry growing the way it has.

Most motor caravans owe their origins to the motor manufacturers' light commercial vehicles like the Volkswagen Kombi and Microbus, the basics of Danbury Conversions, two products which cost £1,280 and £1,320 respectively when finished. Among other vehicles used are the Bedford 15cwt, the Ford Transit, the Commer 1500, the Landrover, and a Mercedes commercial chassis. Some of the vehicles have progressed quite a way from the plain interiors of the early pioneer days, and have standards of sophisticated comfort akin to home, with refrigerators and showers. Other converters have even installed gas fires and water heaters. The last word in luxury is a £15,000 vehicle called the

Auto Roam Land Cruiser, which sleeps eight, has a fully equipped bathroom, a kitchen, a verandah on top of the vehicle and, for the driver, a swivel aircraft-style seat, power steering and closed circuit television for rear vision. The caravan converters have clearly learned that, like selling conventional cars, you need to keep the market stimulated with new models, ideas, and innovations.

The great selling point of the Dormobile Elba (basically a Ford Escort de luxe 8cwt van with a 1600cc Ford Cortina GT engine) was its speed. I described it in a *Sunday Times* report in October 1969. 'The fastest bed-sitter in Britain has extra straps to hold its roof on. Since it is capable of 100mph this seems a sensible precaution. For faint hearts like me, nurtured in a staid, immobile, semi-detached, the idea of a GT model pied-à-terre takes some getting used to. But for the country's youthful motor caravan industry and its clients, there is, it seems, both money to be made and a measure of upmanship to be enjoyed, in opening the throttle and having a double bed show a clean pair of castors to pretty nearly everything else on the road!'

George cut his teeth selling motor caravans in a market which he calculates was worth a total of about £350,000 a year in retail sales. In the late 1950s motor caravans were exhibited at the London Motor Show for the first time, and he thinks that just after this there must have been about 3,500 registered. It is impossible to get precise figures by looking at the car registration statistics because motor caravans are not listed separately as a class, but the Society of Motor Manufacturers says over 6,300 were converted in 1970. What is certain is that in the last four and a half years, Danbury Conversions has contributed over 4,000 motor caravans to that figure. It is an achievement which affords George nothing but satisfaction now, although the crisis which ultimately led to it still rankles.

At first, after parting company with his employers, he trudged round knocking at the opposition's doors in search of a job. 'I had an investment in the expertise I had acquired in the motor caravan business and didn't want to throw it all overboard,' he says. 'But the interviews were rather like auditions—don't call us, we'll call you.' He was looking for a job for nearly four months.

At the same time he had been talking about buying into Danbury Conversions, a small firm which had been going for a couple of years with two partners, one of them more or less on a part-time basis. This partner eventually pulled out, while the other remained. The business the company was doing was not particularly encouraging. George could see the potential but had no money to buy in. He had £200 in the bank and a wife and three children to support. All he could offer the firm was sales expertise, and the promise to pay for his shares out of his earnings as he went along. Once he was in the firm it took him three months to restructure it as a limited company because of various complications, not the least of which was the legacy of a £2,000 overdraft at the bank in Chelmsford, another £2,000 owing to suppliers for materials and only one demonstration vehicle.

This was the point at which he made his memorable visit to the bank. Not only was the money needed to pay off some of the firm's debts put George felt it was vital that Danbury Conversions should exhibit at the London Motor Show in the autumn of 1967, and he knew this would set the firm back about £1,250. Before he could even buy stand space the company had to be a member of the Society of Motor Manufacturers, and before being accepted as a member, it had to be able to meet certain requirements. These involved the society in sending one of their officials to Danbury to inspect the enterprise. What Danbury Conversions had to show was pretty rudimentary, especially in the way of production facilities. There was scarcely an office you could call an office, and when it rained most of the ground turned into a morass. So George went down the village and bought an 8ft garden hut from Poulton Portables and set it up as an office. When the inspector arrived from the Society of Motor Manufacturers he was clearly taken aback at being conducted down a lane, into an old gravel pit, to the creosoted hut. Fortunately he was a man of rare imagination and perception and when he put in his report recommending Danbury Conversions should become a member of the society he described the garden hut, the straggle of old buildings and the swampy gravel pit as a 'mini-industrial estate'. Danbury Conversions appeared at the 1967 Motor Show.

In 1968, for the first time, Danbury Conversions was in the black, even though the balance was only about £5. From then on the business prospered and the company's bank balance got fatter and fatter. The day George, Charles and Joy talked to me, four years to the day the company was formed, Danbury Conversions had something like £160,000 on deposit, £20,000 on current account, and had just paid a total of £40,000 for an old mansion, cottages and ground in Danbury with a view to using it as a new office headquarters, and to provide housing for some of their workpeople.

Naturally, in between the two dates there had been moments of acute anxiety, crises which afflict any firm which is growing, and which seem all the more traumatic at the time than perhaps they do in retrospect. Curiously, one of the hazards of running a motor caravan business centres quite explicitly on one of the main reasons why it thrives. This is purchase tax. I have already pointed out it is not levied on a motor caravan, unlike a car, and for many buyers this is an attractive consideration. None the less it is a fact which make George, Charles and Joy thoroughly nervous before a budget. Who knows what dark thoughts the chancellor of the exchequer may harbour about motor caravans? 'It might not kill us now, but it wouldn't do us much good,' says George. 'But in the early days if the chancellor had clapped on purchase tax it would have flattened us.' There was a year when the firm had a stack of vehicles awaiting conversions and budget day was getting nearer and nearer. The hold up was due to a shortage of cookers, sinks and some other pieces of equipment. So George got up at four one morning, drove in a motor caravan to Stockport for the cookers, then to Cirencester for the sinks and on to Kentish Town for the last pieces of equipment. It was a long, hard, slow journey. When he got back he was told he need not have bothered because there were no drip pans for the cookers. Despite this George managed to make 139 deliveries between January and March prior to the budget. In the event the effort was not necessary, but who was to know?

The response George received after his marathon rally round manufacturing Britain getting the bits and pieces for the vehicles was enough to convince him he and his partner should part company. It was a pity because George says he was a pleasant, gentlemanly chap, but as business partners they were ill suited. George felt that in crises he failed to respond in a positive way; 'it seemed to me that the common-sense thing to do was to make the conversions, sell them, get them promptly delivered and get the brass in smartly,' says George. One day it got to the point when George lost his temper, found himself gripping the other man by the lapels and had to be persuaded to let go. He is not particularly proud of this. The upshot was an agreement for George to buy his partner out for £7,500; he borrowed £2,500 and contracted to pay the rest off in two years, and did it in fifteen months. It was quite a gamble because at this point he had committed himself to a large sum of money, but the firm was not yet an officially appointed converter for Volkswagen.

Like the Society of Motor Manufacturers, Volkswagen Motors arrived on a tour of inspection. By this time there were two sheds, an acre of mud (because it had rained just before they arrived) and only five vehicles on the site; and Danbury Conversions was only one of four companies vying for the appointment. However, it so happened that the inspection occurred at a time when Volkswagen was undergoing a management reorganisation in Great Britain. For George the timing was meticulous. He did his great selling act, the new broom at Volkswagen took over, and four months later Danbury Conversions was appointed as official converter. This was a tremendous landmark in the company's development, because it meant the whole Volkswagen dealer network was open to it, and it got official backing in things like advertising.

Winning this would not have been of much value if the product had not been both right for the market and competitive. Four days before the 1969 Motor Show George was told by Volkswagen that the chassis prices of the Kombi and Micobus were to be increased by £115 and £120. 'We did some sums, slanted our price in favour of the Microbus and we were still £25, £75 and £125 cheaper than the leading competitive models,' says George. Danbury Conversions was the first company to design forward-facing locker seats into its motor caravan, and in this particular feature had the market to itself for almost three years, until the competition followed suit in 1970. Forward-facing seats were a bull marketing point because, according to the motoring caravan cognoscenti, they reduced travel sickness, but even more appealing was the fact that the conversion could be used as a caravan for a couple of months of the year, and as a family estate car in which to do the shopping and fetch the children from school in the other ten months. It is the sort of unique selling proposition into which salesmen can really get their teeth.

Danbury Conversions thrives on excitement, fun and hard work, though there are times when the three directors get the feeling they are trying to run a railway engine over a bridge of twigs. Charles says they like the business because they like the people they meet in it, and they reel off the names of jolly characters who run Volkswagen distributorships all over the country. All three are away a lot, demonstrating vehicles, exhibiting at caravan and camping shows. Between the London Motor Show in the autumn of 1970 and March 1971 Joy had been away virtually every weekend. She says it is fortunate she has a husband who likes to work hard and puts in long hours himself. This means she is often home before he is because she only lives ten to fifteen minutes drive away from Danbury. When they do have a weekend together they enjoy it all the more and the marriage has no chance to get dull or strained, with her complaining about being trapped between four walls and the kitchen sink.

Even so she has paid a price: she has no children. She is sad about this. She knows she could get away from the firm, have a baby and then come back again; 'but the idea of someone else looking after my children is alien. I would be too possessive about them. I feel the same about my job. I'm possessive about that too.' The human cost of committing themselves totally to the company, the social deprivation, the family difficulties it causes, was something which they had not thought about very hard. They discussed it with sorrow, perhaps even remorse, I do not know. George says he paid the price of his two elder children growing away from him, thinking he does not care about them. His little girl? 'That's all right, she knows I love her.' Both he and Joy say Charles is a better person than they are in a family sense. When he goes away he always tries to take his wife with him, or, if not, he makes sure he flies back home that night if at all possible. If they could start again, and order things differently, both Joy and George would try to love their own people more than they have.

As a company Danbury Conversions seems to generate strong feelings and breed determined people. The directors identify with the firm in a very positive fashion. You would expect them to be interested, devoted and absorbed, but what comes as something of a shock is their intense passion for it. They have this anxiety that as it grows it will lose the flavour and spirit of the early days, the days when Joy knew all the men on the shop floor by their Christian names. There was a time when George, suffering his usual pre-budget twitches, looked at all the vehicles they had waiting to be converted, called the men together, told them he had the wind up about the chancellor's intentions and asked if they could help in any way. (This was before Charles had arrived to organise production.) The men decided to work right through, not on a rota of eight-hour shifts, but twenty-four hours at a time. They worked it all out by themselves and set to, the stubble growing steadily on their chins as they worked, and George got his deliveries in time. Nowadays he has the capacity to do twenty-two conversions a day if needs be, 5,000 vehicles a year.

Capacity is one thing, selling the vehicles is quite another. What happens is that George sets the year's targets using an amalgam of expertise and intuition. 'Look,' he says, 'if we did 1,100 units last year surely we can do 1,500 this.' Anyway, as he is fond of saying, there are no absolutes, everything is relative, and business decisions are not all taken according to the precepts of the Harvard Business School, a lot of them are made irrationally and emotionally. He is suspicious of hawk-eyed, incisive decision-making where people are always right. When the sensible things have been done, like assuring finance and supplies, controlling stocks, meeting production schedules and delivery dates, then he still falls back largely on the intuitive, a-sniff-in-the-air-and-a-feel-of-the-market style of management. That, plus some gambling, plus some good luck and sheer hard work.

The whole ethos of the company is selling. If George and his co-directors have no clear idea of its long-term objectives, they see the short-term ones with great clarity: selling more units than the year before. Not building them, but selling and delivering them. They keep the running totals on blackboards in the office. Those blackboards are their management information system, with at-a-glance retrieval and a quick scratch of chalk to keep the information up to date. The figures on them present an historic picture. They show how Danbury Conversions, in the space of four short years, hauled itself from being a virtual nonentity in the business to being top position as a Volkswagen converter. The blackboards even have other firm's fortunes encapsulated in chalky white. There is an entry showing how many Volkswagen shells Danbury Conversions took in 1970, which were originally destined for their largest competitor, but which that firm did not take up. George took them instead. When I was there a German buyer was due to visit them the next day. 'We'll leave that figure up,' said George. 'It will give him something to think about.'

Of course, they have made mistakes, but ask about their strengths, and they say that in every proposition there is an opportunity, and one or the other of them will see it, and one or the other of them will recognise it if it is the right one for them. Yet the way they regard the business goes deeper than recognising the right proposition when it comes along. This was how Charles described it. 'We are exceptional, and we have something going for us, because we care. We feel we owe something to every person who buys one of our conversions. The three of us feel we have a total commitment to thirty-odd other people. As long as the product is a benefit to us and to the people who buy it, and we are backing it, not with a written guarantee, but with our belief, this is what is important. This company enables us to express ourselves, to satisfy our ego. Joy and I have ability, and Danbury Conversions has given us the opportunity to use it. This is nothing to do with having shareholdings in the company, it's nothing to do with finance, or making loads of money.' As it happens Charles has just one share. So does Joy. Also, as it happens, this particular fact produced in our conversation a long, involved argument and counter argument among the trio in which George and Joy tended to shout at each other. George exhorted me to tell her what happened in industry, how directors took up shares, were given stock options, and all the rest. It finished with Joy saying, 'You two still regard me as a bloody kid, patting me on the head, and not taking my money and treating me as if I were a little girl.'

The argument goes back a few years ago when the company needed money, and Joy offered her savings, £300, and George refused point blank to let her risk them. 'He said he was the one who took the risk, and I was only a bit of a girl and it was all I had in the world.' Now George wants the directors to have some shares Joy, being female, unpredictable and proud, says she was refused once so she is not going to have any now: so there.

They are not ones for writing memos to each other, or having stiff, formal meetings to discuss policy. They do this over lunch at the Army and Navy or the Blue Boar in Maldon, or over a few drinks at the Bell in Danbury. Their relationship with each other is deep and personal, and it is important because without it Danbury Conversions could not be what it is. Joy says, 'We are three mates together,' an unexpected thing for a woman to say. Charles's son, who is eighteen, says they all love each other. On top of that there is respect, admiration, protectiveness and honesty.

There was a time, not so long ago, when Charles had the feeling, and so did the others, that they were not talking to each other properly, they were not communicating. It was a period when they had all been working enormously hard, with two different shows close together, something like twenty days of working eighteen hours and more each day. On top of that a wall in the yard collapsed on twenty-five vans waiting to be converted. Everything seemed to be running at an unprecedented frenzied level and Charles told the other two, 'Look, you can shoot me if you like, but we are getting overworked, we've stopped talking to each other, we are starting to blame each other, so for Godsake let's remember we are not in this for the money, but for us.' He reckons that if the heart of something is right and the bits on the fringes are wrong the situation is by no means impossible, but the opposite way round it is. This was a case of Charles being a sheet anchor, not just the production director; the man with an immense capacity for listening, for thinking and then pronouncing on a problem with a degree of finality which makes it hard to say any more about it. He is frequently cast in the role of adjudicator between the other two, the man who is asked to judge one course of action against another. He will tell you that George, with his drive, and Joy with her razor-sharp mind, are the two who set the pace: he follows and does his bit. This is greeted with loyal protestations from Joy and 'Silly bugger' from George. But Charles sticks to his guns and says it truly is the way it works. 'With this kind of lead we are able most of the time to find the right solutions to our problems,' he says.

To an outsider some problems might seem small, not much more than pinpricks really, but they can build up to something quite large in the minds of people running a firm. They have been having trouble with a man whose house backs on to the old gravel pit where they have their workshops, and he is always writing letters to George, to the local council and the newspapers complaining about something or other. George wanted to build a cover over the yard which would have cut down a lot of the noise, but this man's intervention stopped it. George says his men have their transistors on, playing them loud; he turns them down a bit as he passes, but being young they turn the volume up again, and the man over the back doesn't like that. Nor does he like it when the lads hit their thumbs with a hammer and understandably, says George, give forth with a few expletives. Obviously this fellow was beginning to get George down, which was odd when you consider there are many bigger problems with which he copes happily. He says it is because he has got a thing about people being negative, putting up blocks to this or that, and not offering anything constructive in its place. Yes, negativism. He goes on quite a lot about it.

At least money is not one of their problems any more. It is more a matter of knowing what to do with it. They realise the latent danger in the purchase tax situation, and the fact that it is essentially a one-product company which makes them vulnerable both to chancellors and a change in public taste. They often talk about diversifying but have not found anything which really convinced them yet. This is why they put the money which was mounting up in the bank into property, the large old house they bought in the village. 'It makes us feel we have something behind us, something solid. It's a reassurance,' says Joy. Actually, they talk about money in a slightly obtuse, sideways fashion, as though it were something which came with the job coincidentally, and which they have learned to live with. George declares that the other two pay him £120 a week, and he pays them £60 a week each, and they have a share out at the end of the year. (George's wife Ellen is also a director.) In 1970 the directors' emoluments, as accountants like to phrase it, were £27,000.

They all have nice cars and live comfortably, but the idea of making untold fortunes, of succumbing to the velvet-tongued blandishments of the merchant bankers, of selling out or going public, leaves them feeling quite indifferent. It is not what they want. They want to continue doing what they are doing now, running Danbury Conversions the way they have been. The reason is clear and uncomplicated. It is fun, it is satisfying and the business sustains friendship, loyalty, affection and respect for each other. You see, even in business people find a time and place for enchantment.

Chapter 16

The perennial problem of money

The experience of Contemporary Industries shows the importance of having the right money at the right time. It is a problem which afflicts countless small firms. Their lack of capital, difficulty of knowing where to go for it, dependence on bank overdrafts and big firms paying their bills, makes them especially vulnerable during credit squeezes. They have long felt the tax system discriminated against them, hazarding their continued existence and profitability, a serious restraint since profits are their life blood and most small firms rely on them to finance expansion.

IN many respects Danbury Conversions is an uncommon firm and one of the more uncommon things about it is that it is singularly unworried about money. Except for the very early days when George Dawson had to argue for an extension of an overdraft in the bank manager's office, it has put up a profits performance of such impressive calibre, sustaining its own growth from its own resources, that had it felt the need for outside backers to finance further expansion it would have had little trouble in raising the money. But the firm chose a different course. It preferred to fund its own growth and carry on the way it had been without being committed to outsiders. This is by no means unusual among small businesses, where the desire for independence and the emphasis on personal values shine out like beacons. But whether a company like Danbury Conversions could have afforded such an autonomous posture, whether its business philosophy would have evolved differently, if the hard cash had not been available to subsidise its attitude, is a matter of speculation. The truth is that while independence is a flame which a host of small businessmen are determined will not be snuffed out, it is equally true that many of them do not make sufficient profit to fan and fuel it. Small firms tend to operate under pinched financial circumstances and for innumerable owners of small businesses money is a source of constant anxiety, frustration and dissatisfaction. The evidence suggests that the experience of firms like Danbury Conversions is rare, especially so over the last four or five years of the 1960s when the company was forging ahead while other small firms were going to the wall in mounting and unparalleled numbers, the victims of severe deflationary policies.

For starting, running and expanding a business, money is an essential fuel. Having the right type of finance at the right time in the requisite amounts is a problem which increasingly occupies the minds of small businessmen. Allied to those two other factors in the tedious and persistent trinity of difficulty—premises and staff—it is a problem which is never completely solved. You only have to read through the evidence submitted to the Bolton Committee by organisations like the Smaller Businesses Association, the Confederation of British Industry and the Institute of Directors to realise that it has come to occupy an almost obsessive place in small business thinking.

The story of Wally Orner, the predicament he found himself in because of the lack of money and his search for it, is the story of scores of owners of small firms whose endeavours to walk a financial tightrope produces an uncertain and erratic performance with the prospect of a nasty fall apparent in every step. Fortunately Wally was lucky and intelligent enough to regain his balance almost at the last moment. How he managed to do it is worth recounting because there are lessons in it for everyone in a similar situation and warnings for those who might be.

Wally's business grew from a hobby and it nearly collapsed because of it. There was a time when, if you had chucked Wally in at the deep end with all his debts hanging round his neck, he would have plummeted to the bottom like a stone, producing a spectacle as sad as it would have been inapposite, since Wally is something of an expert on deep water and diving into it. For years he was an amateur diving coach and among his star pupils was diving champion Brian Phelps. While he was coaching, Wally was also running his company, Contemporary Industries, which makes top-quality springboards and other swimming-pool equipment. Unfortunately Wally was treating it more as a vehicle for his coaching activities than his business ambitions and while his protégés were winning medals, he was losing money and acquiring debts. When he decided eventually to stop coaching and concentrate his efforts on running his business it didn't take him long to realise he was desperately in need of financial help, and that he had left it rather late in the day to get it. But everywhere he went the price of funds to rescue the business was the surrender of his controlling interest and the loss of his independence. It was a notion he disliked thoroughly.

How Wally, a slightly-built, bright and lively chap, got into business in the first place, is linked directly to his efforts to improve standards in his sport. It was while he was a member of the Highgate Diving Club in London that he designed and produced (as a club project, not a business operation) a new type of aluminium springboard in which he brought together his diving expertise and an engineering background. In the early 1950s the quality of diving equipment was poor. It had not advanced much since the 1920s and, according to Wally, the manufacturers' attitude to design was, 'if boards break we'll make them thicker.' None the less wooden boards still kept breaking. These springboards, built like bridges, were, in the opinion of Wally and his diving friends, severely curtailing the improvement of diving standards in the country. Better boards were being built in America, but Britain's trade balance was not healthy, dollars were not available to buy them.

The springboard which Wally and a couple of other chaps built in 1953 filled a gap in the market, and it was bought and installed in its baths by Finsbury Borough Council, a fact which illuminated its commercial possibilities. So Wally started a small business with an accommodation address in London and put an advertisement in the *Baths Service Journal*. Things went fairly well and he sold boards and even exported them to places like the Soviet Union.

'But I was not a 100 per cent dedicated businessman and for about eleven years I split my interest between business and the sport and as a result the annual turnover of the company languished at about £10,000,' says Wally.

When he gave up coaching in 1964 to concentrate on his business he started to develop a range of products other than springboards for the wet areas of swimming pools. The next few years were complicated and difficult. There were quality control problems with subcontractors and long production delays. At one stage Wally and the contractors merged their interests, but this did not work and had to be unravelled with the consequence that for five months in 1967 there was virtually no production.

During this time Wally was encouraged by the reception his boards were getting. If he failed to get an order first time round, he tended to get it the second. Sometimes because of the delivery problems baths' superintendents would get their local council committees to wait for a board from Contemporary Industries rather than buy a more readily available replacement. Wally never took much notice of what the existing makers were doing, or what they were charging. He costed his equipment and charged accordingly. He considered it was the best on the market and could therefore stand the premium price.

Encouraging as all this was, he found himself getting caught up in successive credit squeezes, increasingly being cut back on the traditional source of funds for the small business, the overdraft from the local bank. The business tottered along financially with some private people putting in money because of their interest in the sport. In all a total of £5,000 was injected in the business like this. The backers felt that if Contemporary Industries folded it would be a death blow for British diving.

With the help of these loans and bolstered by the combined goodwill and credit of his suppliers, Wally somehow managed to survive. Roughly speaking the yearly losses were covered by the loans, but even so at the end of 1967 the firm's cumulative loss was £21,000. In the following year, the year when the company was disentangled from its involvement with its previous firm of subcontractors and the first year in which it undertook its own engineering work, there was a small profit; things looked brighter than they had done for some time. There was even some slight government relaxation which made credit a little easier and after two years of slog prospects were improving. It was then that Wally was dealt a hard knock by circumstances quite outside his control. World nickel prices started to rocket upwards with the consequence that stainless steel prices rose by 50 per cent. Wally used a lot of stainless steel and he was working on fixed price contracts. The company found itself back in the red to the tune of over £7,000.

Again Wally found himself in an unenviable and frustrating position. For in 1970 more and more baths wanted Contemporary Industries' fibre-glass springboards, and the orders arrived in a steady stream. The market was clearly opening up. But there was an urgent need for money to be pumped into the business in order to pay off debts to private individuals and to suppliers, and to be able to expand it in terms of machines, men and larger premises in order to take advantage of the opportunities.

Wally freely admits he was inexperienced in raising money. It took time and effort. It meant telling the Contemporary Industries' story over and over again; being questioned on its prospects; explaining its problems. And, of course, all the time this was happening the business still had to be run and the problems were getting larger. Finding financial backers took much longer than he thought. With hindsight he now realises that instead of just approaching one financial institution at a time he should have been opening up several avenues. Even when he did find the right sort of backer, who was prepared to come in and be content with a minority interest, it still took much longer to actually get the money than he imagined.

In all he spent about six months trying to raise funds. 'And during that time you are running down,' he says. 'If you knew how long it would take you would make different decisions along the way than the ones you did. You are asked to provide figures, budgets and sales forecasts and then they get out of date and you are asked to do them again.' Wally had no department of backroom boys to do the job; as managing director he had to sit down and do it himself. The ironic thing was that to raise money it cost him money he did not have, especially in the diversion of management effort.

The situation also imposed a strain on his credibility with suppliers. Wally had gone to great pains to keep them posted, to tell them what was happening and how they would get their money shortly. But when it took longer than he anticipated he had to write to them again, saying how sorry he was for the delay, but the money would be coming. Being an honest man, sensitive of his integrity, he found the situation very worrying personally. In fact he could have gone into liquidation a lot earlier and solved his problems, but he strongly felt the commitment to suppliers and to private individuals who had put money into the business—one of them was a schoolteacher who invested £1,000—to struggle and carry on.

Wally's new shareholder was the Small Business Capital Fund, a newish company supplying risk capital to firms in which it considered there were good prospects of growth. The fund is backed by Co-operative Insurance Society money and the Taylor Nelson market research group. It appealed to Wally because it was prepared to take a minority holding and give management advice if needed. The Small Business Capital Fund was prepared to support Contemporary Industries because it was impressed by its first-class product, by the prospects for it and by the sheer resilience and dynamism of Wally himself. To the Small Business Capital Fund, Contemporary Industries was the classic small company which had gone as far as it could on the limited resources available to it.

So at the beginning of 1971 it took a £50,000 stake in Contemporary Industries. The money made an enormous and immediate difference. Most important of all, it unlocked Wally's suppliers of material from what might be called a seized-up state. There was between £8,000 and £10,000 owing to them and some accounts were a year overdue. With one exception the money enabled Wally to win back his credit rating with them, and there were no further restraints on getting materials.

The second pressing problem it helped solve was the question of machines. The machines which Wally had been using all during this period had not been properly repaired when they broke down because there was no money to do it. So the chaps working them had to improvise and do the best they could, which was inefficient and in the long run costly. So the money also financed new machines.

Then there was the outstanding problem of staff. Wally was able to take on a full-time draughtsman instead of farming out the work, and he was able to fill a gap on the accounting side to help get a grip on the administration and produce something better than the crude costings which had been used previously. Prior to the Small Business Capital Fund coming in morale in the works had been at a low ebb, and good people had been leaving the company. When the word filtered through that money was coming it helped remove the uncertainty that some of the workpeople must have felt, and from then on there was a much better spirit in the place.

Lastly it solved the problem of space. Wally's premises in London were cramped and room to expand was vital if the firm was to take advantage of the unsatisfied demand for its equipment. So Wally was able to extend into new premises a few doors along the road, and by the end of 1971 he was expecting that the expansion, fuelled by the all important new funds, would bring in sales of £153,000. Future prospects were even brighter. The pool equipment business was growing at such a rate that in another five years Wally reckoned the firm could be winning sales of nearly £500,000 a year.

The message which comes out of Wally's experience is clear enough and it goes back to the proposition with which we started the story of Contemporary Industries: the need to have the right money, at the right time, in the right amounts. As a basic business requirement it sounds simple, but in practice it is exceedingly difficult to attain. This is not just because of the failings of small businessmen themselves in not budgeting and planning properly, of not making critical assessments of the ifs and whys of needing money and on what sort of terms, although this is part of it, but because they mostly start with the firm conviction that when it comes to raising funds the dice are loaded against them.

It is impossible to escape the impression that many of the people who run small firms see themselves rather like the prey of the shrike, a bird which has the unappealing habit of impaling its victims on sharp and prickly thorns. In this instance the government is represented by the little butcher bird while they, its victims, are transfixed on two very spiky thorns, one being the inadequacy of the financial mechanism to meet their needs, the other being a tax system which discriminates against them.

The small man has long harboured the suspicion that the financial machine is geared to serving the needs of big business, not him. He sees the two joining in a powerful alliance unhelpful to him, a view in which it is possible to discern strands of truth, especially in some of the less reputable and murkier areas of business financing. But largely the attitude is engendered by misunderstanding and fundamental lack of knowledge of how various institutions work and what, in terms of supplying money, their function is. Understandably he relates his financial difficulties to his own situation. There is nothing else to which he can relate them.

The details which compound the general problem are plain enough. First there is the small firm's lack of capital and the difficulty of raising it. There is its substantial dependence on trade credit and on firms paying their bills promptly. The paucity of capital is inevitable because of the inherent nature of the small firm, launched as it mostly is on the savings of its owner, on a loan from the family and a bank overdraft, but these are rarely substantial enough to meet the financial demands of a growing business. Secondly the difficulties he experiences in raising money are directly related to the limited economic base of the small firm, the fact that it does not enjoy the name and status of a large concern and it cannot offer the same security. Bank credit, for instance, may be more costly to the small firm for the simple reason that transaction costs are proportionately higher for small than for large loans. Experience makes it clear that small firms do experience difficulty in obtaining risk capital, but the difficulties may well be due less to the lack of a supply of capital for small business and more to the economics of providing financial information services.

The point is that it must be relatively more expensive to keep small firms informed about financial facilities open to them than large ones. Similarly on the small man's side of the fence it is relatively more costly (and you will recall this was a discovery Wally Orner made when he was searching for backing) to tell potential lenders about the company's performance and prospects.

In addition it is argued that certain conventions adopted by financial institutions restrict the flow of finance to smaller companies. While transaction costs are relatively higher for small loans than large ones, the narrow differential charged on smaller as against larger loans does not seem to reflect this. Therefore it could be of advantage to small firms if they paid a higher rate for their money, a more realistic charge considering the work involved in it, rather than being refused money outright at some conventionally fixed lower rate. It is sometimes forgotten that the price charged for money is only dear or cheap relative to the results you get using it. Borrowing at 18 per cent, high as the rate may seem, cannot be too onerous if you are earning 36 per cent on it. Another instance where financial convention slows the flow of money to small companies is that the lower limit set by insurance companies and pension funds for mortgage is often unnecessarily high and the valuation of properties on the conservative side.

Thus both the facts of life of being small plus the established and conventional attitudes of money lending institutions tend to make life difficult for the small firm. On top of these are the effects of public policy. In recent years the general financial problem of small companies has been exacerbated by successive credit squeezes, although this is not a phenomenon which is confined to the United Kingdom alone. The OECD study which looked at the problems and policies relating to small and medium-sized businesses on an international basis found that the volume of investment loans to smaller enterprises is apt to fluctuate because financial institutions have a tendency to start by cutting their money supply to the smaller enterprises when the money market becomes tight and to increase it when the money market becomes easier.

Clearly when a small company depends on bank credit as an orthodox and traditional mechanism for financing its business, anything which disturbs or restrains the flow of that credit will have a proportionately greater effect on the small concern than a larger one with recourse to other sources of finance. This is largely what so much of the bitterness among small businessmen has been about in recent years. It becomes increasingly clear the more one studies small firms that the major difference between the investment behaviour of a small and a large concern is in their methods of financing. An almost exclusive reliance on bank lending makes them all the more vulnerable when the Bank of England puts the pressure on banks and directs them to keep their overdraft levels down. Small businessmen point to a variety of fiscal measures introduced in the 1960s—import deposits was a particularly unloved one—which meant they had to use banking facilities more often than they might otherwise have done. So when the facilities were rapidly withdrawn because of the credit squeeze, many small concerns found themselves in acutely difficult circumstances. When a credit squeeze removes the small man's local bank as a simple and uncomplicated source of finance, it produces a vacuum which it is scarcely possible for other financial institutions to fill.

In any case the owners of small businesses tend to be conservative in their attitudes to obtaining alternative finance either because they believe it to be too expensive, or they are convinced that the price of the money advanced will be too much interference in their affairs, or loss of control of their firm. This was an important consideration for Wally Orner when he was searching for money. The fact is that their local bank has always been the place where they have raised money when they needed it, and they scarcely think much beyond it. They are well aware that there are inherent financial drawbacks in being small, and they have learned to live with them. What they have not been successful at doing is coping with the bewildering situation in which they find themselves when this traditional, almost taken-for-granted source of funds is instructed from loftier heights to turn off the tap. This was demonstrated by the authors of one of the Bolton Committee's research reports[1] who interviewed a number of small businessmen. This was the view of the managing director of a firm manufacturing jewellery in the Midlands.

'It's not just government SET and so on—government policy generally makes it very difficult for the small firm to exist. We haven't got the collateral the bank manager wants. He just assesses us personally. You need credit to pay purchase tax, but my bank manager says nothing over £4,000 can be advanced, and that it's nothing to do with him. My turnover increases by over £5,000 per year which I have to finance. How can you do this with a reduced overdraft? People are being squeezed out. There've been 210 jewellery firms which haven't survived since 1961 because they couldn't get credit.'

The owner of a wholesale distribution firm, also in the Midlands, thought that the risk was now too great for a small man to start up. 'When you think of salaries and rents and not being able to get credit. You could build up capital in the late 40s—that's all finished now.' And from a hairdresser in Cheshire: 'We'd like to expand but you've got to have the bank behind you and they'll only lend when the sun shines—when it rains pass it on to you. They're screaming now because I'm overdrawn, so that means I can't get new premises.'

Government fiscal policies and the way they seem to the owners of small businesses to be designed to lay a disproportionate burden on their shoulders are a major cause of discontent. If you are looking for something which triggered off the complaints, the 1965 Finance Act is as good as anything. There was particular resentment for the section dealing with close companies—those with five or fewer controlling shareholders—which required that such a company had to distribute to shareholders a fixed proportion of its income after paying Corporation Tax.

Obviously the term 'small firm' is not a fiscal any more than it is a legalistic concept. The tax problems of small concerns have not arisen because the tax measures were directed at small firms as such. The central point hammered home by all those who argue for corporate tax reform is that the system weighs disproportionately on small firms by virtue of their size and their character.

This was how the Taxation Committee of the Confederation of British Industry put the case to the Bolton Committee.

'The two most important characteristics of a small firm for present purposes are the independence it offers to the entrepreneur and his family and the frequent necessity to raise finance from within the family circle or the firm itself. The desire for independence is a powerful incentive to enterprise and one that we believe should be encouraged, particularly if monopolies legislation and other forms of state surveillance and intervention are directed at large firms merely by virtue of their size. If the proprietors' wish to retain control of their business is frustrated by fiscal means, the scope for personal initiative is reduced in an economy where the opportunities to be one's own master are already too few. But the retention of independence for the family firm poses financial problems from which larger firms are substantially immune. We are not basically asking that small firms should be accorded preferential treatment, although we believe a strong case could be argued for such a preference. We are simply asking for the removal of disadvantages inflicted on them by the present system.'

Taxation is a large, knotty and complicated subject which would easily consume several volumes on its own. So without getting bogged down in too much detail I shall try to paint a broad picture of the tax measures which have produced such simmering resentment among small businessmen ever since the mid 1960s; to show how they have worked to the disadvantage of smaller firms; and to indicate what the Anthony Barber budget of 1971 has done to alleviate the situation of small companies. In this context it is worth returning first to the Taxation Committee of the CBI and its submission to the Bolton Committee. In examining the characteristics of the United Kingdom tax system it says:

'The UK tax system is distinguished from those of most other developed economies by being more burdensome on saving and capital and having higher rates of tax at the top of the scale on earned income, investment income and inheritance. These qualities of the system are particularly inimical to unincorporated businesses but are also damaging for small firms more generally. The complexity of the tax system constitutes an administrative burden that is relatively heavier for smaller compar plexity is largely due to anti-avoidance legislation, lative pursuit of avoidance has been carried on with its cost. The complexity of investment grants and s ployment tax is also burdensome for small firms.

'It is difficult for the small potential entrepreneur ever to save enough capital to begin. The scales are loaded against him; if the business fails he obtains no tax relief on his losses, but if he succeeds the profits are heavily taxed; the state shares the profits but not the losses. This general characteristic of the tax system is especially harmful to potential entrepreneurs since their risks are high. Valuation and other problems make estate duty a more burdensome tax on unquoted than on quoted securities. Family businesses incur this burden every generation.

'The small firm loses as a sole trader or partnership by paying surtax on all reinvested funds and as a company by incurring a double charge to capital gains tax, a charge which is more onerous for small companies than large. The shortage of funds caused by high rates of taxation constitutes an obstacle to the expansion of established small firms.

'The average rate of tax on corporate profits, distributed and undistributed, is now some 60%; this and other taxes were cited as obstacles to expansion by a large proportion of the respondents to our general questionnaire addressed to all small firm members. These problems of the small firm are aggravated when, as at present, credit is scarce and dear.'

It was economist John McCulloch, one of Gladstone's contemporaries, who wrote: 'Oppression either raises men into heroes, or sinks them into slaves; and taxation, according to its magnitude, and the mode in which it is exacted, either makes men industrious, enterprising and wealthy, or indolent, dispirited and impoverished.' There are no prizes for guessing with which bit of the quotation small businessmen identified themselves in the second half of the 1960s. Of all the new tax measures which were introduced in that period it is possible that Selective Employment Tax, introduced in September 1966 and by far the most sensational feature of the budget of that year, will ultimately get its rating in the fiscal history of the post-war years as one of the most universally despised taxes to come out of a chancellor's dispatch box. Basically SET was a payroll tax on all industry and commerce. Manufacturers, three months after paying the tax, had it refunded plus premiums if they were situated in a development area. A second category of enterprise which was neither manufacturing goods nor supplying services also qualified for the refunds, but received no premiums. The service industries were the hardest hit. They paid the full tax without any refunds at all. The purpose of the tax and the philosophy behind it is beyond the scope of this book, but for small business it produced a number of extraordinary anomalies. One case will suffice to show just how extraordinary.

Two small businesses, one called McTavish's Kitchen, the other Archibalds, were occupying premises next door to each other in Argyle Square, Oban, Scotland. Both places served meals and their menus and price lists were displayed within a few feet of each other. If you went into McTavish's Kitchen for a bite to eat, scrambled eggs and chips would cost you 4s followed by apple pie and cream for 2s 9d. The same dishes at Archibalds cost only 3s and 2s respectively. The discrepancy in prices was both upsetting and uncomfortable for McTavish's as well as reducing their business competitiveness. Customers accused them of charging too much because their prices appeared out of line with Archibalds. The position in a nutshell was that Archibalds business was being boosted by government subsidies via SET, while McTavish's was falling off because it received no subsidies and could not meet the competition from the neighbour who was.

Archibalds, more of a bakery than a restaurant, was classified for SET purposes as a manufacturer, and SET and returns, plus regional employment premiums, gave it a £3 2s 6d advantage over its next-door neighbour each week on each of its male employees. McTavish's was more of a restaurant, though it employed a baker for its restaurant baking; it was classified as a service industry, had to pay SET and received no regional employment premiums. This discriminated against it financially to the tune of minus £3 2s 6d on each male employee per week, and if customers at that time wondered why the apple pie they were eating cost 9d more in McTavish's Kitchen than it did next door, it was mostly because it was baked in an old oven that would not qualify for an investment grant if replaced, was baked by a baker, cut by a cook, served by a waitress and the crumbs swept up by a cleaning woman—all of them costing their employer SET payments without any refunds or premiums.

Curious anomalies like this apart, the overall argument against SET from the standpoint of the small man was that since the tax fell primarily on employers in service industries this meant that it fell on a higher percentage of small firms than large ones, since service industries, which do not normally require a lot of capital and equipment in which to set up and which produce a fairly immediate cash flow, are favourite areas of small business enterprise. In the case of manufacturing firms SET was in effect a forced loan to the government for a period of three months which they had to make at a time when there was heavy pressure on their cash resources and credit was both short and dear.

For many small firms estate duty is the ultimate fiscal ogre. The death of a proprietor or a major shareholder, or several large shareholders within a short space of time, can eventually mean the death of the firm as well. In Chapters 7 and 8 reference was made to the particular anxieties and difficulties imposed by the prospect of, and the actuality of, estate duty on family controlled firms as small as Taylors of Abberton and as large as Pilkingtons of St Helens. It is hardly necessary to parade their specific problems again, but there are a number of general points which need to be made about estate duty and which, indeed, were made by the Confederation of British Industry in its evidence to the Bolton Committee. 'It clearly presents the gravest obstacle to the continuation of the family business from one generation to another,' it said. 'It involves the taking of precautions against the future inevitable tax demand which are heavy in their incidence and may be crucial in their effect. It may, notwithstanding the measures taken, involve the disposal of the assets of the company in whole or in part on highly disadvantageous terms and is a major disincentive to the consolidation and expansion of a business built up in earlier years by the founders when they approach retirement. The only way in which the senior generation in a family business can safeguard against a forced sale on their death is to accumulate sufficient capital outside the business. The rates of personal taxation are such that with an expanding business their savings cannot keep pace with the increasing paper value of their shares. While it is possible to rearrange an estate to lessen the effect of estate duty, this is a complicated process, the rules are constantly changing, and the scheme is out of date as soon as the business expands again.'

From this it begins to be apparent why so many small firms regard estate duty as a killer. When you consider the various readily identifiable stages in the development of a firm it is possible to conduct an exercise which not only shows the impact of estate duty on a small concern, but also capital gains tax and the interlocking of other taxation. This was the method employed by the Smaller Businesses Association in showing the implication of these taxes for small firms when it submitted evidence to the Bolton Committee.

The first stage is one of direct involvement where the proprietor works long hours for a small return, where all his savings will be put in the business and every penny he can spare is left in. The next stage is supervision where the business has grown and the boss has learned to delegate. The product is established and there is a firm base on which to grow. Whereas in the first stage it was difficult to borrow money, he is now much more strongly placed to do so, but he still probably leaves most of his earnings in the firm, cannot draw much out, mostly because his rate of expansion is often determined by the finance available. The third stage is where the firm gets a proper management organisation and structure, and at this point the proprietor is in a position to draw more money from the business which may be on the threshold of going public.

Certain tax implications emerge from this pattern of growth. In the early stages because he leaves his earnings in the business he is unlikely to have any outside cash of consequence, and it is unlikely that he will have made any worthwhile provision for his retirement—or indeed for death. It is only towards the end of the second stage that he can start to pay himself more handsomely, but then heavy surtax prevents any build up of personal cash, and if he decides to forestall the inevitable estate duty by giving away a share in the firm this immediately involves (unless it is a gift to his wife) heavy capital gains tax, and he is unlikely to have the cash to meet it.

If he dies in the first or second stages of the firm's development there are not likely to be spare funds to meet estate duty and to borrow the sums—often quite substantial—to pay the tax is not easy. If his heirs are forced to try to find a buyer for the firm they are handicapped by all the bargaining disadvantages. Added to this is the difficulty of putting a valuation on non-quoted shares.

The threat of what estate duty might do to a business has more than once contributed to a company deciding to go public, even though there might have been no great inclination on the part of its owner to do so. The other way of avoiding what seems to be inevitable is for the fast-growing and successful entrepreneur to sell out while still young, make a capital killing, cheerfully pay the gains tax and then go and live permanently in a tax haven like Jersey or Guernsey, where income tax is minimal and estate duties do not exist.

Corporation tax and its close company provisions which were introduced in 1965 have attracted bitter criticism on a number of counts. The arguments against it can be summarised as follows. Firstly, the high rate at which it is levied (it commenced at 45 per cent and is now 40 per cent) taken with the full rate of personal taxation on dividends has produced a total burden of taxation on small company shareholders which is unequalled elsewhere in Europe. Secondly, where profits are running at a low level, especially in close companies, the proprietors of the firm have to bear a higher rate of tax than if they were partners or sole traders. Thirdly, the close company provisions, perhaps one of the hottest of corporate tax potatoes to drop into the laps of businessmen, make a nonsense of one of the purposes originally envisaged for the tax. Namely to encourage the ploughing back of profits for use in the development of the business, rather than have them accumulating and being hoarded within the business as a means of avoiding payment of both income tax and surtax which would have been payable if they had been distributed as dividends. The requirement is that 60 per cent of the profits of a company after corporation tax must be distributed unless it can be proved that such money is required for the maintenance and development of the business.

Here there are two considerations which are crucial. If the use of the company as an instrument for the avoidance of paying surtax and income tax is disregarded, there remain a great many small firms who, as close companies with their five or fewer controlling shareholders, have to depend more on their own resources for financing development than a public company does. The directors tend to adopt conservative dividend policies in order to build reserves for future investment. They say if they are making, for instance, 15 to 20 per cent return on capital employed and are forced to make distributions there is scarcely enough money left for reserves in which to maintain the business in times of inflation and virtually nothing to finance expansion.

In the end it comes down to a matter of degree, the attitudes of individual tax inspectors and their interpretation of the strength of a firm's case for retaining profits in order to develop the business. Accordingly, one firm may find it impossible to save money for future projects which have not yet reached a definite stage, because it is compelled to distribute its savings. Another tax inspector may consider the retention justified. At worse the present position means that a close company must function with only a minimum bank balance or overdraft to avoid compulsory distributions, and living on overdrafts is a dangerous position to be in when sudden squeezes are part of the pattern of economic life. In some cases companies faced with having to make compulsory distributions adopt a more cavalier and extravagant attitude to expenditure as a means of avoiding them. This can range from all the directors having new, expensive cars more frequently than they otherwise might, or to increasing the amounts spent on advertising or promotion. In this sense it is reducing resistance to what could be considered unnecessarily increased costs.

Thus it is argued that corporation tax bears most heavily on the efficient company, preventing it from expanding as it might, while the inefficient company pays little or no tax and is therefore in effect subsidised in its operations. The tax as such certainly appears to have achieved little in simplifying the tax problems of close companies, and there is no question that it is held to be negative and discriminatory against them. Specifically the close company provisions have merely served to confirm the suspicions of the owners of small firms that those responsible for the measure are totally out of tune with the realities of running such companies.

There have been, however, various changes since corporation tax was first introduced which have helped ameliorate the position of small firms and their owners. One example of this is the lifting of the tax limitation on the salaries of directors of close companies. As things stood there was a 'ration' for directors' remuneration and any amount paid above this was not allowed as an expense for corporation tax purposes. Another example is the interest paid on a loan made by a director-shareholder of a close company to his company. This was not allowed for relief against corporation tax. Now it is, providing the interest is at a reasonable rate.

The one event which did more to encourage small businessmen than any other in recent years was the 1970 budget which promised and started to perform perhaps the biggest fiscal reform of this century. The main elements in it were the reform of personal taxation, a major revision of company taxation and the introduction of a value added tax to replace purchase tax and the cumbersome and loathed selective employment tax. For small businessmen the major effect was to give them a psychological shot in the arm, something to relieve the depression into which so many of them had drifted.

They also felt that it served to strengthen something which had been weakening over the previous difficult years—the satisfaction and gains of being in business for themselves. For along with the psychological restorative the budget provided specific and calculable benefits. Selective employment tax rates were halved. Corporation tax was cut to 40 per cent with the promise of government reform of the tax in the future. The starting point for estate duty was raised from £10,000 to £12,500 and there was provision for the spreading of the payment of the duty over an eight-year period for unincorporated businesses and for certain unquoted shares in family companies. The limit was increased from £1,500 to £5,000 below which close companies do not have to justify their level of distributions to the tax man, a measure which was more significant for small business than was generally realised at the time since it removed altogether more than half the trading companies which previously fell within the scope of the enforced 60 per cent distribution of profits.

The promised reform of personal taxation, one of the main features of which is a single graduated personal tax replacing both income tax and surtax in 1973, bears directly on the small firm since it is widely held that the high levels of personal taxation reduce the supply of private, non-institutional risk capital important to the growth of small firms in the past.

One of the most welcome benefits of the budget for the small man was the effect it had in lessening the pressure on his liquidity, something which was further assisted by the increased level of bank lending which the chancellor allowed. In this context both the reductions in SET and corporation tax had a direct impact, and anyone who has witnessed the sort of manoeuvres in which companies indulge when the annual January corporation tax reckoning comes round will know how even a small 2½ per cent cut helps. The pattern is fairly common. As the time gets near a firm, if it is prudent, starts to build up a fund, since it is unlikely to be holding the tax money in a lump sum, having better things to do with it. The less prudent firms find themselves shopping round to pay the money. Sometimes to get the last bit of it one of the firm's suppliers may be kept waiting longer than usual for his money, or only half a bill is settled. Small firms, of course, are notoriously prone to this sort of pressure, especially from larger ones. In many cases it is a matter of what you do unto others being done unto you, but it all serves to make life and liquidity difficult at tax-paying time.

While this important budget offered signs for the first time for a long time of small businessmen being brought in out of the cold it also raised something of an unknown quantity for many of them. The effect on small businesses of the switch to value added tax in April 1973 can at this stage only be assessed in the light of how it has worked in Europe since the French first took to it in 1954 and most of the Common Market members followed. Basically the tax is a simple, effective and relatively painless way of taxing goods and services. It is a way of collecting money by instalments, a little bit from everyone involved in producing each item as it moves from a raw material to a final product and the customer. It will be paid on virtually everything bought and sold, except food, books and newspapers.

The promise is that small traders will be exempt from it, but the suspicion is that this is because there will be substantial administrative savings in not having to keep tabs on millions of minor transactions which take place, rather than for any sympathy with the smallness of their state as such. One of the tricky areas of value added tax will be the exemptions. The way the tax works there are likely to be disadvantages for the small man if he is exempted as an intermediate supplier. In this situation, when he sells his product to the next firm in the chain he has no previous tax payment to include on his invoice, which means that the next man in the chain has nothing to offset against his own tax payment which therefore becomes much bigger. From this one can visualise the possibility of people buying from a competitor intermediate supplier who offers 'tax credits' as a form of discount. In this way the system will discriminate against the small, exempt operator. However, these are technicalities which it should not be impossible to iron out. The main thing is that it will be far less clumsy than SET.

It also enjoys the substantial bull point of being totally rebatable to exporters and chargeable to importers without upsetting all the plethora of international regulations directed towards protecting free trade. By its simplicity alone it should be time and energy saving for the small firm and thus in the end prove a help rather than a hindrance to profitability.

One of the realities of business is that it is profit which makes the business world go round. The importance of profitability and the effect taxes have upon it in determining the performance of small companies, and in influencing the decisions of owners in the courses of action they follow, is central to any discussion about money and the small firm. Various surveys and studies have been made which show that small firms show up well in the profitability league tables compared with large, publicly owned ones. One study concluded that profit rates and firm size were inversely related, and that smaller firms enjoyed a higher rate of profit.[2] The Industrial and Commercial Finance Corporation's Small Firm Survey 1970, although confined to firms which have been financed by the Corporation, provides a useful if not perfect guide (the fact that ICFC invested in them suggests their performances were better than average for firms of similar size and type) to small company profitability. In the period 1964–5 to 1967–8 ICFC firms produced a growth in profits of 21·8 per cent while the figure for all United Kingdom as a whole was 1·7 per cent. The profitability of ICFC firms, measuring it as a ratio of net profit before interest to total net assets plus bank borrowing, for the same period was 13·5 per cent compared with 12·3 per cent for quoted UK companies. A survey undertaken by ICFC covering the period 1961–2 to 1964–5 produced a figure of 14·8 per cent for ICFC companies and 12·7 per cent for UK quoted companies. The closing of the gap between the two sorts of companies reflects a deteriorating economic position in a period when it became increasingly difficult for smaller firms to survive.

Clearly profits are the life blood of any firm, and any fiscal barrier or restraint which hinders their use for further investment—and therefore greater profits—tends to slow down the growth of the small company. Some economists do not place much credence at all on studies aimed at establishing the relationship between a firm's size and its profitability and rate of growth, and argue that the problems of comparison are so difficult that it is hard to establish any general link at all. This problem is expressed by the authors of the Bolton Committee's Research Report No 11[3] in these terms.

'The ambiguous nature of directors' remuneration (part salary, part interest, part profit) hinders the drawing of meaningful comparisons between the profitability and appropriation of income of small firms and large public companies.' As anyone knows who has talked with small businessmen on this subject it is a difficult area to chart with any degree of accuracy. The fact is, that there are benefits which accrue to the owner of a small firm which are inextricably enmeshed with profit and remuneration, and which have specific values, but which for reasons which will become plain they have no wish to spell out in precise terms. This reluctance springs from the fear that the tax authorities might take a jaundiced view of their activities.

It is clear that many small businesses provide opportunities for expenditure on the part of their owners which falls in the marginal area between business, private life and pleasure. This is especially so in the case of self-employed, own account traders. Because a man utilises part of his home for business, he may then be able to afford a larger, more luxurious house than he would have normally because he can justify parts of its upkeep and running expenses being chargeable against tax. Much the same goes for travel. A visit to an exhibition or trade fair pertinent to his business in America or Europe may be justified as a legitimate expense whereas he might not bother with a similar exhibition in, say, Liverpool or London. Sometimes hobbies and interests can be subsidised through the business. A man with an interest in Venetian architecture may consider it worth while developing an import side to his business, bringing in Venetian glass for example, which in itself is perfectly genuine as a business operation, but which is none the less a vehicle for his interest and which would justify forays to Venice as legitimate business expenses. In other words there are many ways of running a small business which provide tax-free bonuses.

With a good accountant behind you it is possible to run a small concern so that when you have taken your salary out of it, covered expenses and ploughed back some of the profits, everything balances out neatly so there are no profits on which tax has to be paid. If profits start to exceed the point of ideal balance which most efficiently minimises the tax burden, it is possible to mop up the excess either by spending money on something like advertising or an export selling mission, or indeed to reduce the price of a product, though this may well have the effect of producing greater profits the year after. But for most people with average drives and ambitions holding this balance year after year would be a tedious and ticklish business and not very satisfying, since it largely negates one of the main satisfactions of having a business: seeing it flourish and grow.

None the less the ability to do this illustrates a point which is often forgotten. An audited profit and loss account is much more flexible than most people realise and various, quite legitimate, accountancy tricks can be employed and only need to be as consistent as the company's shareholders and taxation authorities expect. This means that within certain limits the profits of a firm can be very much what the owners want them to be.

It brings us back to the ambiguous nature of directors' remuneration. A company may pay low salaries to its directors, perhaps at quite uncompetitive rates considering the calibre of the people. If it makes a good profit, directors' fees can be paid. If it has a bad year, then the total remuneration directors receive is unrealistic and below the market level. In the normal run of events this would be unacceptable. But there may be other incentives such as capital growth. One day the directors of a small growing company might expect to go public or get taken over. Then they can look forward to making a capital killing, subject only to capital gains tax.

It is easy to make other adjustments to profits, by variation in depreciation policy or stock levels for example. Thus to impress an outsider, perhaps a potential bidder for the firm, it would be possible to pull in greater profits in any particular year. Conversely, by depreciating stock and equipment rigorously, providing bonuses for hard-working staff and so on, it is possible to deflate profits. The fact that a firm may not decide its profits policy until two or three months after its financial year ends means that, in this context, it is difficult to say exactly what *real* profits are, other than that they are elusive and difficult to pin down. The one sure thing is that profit, or the prospect of it, becomes a salient consideration with merchant bankers when they are running their measure over the man who wants their money.

NOTES

1 Page 307. C. W. Golby and G. Johns. *Attitude and Motivation.* Committee of Inquiry on Small Firms. Research Report No 7 (1971), HMSO.
2 Page 318. J. M. Samuels and D. J. Smythe. 'Profits, Variability of Profit and Firm Size', *Economica* (May 1968).
3 Page 318. P. Lund and D. Miner. *Three Studies on Small Firms.* Committee of Inquiry on Small Firms. Research Report No 11 (1971), HMSO.

Chapter 17

Help and how to help yourself

The bank manager is an important source of credit and advice, but there are others to which the small man can go. Researches show it is not so much a lack of money to finance small business which is the problem, but lack of knowledge about the various facilities available. These range from hire purchase and factoring to long-term fixed interest loans and the proceeds of going public. One of the most important institutions for the small man is the Industrial and Commercial Finance Corporation. Similarly there are bodies which offer a wide range of assistance in the broad field of management, training and education.

As we have seen in terms of everyday business, it is not the merchant banker but the local bank manager who is the most important source of external finance for the small firm. The overdraft is his most important instrument for granting it, and to the small businessman the manager himself is regarded as a fountainhead of financial advice and wisdom. For all these reasons the local bank manager is in a good position to view the progress and observe the weaknesses of small concerns, and his relationship with them extends far beyond the man who merely has his finger on the money bags. The fact that people who run and own small companies report differing attitudes shown towards them by bank managers is not surprising, because the service and availability of finance is partly determined by the experience and expertise of a particular manager, and how rigidly and flexibly he interprets the bank's role as a provider of short-term credit. Even bank managers are human, and an ambitious man may well want to build up his accounts by making loans to small firms. As such he may be prepared to take risks which are marginally greater than banking convention would consider appropriate.

Again, while the local manager has discretion for small sums, he may have to refer large amounts to his regional or head office. In any event the discretion limits vary between the banks. Obviously a manager carefully weighs the solid business and financial factors before he grants an overdraft or makes a loan. Normally he will want to see several years good trading results, though occasionally he will help a firm out of serious financial trouble and assist it with new ventures. He undoubtedly gives unsecured loans, but the growing practice is for the bulk of loans made to small firms to be secured. When he does advance money on an unsecured basis it is because he has confidence in the man, and knows him and his firm. The ease or difficulty which the small man experiences in raising money through the bank must, in the last resort, depend on the bank manager's assessment of his integrity and general business ability. It comes down to a decision based on highly personal judgements rather than one rooted in sophisticated and analytical financial techniques.

The personal nature of the service the bank gives is important too—as much to the bank as to the businessman. A private survey undertaken for Lloyds Bank by Market and Opinion Research International revealed that the proprietors of small businesses had explicit ideas of what made a bank a good one. Above all else they regarded the quality of staff and management of paramount importance. Even good overdraft facilities, so vital to them, were regarded as less important than courteous and efficient staff, an understanding and available manager, and helpful financial and investment advice. In a nutshell, to most small business customers, the bank is more a service institution than a financial one.

The strength of this special relationship is confirmed by the findings of research undertaken for the Bolton Committee into the financial problems of small businesses. Nevertheless there lurks the suspicion that the banks did not lean over backwards to do all that they might have done to save so many of their small customers from the worst effects of the successive credit squeezes in the second half of the 1960s. The suggestion is not that they held back because of a perverse delight in seeing their small customers driven into the ground, but that they did not do enough to point them in other financial directions when they, because of the lending restraints imposed upon them, were no longer able to help. Various reasons have been advanced for this: the fact that ingrained banking conventions and attitudes prevented it; or more serious, that the managers themselves were just not sufficiently aware of the availability of other sources of finance. Understandably the banks are not overjoyed with this assertion and reply that their managers do proffer such advice, and that in any case they start from the proposition, 'How can we lend to this man?', not 'What are the reasons why we can't?'

The specialist financial institutions, however, will tell you that the quality of advice about other sources of finance which is given by the bank manager is poor. This is a contention which underlines one of the very real problems of the small business. All the evidence supports a view that it is not so much a lack of funds available to small firms which is the difficulty, but the general inadequacy of information about them. The Bolton Committee Research Report on Financial Facilities for Small Firms sees no need for new financial institutions to serve small business, but it does identify a need for a government-backed central agency which would have as one of its functions the dissemination of information about sources of finance and the extent of its supply. In particular, it would be aimed at improving the knowledge of solicitors and accountants in these matters, so that they might better advise the small businessman. The agency's other function would be the education of managers of small firms in techniques for evaluating their development proposals, and the presentation of these to financial institutions. It would also encourage the keeping of day-to-day financial records and making cash flow projections, without which potential lenders are discouraged.

It would be wrong to tar all bankers with the same criticisms. In the past some banks have shown imagination and flair in the service they offer their customers. One of the most fascinating manifestations of it occurs in the Orkney Islands, off the north coast of Scotland. There the problems over the past few years have, perhaps, been less those of the bank having to shut off credit to its customers because of the squeezes, but more a matter of the bank on occasions not being able to physically reach the customers. For it only needs a force 7 gale and a spring tide and the bank cannot sail.

The bank is a 6½ ton, four-berth cabin cruiser, owned by the National Commercial Bank of Scotland. In the summer months it sails from Kirkwall round the remote northern isles of the Orkneys bringing the benefits of current and deposit accounts and overdrafts to the crofters, along with the seagulls which fly in its wake. Without the floating bank the crofters would either have to leave their money under the mattress or take the aeroplane or mail steamer to Kirkwall, which sometimes means an overnight stay or longer. Naturally, the floating bank makes a splendid story and it has won a lot of publicity for the National Commercial Bank of Scotland, seeing that it is the only one in the United Kingdom, whose opening hours are dictated by gale warnings and the state of the tide. It also carries the only bank manager who dons oilskins and seafarers clobber between professional appointments and provides the only known example in Britain of the unique nautical cry, 'Bank Ahoy.' But when you have said all this, the fact remains that to the crofters and small shopkeepers on the islands it is an important and useful service, not a publicity gimmick.

Since, as a matter of necessity, the local bank occupies a crucial place in the affairs of any small business it is surprising how many small businessmen fail to actively enhance their relationship with it. Norman Jones is manager of London's Threadneedle Street branch of Lloyds Bank. He has been with Lloyds over thirty years, and in previous branches has had a lot of experience in dealing with small firms and seeing their particular problems and difficulties. His message to anyone with a small firm, either trying to launch it or develop it, can be simply summed up as: 'Make friends with your bank manager.' He says it is always sensible to bank locally where your business is, and he says that if you have the notion you will do better in terms of getting money by banking with a bigger branch elsewhere forget it, because the position is quite the reverse. Being part of the community and entrenched in the locality both you and the bank manager get to see and know each other. If you deal with a bank at arm's length, and only appear in the manager's office for the first time when you want money, he really has had no chance to get to know you and may well be forced back on making decisions on the basis of hearsay.

There is only one yardstick for raising more money and this is that the purpose for which it is needed, whether it be machinery, new premises, or the manufacturing rights to a new product, should add to the company's profits at a satisfactory rate. There is little merit in raising money to finance a new development, and then find that the return being earned on it is scarcely enough to repay the interest on the capital, leaving nothing over to cover the new risks and responsibilities. But if the new project or investment opens up the possibility of earning profits which, when everything else has been taken into account, will yield a good margin, then there is every reason to go shopping for money.

That is so long as the company has followed the elementary drill of making sure that it cannot finance what it wants to do without recourse to outside funds. This may seem a very obvious point, but it is usually only obvious to those experienced in business. In practice there are nearly always opportunities for finding some, if not all, the finance from within a firm. It might, for instance, be possible to unlock money sufficient for the need in question by reducing stock levels which may have grown over the months and become out of phase with requirements. Or the boss might consider taking less in salary, leaving more of his money in the firm than he has been. A quick survey of debts due to the firm might throw up a substantial amount of money which could be got in much more promptly than it has hitherto. These are all important considerations which need thinking about before owners start embarking on fund-raising safaris to the City of London, or elsewhere.

There is a significant link between maximising financial resources within a company and going outside to bolster them further. The man who has used his skill and intelligence to stay solvent, to avoid the hazards of overtrading, who has taken pains to keep the amount of his indebtedness to trade suppliers (itself an important source of short-term finance) known and controlled, is better placed to get a tangible response from others who grant credit. Because of his record a supplier may be persuaded to give longer credit. Because of his responsible attitude to indebtedness the bank will have few qualms about extending his overdraft. On the other hand the man who has allowed his indebtedness to accelerate away and is tardy in discharging his obligations soon discovers that trade credit, instead of functioning as a smooth and accepted piece of the financial mechanism, stops and falters at the most inconvenient moments. What is basically at stake is confidence, something which is of immense value to the small firm. It is the fundamental reason why a supplier gives credit, and anything which undermines it is likely to have a serious and upsetting effect on the running of the company. By adopting a responsible attitude to indebtedness the owner of a firm is in fact protecting and nurturing his credit standing which is an integral part of his firm's goodwill. It does not require a major intellectual effort to safeguard this important source of finance, and there is no lack of advice available on the subject. In fact the points made above, and many more too (such as the basic principles of accepting credit from suppliers, the yardsticks to apply and the ways to control it), are concisely and usefully made in one of the British Institute of Management's splendid little four-page leaflets. It is one of the Guidelines for the Smaller Business series. All the leaflets deal with typical small firm problems. Examples of other titles are *Planning in the Small Firm* and *Cost Reduction and Expenditure Control*.

There comes a point, however, where generous trade credit and bank overdrafts on their own are no longer adequate for the growing firm. It is the point at which it helps to have a clear understanding of the function of different sorts of money. The bank overdraft is a short-term facility which in its classic use provides a firm's working capital; in a situation where possibly an increase in trade means that the firm needs to increase its stock levels because it has more work going through its factory. It is quite wrong to use it for fixed assets like plant and machinery. It is a valuable liquid resource and as such it should be used to pay accounts and settle suppliers' bills, not locked up in machines or bricks and mortar, for it can be withdrawn as readily as it is given, and this is where the danger lies in using it in a function for which, by its very nature, it is not intended. At the other end of the scale long-term money, loaned perhaps for fifteen or twenty years, is intended for fixed assets, the rate of interest once fixed will not change and it cannot be suddenly called in. Therefore it is possible to plan well into the future. Of course, long-term, fixed interest money is more expensive, and often small businessmen go for the overdraft because they think they are saving a per cent or two, without realising it is vulnerable, subject to vagaries outside their control. Placing reliance on it, largely through not understanding its limitations, means they end up in an unpleasant crunch situation.

Before banking services were developed and sophisticated enough to provide things like overdrafts, the bill of exchange, the granddaddy of all methods of financing credit sales, was used for centuries to smooth the way of trade and commerce. They still are, in their various forms, providing a convenient way of bridging the financial gap between the seller of goods requiring immediate cash, and the buyer needing a period of credit. The central point about a bill of exchange is that the right to a future payment is exchanged for present cash. Precisely the same principle applies in factoring, although there are differences in the mechanics of both of these sources of working capital. The basis of factoring is that the firm undertaking it buys the obligations of a client's customers, who are told that payment must be made to the factor and not the client. Unlike the bill of exchange this is a relatively new form of financing, one which is rapidly expanding in the United Kingdom. For the small man in business it is not essential to know how these work in detail. The salient point to grasp is that they exist, are part of the financial mechanism and can be used to advantage to solve some of his short-term financing problems.

As a company grows and develops, its business horizon widens. It may venture into the export market and is immediately faced with a new type of financing problem and a new type of risk which it has not had to cope with before. What happens if the firm's customer in Punta Arenas defaults on payment? Or if there is a revolution in one of the countries he is supplying? Or if the country receiving his goods suddenly slaps on an import surcharge which his customer there either will not or cannot pay? This is where the Export Credits Guarantee Department (although it is not itself a lending institution providing direct finance) is of central importance. The facilities this government organisation offers in smoothing the risky paths the exporter sometimes has to tread are varied and complex, but their significance to the small firm which is exporting is explicit. ECGD conducts a commercial business providing insurance for exporters against the risks of selling overseas. Full details of its service are available from its head office in London or from its local offices in most of the leading provincial cities. All these details provide an impressive example of the sophistication which exists in various bits of the British money machine devoted to financing business and industry. Within the whole of the borrowing spectrum, from flexible, cheap and informal overdrafts, via plant and equipment leasing and hire purchase, nursery finance from merchant banks for firms growing towards the size when they can go public, and to the larger, more ambitious and formalised procedures of a public flotation of a company's shares, there exist virtually all the financial facilities which cater for the money-raising requirements of firms in all their various stages of growth. Facilities which even identify and specialise in the provision of funds for firms of a specific type and character; and facilities which are even geared to resolving highly specific problems.

To take the last point first, it has already been shown that the prospect of death duty is a spectre which haunts many small family companies. A number of the city institutions will tailor their lending arrangements with a view to lessening the burden of this problem on the remaining family shareholders in a firm. One of the ways to minimise its effect, for instance, is for the institution to buy some of the owner's shares. He takes the money from the sale and gives it to his children, who then use the cash to buy more of his shares. By doing this the family minimises the liability to pay both death duty and capital gains tax. This is a very simple example. In practice the death duty problems of many small firms are incredibly involved and tangled and therefore individual situations have to be dealt with for what they are. This is where the advice and help of an institution like the Estate Duties Investment Trust can be of help by arranging matters in such a way that the duty may be raised by the family selling only parts of its interest in the firm, and at the same time retaining control. EDITH, a public company which is managed by the Industrial and Commercial Finance Corporation, was originally formed to help in this way. It becomes a minority holder in a firm, provides funds for meeting estate duty and—a substantial bull point for many people who own small firms—does not seek to take part in the running of the business.

Other specialised lending services are aimed at financing technical innovation. The two most important ones in this sphere are the government-backed National Research Development Corporation and Technical Development Capital, an offshoot of the Industrial and Commercial Finance Corporation. Taken together the two of them account for the bulk of institutional lending to small firms needing money to develop a new idea or product. Sometimes they will get together and back a venture jointly. Bernard Hunn's company, Revenue Systems, mentioned in Chapter 13, is a case in point.

Merchant banks, with their multiplicity of functions, do not make ideal prospects for the mass of small businessmen searching for funds. In general they do not like start-up situations, which are after all the riskier sorts of investment, and if they are going to talk turkey with a small firm, both in terms of supplying equity and loan capital, they will want to see a good track record and pre-tax profits starting from minimum levels which vary, according to the bank and the nature of the business, of between £25,000 and £150,000. Equally they are disinclined to mess about with small loans or participation, for the very simple reason that it takes as much effort to oversee £20,000 as it does £200,000. Which is why it is mostly easier to borrow £500,000 in the City of London than £5,000.

Because of this there have grown up in the last few years a number of what are known as 'venture capital' companies. The term is somewhat imprecise but is generally applied to the financing of new or risky projects. Some of the merchant banks have their own venture capital offshoots, but some like the Small Business Capital Fund are far removed from the traditional bankers' parlours. SBCF was set up jointly by the Co-operative Insurance Society and the Taylor Nelson Group, a market research and marketing company which, through one of its subsidiaries, supplies among other things, the monthly survey of business opinion published in the *Financial Times*. It is this fund which backed Wally Orner's firm, Contemporary Industries, which appears in the last chapter.

The fund was formed in October 1969. The argument for its formation was that there are many thousands of small companies with short track records, or with none at all, who are looking for finance. They are able to raise £5,000 to £10,000 through traditional sources but have trouble when it comes to the £10,000 to £20,000 range. Unlike some venture capital institutions SBCF believes that taking a company from third to first division requires not only money, but management support as well. So, along with the minority interest which it asks for in the firm, it also requires that an SBCF executive is appointed to the board. The fund is not looking for dividends or a return in the short term. Its aim is to help the company in which it invests to expand rapidly so that after four or five years SBCF will make a capital appreciation on its investment by way of public flotation, or by arranging a merger or whatever method is in the best interest of the shareholders.

By far the most important of the institutions lending to small business is the Industrial and Commercial Finance Corporation, which accounts for about five times as much new business as all the other venture capital institutions taken together. In 1969–70 the value of new business transacted by ICFC was nearly £29 million, compared with an estimated total for eight other venture capital operations of £5 million. The respective number of new cases contracted was 250 compared with 50.

For anyone running a small, growing business it is an institution which repays some study. For in the future it may well hold the financial key to the further growth of any firm which believes it is capable of doing more than it is. I am not claiming any influence with ICFC—far from it. But because of its importance it can scarcely be unhelpful to anyone hoping to get money from it to know what it is, how it works, how it evaluates the people who come knocking at its door; and, indeed, how swiftly it helps once the door is opened.

ICFC is in Copthall Avenue, off London Wall, in the City. Piercy House, which is the name of its headquarters, does not have the solid, slightly forbidding air which so many City financial institutions seem to delight in cultivating. The organisation advertises regularly in the *Financial Times* with a nice blend of fact and humour and this, coupled with the relatively informal atmosphere at head office, allays many of the worries which normally beset people faced with a fund-raising visit to the City. Peter Gummer is the man who has been working hard to give ICFC a reassuring image, and in the world of finance there has never before been anything quite like the ads he and advertising agents Doyle, Dane Barnbach devised. Gummer, young, articulate and impressively knowledgeable about what ICFC is, what it does and how it works, is a marketing man. A man you might expect to find obsessively talking of dog foods, breakfast cereals or cosmetics, but not actually marketing money. It shows how competitive things are in the City of London these days when financial institutions have to pay for expertise for reassuring, persuading, and selling firms the idea that they should borrow money from them. It extends to ICFC having a string of branch offices throughout the country where the local managers are busy selling the idea of your needing their money. Although they do not go knocking on doors like a brush salesman drumming up business, they do it in countless, subtle other ways.

There are eighteen ICFC branches, from Brighton to Glasgow, largely because of a cri de coeur which was put up by businessmen as long as forty years ago, and which was reflected in the report of the Macmillan Committee on Finance and Trade. It spoke of gaps in the capital market, spotlighting exactly the same financial quandaries with which small concerns are beset today, and it referred to the need for a finance company to provide long-term money for small companies which could no longer raise it privately and which were too small to go to the Stock Market. It was a phenomenon which became enshrined in a succinctly descriptive phrase, the Macmillan Gap.

ICFC is classically a Macmillan Gap company set up to meet precisely the needs of smallish companies. A later inquiry, the Royal Commission on the Working of the Monetary System, under the chairmanship of Lord Radcliffe, identified the need for a risk finance company, which is how Technical Development Capital, now an ICFC offshoot, came into being. ICFC was established in 1945. Among its shareholders is a phalanx of some of the most prominent and impeccable members of the city establishment—the Bank of England (only a very small holding), the Bank of Scotland, Barclays Bank, The British Linen Bank, the Clydesdale Bank, Coutts and Co, Glyn Mills, Lloyds Bank, Midland, National, National Westminster, the Royal Bank of Scotland and Williams Deacon's Bank.

ICFC, of course, has competitors but none operate on a comparable scale. On 31 March 1971, it had 2,238 current customers on its books and in total it had lent money to nearly 3,000 companies. It had over £150 million outstanding in advances to small and medium-sized firms. It prefers not to get involved in the management of companies and is concerned with lending money at fixed rates. It makes the point that the scale of its operation is such that if it were involved in day-to-day management life would become very difficult, and it would limit its growth in satisfying its main purpose, providing long-term capital to small and medium-sized firms able to prove they will make profitable use of it. Some companies do, to such good effect that they have returned to ICFC many times for funds.

ICFC's argument for its branch system, though it obviously increases office and staff overheads, is a convincing one. The managing director of a small business is often a lonely man. He runs it, is the driving force and supplies it with its impetus. But he has no real sounding board in the business, no one with whom he can freely discuss his worries, test his ideas—or even seek reassurance that a particular course of action he is undertaking is the correct one. All that ICFC asks is that the people to whom they lend money pay it back—and that they get some sort of annual report on what progress is being made. But branch managers who are on the spot, often part of the community, can pay informal visits—liaison visits—and talk quite easily, freely and informally with their clients. In this way they help to solve many problems.

Some clients may want to take ICFC's money and run. They will not brook even the idea of anyone being involved in their affairs—and in any case it might have been precisely this which attracted them to ICFC in the first place. Well, ICFC says that is perfectly acceptable, but they do make the point that informal chats from branch managers are quite a different kettle of fish from formal advice from an outside director.

It works on the entrepreneurial truth that good, well-run companies do not usually stay small for long, and have a habit of growing into larger successful ones. It is precisely this which provides the background, in a grass roots sense, of ICFC's operations. Its lending spectrum, for example, is £5,000 to £500,000. If this kind of money is relevant to you, and you can show it will be profitably employed, on a long-term basis (which means anything from ten to twenty years), then you are a potential ICFC customer.

Clearly the ICFC staff are well placed to observe the type and character of a small businessman who comes to them, and the problems he carries with him in his brief case. He will probably be a dynamic personality, who was employed by a big company when he spotted a gap in the market which the large concerns either could not or would not fill, so he left and started up on his own. For the first few years his sheer technical ability is enough to plug the gap and show the growth potential which exists. Then one day this ability becomes less sustaining than it was—a lot of bright twenty-four year olds have come down from university and are way ahead in that area of technology. So now there has to be greater reliance, not on sheer technical ability alone, but on production, finance, marketing and personnel functions. Which all turn out to be problems too. Because of this the company changes its shape, and begins to take off.

In ICFC's experience, and especially that of its branch managers, most of the people they deal with have these difficulties, do recognise the problems and like to talk them through. In the ICFC structure this puts a lot of the onus on the branch manager, and in many senses he is the most important man in its operation. He tends to stay in one place for about seven years which enables him to become fully acquainted with it, and to become part of the local community. He is paid good money, gets good expenses and a car. Three days out of five he should be out of the office. He is encouraged to canvas for custom.

Surprisingly marketing a product like money is not as easy as you would imagine. It is not really something about which you can knock on a man's door cold, burst in and start talking. This is why ICFC holds eighteen to twenty regional conferences each year which are based on company case studies and to which members of the local business community are invited. This helps make contacts and opens up numerous opportunities for future business. Additionally a lot of ICFC clients come via their own professional advisers—bank managers, accountants and solicitors in that order of importance. They get no form of commission from ICFC for introductions.

Obviously ICFC is not lending money for fun. It is there to make a profit from efficient firms, not subsidise inefficient ones. Indeed, a study of the company's trading results over the last ten years shows a steady climb in pre-tax profits, without any erratic ups or downs. In 1961 they were £2 million, in 1970 £4·7 million. The growth in profits is dependent on winning new business and this is why, when you get down to cases, the branch occupies such a strategic position in the ICFC structure. Exercises like regional conferences give the branch managers the excuse to knock on doors to get to grips with his market. Which is why he will move the conference round in his area, holding it in different towns and cities. It is also why his branch office is unlikely to be a version of a city banker's office, oak panelling and all, and why he pays some attention to dress. Just about the last outfit which the man in Wolverhampton or Glasgow would affect would be black pin stripes with a rolled brolly and bowler. It is not how you would dress in places where there is a traditional distrust of the City.

This distrust is a very real factor and stems from a number of worries which ICFC seems to have identified, and which it has set out to allay in various imaginative advertising campaigns. The first is that customers do not want to lose control or authority in the business, and with an outside director coming in they often feel they are. Secondly, they do not want to be publicly floated. According to ICFC this is a feeling which it is important not to underestimate. It is underlined by the number of times a firm will come to ICFC before taking the step. One company returned fourteen times for more money before going to the Stock Market. Thirdly, they dislike the idea of a legion of bright, sharp young consultants coming into their company to clean up the business before an investment is made. Emotively this means sackings. Although ICFC fields a consultancy service, clients do not have to have it. Fourth, they hate the idea of a long-standing association with their traditional professional advisers being disturbed. It is a difficulty which ICFC tries to scotch as early as possible by bringing the traditional advisers into the discussions. Lastly, there is the worry about money; that once they have borrowed it they cannot do so again. It is a hark back to the old ethic of neither a borrower, nor a lender be.

What are your chances of getting money from ICFC? To understand this you have to understand the way it evaluates a potential investment. The most important element it examines is management ability. This covers a lot of shades and meanings. But it does mean the management of men, evidence of planning, forward thinking and of the ability to communicate. It means above all entrepreneurial drive and the ability to push on against adversity. Then there is the assessment of the business itself. Where do the resources lie—in technical ability, marketing skills? How is the product structured? Are there resources, or reasons, to improve and adapt it? Can it respond to market change faster than any big competitor? Finally there is the market itself, which involves an assessment of the future growth potential of the product.

Obviously ICFC takes prudent measures to try and secure the loan. It may be equity in the company, or another possibility is some sort of sandwich deal with the local bank manager, where an overdraft may be covered on a first mortgage and ICFC takes a second mortgage. But the likelihood of failure seems to be minimised by the evaluation made in the first place. In addition the local ICFC branch manager can soon spot signs that all is not well and can stave off total disaster by giving advice and help. The company does not often seek the right to appoint a director to the board of a customer. When, in special cases, it does so, the nominated member is not a member of ICFC, but an outsider. He meets the company and the company either likes him or not, and has him or not, as it pleases.

What happens if you have taken their money and things start to go wrong late in the day? Then the tendency is to tackle the problem by providing more money and management. Once the company admits it has a problem, then it is easy, and there are other bits of ICFC, for example the combined NUMAS and ICFC Management Advisory Service, which can give help.

For many businesses needing financial help the length of time it takes to actually get their hands on the money can cause problems. In ICFC loans below a certain level can be authorised by the branch manager, but above that a policy group makes the decision at area level. For even larger sums the decision is referred to a London committee which consists of some of the company's top brass. The branch manager makes his submission to this committee. It is heard on a Friday, considered over the weekend, and an answer given on the Monday. The branch manager is telephoned and told what it is in the afternoon. ICFC says that once it has said yes, the client can operate as if the money is in the business with every assurance of being backed. Of all its investments, 22·3 per cent are for under £10,000, 19 per cent between £10,001 and £20,000, and 24·2 per cent between £20,001 and £50,000. In total 65·5 per cent are for under £50,000.

With more competition and more funds available the problem for smaller companies may well be choosing between the people who are offering them. How a company chooses depends very much on the attitude of its owner, whether he wants to keep all his equity, keep soldiering on, as he is, not entertaining the idea of selling, merging or giving up control. Or it may depend on whether he decides to grow a business swiftly and then sell out by the time he is forty. In an era which has seen the collapse of blue chip companies like Rolls-Royce there seems a risk in whatever you do. But in making the choice the owner of a small firm should pay as much attention to the status, record and reputation of the prospective lender as the lender will be paying to him and his record.

It is obviously sensible that the successful growing company should shop around for its finance. Because it has a good record with plenty of prospects for further growth under its belt there is no earthly reason why it should take the first offer it gets. Nor why it should take any, if it really feels the deal is a bad one. Christian Brann, who appears in the earlier chapters of this book, made attempts to raise long-term capital from merchant banks but most of them declined on the grounds they were only interested in companies making a profit of £50,000 a year or more. He approached ICFC and they offered, after exhaustive inquiries, to provide £50,000 of loan capital secured by a 25 per cent share in the equity. For this they offered £3,000. Brann decided it was a bad proposition, and elected to struggle on financing expansion out of retained profits, with the hope that the credit squeeze would lift (which it did) and that additional finance might be obtained from the clearing banks.

When David St John Thomas (Chapter 11) was shopping for finance he approached four merchant banks and in his view the one which won, Hambros, did so because it did its homework more thoroughly, and in the end really knew something about David & Charles. David has some useful advice for others who might want to go shopping for money: plan well ahead, do your homework thoroughly so that you are clear about your needs and objectives; approach four, or maybe more, of the financial institutions; and leave yourself a large slice of free time during the negotiating period (which tends to spread over months rather than days) so that you are free to fit in with the bankers' schedules and do not contribute to delays which make it difficult to keep negotiations with different banks running at the same time. The last and encouraging point David makes is that in his experience you do not have to have contacts in the city. Hambros knew nothing about his publishing firm until he wrote to them asking if they would be interested in putting money into the company. So it seems that when you are knocking on doors in the city, it is not necessarily so much who you know which counts, but whether the bankers judge you to be the man who can make money for them.

In many respects solving the management problems of a business is a more difficult proposition than dealing with the financial ones. Even if there is a lack of knowledge about all the available sources of finance open to a small businessman, it is an area in which large tracts are criss-crossed by a number of well-trodden paths, and geographically it is well defined, particularly if you think of the City of London and the concentration of money-lending institutions which are found there.

Sources of help, other than financial, are quite a different kettle of fish. They are fragmented, geographically dispersed and very wide ranging, from government departments, government sponsored agencies and training boards through trade and industrial associations and beyond to private enterprise consultants, universities and educational institutions. They cover the full spectrum of advice, consultancy, training and education and to describe them all in the space available would be impossibly tedious, and a little pointless since there is an excellent publication, *Business Efficiency: An ABC of Advisory Services*, available at HM Stationery Office. It lists a formidable number of them, especially government sponsored and voluntary services which can help industry increase its efficiency and productivity. However, I shall give some of the more important and useful sources of help, but since the type in this chapter is not elastic you will find them in Appendix 2. *Business Efficiency* covers an enormous range of information and is a weighty counter to those who believe there is a paucity of such advice. The position is quite the contrary. There is a wealth of assistance available for the small man if he only has the wit and intelligence to ferret it out.

But you come back to one of the central problems of the man

running a small firm, where all the functions which a big company employs departmental heads to cope with fall on his shoulders. Time is the essence, and it is an essence he does not have. This is a pity because it is one of the ironies of small business life that the firm most in need of help—and the one most likely to show swift and markedly beneficial results for it—is precisely the one which does not get it, not for any lack of facilities but more because of the fear of outsiders coming in and showing up the owner's inadequacies. This is a recognisable situation in the great middle mass of firms. It is noticeable that the more efficient, thrusting small firms are much more disposed, for example, to call in consultants to help them—often to help solve a problem which the firm itself has already defined. Or to undertake a piece of highly specialist problem solving. The PA Management Group has an offshoot based in Cambridge called PA Technology. Basically it is a think tank, contract research organisation, call it what you will, which will invent or innovate to order. Again, it is only the lively, outward-looking small firm which will make use of a facility like this. In stark contrast, and at the other end of the scale, is the firm which calls in consultants as a last resort, usually when it is too late and because it is in a desperate financial plight.

One of the main excuses advanced for not employing consultants is that the firm cannot afford them, and that the fees charged are geared more to the economies of large companies than small ones. The larger consultants themselves will admit that from their point of view a small company is not quite so profitable as a large one. To give just one example, while the regional office of PA Management in Bristol, which covers the south-west and Wales, does about 50 per cent of its work in companies with under 300 people, it seldom goes into companies where the labour force is under thirty. Although they may well be in need of PA's expert advice, it is just these companies which either genuinely cannot afford the fee, or in their heart of hearts do not really want people from outside poking about. In defence of the companies it has to be said that sometimes the consultant's style of working is not relevant to the small firm. It may not really want a major, across-the-board investigation followed by a report and recommendations, but may be more concerned with someone showing it how to solve its particular problem virtually on the spot.

In this context, therefore, the existence of consultancies like NUMAS geared to the needs of the small firm is important. But even so its service is not cheap. The problem of consultancy in, and for, small firms has given rise to a handful of small business centres or units which are part of universities, usually those with technological roots, and colleges of technology. The staff of these centres undertake both research on the management problems of small firms and also run consultancy services for small companies in their area. These centres are operating at both Bristol and Sheffield Polytechnics and at the University of Aston in Birmingham, and other colleges and universities are thinking about establishing them.

At Aston the Small Business Centre is part of the Department of Industrial Administration. When it was formed in 1967 with a grant from the Department of Economic Affairs, it was the only professional service of its kind in the United Kingdom provided by a university. It had rich country in which to prospect, for it was estimated there were between 4,000 and 5,000 small firms within convenient distance of the university. It is staffed by men who are well qualified academically and who have spent most of their lives in industry, with particular experience of the problems of small businesses. It has tackled two of the main consultancy problems associated with small firms by pitching its fees at a modest level (it charges £40 a day which is about half the daily fee of the leading consultancy firms); and it tailors its services to meet the intermittent and recurring needs of the small firms. Bearing in mind that a managing director of a small company still has to run it, it tends to arrange courses accordingly between 4pm and 6pm one afternoon a week, and it is prepared to organise courses within the firm. The centre has helped over 300 small businesses with consultancy services or specialised training courses since its inception and is now self-financing.

Its success demonstrates the fact that academic communities can build up mutually rewarding relationships with small business. Its achievements also provide proof that the assumption made by so many small firms, that professional help is not likely to be relevant to their needs, is a totally false one. This probably has its roots in the fact that the only contact many of them have with any outside specialist is their auditor, whom they have usually appointed at as low a fee as possible, and they are disappointed when they ask him questions about the actual operations of the business and he is unable to be of any significant help. A. E. B. Perrigo, director of the Aston Small Business Centre, says: 'Small businesses do not use the services of outside specialists anything like as much as the cost/benefit situation demands. But by providing consultancy services at moderate fees, the Small Business Centre helps give them greater insight into the advantages of using such services when and as needed.'

Local authorities and new towns are starting to provide useful and practical help for small business. A programme called 'Enterprise Lancaster' is a joint scheme between the university and the city of Lancaster to attract new industry to the area with particular emphasis on small science-based industrial units. The university offers assistance to the managers of small firms coming to the area, not only from its departments of science and technology but also from departments concerned with business administration. For its part, the city offers assistance with premises (factory space, new buildings on lease or mortgage) and housing for key staff which is immediately made available.

The accolade for one of the most imaginative direct assistance schemes in the broad local authority/new town sector must go to the Glenrothes Development Corporation, Fife, Scotland. The scheme is quite novel; the provision of special facilities as an encouragement to individual inventors to carry out original work that might develop into a commercial proposition. The aim is to enable 'ideas men', who lack the finance to make an independent start, to launch themselves. To overcome the problem of high overheads incurred by inventors starting up the corporation is offering individual workshop units of 400sq ft, close to the town centre, at a nominal rent. These will be linked to general office facilities for which each inventor will pay separately. Because these will be akin to the typing pool in a large company, the cost will obviously be less than if the inventor had to provide his own office staff. Applicants have to go through a screening process, since there is not an unlimited supply of units. Six months after announcing the scheme the corporation had over 100 applicants on its books. An important feature of the project is that management and marketing advice will be given by a group of local industrialists.

The rent paid depends on the means of the applicant but does not exceed £3 a week, plus rates in the order of £30 a year. The real importance of the scheme is that it helps the inventor over that awkward period between having an idea and developing it to the point where manufacturers are likely to show interest. I said the scheme was novel but I had forgotten for the moment that over a century ago Thomas Edison pioneered a similar arrangement, putting a laboratory at the disposal of inventors who would not otherwise have been able to afford such facilities. The story is that he took 50 per cent of any subsequent profits. The Glenrothes Development Corporation makes no such conditions. Nor does it impose a fixed time in which to succeed, and there is no compulsion to leave the premises once production starts. Indeed, there is no requirement that the inventor should stay in the new town once the business is ready to expand.

In the same way that consultancy services need to take account of the difficulty and character of small firms, so do training programmes. One of the reasons why so much training undertaken by the Industrial Training Boards is inappropriate to the needs of the small firm—and has attracted so much criticism from them especially when they weigh it against what it costs—is that so often it consists of big company techniques and practices watered down for the little chaps. Large sections of this book are devoted to showing how little companies are essentially different from big companies, and it is as true of their training needs as anything else. In spite of the Industrial Training Act there is still a gap. Much of the training for the smaller small firms is not basically the sort which helps them at grass root levels. What is the point of training the owner-manager in a sophisticated management technique like corporate planning when the nature of his business demands that he spends something like three-quarters of his working day on the telephone? In such circumstances there must be a case for training which helps improve his telephone technique; showing him how more efficiently, lucidly, persuasively to give or glean information, and issue instructions. The example is an extreme one, but the problem with so much training is that it is pitched above the heads of the recipients, and is not really suited to their needs. Obviously it is not easy to cater for small firms and small businessmen, for in all their variety and diversity they make a nonsense of any general formula of needs.

One answer to the dilemma for companies at the lower end of the spectrum might be greater emphasis on education, on pointing them in the right general direction, rather than unsuitable training. The trouble is that colleges of technology and the like have to present programmes which do all things for all comers, not just subjects which service the interests of small business as such. Specialist courses are another matter. Then there is scope to get somewhere. The Bournemouth College of Technology, for example, runs courses in hairdressing management, and from this hairdressing base it has been able to extend to subjects like staffing and financing. The success of the course is that it is not just a technical course alone. It is conducted by a man who knows hairdressing in concert with a man who knows management.

The problem of training for the small firm emphasises yet again, as do so many other problems which are specific to it, its unique and individualistic character. There are some problems which are so specific that it is an easy bet that even the Bolton Committee has not stumbled across them. There is the one which Richard Lamb of Adcola Products (Chapter 7) found himself having to face, and the extraordinary way he resolved it.

Strange things started happening in the building where the firm produced its soldering instruments. Doors opened on their own, there was the sound of mysterious footsteps, and it was all a bit of a joke. 'It's the ghost of Grandfather Cross,' they used to say, referring to the original owner of the old building. It was not the ghost which particularly worried Richard Lamb, but it did worry the girls who worked for the firm on wiring assembly. When it came to overtime in the evenings or at weekends they just didn't want to know. It was the sort of problem which never appears in manuals on productivity or industrial relations, so Richard Lamb called in a well-known lady medium his wife knew. She made a tour of the plant, had a vision in which she saw a friendly old man sitting at a brazier, went into a trance and politely called upon him to go on to the beyond. 'Since that day we have never had any more problems and the girls work overtime quite happily,' says Richard.

Postscript

The future for small business

The researches of the Bolton Committee have filled a major gap. Its main findings and recommendations are presented below. So are examples of immediate government action which followed it. Yet in some respects it was out of date before the ink was dry on its pages. In the autumn of 1971 the small business situation was changing. Many of the problems it analysed in detail were being resolved, thanks to more enlightened policies from government and credit institutions. Events were attacking ingrained attitudes about job security and risk. Unemployment was spawning new businesses, and a new breed of technically qualified and management trained entrepreneur was appearing in the ranks of small business. The future for it hadn't looked so encouraging for a long time.

AFTER over two years of investigation and research the Bolton Committee of Inquiry on Small Firms published its report on 3 November 1971. It was 436 pages long, weighed 1lb 4oz, cost an estimated £149,585 to produce and £2.55 to buy. The material within its pages was backed by eighteen separate research reports which were commissioned to assist the committee to arrive at its own conclusions.

It was the first detailed and comprehensive study ever made in the United Kingdom of the world of small business, its importance and its problems, and it filled many gaps which had hitherto existed in the body of information and research previously available on the subject. Page 1 of the report carried a passage which bears repeating because it helps pull together what a large part of my book is about—the extraordinary pervasiveness, ubiquity and, paradoxically, the sheer size of the small business sector in the United Kingdom.

'It soon became obvious that we had undertaken a massive task, and one of great difficulty, for the small firm sector is extremely large and remarkably heterogenous,' says the report. 'On any reasonable definition, small firms count numerically for the vast majority of all business enterprises. Their diversity is even more striking than their numbers. Small firms are present in virtually every industry and the characteristics they share as small firms are sometimes not apparent because of the differences arising from the contrasting conditions of different industries. A proper study of the small firm sector therefore requires study of many industries. There is also extreme variation in the sector as regards efficiency, methods of operation, the nature of the market served and the size of the resources employed. Thus a manufacturing business employing up to 200 people has very little in common with a small shop owned and run by a married couple. Were it not for one characteristic of prime importance, it would be difficult to point to any similarities between them. The all important characteristic which is shared by these highly disparate enterprises, and by all small firms as we are using the term, is that they are managed by the people who own them. It is this which gives unity and meaning to the elusive concept of the small firm sector, and which distinguishes the independent small firm from the subsidiary of a big company.'

It was with these owner-managers that Bolton essentially concerned itself, but since quantitative definitions were required for statistical purposes it adopted the following yardsticks of size: manufacturing, 200 employees or less; retailing, a turnover of £50,000 per annum or less; the wholesale trades, a turnover of £200,000 per annum or less; construction, 25 employees or less; mining and quarrying, 25 employees or less; the motor trades, a turnover of £100,000 or less; road transport, five vehicles or less; and for catering it included all firms except multiples and brewery-managed public houses.

In quantitative terms the report strikingly confirmed the role and importance of small firms in the economy. Taking all the categories listed above, plus agriculture and the professions, there were 1·25 million small firms which accounted for 19 per cent of the gross national product and 24 per cent of the output of the private sector. They also provided work for 29 per cent of the employed population—more than the entire public sector. As it happened Bolton did not study agriculture and the professions in its inquiry. But even without these two there remained 820,000 small firms, which accounted for 14 per cent of the gross national product and 18 per cent of the net output of the private sector. Between them they employed 4·4 million people. The committee also found that as a group these small firms were not inefficient in the use of resources and they won a better return on their capital than larger companies, although output per person was on average lower. This was partly explained by the labour intensive nature of the trades in which small firms predominate, and by differences in the composition of the labour force—the use of more part-time labour, for example.

But despite the small firm sector being a large and important component of the country's industrial structure, the main finding of the committee was that it was in a state of long-term decline, both in size and in its share of economic activity, and while the same was true of most other developed countries throughout the world, the process appeared to have gone further in the United Kingdom than elsewhere. The committee thought it was possible to foresee a time when the small firm sector would cease to be viable, if trends it observed at the time were to continue unabated. Since the committee considered a lively small firm sector vital to the health, if not the existence, of the private enterprise system, the main problem they faced was whether the situation justified special measures of support for the small firm.

With some forebodings, they decided there was no case at that time for discrimination in favour of small firms. The decline was largely attributable to inevitable and even desirable changes, in technical processes and in the size of markets for example. It believed that before it reached dangerous proportions the natural resilience and the inherent strength of the small firm would assert itself. Thus it was against subsidies, tax concessions or other differential measures, while its positive recommendations were designed to remove the inequities and disabilities which small firms had suffered, usually as a result of unintended neglect by the government. This would give them a chance to compete on equal terms with the large.

None the less to guard against the possibility that the decline might continue past danger point, it recommended the setting up, within the Department of Trade and Industry, of a Small Firms Division under the aegis of a minister designated as responsible for small firms, whose main function would be to monitor the health of the sector and to ensure that in future its interests would not be allowed to go by default. In fact, with uncharacteristic speed and almost within minutes of publication the government set up a brand new Small Business Division and appointed Nicholas Ridley, Parliamentary Under Secretary for Industry, as protector of the small firm. This was the main recommendation among a total of sixty made by the Bolton Committee, and it represented the first positive and specific step taken by a recent government on behalf of the country's small companies. Other recommendations—that a network of advisory bureaus should be established in important industrial centres and that measures should be undertaken to reduce the burden of form filling on small businessmen—also received swift and sympathetic responses. Additionally, companies with a turnover of less than £250,000 a year were promised exemption from the obligation to disclosure under the 1967 Companies Act, and also from showing information about the remuneration of individual directors when the total remuneration of their boards did not exceed £15,000, compared with £7,500 at the time. By the end of the week in which Bolton was published there was a feeling in the air that the government would be taking note of many more of its suggestions which ranged over the full spectrum of small business problems—from enabling small firms to compete more effectively for government contracts to changes in close company legislation, capital gains provisions, estate duty relief and the exemption of small firms from the industrial training levy and grant system. None the less, there was one major omission. Or, if not an omission, a piece of buck-passing which by the time action was taken on it was not likely to be of much value. Bolton recommended that the new Small Business

Division should immediately set up a study of the impact of entry into the Common Market on small firms. In view of the urgency it seemed a curious responsibility to shove on to someone else's shoulders at that stage. In November 1971 it was a question on which many small businessmen wanted immediate, not belated guidance. Even more so, because of all the argument and counter argument for and against Britain's entry. In its report Bolton said it was evident that entry into EEC would accentuate some of the processes which had contributed to the decline of the small firm in the United Kingdom, as well as providing new opportunities for the most enterprising. Then, in a few brief throw-away lines it hinted at some of the problems in store for the small firm—which will result from an event which many people believe will have more effect on the nation's business life than any other this century. 'We are informed that in the Netherlands the formation of EEC was followed by a tendency to larger-scale production and an increase in the number of mergers and takeovers, and that in general the relative position of small business has deteriorated. Adaptions to the demands of the wider market impose an additional strain on the slender management resources of the small firm. The national Governments of the Six and the EEC Commission have shown appreciation of these problems of the small firm and various studies have been undertaken by the Commission of ways in which small firms can be assisted to adapt to the new circumstances.' It was a passage which cried out for exposition. It triggered off all the questions small businessmen in Britain were asking about the Common Market and its effect on their firms. It supplied no answers and offered little reassurance.

In some ways the nature of the main piece of help recommended by Bolton seemed strangely out of line with the picture it presented of the man towards whom it was directed. For the small businessman is jealous of his independence, mistrustful of outside intervention of any sort and so burdened by the day-to-day running of his business that it is doubtful whether he will have the time or the inclination to trot off to government advice bureaux manned by retired executives, any more than he has the time to attend management courses or keep up with the flood of management and technical literature which drops on his desk. Indeed, some owners of small firms tell you the most sensible and useful bit of help the government could give them would be a telephone service which worked efficiently. In practice it is the man most in need of advice and help who eschews it. The point was neatly put in a letter to the *Financial Times* a few days after the Bolton Report was published.

'If the Department of Trade and Industry is going to make Bolton work, then the setting up of regional bureaux, suggested in the report, needs to be backed up with a giant educational exercise, not just a few strategically placed posters and newspaper ads,' said the writer. 'This sort of campaign, whether it applies to rent rebates or to subsidised consultancy, has long since proved to be inadequate. Not that there will be any shortage of companies taking advantage of any new facilities offered by the regional bureaux. The problem will be, as Bolton rightly points out, that these companies will be the high fliers; those who know what it is all about anyway. The ones that will be the most difficult to help are those that have traditionally shied away from any help and assistance from government agencies. The companies in fact who do not know their Industrial Liaison Office, have serious doubts about how much their Training Board can help, and are neither affiliated to the Productivity Council or the CBI, and have not heard of either the Council for Small Industries in Rural Areas or the Industrial and Commercial Finance Corporation. These are the firms which are too busy to sit on the regional committees of their own Employers' Federations. Yet these firms constitute the majority of Britain's small businesses and these are the ones the new division will need to get through to if Bolton is to work. What is really needed is a package which will reach small businessmen where he needs it. At his works.' But even with its deficiencies the Bolton Report must be required reading henceforth for any serious student of the small business scene, for it has revealingly and factually spotlighted so many aspects of small business which were previously the subject of hazy half-truths or matters of opinion. It was a large, ambitious document which not only charted the major trends which were occurring in the small business sector, but also tackled in immense detail the minutiae of small business life. It went to enormous pains and took a great deal of space to analyse the problems small businessmen had been vociferously complaining about for so long. Yet, by the time it was published, there were already signs that the situation was changing. Much of the pessimism which lies just beneath the surface of the report was in actuality already being dispersed by a fresh and encouraging climate of public opinion and a better and more sympathetic understanding from government of the difficulties of small firms. The very fact of Bolton sitting—long before it started recommending—was part and parcel of this. As a result, for the first time for a long time, small businessmen felt they had just cause for a new felt optimism. Those seemingly intractable disadvantages suffered by small firms to which Bolton devoted so much analysis—a tax system which discriminated against them, and the belief that the financial mechanism was geared to the needs of big rather than small firms—suddenly seemed in the autumn of 1971 less immediate, less persistent and less acute than hitherto.

The spring budget did more to bolster this feeling than any other fiscal bag of tricks for a long time. From it sprang a more relaxed and easy credit climate. Indeed, by the time Bolton was published the banks were falling over themselves to lend money and woo customers from wherever they could. It is just possible that if they had been a little more unbending during the harsh years, not quite so conservative in their attitudes and prepared to point some of their more desperate clients in the direction of other forms of finance, the ranks of small business might not have been decimated to the extent they were. Anyway, for most small businesses, the gentle and warm caress of the wind of change which had started to blow was a welcome relief from the inclement mistral of the previous decade, and they had reason to take heart from it. Despite trials and tribulation, and a high level of business failures, the great mass of them had shown enormous resilience in adverse conditions and a bulldog-like ability to hang on and survive in spite of the benign neglect and grey disinterest of both public and government. As such the survivors emerged, lean and sinewy, adept in the skills of business endurance, both more experienced and wiser, and with an edge which placed them in a position to benefit all the more from the promise of forthcoming measures designed to bring about a real improvement in the growth of the economy and produce a more beneficial business climate. For them it was like responding to the first stirring of spring after a long, hard winter of discontent, and it was largely this climate of winter which the Bolton Committee described, disclosed, and prescribed for. Springtime, which offered new hope and the renewal of old ones, was just around the corner and Bolton largely ignored it.

It was not an easier monetary policy in isolation which was responsible for the change. There was increasing evidence in reports of company chairmen that large companies were abandoning unprofitable and marginal activities—classically the sort which small firms can often operate more swiftly and efficiently—and rationalising their product lines. Giving up the jobs which they had no business doing, by virtue of their size and scale, in the first place. Even in the changing industrial structure and the decline in the importance of the small firm there were new opportunities for it as merger, rationalisation and amalgamation of small units into larger ones sometimes left a vacuum which a new, small firm was able to fill, giving a similar service or making the same product that the previous small firms supplied before they were merged into something bigger.

There was an additional stimulus to the health of small firms in that the number of people who, despite high levels of personal taxation, seemed to be able to raise sufficient money from their own resources to start a business—and to have sufficient funds to live on for a year while they were getting it off the ground—remained amazingly high. Mounting unemployment, both among workers and executives, gave further impetus to this trend since those without jobs were faced with the pressing necessity of earning the groceries, or going on the dole. For many of them a business of their own became a practical proposition because ever increasing redundancy payments and golden handshakes were available to finance it.

People's attitudes counted too. Old values about security and a pensionable job for life were given some hard knocks in 1971.

There were some notable and outstanding failures in big business, the most shattering of all being the collapse of Rolls-Royce. With it the old, assumed, taken-for-granted confidence that if you worked for a blue chip firm you had a blue chip job flew right out of the window. After the famous engineering firm's failure it was a notion to which many people in industry would never give much credence again. Viewed against such an unhappy event the risk of being in business for oneself, where a man at least had some command over his own destiny, paled in significance.

Allied to this was the emergence of a middle-class generation for whom the depression years, with their hunger marches and closed factories, were incidents of economic history, not experiences which had been lived through. Their attitudes, therefore, about taking the plunge and starting up on their own were less inhibited and cautious than those of their fathers. Their priorities were different and for them job security with a solid firm was not a factor which weighed as heavily as it did with their dads. In any case it was a time when the mass media, both newspapers and television, devoted more and more of their space and time to business as a subject in its own right. How money was made, turned over (and sometimes lost) was a staple part of readers' and viewers' diets. Successful entrepreneurs were paraded before them. So were wicked villains intent on separating men from their money. There was encouragement to emulate the high fliers in every other line; there were plain warnings to steer clear of the crooks. It was a time when people avidly read, studied and inwardly digested the creeds of business. It was a time when a newspaper columnist had only to chart the progress of one successful entrepreneur, to have a score of potential ones writing to him with their ideas—all fired with the feeling there was money to be made and a wide range of highly personal gratifications to be enjoyed by working for themselves rather than anyone else.

Also important was the increasing presence of a new style of small businessman, who at the beginning of the 1970s was certainly better educated, more technically expert and often managerially experienced and qualified, altogether more worldly in the ways of business and more articulate about it than his predecessors. Often he had big company training behind him, and was able to translate and adapt the sophisticated management techniques of big business with a gratifying quality of results to his own small firm. Often, too, he was a scientist or technologist whose field was so specialised and expert that there was every opportunity and scope for him and his firm to make their way in a world where business was getting bigger all the time. He was very much a new breed, a different animal to Bolton Man, with his lack of higher education, his average age in the middle fifties and a business probably older than him. Time, a better education and a changing industrial structure made him less dependent on the old entrepreneurial attributes of flair, drive, unorthodox seat-of-the-pants style management. He was better equipped to clearly identify his business goals and objectives, make use of every appropriate source of help, from organisations like the British Institute of Management to public relations consultants who know their way about the corridors of Whitehall. In his highly specialised field he knew where to look for the gaps and which ones to exploit—and in that he was no different from any other man who ever had an idea and made it into a business.

It would be easy to oversimplify the argument and take it to a conclusion where old-time entrepreneurial intuition plus shrewdness and drive were replaced by technological knowledge, organisation and professional management techniques. But it is an argument which will not do at all. For even the new-style entrepreneur can do with some of the old-style attributes. There is not a business textbook yet, when all the accounting and all the corporate planning has been described, which has successfully identified and reduced to a handy formula the magical, X-plus quality which makes one small businessman outstandingly successful and another a barely competent mediocrity.

For all these reasons it is not difficult to believe that Bolton came in at the tail-end of a situation which had started to change; a situation which, in another five years time, will make the reading of the report an historical exercise. For, in my view, the pendulum has commenced to swing in the other direction, away from the 1960s which rang the death knell of so many small firms, towards the 1970s which offer more hopeful and happier horizons. This is despite the statistics of decline and extrapolations of ultimate doom for the small man. Time, of course, has made many a monkey out of pundits and soothsayers but in this case there is comfort in the sheer historical persistence of the small firm, and there is even a modest piece of insurance for holding a belief in its future. This is in the form of just thirteen words buried away in the ocean of words which make the Bolton Report:

> 'If small firms did not exist it would be
> necessary to invent them.'

Further reading

UNTIL the publication of the Bolton Report, research into the character and problems of the small firm was sparse and patchy. Now this gap has been filled and for serious students of the subject the report and its associated research studies must be standard reading.

The full title of it is the Report of the Committee of Inquiry on Small Firms. It is published as Command Paper 4811 by HMSO. The eighteen research reports are listed below:

1 The Small Firm in the Road Haulage Industry. B. Bayliss.
2 Scientific and Engineering Manpower and Research in Small Firms. J. G. Cox.
3 Small Firms in the Manufacturing Sector. J. R. Davies and M. Kelly.
4 Financial Facilities for Small Firms. Economists Advisory Group.
5 Problems of the Small Firm in Raising External Finance—the Results of a Sample Survey. Economists Advisory Group.
6 The Role of Small Firms in Innovation in the UK since 1945. C. Freeman.
7 Attitude and Motivation. C. W. Golby and G. Johns.
8 The Small Unit in the Distributive Trades. Margaret Hall.
9 The Small Firm in the Motor Vehicle Distribution and Repair Industry. J. Hebden and R. V. F. Robinson.
10 Small Firms in the Construction Industry. P. Hillebrandt.
11 Three Studies on Small Firms. P. Lund and D. Miner.
   i Previous Surveys of Small Firms

ii Comparisons Between Firms of Different Size using the CBI's Industrial Trends Surveys

iii The Investment Behaviour of Small Firms

12 Dynamics of Small Firms. Merrett-Cyriax Associates.

13 Aspects of Monopoly and Restrictive Practices Legislation in Relation to Small Firms. S. Moos.

14 The Small Firm in the Hotel and Catering Industry. J. F. Pickering.

15 Small Retailers: Prospects and Policies. A. D. Smith.

16 A Postal Questionnaire Survey of Small Firms: An Analysis of Financial Data. M. Tamari.

17 A Postal Questionnaire Survey of Small Firms: Non-Financial Data, Tables, Definitions and Notes. Research Unit.

18 The Relative Efficiency of Small and Large Firms. D. Todd.

General Interest and Background

For readers with a general interest in the subject wading through Bolton is not likely to prove very rewarding. Unfortunately there is a dearth of books for non-specialists which give a viable coverage of the subject and it is therefore not easy to suggest a comprehensive reading list. There is no popularly written all-embracing work which makes the world of small business intelligible. The books which do exist are either pitched at an academic audience or tackle the subject from a make-yourself-a-fortune-by-the-time-you-are-forty angle. There is nothing which steers a middle course, although the *Sunday Times Business News*, the *Financial Times, The Director* and *Management Today* frequently feature small firms in their editorial pages. At an academic level *Problems of a Mature Economy* by F. V. Meyer, D. C. Corner and J. E. S. Parker (Macmillan, 1970) gives an understanding of the economic backcloth to small business. It deals with the principal problems of the British economy over the last twenty years, makes an analysis of the causes and suggests remedies. The first part of the book is the most valuable in that it makes a micro-economic study of the firm and the factors affecting its growth. Both *The Structure of Industry in Britain* by G. C. Allen (Longmans, 3rd edition 1969) and Graham Turner's *Business in Britain* (Eyre & Spottiswoode, 1970) make sensible complementary reading. For the European background read *An Economic History of Western Europe 1945–1964* by M. M. Postan (Methuen, 1967). It is also worth reading selected sections of *The Financing of Small Business* (Collier-Macmillan, 1967) which is one of the studies by the Columbia University Graduate School of Business in its Modern Corporation series. Although the book is an assessment of American experience, Part 1, especially the chapter on the Position of Small Business in the American Economy, contains much material which is germane to small business everywhere. Both Edith Penrose's, *The Theory of the Growth of the Firm* (Blackwell, 1959) and *Attitudes in British Management—A PEP report* (Penguin, 1966) originally published by PEP and George Allen & Unwin as *Thrusters and Sleepers* are studies of what makes firms grow. *The Private Company Today* by A. J. Merrett and M. E. Lehr (Gower Press, 1971) is an investigation into the economic position of the unquoted company in the UK, and within this compass it does, of course, include large unquoted companies as well as small ones. The Confederation of British Industry's simple and uncomplicated little book, *Britain's Small Firms—Their Vital Role in the Economy*, makes a starting point for beginners in the subject. On the more popular level of books there is *Fortunes to be Made* by Raymond Painter (Arthur Barker, 1970) which traces the case histories of many new entrepreneurs who have succeeded in making a fortune in recent years. It does not pretend to be an in-depth analysis and the reading is easy and undemanding.

Practical Management

I have not yet discovered a simpler small book on the subject of running a small business than *Developing a Small Firm* by Tony Matthews and Colin Mayers (BBC Publications, 1968). Anyone with a small business starting to take off should take an afternoon off to read its 150 pages which cover everything from opportunities for small firms to making growth decisions. There is no shortage of other books in the How To Do It genre: Westropp's *Starting Your Own Business* by Hugh Dykes (Oldbourne Books, 1967); *Buying and Running Your Own Business* by Ian Ford (Business Books,

1970); and *A Business of Your Own* by Brian Fraser Harrison (The World's Work, 1968). Since it behoves anyone starting or running a business to learn enough about accounting, without getting bogged down in a morass of technicalities, to know whether his accountant is doing a good job or making a hash of it, a book like L. E. Rockley's *Finance for the Non Accountant* (Business Books, 1970) should point him in the right direction. It is less concerned with the mechanics of accounting than with showing how to use balance sheets and statements and how to look at them critically. In the practical books sector the management booklets published by the Industrial and Commercial Finance Corporation give much helpful information. Sample titles are *Making an Idea into a Business, The Monthly Statement, Budgetary Control, Growth by Merger*. Similarly the British Institute of Management has an excellent portfolio of practical publications. Its Guidelines for the Smaller Business series of leaflets which deal with typical problem subjects; its checklists, thirty-four of them, which ask a range of questions about subjects as diverse as report writing and packaging; and its Management Information Sheets on topics like Luncheon Vouchers and Management By Objectives are all well presented down to earth aids. Lastly the Pan Books Management Series in paperback has over twenty-five titles ranging from the *Practice of Management* to *Selling and Salesmanship*.

Retailing

For the historic background and the main trends, *High Street Retail Trading in Britain 1850–1950* by J. G. Jefferys (Cambridge University Press, 1954) is a good standard reference. Much more contemporary, and popularly written, is Greville Havenhand's *Nation of Shopkeepers* (Eyre & Spottiswoode, 1970). For a single study of a little shop which grew into a national chain, *JS 100—The Story of Sainsbury's* (J. Sainsbury Ltd, 1969) is a company publication which gives a brief account of the firm's first century of growth.

Invention and Innovation

The National Research Development Corporation's leaflet,

Help for the Inventor, presents in question and answer form the basic facts an inventor should know about patenting and explains what NRDC and other bodies can do to help the inventor. For general reading Peter Fairley's *Project X—The Exciting Story of British Invention* (Mayflower Books, 1970) covers the story of major inventions like the hovercraft, penicillin and the fuel cell and the problems and triumphs in the fight to commercialise them. More academically pitched is a pamphlet by William Kingston, *Invention and Monopoly* (Department of Economic and Business Studies, Woolwich Polytechnic). For those who wish to pursue the subject in greater depth *The Sources of Invention* by J. Jewkes, D. Sawyers and R. Stillerman (Macmillan, 1969) is an essential source.

Government Policy

In recent years there has not been a government policy which you would notice for small business, so it is hardly surprising there is no standard book about it. However, Frank Broadway's *State Intervention in British Industry 1964–1968* (Kaye & Ward, 1969) charts the rising tide of intervention in this period, pin-pointing so many of the measures and bodies, fiscal and otherwise, which legions of small businessmen came to so heartily dislike and resent.

Finance

For specialist readers I suggest *The Financing of Small Business* by James Bates (Sweet & Maxwell, 1964) and the American book of the same title mentioned in the section on General Interest and Background. On a practical note readers can do no better than the concise and excellent breakdown of sources of finance in *Financing Your Business* (Engineering Industries Association, 1968). The Bolton Committee Research Report No 4 is a detailed and comprehensive study of existing Financial Facilities for Small Firms. It repays reading by anyone looking for money because it does what so many books on the subject don't do—and that is to suggest an ambiance for each of the money-lending institutions. This plus its factual findings make it a splendid guide to raising money if it is used intelligently. For an interest beyond the small firms' financial problems there is still no book to beat *The City* by Paul Ferris (Penguin, Revised Edition 1965) for a highly readable and fascinating insight into this esoteric world.

Official Publications

1 Report of the Committee on Finance and Industry (The Macmillan Report) 1931. Command Paper 3897. HMSO. This was the report which spotlighted as long as forty years ago the difficulties small and medium-sized firms were having in raising capital.
2 Report of the Committee on the Working of the Monetary System (The Radcliffe Report) 1959. Command Paper 827. HMSO. This report again stressed the problems and difficulties small firms had in financing their growth.
3 The Annual Companies Reports of the Department of Trade and Industry. HMSO. These give basic statistics of the numbers of companies registered, the trend of company registrations, and figures for company liquidations.
4 Reports on the Censuses of Production and Distribution. HMSO.
5 Annual Abstracts of Statistics. HMSO.

Appendix I

The small firm in other countries, official attitudes to it, and how it is represented

The Common Market

THERE are no special provisions under the Treaty of Rome for small firms, but there are arrangements in individual member states which are designed to favour them. There has, as yet, been no harmonisation of these, and they are by no means identical in each country. The only specific arrangements to assist small firms are certain forms of agreement (not normally allowed on the grounds that they might limit inter-state trade) which permit them to enter into arrangements relating to the exchange of information on market research, agreements on common sales and after sales services and other forms of co-operation. It has also been proposed that there should be a regulation granting small firms exemption for agreements relating to standards, to research and development and to common purchasing and selling. Member states have also been encouraged to introduce national rules which would favour small firms.

The following action has been taken by the European Economic Commission:

Finance: The Commission has documented national measures for establishing machinery for assisting small firms to secure the finance they require. These cover organisations or rules which enable funds to be raised at specially low interest rates, or on other particularly favourable terms. Certain experiments have been made in the Community to make provision for funds for rapidly developing small firms, and these are the subject of a special study.

Associations of small firms: The Commission is encouraging other states to follow the example of the French who have established associations of firms known as 'Groupements d'Intérêt Economique'. These were designed to provide a suitable legal form in areas where companies might wish to co-operate, for example, in sales or research, without losing their identities or going to the length of a merger until they had had a trial period. The resulting body comes somewhere between a company and an association, avoiding the rigidity of the first, without suffering the incapacity of the second, and it can be used in the profit-making objectives of a company, or the non-profit-making objectives of an association. It is available without restriction or discrimination to all undertakings whatever their form or structure, as well as to individuals, and it has full legal capacity and identity of its own. It may be formed with or without capital, and may or may not give rise to the making and sharing of profits. Its members are fully responsible for its debts up to the limit of their own resources. It is subject to the same fiscal laws as associations and individuals. The profits or losses from it which fall to each member is part of the taxable revenue of that member, and is subject to the fiscal rules applicable to the member. Thus the GIE is particularly useful as an instrument of trans-frontier co-operation.

Harmonisation of company and tax laws: Little progress has been made to date and this will be a lengthy process because of the inherent difficulties. There has been much debate about the possibility of devising a standard form of company, a 'European Company', to overcome them, but so far draft proposals suggest this would be more suitable for larger and medium-sized companies rather than small ones. Accordingly the Commission is studying the possibility of a 'European GIE' which would probably better suit the needs of small firms.

Measures to encourage co-operation: The basic ones which are most likely to assist small firms to benefit from the Common Market have been identified by a working party set up by EEC as:

1 Measures designed to encourage the formation of bureaux to facilitate the exchange of information and the establishment of

direct contact between small and medium-sized companies in different member states.

2 Measures, including the establishment of bureaux, to facilitate sub-contracting by small firms.
3 Measures to encourage the availability of forms of finance particularly designed to assist small firms.
4 Other measures designed to encourage co-operation between small firms.

Although most of the member states of the Common Market have introduced measures to assist small firms they are not necessarily in the same fields or similar in character, and they are, of course, individual national arrangements which have not resulted from action of the Commission. It is only possible to give a brief pointer rather than a comprehensive guide to some of them. Broadly speaking, they can be categorised as measures concerned with political action, legislation on business competition and concentration, the taxation treatment of small firms, financing facilities favourable to small firms, and management training and education.

In *France* a Secretary of State for Small and Medium-sized Industry has specific responsibility for defining, co-ordinating and implementing action to encourage the contribution of small businesses to economic growth. On the fiscal front there is scope for certain small businesses to be assessed on a basis which is different from real profits and real turnover, and which has the effect of abbreviating and simplifying the returns which have to be made to the tax authorities, and therefore absolves small business from keeping full accounts. On the question of finance the French attitude is that because smaller firms are often not able to offer sufficient security to raise a loan under the normal system, they should be given special credit facilities. For example, loans are available to such firms if they are members of a Mutual Guarantee Society—there is one specifically for small and medium-sized enterprises—which for a small commission guarantees loans granted to its members, who can then obtain two to seven year professional credits for equipment and light construction from banks at rates of interest believed to be a little below those normally charged. Reference has already been made to the Groupements d'Intérêt Economique which have been formed in France. These are mainly concerned with the production and supply of goods. A similar form of association is the Société Conventionée which is a combination of firms formed for the purpose of co-operative research, marketing research and the encouragement of specialisation. This type of association is specially adapted to the needs of small firms and its advantages are becoming increasingly recognised in France.

Germany has successfully pursued a policy of promoting co-operation agreements between firms in general, and small businesses in particular, through a whole range of measures. More than 1,000 agreements are estimated to have been concluded in 1968, about two thirds of them concerning small and medium-sized businesses. Also government guarantees given to industrial associations in respect of loans granted by them have helped small businesses lacking sufficient security to find loans more easily. In *Belgium* small businesses enjoy favourable credit terms because of a system where the government pays part of the interest on loans over a given period.

It is clear that both on an individual country basis and on a Community level the importance of small firms has been recognised in Europe. So far more positive steps have been taken by individual governments than concerted ones by EEC, though the Commission has undertaken a lot of valuable groundwork.

United States: In America the general climate towards small business is favourable. Extensive anti-trust legislation is one example of this and both the Senate and the House of Representatives have powerful Committees on Small Business. The US also provides the most striking example of government action to encourage small business in the shape of the Small Business Administration. The basic reason for the existence of this body, which was set up in 1953, was the widespread recognition that the achievements of small business had been accomplished in the past against heavy odds. For instance until the SBA started its regular business lending programme, the provision of long-term loans to small businessmen was rare and many of them, with good security and good prospects and in need of long-term money, had to use short-term funds, with all the attendant disadvantages, instead.

SBA is an independent government agency, which receives its money on an appropriation from the federal budget. Its declared purpose is to help in the setting up, the continuance and the growth of small business, as well as to assist with management education.

It administers the Small Business Investment Act which is designed to encourage the flow of private capital to small businesses via Small Business Investment Companies, of which there are several hundred. These lend money in the form of equity, or make five to twenty year loans. The SBIC can obtain funds from the SBA to lend to small businesses at advantageous rates—and both the SBIC's and private investors gain tax concessions when they sell their securities.

The SBA also makes available the results of federally sponsored research and development to small business and deals with requests for scientific and engineering information. It is active in disseminating information on management research, publishes free booklets on the subject, and operates a data bank to provide management and economic information to small firms. It also publishes management aids on subjects like exporting and productivity which are free, as well as a whole range of publications, for which it charges, on every conceivable topic likely to interest small businesses.

Small firms in the USA also receive favourable tax treatment, whereby both new and established small businesses are allowed to select the tax structure most beneficial to them.

Japan: The spectacular growth of the Japanese economy since 1955 has resulted in large structural changes in industry which have had significant effects on small business. In many instances small firms had to modernise and expand. This called for large investment programmes and accordingly a number of government financial institutions have been established to supplement the conventional sources of finance. For the most part these confine their lending to small business.

The Central Bank for Commercial and Industrial Co-operatives has mixed ownership—both public and private—and its operations are supervised by the government. It also provides financial assistance and it extends credit to its member organisations in five to twenty year loans as well as overdrafts.

The Small Business Finance Corporation is a financial agency of the government and was established in 1953 to supply funds to small businesses which would have had difficulty in raising them through other channels.

The People's Finance Corporation is another government agency which lends for business purposes to private individuals who encounter difficulties in borrowing from ordinary financial institutions. Both of these institutions are supervised by the Ministry of Finance.

The Japanese Government encourages small businesses to co-operate in production, purchasing and sales by forming joint business operations (through co-operatives) and to avoid excessive competition (through commercial and industrial associations). It also gives preferential tax treatment—lower rates of corporation tax are payable by companies with a capital of £117,650 or less on distributed and undistributed income up to £3,500—and guidance on management and production techniques through local government agencies throughout the country which are partly supported by central government funds.

Small Business Representation

Here we are referring to organisations formed by smaller businesses themselves, not by governments. The largest international body representative of small firms is the International Association of Artisans and Small and Medium Businesses to which small business associations in fourteen countries in Europe and seven outside Europe are affiliated. The International Union has a membership of over 6 million small firms.

One of the strongest and most influential of these is in France—La Confédération Générale des Petites et Moyennes Enterprises, which was formed in 1946. It is an important body, maintains a large research staff and is capable of exercising some influence on government policies. It has a membership of over 1 million industrial and commercial enterprises. Its objectives are the expression of the social and political ideas of small business; the provision of information and services to members; and the promotion of international interest and understanding between small firms of various countries.

Appendix 2

Sources of help for small firms

Financial

It is impossible to list by name all the institutions involved in financing industry. Mention has already been made of the Engineering Industries Association booklet, *Financing Your Business*, which surveys every sort of credit-raising technique, gives details of each facility, the terms on which it is available and explains how and where to apply for it. The booklet costs 50p and is available from the Association at 3–7 Portman Square, London W1.

The following are brief pointers to some of the money-lending institutions mentioned in the main body of the book.

1 The Industrial and Commercial Finance Corporation, 7 Copthall Avenue, London EC2, makes long-term fixed interest loans in the £5,000 to £500,000 range.
2 The Estate Duties Investment Trust (address as for ICFC) will invest in small firms where money is needed to pay off estate duty, or where funds are required for future payment of duty.
3 The Small Business Capital Fund, 88 Baker Street, London W1, invests in any field of activity including new ventures. There is no set upper or lower limits as to amounts.
4 The two main sources of finance for innovation are:
   - i Technical Development Capital (address as for ICFC) provides risk capital to firms developing a new idea or product. Preference is given to projects which have passed the development and prototype stage.
   - ii National Research Development Corporation, Kingsgate House, 66–74 Victoria Street, London SW1, in-

vests on the basis of recovering its outlay if a project is successful. If it isn't, it doesn't seek to recover its money.

Services for small firms partly or wholly Government financed

1 Industrial Liaison Service: aims at assisting small manufacturing firms to improve efficiency and technological strength. There are 75 Industrial Liaison Centres based on colleges of technology and universities. The service is free. Addresses are available from Department of Trade and Industry or its regional offices.

2 Low Cost Automation Centres: provide information and consulting services on inexpensive use of mechanisation and automatic controls in relation to the problems of small firms. There are 18 centres (addresses from DTI and regional offices) and fees are charged for consulting.

3 The Council for Small Industries in Rural Areas: provides advisory, consultancy, training and credit services (loans up to £25,000) for small firms employing less than 100 persons in all and less than 20 skilled workers. Address: 35 Camp Road, Wimbledon Common, London SW19.

4 Small Industries Council for Rural Areas in Scotland: the counterpart in Scotland of COSIRA. Its aims and methods are broadly similar. Loans range from £250 to £25,000. Address: 27 Walker Street, Edinburgh.

5 Highlands and Islands Development Board: operates in the crofting counties and the islands as a development agency to assist economic and social growth, encouraging industry to set up in its area. It offers management services and makes grants and loans for approved projects up to £50,000. Address: 6 Castle Wynd, Inverness, Scotland.

6 Government export services: these are fully described in *The Export Handbook: Services for British Exporters* which is avail-

able from the Department of Trade and Industry, 1 Victoria Street, London SW1.

Guides to Services

Business Efficiency: an ABC of Advisory Services. HMSO. This is a comprehensive treatment of sources of advice ranging from government agencies to individual industry research and information services.

Technical Services for Industry is a booklet which gives all the technical services available from government research establishments and from other government departments. Available from the DTI.

Consultancy Services for the Small Firm

1 ICFC/NUMAS: from general management consultancy to specialist areas of work study. Available through over 20 offices in the UK. Details from 7 Copthall Avenue, London EC2.
2 The Small Business Centre, The University of Aston: provides a management consultancy and training programmes for small firms. Details from Maple House, 158 Corporation Street, Birmingham 4.
3 The Small Business Centre, Bristol Polytechnic: provides similar service to above. Details from 3 Great George Street, Bristol.

Organisations of interest to small firms

Confederation of British Industry, 21 Tothill Street, London SW1.

Smaller Businesses Association, 6 Holborn Viaduct, London EC1.

The Institute of Directors, 10 Belgrave Square, London SW1.

British Institute of Management, Management House, Parker Street, London WC2.

The British Productivity Council, Vintry House, Queen Street Place, London EC4.

Appendix 3

How to find out about your own company

TIME and again during the course of the many interviews I conducted in gathering material for this book small businessmen told me the questions forced them to think about aspects of their companies to which they had never given much thought before. One man, who had been in business for some years, said the interview was rather like a voyage of rediscovery and it had prompted him to make a number of decisions about the running of his firm, and its future development, which might otherwise have gone by the board. Another said it gave him an opportunity to gather his ideas and clarify them, to take stock of his situation and see it in relation to his original plans. All in all he felt it had been a most valuable exercise. On the other side of the fence a public relations consultant with a new, small-firm client in whom I was interested found my interview outline extremely useful in enabling him to swiftly get a complete picture of his client and his firm.

I am not claiming it is perfect or cannot be faulted and it was not designed as a rigid questionnaire, but it did help me in the formidable task of researching this volume, and it has evidently been of some use to small businessmen themselves and those who service them. So here it is, slightly amended, in the hope it may be of use to a wider audience:

The Beginnings of the Company

Where it started, in what circumstances, and by whom.
How was it financed? Its first products or services.
Early problems and achievements.
The degree of ease or difficulty with which it was launched.

What part did family and friends play in early days?
Relationship of present owners and managers to founders where applicable.

The Growth of the Company to the Present Time

What are the main landmarks or breakthroughs in its development? In terms, perhaps, of new products, innovations, ideas, designs; or new financing, new management or change in public tastes and requirements.

How has the company grown in terms of (a) Turnover
(b) Profits
(c) People
(d) Premises
(e) Reputation

Assessment of part played by flair, opportunism, luck, sheer hard work etc.

The problems and difficulties of growth—what are they, how have they been resolved?

The Background to Growth

The part played by external matters over which company has no control, eg the economic climate, the tax structure (how penal), the importance of timing (ie in terms of cashing in on, say, changing tastes), weather, wars, advances in transport etc (jets, containerisation, roll-on, roll-off ferries), television.

Where the Business Stands Today

What position does it hold in its industry?
What marks it out in a special or unique sense from its competitors?

The Style and Character of the Business

The image created by its letterheads, emblems, advertising.
The manner and the flavour of the business in the way it is run, eg by one man, by committee, by partners. Informally, or formally. Is it a word-of-mouth company or a memorandum-

writing company? Who decides policy and how, compared to the taking of daily decisions? How is the management organised? How is the decision taking apportioned? In the case of partners, or working directors with equal shares, how are differences resolved?

The Company's Markets

To whom does it sell and how? Direct or through distributors. What is its pricing policy?

Is its market changing? Has it changed?

What is the record of new company products or services?

How has it been affected by new products or services from competitors? Who are the competitors? How strong are they?

How do you know what to produce—does market research tell you, or experience plus intuition?

What is the company's export story?

Production

On what is the product based, eg special recipe, formula, design, invention, patent, service?

Is its production weighted towards modern technology or old established techniques?

How is production organised and controlled with reference to planning, purchasing, cost and quality control, stocks etc?

Working with Money

Is, or has, money been a major problem? How has expansion been financed? What has been happening to the level of profits in terms of the return on capital employed? Has the percentage been dropping, rising or remained static? What is the attitude to raising outside money ranging from overdrafts to having outside shareholders? Are there special problems about cash flow and credit giving in the trade (perhaps to do with its seasonal nature)? Has the company benefited from special assistance from government or semi-official sources, eg subsidies, loans, grants? How important have these been?

The Future Growth of the Company

Where is the company going? Where does it see its greatest opportunities? What are its objectives and targets?

What are the present strengths of the firm? What are its weaknesses?

Is management succession a problem? Has it been assured?

Will the shape and structure of the company have to change to meet future needs? If so, in what way?

The Company, Its Proprietors, Its People

Is there a sense of family? Has it a stable work force? Is long service a characteristic of the company? Does it promote from within or bring in outsiders? Does a sense of loyalty matter in a small business? To what extent is authority delegated from the top? On what sort of matters? Is it easy or difficult to delegate?

Is there a training scheme? How benevolent is the company—helping workpeople in trouble, loans etc?

What is the background of the owner/managers? Do the jobs they do suit their personalities? What do they get their satisfaction from? In what sort of proportions are pride, enjoyment, hard work and slog mixed?

The Social Profit and Loss of Running a Small Business

How has the business affected the lives of the people running it? How demanding has it been and what has it cost, or what has it enhanced, in terms of family life, friends, other pursuits and interests? Can you give examples of this?

Summing up, has it made for happiness, unhappiness, fulfilment, frustration?

The Lesson of Experience

If you were to start again from scratch what would you do differently and why? Would you even start a business in this day and age?

Appendix 4

Addresses of firms featured in the text

(*Listed in order of appearance*)

1 Caterpillar Products, Flaunden, nr Hemel Hempstead, Herts.
2 Danbury Conversions Ltd, Danbury, Chelmsford, Essex.
3 Chalk Drillcater Ltd, Oil Field Depot, Battery Road, Great Yarmouth, Norfolk.
4 Phase Separations Ltd, Deeside Industrial Estate, Queensferry, Flintshire.
5 Horizon Holidays Ltd, 17 Hanover Street, London W1.
6 Underwater and Marine Equipment Ltd, 61A Fleet Road, Farnborough, Surrey.
7 Revenue Systems Ltd, 59 Hitchin Road, Luton, Bedfordshire.
8 Benjamin Shaw Ltd, Willow Lane, Huddersfield.
9 J. Taylor and Sons, Abberton, Colchester, Essex.
10 H. Crabb and Son, 158 Liverpool Road, Islington, London N1.
11 Sykes-Robertson (Electronics) Ltd, Sanday, Orkney Islands, Scotland.
12 Ben Jones and Company, Nayland, Colchester, Essex.
13 Individual Shipments Ltd, 385 Green Street, London E13.
14 Christian Brann Ltd, Blackjack Street, Cirencester, Gloucestershire.
15 Richmond Marine Ltd, 48 The Green, Twickenham, Middlesex.
16 Lyric Pattern Services, Northway Crescent, London NW7.
17 The Beck Kindergartens Ltd, 9 Widmore Road, Bromley, Kent.

18 David & Charles (Holdings) Ltd, South Devon House, The Railway Station, Newton Abbot, Devon.

19 Newtown Oyster Fishery Co, Newtown, Isle of Wight.

20 Balding Engineering Ltd, Beaver Works, Sweet Briar Road, Norwich.

21 Wilkin and Sons Ltd, Tiptree, Colchester, Essex.

22 Seacrete Ltd, Port of Wroxham, Wroxham, Norwich, Norfolk.

23 G. E. Cook and Sons Ltd, Tidings Hill Brewery, Halstead, Essex.

24 Adcola Products Ltd, Adcola House, Gauden Road, London SW4.

25 Panavista Ltd, Old Stone Link, Ship Street, East Grinstead, Sussex.

26 Spearhead Chemicals Ltd, Heathrow House, Bath Road, Cranford, Middlesex.

27 Watercraft Ltd, The Barge Walk, East Molesey, Surrey.

28 Richard Atkinson and Co Ltd, Irish Poplin House, Donegall Road, Belfast.

29 Roys (Wroxham) Ltd, Wroxham, Norwich, Norfolk.

30 Archie Smith, Queen's Corner, West Mersea, Colchester, Essex.

31 Trago Mills Trading Estate, Two Waters Foot, Liskeard, Cornwall.

32 The Hire Shop, 16 Station Square, Petts Wood, Kent.

33 A. L. Harper (Wimpy Bars), 40 High Street, Gosport, Hants.

34 Sidney Searle, Martins Five, Birdham, Chichester, Sussex.

35 Axess Turntables, Kymore House, North Street, Axminster, Devon.

36 The Travel Club Ltd, Station Road, Upminster, Essex.

37 Wimpy International Ltd, 214 Chiswick High Road, London W4.

38 Contemporary Industries (Engineering) Ltd, 347 City Road, London EC1.

Acknowledgements

WITHOUT the support of the *Sunday Times* this book would not have been written. In particular I must thank the editor, Harold Evans, for his generosity in granting me time off to tackle it, and my colleague, Peter Wilsher, editor of *Sunday Times Business News*, for his interest and suggestions. At the outset it was he who prevented me from galloping off in unfruitful directions. Nicholas Faith, deputy editor of *Business News*, has my gratitude for some stimulating ideas which made the tail-end of the job that much easier. All my other colleagues on *Business News*, whose sum total of knowledge about every conceivable corner of the business scene never ceases to astonish me, and who willingly fortified me with their expertise, also have my thanks. I must also mention an admirable quartet of secretaries—Susan Darke, Noreen Linnane, Caty Stubbs and Sheila Smart—who undertook countless tedious and unrewarding tasks. There is also my debt to a regular weekly column called *Prufrock*. Much of what I have learned about small businesses and how they tick is directly attributable to it, and some of the small firms which are featured in this book first made their appearance under its logo.

Indeed, it is to all the small businessmen who appear in this book (and to some who, because of pressure on space, do not) that I owe especial thanks. They were most generous with their time, but above all it was their patience in answering my questions and their interest in the project which made my meetings with them both agreeable and profitable. The contribution they have made to these pages is most substantial.

David St John Thomas, the publisher of the book, has a place here on two counts: his contagious and encouraging enthusiasm for the project, and the fact that he gave a passable imitation of a man remaining calm and unruffled when I presented him with a manuscript three times as long as the one he expected. In Norfolk John Myatt of the Great Yarmouth Press Agency undertook some important and productive reconnaissance work for me.

My children deserve a word of praise for genuinely and valiantly trying to reduce the accustomed noise level of their daily lives a few decibels and my wife for so cheerfully coping with the ill-tempered churl which the writing of a book occasionally makes a man. Without her administrative talents I would have long since subsided in a sea of paper, and it was her work on the typewriter which produced the bulk of the final manuscript.

Index

All entries referring to small businesses are listed under relevant subject — eg *Financing of*, *Management of* etc etc